D1552736

SOCIALISM

Key Concepts in Critical Theory

Series Editor
Roger S. Gottlieb

JUSTICE
Edited by Milton Fisk

GENDER
Edited by Carol C. Gould

DEMOCRACY
Edited by Philip Green

IMPERIALISM
Edited by Ronald H. Chilcote

RACISM
Edited by Leonard Harris

ECOLOGY
Edited by Carolyn Merchant

EXPLOITATION
Edited by Kai Nielsen and Robert Ware

ALIENATION AND SOCIAL CRITICISM
Edited by Richard Schmitt and Thomas E. Moody

SOCIALISM
Edited by Michael W. Howard

Key Concepts in Critical Theory

SOCIALISM

EDITED BY **Michael W. Howard**

Humanity Books

an imprint of Prometheus Books
59 John Glenn Drive, Amherst, New York 14228-2197

Published 2001 by Humanity Books, an imprint of Prometheus Books

Inquiries should be addressed to
Humanity Books
59 John Glenn Drive
Amherst, New York 14228–2197
VOICE: 716–691–0133, ext. 207
FAX: 716–564–2711

05 04 03 02 01   5 4 3 2 1

Library of Congress Cataloging-in-Publication Data

Socialism / edited by Michael W. Howard.
      p. cm. — (Key concepts in critical theory)
    Includes bibliographical references and index.
    ISBN 1–57392–956–5 (paper : alk. paper)
    1. Socialism. 2. Critical theory. I. Howard, Michael Wayne, 1952- II. Series.

HX73 .S615 2001
335—dc21   2001039070

Printed in the United States of America on acid-free paper

CONTENTS

PART II: RETROSPECTIVE ASSESSMENTS

PART III: MODELS OF SOCIALISM

PART IV: FREEDOM AND EQUALITY

PART V: DEMOCRACY AND COMMUNITY

SERIES EDITOR'S PREFACE

THE VISION OF A rational, just, and fulfilling social life, present in Western thought from the time of the Judaic prophets and Plato's *Republic*, has since the French Revolution been embodied in systematic critical theories whose adherents seek a fundamental political, economic, and cultural transformation of society.

These critical theories—varieties of Marxism, socialism, anarchism, feminism, gay/lesbian liberation, ecological perspectives, discourses by antiracist, anti-imperialist, and national liberation movements, and utopian/critical strains of religious communities—have a common bond that separates them from liberal and conservative thought. They are joined by the goal of sweeping social change; the rejection of existing patterns of authority, power, and privilege; and a desire to include within the realms of recognition and respect the previously marginalized and oppressed.

Yet each tradition of Critical Theory also has its distinct features: specific concerns, programs, and locations within a geometry of difference and critique. Because of their intellectual specificity and the conflicts among the different social groups they represent, these theories have often been at odds with one another, differing over basic questions concerning the ultimate cause and best response to injustice, the dynamics of social change, and the optimum structure of a liberated society, as well as the identity of the social agent who will direct the revolutionary change and in whose interests the revolutionary change will be made.

In struggling against what is to some extent a common enemy, in overlapping and (at times) allying in the pursuit of radical social change, critical theories to a great extent share a common conceptual vocabulary. It is the purpose of this series to explore that vocabulary, revealing what is common and what is distinct, in the broad spectrum of radical perspectives.

9

For instance, although both Marxists and feminists may use the word "exploitation," it is not clear that they really are describing the same phenomenon. In the Marxist paradigm the concept identifies the surplus labor appropriated by the capitalist as a result of the wage-labor relation. Feminists have used the same term to refer as well to the unequal amounts of housework, emotional nurturance, and child raising performed by women in the nuclear family. We see some similarity in the notion of group inequality (capitalists/workers, husbands/wives) and of unequal exchange. But we also see critical differences: a previously "public" concept extended to the private realm; one first centered in the economy of goods now moved into the life of emotional relations. Or, for another example, when deep ecologists speak of "alienation" they may be exposing the contradictory and destructive relations of humans to nature. For socialists and anarchists, by contrast, "alienation" basically refers only to relations among human beings. Here we find a profound contrast between what is and is not included in the basic arena of politically significant relationships.

What can we learn from exploring the various ways different radical perspectives utilize the same terminology?

Most important, we see that these key concepts have histories, and that the theories of which they are a part and the social movements whose spirit they embody take shape through a process of political struggle as well as of intellectual reflection. As a corollary, we can note that the creative tension and dissonance among the different uses of these concepts stem not only from the endless play of textual interpretation (the different understandings of classic texts, attempts to refute counterexamples or remove inconsistencies, rereadings of history, reactions to new theories), but also from the continual movement of social groups. Oppression, domination, resistance, passion, and hope are crystallized here. The feminist expansion of the concept of exploitation could only grow out of the women's movement. The rejection of a purely anthropocentric (human-centered, solely humanistic) interpretation of alienation is a fruit of people's resistance to civilization's lethal treatment of the biosphere.

Finally, in my own view at least, surveys of the differing applications of these key concepts of Critical Theory provide compelling reasons to see how complementary, rather than exclusive, the many radical perspectives are. Shaped by history and embodying the spirit of the radical movements that created them, these varying applications each have in them some of the truth we need in order to face the darkness of the current social world and the ominous threats to the earth.

ROGER S. GOTTLIEB

ACKNOWLEDGMENTS

In editing this collection, I had the benefit of suggestions from many friends and colleagues. Roger Gottlieb and John O'Neill deserve special mention for their consideration of the entire project and many helpful suggestions. The students in my socialism seminar also deserve thanks for the feedback provided on a first draft of the anthology, and for reading more than, in retrospect, it was reasonable to ask of them in a semester. Eugene O'Connor of Humanity Books was encouraging and helpful at every stage of the manuscript preparation. Others who made worthwhile suggestions include Christa Acampora, Doug Allen, Betsy Bowman, John Brentlinger, Al Campbell, Valerie Carter, Frank Cunningham, Ann Ferguson, Peter Fitting, Nathan Godfried, Alex Grab, Jim Harney, Burt Hatlen, Mary Hobgood, Greg Horowitz, Tom Huhn, Naomi Jacobs, Roger King, Len Krimerman, Oscar Remick, Sonny San Juan, David Schweickart, Bob Stone, and Jeff White. I could use only a fraction of the material suggested, but was able to make a better selection for having perused their suggestions. I of course assume responsibility for the final choices. I am grateful to Brenda Collamore for scanning and editing chapters and typing, to Jeff Wilson for scanning and typing, to Steve Galbraith for tracking down citations, and to Nick Robertson for editing three chapters, preparing the bibliography, and offering helpful comments on the introduction. The editing of the selections from Marx and Luxemburg was made much easier by the availability of electronic versions of texts in the public domain at the Marxists Internet Archive (http://www.marxists.org/). I am grateful to the following for their prior transcription and HTML markup: for the Luxemburg texts, Andy Lehrer and Brian Basgen; for the Marx texts, Zodiac, Brian Basgen, Hinrich Kuhls, Allan Thurrott, Bill McDorman, Bert Schultz, Martha Gimenez, Stephen Baird, Tim Delaney, and M. Griffin. In choosing the Luxemburg texts, I followed the example, with minor additions, of David McLellan, ed.,

Marxism: Essential Writings (Oxford: Oxford University Press, 1988). Special thanks to my wife, Valerie, and my daughter, Emma, for their compassion, patience, and combative spirits, which give me hope.

PREFACE

This anthology is not primarily about capitalism versus socialism, although some essays address this topic; there are many such books already available. Nor is it a collection of socialist classics. Nor is the collection focused mainly on the meaning of the fall of communism, although many of the essays were written since 1989. My goal was first to present socialism as a key concept in critical theory, or more precisely as a family of conceptions of alternatives to capitalist society which play a key role in articulating socialist perspectives in social and political theory on freedom and equality; democracy and community; art, culture, and religion; ecology, science, and technology. Second, I for the most part selected essays focusing on controversies among socialists rather than between socialists and nonsocialists in order to highlight the diversity of views among socialists which is often lost when the theme is "socialism versus capitalism." For example: How should socialism be defined, as public ownership, as material equality, as economic democracy, as working-class rule, as solidarity and cooperation, as freedom from "scarcity, toil, and socially organized repression," or as rational planning, to mention only some of the definitions to be found in the literature? Can/should socialism be wedded to a market economy? (See especially essays by Marx, Nove, Schweickart, Albert and Hahnel.) Can/should socialism be justified as an extension of liberalism, or in terms of a communitarian political theory (Lukes, Williams, Miller, Cunningham)? Are technology and science neutral, or laden with capitalist or socialist values (Feenberg)? How egalitarian can/should socialism be (Lukes, Schweickart, Albert and Hahnel, Cunningham, Marx)? Is religion a form of false consciousness opposed to socialism or a potential source of insight and motivation toward socialism (Gottlieb)? Is mass culture merely manipulative, or does it also contain critical utopian elements (Jameson)? What is the relative importance of freedom, equality, and democracy

(Macpherson, Lukes, Marable, Ferguson, Luxemburg, Cunningham)? How much weight should be given to class when thinking about the politics of socialism (Marx, Luxemburg, Lukes, Marable, Ferguson, Cunningham, O'Connor, Przeworski, Gorz)?

Third, I wanted to frame these discussions in the context of recent retrospective assessments of the experience of Communism and Social Democracy, the two main streams of socialist practice in the twentieth century. Thus the reader will find, after some classic statements by Marx on socialism, and some selections by Rosa Luxemburg representative of the debates over revisionism, party organization, and dictatorship in the first two decades of the century, assessments of Social Democracy and Communism, by Adam Przeworski and Alec Nove, respectively. These essays taken together should give the reader a proper sense of the challenges confronting those who wish to sustain a rational hope for the possibility of socialism at the beginning of the twenty-first century.

One challenge consists in developing models of socialism that promise to overcome economic difficulties encountered by centralized state planning, and that would be clearly preferable to capitalism. A central topic here is the market. Does some form of market socialism hold the most promise for socialism's future (Nove, Schweickart), or is there a feasible form of participatory planning still to be tried that socialists can envision and defend (Albert and Hahnel)? How this question is answered will affect the horizon of discussion of most of the aforementioned topics, because, for many, socialism has meant the overcoming not only of capitalist inequalities, but also market competition, egoism, and lack of conscious collective coordination. The market socialist must either scale back traditional aspirations toward cooperation, sociality, and collective rationality, or show how these can still be hoped for despite market pressures to the contrary.

In the contemporary selections I have avoided comfortable socialists, preferring authors who (while remaining forthrightly critical of capitalism) are troubled by the record of self-described socialist states, vis-à-vis freedom, equality, democracy, community, efficiency, and the environment, or who challenge the marginalization of race, gender, and "superstructural" dimensions of society such as religion, science, technology, art, and culture. That briefly explains the thematic organization of the book. Although (with the exception of the market socialism debate) I have not attempted to present opposing views, I have tried to find selections which, while representing a position, also key the reader in to a range of opposing views. Many of the essays focus on conceptual and normative concerns. But the reader will find ample empirical details along the way about both socialist parties and practices in Western Europe, and socialist states in the Soviet Union, Eastern Europe, Asia, Latin America, and Africa. Authors are from a variety of disciplines including economics, history, literary criticism, philosophy, political science, and sociology.

New directions for socialist politics are suggested by several authors, and the concluding essay offers a new agenda for socialism that picks up on some themes from various essays: the changing conditions of work and leisure, the importance of new social movements, cultures of resistance outside the sphere of work, the deepening problem of commodification in all spheres of life, and a reaffirmation in new terms of ideals of emancipation and solidarity.

In my introduction I address, for readers new to the topic of socialism, some common misconceptions about socialism. I also outline the main problems of capitalism that still motivate people to become socialist by means of a discussion of the centrality in the socialist tradition of Marx, as a thinker who succeeded in weaving together many diverse strands of criticism (Enlightenment, romantic, radical democratic, egalitarian, emancipatory, scientific, universalistic, communitarian, prophetic, critical, redemptive, revolutionary). I suggest that the evolution of socialist thought might be thought of in some cases as attempts to develop this project in the face of historical difficulties, and in other cases as the disentangling of some strands of critique from the others. I also provide some further contextualization of the essays in the book, and additional references for those wishing to dig deeper on particular topics. Links to relevant complementary texts on the Internet are accessible from my Web site at the University of Maine: http://www.ume.maine.edu/~philoso/mikehowarda/index.html.

With the exception of the introduction and the essay by Cunningham, all the selections in this volume have been previously published. Texts reprinted here are unaltered except for conversion of British to American spelling and punctuation, elimination of unnecessary capitalization, and conversion of notes to a consistent style (although in the selections from Marx, Luxemburg, and Williams the intratextual notes have been retained).

SOCIALISM
An Introduction

MICHAEL W. HOWARD

A decade has passed since the collapse of the Soviet Union and other communist states in Eastern Europe. China, Cuba, Vietnam, and North Korea remain nominally communist, but are now embedded in a world capitalist system to which they must increasingly adapt. The twentieth century can thus be viewed as encompassing the first great experiment to go "beyond capitalism." Will it come to be seen as the last? Have we reached the "end of history" as far as it concerns the evolution of politico-economic systems? What is the meaning of the failure of Soviet-style communism? What survives of the socialist idea (understanding socialism to be distinct from, and broader than, communism)?

This anthology is intended to introduce the reader to some assessments of socialism: its definition; various models of socialism both tried and untried, and what it might still promise (or a "socialist perspective" might reveal) with respect to a range of fundamental human concerns and practices including freedom, equality, democracy, community, efficiency, religion, science and technology, art and culture; and what new avenues for socialist practice and new conceptions of the socialist project should be considered in light of the socialist experience of the twentieth century and the current capitalist context.

In this introduction I list some common misconceptions about socialism, define capitalism, and discuss socialism as arising in reaction to capitalism. I distinguish different, sometimes conflicting, tendencies in the socialist movement, and focus on Marx's critique of capitalism as including most of the major problems that socialists have associated with capitalism, and Marx's proposed socialist alternatives. Along the way I will refer to the essays in the book as they develop this socialist critique, or criticize it, or take it in new directions, or offer alternative models of socialism or paths to it.

COMMON MISCONCEPTIONS

In this section I address some common misconceptions about socialism that may be shared by readers who are new to the topic.

1. The first and most common is the equation of socialism with Soviet Communism, particularly the latter's one-party dictatorship and centrally planned economy. Replacement of the market by planning, it is true, was a goal of Marx, Fabian socialists, and most other socialists, but a form of market socialism was also advocated by Oscar Lange and Fred Taylor in the 1930s. Yugoslavia experimented with a socialist market economy for over twenty years, and China now considers itself a form of market socialism.[1]

Socialism, whether defined as material equality, social or state ownership of the means of production, economic democracy, or even rational planning of certain key aspects of an economy (e.g., investment) is compatible with a market economy and decentralized decision making. Thus whatever verdict one makes about central planning is not a verdict about socialism generally.

Dictatorship in the Soviet Union was undoubtedly connected to the economic backwardness of the country at the time of the revolution, its lack of democratic traditions, and the difficult conditions of world war and imperialist encirclement. (The United States joined several other capitalist countries to invade the Soviet Union in 1918–20). With the exception of Yugoslavia, all the Eastern European countries had socialism imposed upon them by force. Cuba has faced a hostile superpower since the beginning of its revolution. These are not conditions favorable to democracy. The socialist states in Asia have emerged from lengthy wars against foreign invaders. Moreover, they should be compared with their capitalist neighbors, many of whom have experienced no less dictatorial governments over most of the last half of the twentieth century.[2]

Just as socialism should not be automatically linked to dictatorship, so, too, capitalism has no necessary connection with democracy, as is evident in the fascistic capitalist regimes that ruled in Argentina, Brazil, Chile, the Philippines, South Africa, Spain, Greece, and elsewhere in the post–World War II era.

2. Socialism should also not be equated with societies where socialist or Social Democratic parties have been in power (such as Sweden, Germany, France, and Austria), for these economies have been unquestionably capitalist in their ownership relations.

3. Socialism should not be confused with state paternalism, though this has been a feature of the Communist and Social Democratic traditions. An important current of socialist thinking, in Marx and in Rosa Luxemburg for example, is a commitment to freedom, both the free development of each individual and the self-determination of workers (more on this later).

4. Socialism is not the same as Marxism, though Marxism has been the dominant tradition within socialism. The British Fabians were distinct (see Lukes's

essay for some discussion of these), as have been Christian socialists and assorted non-Marxist market socialists.

5. Marxism broadly understood should not be reduced either to the orthodox Marxism of the Second International (represented by Kautsky, for example) or to Russian Marxism, not to mention Stalinism, all of which tended to neglect Marx's early humanistic writings. In these early works it is clear that Marx is antistatist, and sees the point of socialism to be emancipation, not just material well-being.[3]

It is also clear from these writings that Marx advocated a radical extension of democracy and does not easily lend himself to defense of dictatorship. A common interpretation of Marx as positivist, reductionist, economistic, and determinist is also revealed as inaccurate in his early works. (By "positivist" I mean an approach that attempts only to *describe* reality, without prescribing or making value judgments; by "reductionist" and "economistic" I mean the view that all political, legal, moral, cultural, and religious phenomena can be directly explained by economic causes; by "determinist" I mean the view that what happens historically is inevitable, as in the prediction that socialism will inevitably replace capitalism.) There is clearly a moral point of view in Marx's critique of alienation and exploitation, a recognition of causality moving from the "superstructure" to the "economic base" as well as vice versa, and a clear role for agency in history.[4]

6. Socialism should not be equated with absolute equality. This simplification of socialist calls for "equality" typically is followed by the conclusion that socialism lacks incentives for hard work and progress, and that it imposes a dreary uniformity on society.

While some form of equality may be the goal of public ownership and/or the curtailment or abolition of market relations, equality doesn't necessarily follow. One can expect—in socialist experiments as well as any socialism advocated in theory—*greater* equality than one finds under capitalism, but this leaves open the question of *how equal* people should be, and *for what reasons*. Socialists differ among themselves in answering these questions. It is probable that any complex society will find it desirable to have some income differentials, and there have been differentials of at least four or five to one in all of the socialist states. Moreover justice, while still supporting socialism, may *require* some inequality. (See Lukes for an argument for the desirability of equality, examination of actual inequality in capitalist and state socialist societies, and criticism of arguments for the inevitability of inequality).

On the issue of conformity, for many socialists it is precisely in order to weaken pressures to social uniformity generated under capitalism and to liberate individuality that they have favored socialism.[5]

7. Public ownership is not the same as ownership by a nation-state. Other possibilities, distinct from individual private ownership, include cooperative ownership, municipal ownership, and hybrids of consumer, worker, and other owners.

8. Socialism is not necessarily "materialist" if what one means by that term

is (a) promoting only the most basic material needs and/or (b) neglecting or suppressing spirituality. This view is a misunderstanding even of Marx's atheism, which sought to bring down to earth fundamentally Christian aspirations. His "materialist" theory of history is a dialectic of needs in which new needs emerge out of practices designed to meet prior needs. Marx is harshly critical not only of the crass materialism of capitalist society, which reduces all human relations to money terms, but also of the "crude communism" of some socialists that seeks to level everyone down to the same minimum (more on this below).

Recent decades have also witnessed the fusion of Marxism and Christianity in Latin America in "liberation theology," showing how these need not be opposed.[6] There are also non-Marxist socialists whose inspiration is Christian, Jewish, Gandhian, or otherwise religious.

9. It is a mistake to assert categorically that socialism is inefficient. There are some ways in which the centrally planned command models in eastern Europe failed in comparison with capitalism, in meeting consumer demand or in innovation. But even these models had countervailing efficiencies, achieving full employment and rapid industrialization (see Nove).

It is also important to note that efficiency, which on one measure has to do with the total produced with a given amount of labor and resources, has to be weighed against considerations of equity—fair distribution—when deciding what is, all things considered, the right thing to do. And socialism may have the edge over capitalism, all things considered, when the focus is not only on efficiency, but also on justice (see Albert and Hahnel).[7] Some form of market socialism may even prove to be more efficient than capitalism, considerations of justice aside (see Schweickart).

10. One of the most common misconceptions is that socialism is incompatible with freedom. The relationship between socialism and freedom depends in part on the type of socialism. The combination of state ownership, central planning, and a single party poses a powerful danger to freedom. But even this model is compatible with individual freedom if the party is itself pluralistic and there is considerable devolution of decision making (see Macpherson). Forms of socialism without some of these features pose fewer dangers and promise to expand freedom.

Market socialism prescribes autonomy of enterprises from the state, thus affording the possibility of a balance of state and economic power (which some have seen as a virtue of capitalism). If the society is also politically pluralistic—and there is nothing in the idea of socialism that precludes multiple parties—then socialism can have the same check against tyranny afforded by competition for rule in capitalist democracies. In addition, greater equality means that more people will have more of the conditions making liberty valuable. And the extension of political rights into workplaces, as in Schweickart's model, is itself an expansion of freedom over capitalism.

Finally, as already noted, capitalism itself provides no guarantee of freedom, having been compatible with some of the most tyrannical regimes in modern history.

11. The most seductive misconception about socialism is that it is passé. On the most superficial level, one should note the reelection of former Communists in Russia, Hungary, Slovenia, and elsewhere after the introduction of multiple parties (though these parties have often abandoned a socialist platform), and the return to power of labor, socialist, and Social Democratic parties in Western Europe in the nineties (though, again, with less socialistic programs than before, in England, West Germany, etc.).

More importantly, (and above-mentioned elections are symptomatic of this) capitalism still confronts us with many problems not easily resolved within a capitalist framework. Foremost among these are the continuing divide between rich and poor, internationally and within nations, and the contradiction between capitalist growth and ecologically necessary constraints on growth. To illustrate, according to the United Nations Human Development Report, "the assets of the world's 358 billionaires exceed the combined annual incomes of countries accounting for nearly half (45%) of the world's people,"[8] and twelve million children die every year as a result of hunger.[9] In the United States, real wages for Americans have been falling since the 1970s, and income and wealth inequality has grown. In 1995, "the richest one half of one percent had a larger total non-residential net worth than the bottom 90%. . . . Wealth is now the most concentrated it's been since the 1920s."[10] Population growth and energy consumption are on a trajectory that is environmentally unsustainable over the next century, with ozone depletion and global warming among the most systemic and threatening consequences already developing. Yet economic growth remains a priority for capitalist economies, without which profit incentives would disappear (on the link between capitalism and environmental destruction, see O'Connor).

Finally, socialism remains a living idea because there remain untried models, some of which are presented in this volume, developed in the light of the initial flawed experiments. Capitalism developed over many centuries, with much human devastation along the way from the enclosure movement in England, through colonization, world wars, and global depression. It is to be expected that this system will not be displaced overnight or without failed experiments as the human species gropes its way toward a peaceful, equitable, sustainable sharing of the planet.

CAPITALISM AND SOCIALISM

"Socialism" (the word, but also the idea and the movement designated by it) arose historically in the nineteenth century in reaction to capitalism. Hence, to understand socialism we need to have some grasp of capitalism. Capitalism is a form of society characterized by the predominance of:

(1) *private property*, specifically private ownership of the means of production (the land, factories, raw materials, and funds to hire workers), i.e., capital;

(2) coordination of supply and demand for goods and services by means of *competitive markets*;

(3) allocation of labor by means of these same markets, such that the predominant production relation is the hiring of workers in need of wages for their survival, by capitalists whose aim is to realize *profit* in the sale of the products of labor.

This system, in place in Europe and America and spreading since the eighteenth century, may be contrasted with precapitalist systems such as the primitive communism of hunter gatherers, the slave societies of ancient Greece and Rome (or in the Americas until the mid to late nineteenth century), and feudalism in Europe, Japan, India, or China prior to the development of capitalism.

More relevant for our purposes are the varieties of postcapitalist society that have been tried or imagined, corresponding to changes in the defining elements of capitalism mentioned above. First, private property might be replaced by state ownership as in the Soviet model, or by municipal ownership, or by cooperative ownership by the workers and/or consumers, or by a hybrid of public and private ownership such as that proposed recently by John Roemer (see Schweickart).[11]

Market coordination could be replaced by centralized, bureaucratic planning, but also by participatory democratic planning such as that proposed by Michael Albert and Robin Hahnel. And planning may include investment, production, and consumption, or only investment (as advocated by market socialists), or merely certain broad parameters such as priorities for innovation, or interest rates that are now subject to state regulation in most capitalist economies. Also, between market and state are many voluntary associations that have economic functions, but operate (or can operate) on other-than-market principles, such as universities.[12]

Wage labor can be displaced by administrative allocation of labor, but also by cooperative association (see Schweickart). And production for profit by individual capitalists can be replaced by the state as collective capitalist, adopting a different principle of distribution of income such as work time or need (see essays by Marx, Lukes, Schweickart, Albert and Hahnel), or a technocratic or meritocratic principle. Or, cooperative firms can seek to maximize income per worker.

The variety of institutional schemes favored by socialists is connected to differences of aim and strategy among socialists. As Raymond Williams has observed (in the first essay in this book), there are two often divergent connotations of the word "socialist." (i) The first takes socialism to be a continuation and perfection of liberalism, the dominant political philosophy of the late eighteenth and nineteenth centuries in Europe and North America, as expressed in the

French Revolutionary Declaration of the Rights of Man and the Citizen, the American Declaration of Independence, or the Bill of Rights. Central to liberalism is the liberty of the individual, expressed politically through freedom of speech, press, and association, and the right to vote and hold office, and economically through freedom of choice and the right to hold and accumulate property. The point of such freedoms, on one classic formulation by John Stuart Mill, is the flowering of individuality in all its variety.[13]

Socialists, including non-Marxist socialists such as Oscar Wilde, Bertrand Russell, and R. H. Tawney, have noted the tension between liberalism's privileging of equal political rights and political democracy on the one hand, and its favoring of the capitalist market economy and property rights leading to inequalities of income, wealth, power, political influence, and economic decision making (both over investment and over management of workplaces). The resources enabling one to make use of one's liberty—income, wealth, a voice in politics, etc.—are the conditions that make liberty valuable, and too great an inequality of these conditions is thus incompatible with the central importance assigned by liberalism to liberty.[14]

(The term "liberal" in popular American political discourse, when it refers to state intervention, and redistributive taxation to curb the worst excesses of capitalism, is a compromise between the "classical liberalism" of the nineteenth century—sometimes now called libertarianism—and socialism, which aspires to move from merely political to social and economic democracy, and from merely political equality to a practicable level of economic and social equality.[15])

(ii) Whereas the first connotation of "socialism" amounts to an extension and fulfillment of liberalism's individualist promise—the full development of individuality through providing not only the formal rights but also the material means for such development—the second connotation involves a break with liberal individualism. Competitiveness, profit seeking, and wealth accumulation are opposed to the essentially social nature of human beings (in Marx's early writings, for example), the latter requiring for its full expression a society structured by cooperation. Most socialists consider this to be incompatible with private ownership of capital (which steers investment and production toward individual profit) and many consider it incompatible also with market coordination which puts in conflict enterprise against enterprise, producer against consumer, worker against capitalist, and worker against worker.

These two connotations are sometimes combined, for example by Marx, but have also corresponded to political differences within the socialist movement. Thus many Communists after Lenin have rejected liberalism as sentimental, historically limited, and ideological, and many liberal socialists have accused Communists of neglecting essential freedoms. Conceptually, two sorts of reconciliation are possible. First, one could argue that the essentially *social* nature of human beings *requires* certain *basic liberties* (ii implies i). Second, one could argue that making good on liberalism's promise of *equal respect* for each requires a large degree of *cooperation* and mutuality, participation and democracy (i implies ii). See David Miller for an example of the second of these.

MARX'S CRITIQUE OF CAPITALISM

One reason that, of all the nineteenth-century critics of capitalism, Marx emerged as the most noteworthy and influential is that he succeeded in integrating these two strands of criticism into a coherent whole. Moreover, he strove to discipline his criticism with a careful analysis of the actual structures and developmental tendencies of capitalist society, and to link it with the aspirations of actual social movements of his day. Earlier socialists such as Robert Owen designed schemes for utopian communities that would break off from the dominant capitalist society. These have historically provided interesting microcosms of alternatives, but have never succeeded in replicating themselves on a scale that could threaten the dominant capitalist order. Socialists with and after Marx have sought to transform capitalism directly.

Hence, despite differences over ultimate aims and strategies (more on this later), most socialists since Marx have shared an emphasis on the centrality of political struggle, struggle for control of the state, as a first step.

Alienation

The ultimate aim of socialism, for Marx, was nothing less than the overcoming of *alienation* in all its forms. The concept of alienation has its origin in religion. The human being is estranged from God, and to return home from this alien land one must reorient oneself to one's true human nature, which is to be oriented toward God. In Hegel's *Philosophy of Right*, the concept is generalized. Hegel's god is an immanent god, revealing and objectifying itself in history, through the development of human self-consciousness. Human social structures, such as the family, the market economy, or the state, are objectifications of this unfolding consciousness. When not understood, they appear as alien oppressive structures, limits on one's freedom. But when understood in their systematic interconnection and historical context, they structure and enable one's self-fulfillment.[16]

Marx followed Feuerbach and left-Hegelian thinkers in criticizing Hegel's philosophy as itself an alienated expression of an alienated world.[17] Religion expresses some of our deepest longings for unity with our fellow human beings and with nature. But insofar as it promises an illusory otherworld as a consolation for the suffering of this world, as does much of Christianity, it numbs us to the pain, renders us passive and accepting of things as they are, and serves as an ideological rationalization for oppression.

Marx's critical theory was to extrapolate this critique of religion to the state, civil society, and morality. The state as it emerged from the Middle Ages, distinct from "civil society," the domain of free association, private property, and market exchange, is not the place where citizens achieve their true universal humanity. Nor is the state bureaucracy truly animated by the altruism of a "universal class" as Hegel characterized it. Behind this misleading self-understanding, the state is a parasitic institution that serves the interest of the bureaucracy, and adjudicates a compromise among the competing interests and classes of civil society, a compromise decidedly favoring the dominant class.[18] Mere "political emancipation," such as that aspired to in the French and American Revolutions, would bring about an equality of citizens, but would leave in place the *inequalities* between classes.

Material equality would be in principle compatible with a continued separation of civil society and state, and continued competition among individuals in the market, as advocated by market socialists (see Schweickart).[19] But Marx is equally troubled by the *individualism* and *egoism* of capitalist society. In the political revolutions of the eighteenth century, "man was . . . not freed from religion; he received freedom of religion. He was not freed from property; he received freedom of property. He was not freed from the egoism of trade; he received freedom to trade." Human emancipation involves not only overcoming the inequality masked by these equal freedoms, but also the egoism:

> All emancipation is bringing back man's world and his relationships to man himself.
>
> Political emancipation is the reduction of man, on the one hand to a member of civil society, an egoistic and independent individual, on the other hand to a citizen, a moral person.
>
> The actual individual man must take the abstract citizen back into himself and, as an individual man in his empirical life, in his individual work and individual relationships become a species-being; man must recognize his own forces as social forces, organize them, and thus no longer separate social forces from himself in the form of political forces. Only when this has been achieved will human emancipation be completed.[20]

Thus the transcendence of capitalism is not only about rectifying inequalities, but also about restoring community. And this involves transcendence of the division between civil society and the state. Ultimately, the state in the sense of a separate entity that aims for the general interest in opposition to the particular interests of civil society (though in reality serving its own interest and the particular interests of the dominant class) will "wither away" as the activities of daily life assume a more universal character.

In the theory Marx developed by 1844, the core of alienation in all its forms is the *alienation of labor*, for whatever else human beings do they must produce their means of subsistence and reproduce themselves. In capitalist society the product of the worker's labor is appropriated by another, as is the labor itself. Both are literally alienated in the legal sense, sold, in the market. This is the basis of *exploitation*. As a worker one is thereby also alienated from one's "species-being," the realization of one's human and social capacities, because these have been appropriated by another, turned to the other's particular ends. "Man makes his vital activity and essence a mere means to his existence."[21] Thus also is the worker alienated from the capitalist, whose appropriation of wealth through exploitation of the worker contributes to an even greater *power* over the worker, and the worker is alienated from other workers, in competition in the labor market. The state is but the symptomatic counterpart of this generalized alienation and competition. The key to transcending the state (and religion) is thus overcoming alienated labor, and the capitalist structures that it produces, "private property." "Socialism," in Marx's earliest work, denotes this overcoming of alienation in various stages and degrees. Ultimately it is the overcoming of all the dualisms characteristic of Enlightenment philosophies and much of the experience of modern life:

> Communism as the positive abolition of private property and thus of human self-emancipation . . . is the genuine solution of the antagonism between man and nature and between man and man. It is the true solution of the struggle between existence and essence, between objectification and self-affirmation, between freedom and necessity, between individual and species. It is the solution to the riddle of history and knows itself to be this solution.[22]

However, unlike many romantics, Marx was not antimodern or antiscientific. Marx saw an intimation of the socialized human being in the form of life of the modern scientist.[23]

"Communism" referred to the radical movement of workers that rose up to resist the capitalists. "Communism is the necessary form and dynamic principle of the immediate future, but communism is not as such the goal of human development, the form of human society." The steps taken by this movement to abolish private property may be partial, deluded, or even constitute a worsening of alienation. For example, Marx criticizes mere calls for the equality of wages, and he rejects the "crude communism" that is "only a generalization and completion of private property," and that "abstracts from talent," in which

> the category of the worker is not abolished but extended to all men. . . . How little this abolition of private property constitutes a real appropriation is proved by the abstract negation of the whole world of culture and civilization, a regression to the unnatural simplicity of the poor man without any needs who has not even arrived at the stage of private property, let alone got beyond it.[24]

It should be clear from these passages how far Marx's idea of socialism is from either mere redistributive income schemes or paternalistic state ownership and control of capital.

Later Marx and Engels distanced themselves from the word "socialist" because of certain connotations it had come to have with reference to other groups.

"Socialism was in 1847, a middle-class movement, Communism was a working-class movement."[25] But the communitarian aspirations are evident in the various conceptions of postcapitalist society that Marx sketches from 1848 onward.

Notably, in the *Critique of the Gotha Program*, Marx posits for the "lower phase of communism," the society that would take the place of capitalism once class divisions have been broken up, a nonmarket planned economy. Producers will produce directly for use, and not for the sake of exchange or profit. Economic transactions, rather than being mystified through commodity prices, will be transparent. The anarchy of the market will give way to rational planning. Workers, hitherto the playthings of economic forces, will become the makers of their own history. However, this will not be a society of perfect altruists. People will still require material incentives for labor. Hence, the principle of distribution is according to work, minus the necessary levies for reinvestment, support for those unable to work, etc. Full communism, characterized by the principle from each according to ability, to each according to need, is the ultimate aim, but possible only after

> the enslaving subordination of the individual to the division of labor, and therewith also the antithesis between mental and physical labor, has vanished; after labor has become not only a means of life but life's prime want; after the productive forces have also increased with the all-around development of the individual, and all the springs of co-operative wealth flow more abundantly. . . .[26]

In thinking that in such a society "bourgeois right," which persists in the lower phase, will cease, Marx reveals a romantic longing for social harmony without any conflicts requiring formal adjudication, rights, rules of justice, and the like.[27] One might think that the remoteness of full communism would render this utopian element harmless. But it serves even in Marx to support a contempt for "ideological nonsense about right and other trash." It can also serve (illegitimately) to rationalize arbitrary suspension of constitutions and legal procedures by those representing, or claiming to represent, the working-class movement whose historic mission is to carry humanity to full communism. A less romantic conception of our human possibilities, that leaves room for serious conflict even in the best imaginable circumstances, will engender more respect for legal rights as part of the permanent furniture of the social landscape.

Some, like Leszek Kolakowski, argue in the light of the Eastern European Communist experience, for the complete abandonment of Marx's communitarian aspirations, leaving standing only the left-liberal egalitarian dimension of Marx's critique.[28] In his essay in this volume, David Miller attempts to preserve the communitarian strand, qualifying it to avoid the excesses of a romantic longing for perfect harmony. For Miller, a degree of community is a necessary condition for realizing even the promise of liberalism, hence those social democrats who wish to jettison communitarianism altogether may be defeating themselves. As we shall see, some degree of community and collectively shared rationality may be necessary for survival of the species, as we confront large-scale environmental destruction.

Democracy

Given the association in many people's minds of socialism with one-party dictatorship, it may come as a surprise that Marx was a radical democrat. His early criticism of representative democracy was that it was not democratic and participatory enough.[29]

In *The Communist Manifesto* Marx and Engels say that the first step in the revolution of the working class is "to win the battle of democracy," aligning themselves in England with the Chartist movement for extending the franchise to workers.[30] In 1848 they naively thought that the expansion of voting rights would immediately lead to a rapid democratization of the economy, along the lines of the communist program sketched in the *Manifesto*. The failure of the 1848 revolution and the experience of subsequent decades of struggle, notably of bourgeois readiness to support dictatorship in order to defend property rights, convinced Marx, by the 1870s that between capitalism and socialism must come a "dictatorship of the proletariat." The term, appropriated by Lenin to denote the dictatorship of one among several *parties* of the Left, for Marx meant rather the dictatorship of one *class*, the working class, over another, the capitalist class, a temporary suspension of the political rights of the latter until their economic, military, and other power could be broken, and the will of the majority secured. Although such an exclusionary regime is not without its dangers, it is clear that Marx had in mind a highly participatory and democratic model, exemplified by the Paris Commune of 1871, in which workers held power for the first time for a brief period.

The Paris Commune, as Marx described it, *displaced* the state apparatus and bureaucracy of the old order. The standing army was replaced by militias; elected officials held relatively short terms, were recallable, and under a mandate from their constituencies. They were paid workers' wages. Lenin himself endorses something like this model, along with worker control of the enterprises, in *State and Revolution*. But in practice the Bolsheviks substituted the rule of the party for the rule of the class, and a highly centralized party at that, for which Rosa Luxemburg, arguably closer to Marx's democratic spirit, took them to task (see essays in this volume). She nonetheless defended a revolutionary road to socialism, against the purely electoral strategy of Bernstein. Rejecting all versions of the idea of "dictatorship of the proletariat," Cunningham nonetheless favors a conception of democracy that includes not only electoral party politics, but also other collective efforts by equals to achieve "joint and proactive control over shared environments," as exemplified in social movement activism. He criticizes those theories of democracy that would narrow its scope; and he considers competing ideals of socialism in order to identify those most compatible with democracy and with value pluralism.

Social Democracy

In *Capitalism and Social Democracy*, Adam Przeworski says that from the mid-nineteenth century onward the socialist movement conceived of itself as completing the revolution started by the bourgeoisie by extending the principle of democracy. Anarchists resisted participation in elections, fearing that this would destroy the movement for socialism. Socialist parties were ambivalent, favoring elections for propaganda purposes while adhering to the goal of revolutionary transformation from capitalism to socialism. The turning point, he argues, was the failure of mass strikes between 1902 and 1926. The revolutionary movement had somehow to steer between the two reefs identified by Rosa Luxemburg: the abandonment of its mass character and the abandonment of its final goals. Deference to representatives demobilizes. Party bureaucracies succumb to embourgeoisement. The promise of elections as necessary and sufficient for socialism, voiced by Engels in 1895, seemed dashed.

The reason, Przeworski argues, is to be found in the relationship of Social Democracy to the working class. Workers need a party to avoid intraclass competition, and to forge a class identity that can resist integration. But such parties face an electoral dilemma. As a minority, the proletariat needs to reach out to non-working-class allies: peasants and the middle class. Even with these, socialists have never mustered more than half the votes in any election. In reaching out, the strong class identity is lost. If the class identity is maintained, these allies are lost. In neither case is there an electoral road to socialism.

Instead, Social Democrats have settled for—achieved—a class compromise: improved conditions for workers, economic regulation for full employment, and egalitarian income distribution. But this has been achieved on the condition that much of the property remains private, and can operate under conditions favorable to profit.

In the postscript to Przeworski's study, reprinted here, he contrasts this compromise with the more ambitious aims of the original socialist movement: not full employment, but "the abolition of wage slavery," not "a movement for efficiency but for collective rationality," "not a movement for equality but for freedom."

Though pessimistic, he hints that these goals may be reclaimed if the socialist movement once again becomes social and cultural, not just political, and that some basis for this reclamation may be found in movements for shortening the work day—a theme taken up in the last essay by André Gorz. The broadening of scope to include culture (popular, scientific, religious) is a position developed in other ways in the essays by Fredric Jameson, Andrew Feenberg, and Roger S. Gottlieb. I will return to these topics after completing my account of Marx's critique of capitalism and his socialist alternative.

Fetishism, Collective Rationality, Ecology

In "The Fetishism of Commodities," Marx returns to the theme of alienation, emphasizing the alien or fetishistic character of the commodity in which "the mutual relations of the producers, within which the social character of their labor affirms itself, take the form of a social relation between the products." Fetishism arises because producers do not exchange their products directly and transparently, but indirectly through the medium of the market and the exchange values of commodities therein.

The model of socialism Marx proposes to overcome fetishism does away with not only capitalist domination but also the mediation of the market, each working in accordance with a common plan that uses labor time both to "maintain the proper proportion between different kinds of work to be done and the various wants of the community," and "as a measure of the portion of the common labor borne by each individual, and of his share in the part of the total product. . . . The social relations of the individual producers, with regard to their labor and to its products, are in this case perfectly simple and intelligible. . . ."

By contrast, in capitalist society, the value of commodities, including labor power, is determined by the market, "independently of the will, foresight and action of the producers," "behind their backs," and with that a whole train of unintended consequences for the distribution of wealth and income (via profits, wages, and rent), periodic crises, rates of growth, etc. It is in this sense that the products "rule the producers instead of being ruled by them." It is thus to become free, masters of their own history rather than history's products, that workers need to abolish the market.[31]

Marx's concern is more relevant than ever in the context of the ecological crisis, insofar as large-scale unintended consequences such as resource depletion and pollution are linked to capitalist production for profit and its externalization of costs. But, given the poor environmental record of socialist countries, can socialism be part of the solution? In his essay, James O'Connor addresses the question of why anyone could think of the relation between socialism and nature in positive terms. Lack of democracy, lack of power in the hands of workers, technicians and managers, policies of full employment and job security, the context of the cold war and the global capitalist market giving rise to pressures to "catch up" with the West, are among the factors peculiar to socialist states in the latter half of the twentieth century, but not inherent in socialist economies per se. O'Connor also identifies points of comparison and contrast between labor and environmental movements, and between traditional socialist and modern ecological thinking, and analyzes trends giving rise to the possibility of an ecological socialism.

Reification and Culture

The fetishism of commodities, or reification as it was called by some later Marxists, is also central to many socialist approaches to art and culture.[32] So important has culture become, or come to be recognized, as a basis for identity formation not only within but outside the workplace (see Gorz), that, Jameson argues, "if we want to go on believing in categories like social class, then we are going to have to dig deep for them in the insubstantial bottomless realm of cultural and collective fantasy. . . . [U]ntil the omnipresence of culture in this society is even dimly sensed, realistic conceptions of the nature and function of political praxis can scarcely be framed."

Jameson takes as his point of departure the antithesis between "populist" valorization of popular culture in opposition to high culture, and the approach of the Frankfurt School (especially Adorno and Horkheimer) which focuses on the commodification and instrumentalization of mass culture and finds only in high modernist culture any critical perspective. Both rest on a shared assumption of the duality of mass and high culture, which Jameson calls into question. He builds on the Frankfurt School approach, taking account of the market context of popular media, while detecting utopian yearnings "in the most degraded works of mass culture just as surely as in the classics of modernism," which as he concludes "is surely an indispensable condition for any meaningful Marxist intervention in contemporary culture."[33]

Socialism and Religion

That there should even be a question about the relationship of socialism and religion has much to do with the centrality of Marxism in the socialist movement. Secular anticlericalism of course antedates Marx in the history of European radicalism or even liberalism (it was Voltaire who said of Christianity, "Ecrasons l'infâme"),[34] and the role of institutional religion in propping up the old order of feudalism as well as its capitalist successors could hardly keep from generating criticism among the opponents of those regimes, with or without Marx. But the particular legacy of Marxism has been a suspicion not only of the institutions but of the core belief systems and practices of religion, arguably with a consequent weakening of the potential of the socialist movement.

For Marx, religion was construed as an ideology, a system of belief that distorted the truth in such a way as to reinforce dominant relations of power and exploitation. Insofar as it expresses "the cry of the oppressed creature," it is a source of critique—and in the case of Christianity was indeed radical in its origin—but in practice it is reactionary. The truth in religion is the humanism that must be decoded from religion's otherworldly projections. Once humanity is freed by science from unreasonable superstition, and frees itself from oppressive and mystifying social relations (see Marx, "The Fetishism of Commodities"), religion should fade away.

This brief sketch prompts four questions. (1) Was Marx right about the nature of religion as essentially a distorted humanism? Is it reasonable to expect that as human beings acquire deeper understanding of and control over both nature and social relations, these will be demystified, and religion will give way to wholly secular and atheistic outlooks? One might first question whether the Enlightenment project of understanding and control of nature was not embraced too uncritically by Marx, and may not be fully realizable (see Feenberg and O'Connor).

(2) Beside this, is there a need for spirituality to resist the despiritualization of life under capitalism (which Marx and Engels so eloquently describe in the *Manifesto*), and sustain the "prolonged struggles for a post-capitalist future"?[35] This is one theme taken up in Gottlieb's dialogue.

(3) Can religion be progressive? The egalitarians in the English civil war, the antislavery movement in the United States, the Catholic worker movement, and more recently popular struggles in Latin America, have been centrally motivated by an egalitarian reading of Jewish and Christian scriptures. This line of thinking has been developed recently in the United States by a variety of thinkers who hold that the Left has been debilitated through neglect of a spiritual dimension it can and should reclaim.[36]

(4) Is socialism threatening to religion? It has certainly been perceived as such; for example, the attitude of African American churches toward socialism is one factor Manning Marable cites for why black Americans have not been socialist. But it is hard to see how a socialism emerging from self-consciously religious motivations could undermine religion, unless, in the end, Marx is right that religion will fade away with the progress of science and social justice. The hostility of actually existing socialist states toward religion—the closing of churches, temples, and mosques—has more to do with a particularly crude reading of Marx's atheism, that stresses the ideological role institutionalized religion has played, without giving religion its due as, in part, a cultural product of workers and other oppressed groups. (As Harold Bloom put it, writing about Flannery O'Connor, religion is not the opiate but the poetry of the people.[37]) Ironically, if Marx was right about religion, its persistence under socialism, far from being a pretext for its forceful suppression, would be an indictment of the persistence of alienation (e.g., in its statist form) in the new regime.

Science and Technology as Ideology

The enormous developments in natural science and technology of the last three hundred years have coincided with the rise and maturation of capitalism. Marx was among those who celebrated this development.[38] But the twentieth century has witnessed deformations of the environment and intrusions of technology into personal and family life, and the spread of technological and instrumental thinking into politics and social life generally. Where Marx shared in the "progressivist" acceptance of science characteristic of most nineteenth-century writers, many twentieth-century Marxists, particularly the "critical theorists" of the Frankfurt School (including Adorno, Horkheimer, Marcuse, and Habermas) have taken up the question of whether science and technology are themselves a part of the problem, either as displacing moral and political discourse by expertise, or as embodying values of the class society in which they emerged while simultaneously masking those values. As an example of the latter, think of how the technique of the assembly line embodies capitalist relations of production as an apparently neutral force of production. To the extent that previously existing socialisms have shared in such mystification, they, too, need to be criticized before there can emerge a socialism free of oppressive technology and the scientization of politics. Andrew Feenberg's essay on Marcuse and Habermas is a recent development out of this critical-theory tradition.[39]

MODELS OF SOCIALISM

Insofar as any of the topics in this volume are approached from a perspective that presupposes the possibility of overcoming fetishism and transcending the market, an unavoidable question is whether there is in fact any feasible alternative economic model to replace capitalism. For all the shortcomings of twentieth-century socialist states catalogued by Alec Nove, James O'Connor, David Schweickart, and others, they were planned economies, and some lessons can be drawn from them about planning. Nove cautions us not to compare Soviet reality with the idealized models of neoclassical economics, and reminds us of capitalism's failings, but he considers market socialism as the only alternative to central planning, and central planning—not all planning, but centralized coordination of production of goods and services—he judges to be a failure.

Schweickart defends one model of market socialism, economic democracy, which features worker-managed enterprises, a market economy in consumer goods and services, and democratic allocation of investment funds accumulated through a tax on assets rather than through interest on private savings. He builds on the strengths of the Yugoslavian self-management system, and the Basque cooperatives of Mondragon, while trying to avoid their shortcomings. He also discusses a competing model of John Roemer which does not include worker self-management or democratic planning of investment, but distributes property widely through a socialist stock market, with provisions to sustain egalitarian ownership over generations.

Schweickart also briefly cites China as an example of market socialism that has distributed income widely, maintained state ownership, and sustained a remarkable rate of economic growth.[40]

Some socialists resist these turns to the market in theory as well as practice, holding out hope for some form of planning of the economy that is "participatory" rather than bureaucratic, thereby avoiding the alienation, domination, and inefficiencies of the Soviet model. One example of participatory planning is provided here by Michael Albert and Robin Hahnel, who also provide a good concise argument against the market, showing what is at stake in this debate.

It is useful to reflect on how the market socialism debate intersects with other concerns addressed in this book. Would the persistence of market relations preclude the overcoming of commodity fetishism (Marx), reification in mass culture? (Jameson, Feenberg), the subordination of ecological concerns to the logic of profit maximization (O'Connor)? Could the centralization of political and economic power, albeit "participatory," avoid the dangers of too much power falling into the hands of a political elite (Macpherson)? Is the aspiration to equality, particularly in the strongly egalitarian form advocated by Albert and Hahnel, compatible with pluralism of voluntary associations (Lukes)? If socialism and feminism need each other, would feminism be better served by market or nonmarket forms (Ferguson)? Which model is most likely to satisfy the goals of such social groups as might be emerging with interests that point beyond capitalism (Gorz)? Which form of socialism can better address the deeply entrenched inequalities of race and gender, that markets, especially labor markets, have in part adapted to and in part reshaped and perpetuated (Ferguson, Marable)? Can the democratization of the economy—of workplaces and investment decisions—and the preservation or revitalization of community be better accomplished through market or nonmarket socialism (Cunningham, Miller)?

TRANSITION

The essays by Schweickart and Albert and Hahnel clearly sketch models of socialism that have not been tried, keeping alive the idea of a socialist alternative to capitalism as a long-term goal. However, the way from here to there is less clear. The catastrophic consequences of dictatorship leave few defenders of the idea of a Leninist vanguard party as the agent of transition.[41] More importantly, as Gramsci argued early on, the more developed and entrenched capitalism of Western Europe, and increasingly the globe, is not vulnerable to a frontal military assault like the storming of the Winter Palace in the Russian Revolution. Rather, the struggle for socialism is more akin to a "war of position," on many fronts, at different levels, not only economic or political, but ideological, cultural, and social.[42]

Thus has the focus of many socialist writers shifted to the analysis and critique of art and culture, to the development of the critical potential of religious traditions, and to efforts to build solidarity among oppressed groups distinct from the working class as such, groups that identify themselves not in relation to production, but in relation to family, gender, race, sexual orientation, or the environment.

Can these new social movements lead to socialism? Perhaps, if a number of possibilities, suggested by the essays in this book, are realized: If the specific problems at the center of social movements are successfully linked, in theory and practice, to the dynamics of capitalism (see O'Connor on the environment, Ferguson on sexism, Marable on racism, Feenberg on oppressive technology). If socialist interpretations of freedom, equality, and democracy resonate with the ordinary experience and aspirations of people in these movements better than competing inegalitarian interpretations (see Macpherson, Lukes, Miller, and Cunningham). If spiritual seeking can dovetail with, rather than resist or dissipate the efforts of social movements (see Gottlieb). If the utopian yearnings expressed in popular culture can be unveiled and the ideological distortions and profit-seeking manipulation successfully exposed (see Jameson). If the labor movement can encompass the concerns not only of the fully employed but of the unemployed and marginally employed, and together with the other social movements challenge what Gorz calls "economic rationality" (cf. Przeworski). Then socialism has a future not just as an idea but as a real practical possibility.

NOTES

1. Oskar Lange and Fred M. Taylor, ed. with an introduction by Benjamin Evans Lippincott, *On the Economic Theory of Socialism* (New York: A. M. Kelley, 1970). See Schweickart in this volume for discussion of China and Yugoslavia. For a concise and perceptive overview of the varieties of actual models of socialism, including social democracy, see D. M. Nuti, "Socialism on Earth," *Cambridge Journal of Economics* 5 (1981): 391–403. For an account of the alternating introduction and elimination of markets in Cuba, illustrating the tensions between efficiency and equality, see Carmen Diana Deere and Mieke Meurs, "Markets, Markets Everywhere? Understanding the Cuban Anomaly," *World Development* 20, no. 6 (1992): 825–39.

2. This is not to deny that there were any factors inherent in the kind of socialism adopted that contributed to dictatorship. Cunningham, in this volume, identifies paternalism as a factor internal to these socialist states that also led to dictatorship.

3. Karl Marx, "Introduction: Toward a Critique of Hegel's Philosophy of Right," "Critique of Hegel's 'Philosophy of Right,'" and "Economic and Philosophic Manuscripts," in *Karl Marx: Selected Writings*, ed. David McLellan (Oxford: Oxford University Press, 1977), pp. 63–74, 26–35, 75–112. These and other major works of Marx, Engels, Lenin, Luxemburg, and many other Marxist authors are available online at http://www.marxists.org/index.htm.

4. The base-superstructure metaphor, and a brief account of the materialist conception of history is found in Marx's "Preface to 'A Critique of Political Economy,'" in *Karl Marx: Selected Writings*. As an example of Marxist humanism, drawing upon Marx's early writings, see thinkers in the Yugoslav Praxis group, for example, Mihailo Marković, *From Affluence to Praxis; Philosophy and Social Criticism* (Ann Arbor: University of Michigan Press, 1974). For an antihumanist, see Louis Althusser, *For Marx* (New York: Pantheon, 1969).

5. See for example, John Stuart Mill, "Socialism and Liberty"; Oscar Wilde, "The Soul of Man Under Socialism"; George Bernard Shaw, "Socialism and Liberty"; Bertrand Russell, "Science and Art Under Socialism"; and R. H. Tawney, "Liberty and Equality," in *Essential Works of Socialism*, 3d ed., ed. Irving Howe (New Haven: Yale, 1986), pp. 239–96.

6. For a collection of influential writings in liberation theology, see *Mysterium Liberationis: Fundamental Concepts of Liberation Theology* (Maryknoll, N.Y.: Orbis, 1993). For a focus on Central America and a case for the compatibility of Marxism and spirituality, see John Brentlinger, "Revolutionizing Spirituality: Reflections on Marxism and Religion," *Science and Society* 64, no. 2 (summer 2000): 171–93. For an example of Jewish liberation theology, see Michael Lerner, "Jewish Liberation Theology and Emancipatory Politics," in *Religion and Economic Justice*, ed. Michael Zweig (Philadelphia: Temple, 1991), pp. 128–44. For an argument for a socialist politics in the U.S. context, with broad appeal to the biblical tradition, see Mary E. Hobgood, *Dismantling Privilege:*

An Ethics of Accountability (Cleveland, Ohio: Pilgrim Press, 2000). For an earlier exploration of the affinities and tensions between Marxism and Christianity, see Alasdair MacIntyre, *Marxism and Christianity* (New York: Schocken, 1968). For an important example of non-Marxist Protestant Christian socialism, see Paul Tillich, "Marxism and Christian Socialism," in Paul Tillich, *The Protestant Era*, trans. with a concluding essay by James Luther Adams (Chicago: University of Chicago Press, 1948), pp. 253–60.

7. As an illustration, Cuba, compared with other developing countries, has achieved very favorable levels of life span, infant mortality, basic nutrition and health care, and access to education. Despite some inefficiencies associated with state planning, the mode of production makes possible a distribution scheme favorable to the less advantaged that may more than compensate for any losses in aggregate production.

8. Martin Khor, "Growing Consensus on Ills of Globalization," http://www.twnside.org.sg/souths/twn/title/ills-cn.htm (cited 12 March 1999).

9. Frances Moore Lappé, Joseph Collins, and Peter Rosset, with Luis Esparza, "Twelve Myths About Hunger," *Food First Backgrounder* 5, no. 3 (summer 1998): 1–4, based on *World Hunger: Twelve Myths*, 2d ed., by Frances Moore Lappé, Joseph Collins, and Peter Rosset, with Luis Esparza (New York: Grove/Atlantic and Food First Books, 1998).

10. Lawrence Mischel, Jared Bernstein, and John Schmitt, *The State of Working America 1998–99* (Ithaca: Cornell University Press, 1999).

11. John Roemer, *A Future for Socialism* (Cambridge: Harvard University Press, 1994).

12. See John O'Neill, *The Market: Ethics, Knowledge, and Politics* (New York: Routledge, 1998).

13. John Stuart Mill, *On Liberty* (New York: Norton, 1975).

14. A similar point is made with reference to John Rawls's distinction between liberty and the conditions making it valuable by Norman Daniels, "Equal Liberty and Unequal Worth of Liberty," in *Reading Rawls: Critical Studies on Rawls' "A Theory of Justice,"* ed. Norman Daniels (New York: Basic Books, 1975), pp. 253–81.

15. For a statement of classical liberalism, see Milton Friedman, *Capitalism and Freedom* (Chicago: University of Chicago, 1962), reviewed in this volume by Macpherson.

16. G. W. F. Hegel, *The Philosophy of Right*, trans. T. M. Knox (Oxford: Clarendon, 1942).

17. Marx, "Introduction: Toward a Critique of Hegel's 'Philosophy of Right.'"

18. For a recent development of this theory of the state, see Milton Fisk, *The State and Justice* (Cambridge: Cambridge University Press, 1989).

19. My own case for market socialism is developed in *Self-Management and the Crisis of Socialism: The Rose in the Fist of the Present* (Lanham, Md.: Rowman & Littlefield, 2000).

20. Karl Marx, "On the Jewish Question," in *Karl Marx: Selected Writings*, pp. 39–62.

21. Marx, "Economic and Philosophic Manuscripts."

22. Ibid., p. 89.

23. Ibid., p. 90.

24. Ibid., pp. 96, 87–88; see Gajo Petrović, "Philosophy and Politics in Socialism," in *Marxist Humanism and Praxis*, ed. and trans. Gerson S. Sher (Buffalo, N.Y.: Prometheus Books, 1978), pp. 7–18.

25. Frederick Engels, "Preface" to Karl Marx and Frederick Engels, *The Communist Manifesto* (1888; reprint, Chicago: Charles H. Kerr Publishing Co., 1984), p. 7.

26. Karl Marx, "Critique of the Gotha Program" [1875], in Karl Marx and Frederick

Engels, *Selected Works*, vol. 3 (Moscow: Progress Publishers, 1970), pp. 13–30; excerpts reprinted as chapter 2 of this volume. Following Lenin, it has become commonplace to refer to the "lower phase of communism" as "socialism" and the higher phase, the ultimate goal, as "communism," thus in effect reversing Marx's 1844 usage (*State and Revolution*, p. 81).

27. Allen E. Buchanan, *Marx and Justice: The Radical Critique of Liberalism* (Totowa, N.J.: Rowman and Littlefield, 1982).

28. Leszek Kolakowski, "The Myth of Human Self-Identity: Unity of Civil and Political Society in Socialist Thought," in *The Socialist Idea: A Reappraisal*, ed. Leszek Kolakowski and Stuart Hampshire (New York: Basic Books, 1974), pp. 18–35.

29. Marx, "Critique of Hegel's Philosophy of Right."

30. Marx and Engels, *The Communist Manifesto*, pp. 42, 58.

31. Or, at least they need to subordinate the dynamics of the market to conscious political will. For debates on the market, including debates about Marx's position, see Bertell Ollman, ed., *Market Socialism: The Debate among Socialists* (New York: Routledge, 1998). The Schweickart essay is from this debate. See also Stanley Moore, *Marx versus Markets* (University Park, Pa.: Pennsylvania State University Press, 1993); and Michael W. Howard, *Self-Management and the Crisis of Socialism*, chap. 4. For additional examples of antimarket socialists who also distinguish their models from the Soviet model, see P. J. Devine, *Democracy and Economic Planning: The Political Economy of a Self-governing Society* (Boulder, Colo.: Westview Press, 1988); W. Paul Cockshott and Allin Cottrell, *Towards a New Socialism* (Nottingham, England: Spokesman, 1993), also available online at http://ricardo.ecn.wfu.edu/~cottrell/socialism_book/index.html, along with other relevant papers.

32. Georg Lukács, *History and Class Consciousness: Studies in Marxist Dialectics* (Cambridge: MIT Press, 1968).

33. Max Horkheimer and Theodor Adorno, *Dialectic of Enlightenment* (London: Allen Lane 1973). The influential essay from this book, "The Culture Industry," is also available in *The Cultural Studies Reader*, ed. Simon During (New York: Routledge, 1993), and online at http://www.marxists.org/reference/subject/philosophy/works/ge/adorno. htm. An anthology of classic works by socialist authors on art and aesthetics is Berel Lang, *Marxism and Art: Writings in Aesthetics and Criticism* (New York: McKay, 1972). Among practicing artists, William Morris stood out at the end of the nineteenth century as a critic of the corrupting effects on the quality of art (and craft) of the capitalist economy. See for example, "Art and Socialism," "The Lesser Arts," and "Useful Work versus Useless Toil," all online at http://www.marxists.org/archive/morris/works/index.htm.

Morris's optimism about reviving craft is hard to sustain after a century of the degradation of skilled work. See Harry Braverman, *Labor and Monopoly Capital: The Degradation of Work in the Twentieth Century* (New York: Monthly Review Press, 1975). Thus others have sought positive potential within these very processes of technological change. See Walter Benjamin, "The Work of Art in the Age of Mechanical Reproduction," in *Illuminations: Essays and Reflections*, ed. with an introduction by Hannah Arendt, trans. Harry Zohn (New York: Schocken Books, 1968), pp. 217–52, for identification of utopian possibilities in the radical transformation of the context and nature of art works brought about by mass reproduction. For an interesting exploration of the relationship between modernist painting and the socialist movement, see T. J. Clark, *Farewell to an Idea: Episodes from the History of Modernism* (New Haven: Yale University Press, 1999).

34. "We must crush the vile thing," a phrase Voltaire used to end his letters. André Maurois, "The Sage of Verney: An Appreciation," in Voltaire, *Candide*, trans. Lowell Blair (New York: Bantam Books, 1959), pp. 1–15.

35. Brentlinger, "Revolutionizing Spirituality," pp. 171–93.

36. See references in note 6. For the importance of the Exodus story in the English civil war, the antislavery movement, etc., see Michael Walzer, *Exodus and Revolution* (New York: Basic Books, 1984); cf. Said's review in Edward W. Said and Christopher Hitchens, *Blaming the Victims: Spurious Scholarship and the Palestinian Question* (London: Verso, 1988). Information on the Catholic Worker movement is available at the following Web site: http://www.catholicworker.org/.

37. Harold Bloom, *How to Read and Why* (New York: Scribner, 2000), pp. 51–54.

38. The following passage from *The Communist Manifesto* (p. 19) is characteristic:

> Subjection of Nature's forces to man, machinery, application of chemistry to industry and agriculture, steam-navigation, railways, electric telegraphs, clearing of whole continents for cultivation, canalization of rivers, whole populations conjured out of the ground—what earlier century had even the presentiment that such productive forces slumbered in the lap of social labor?

39. Taking science in a more positive light, John O'Neill, in *The Market*, chap. 11, offers an antimarket socialist perspective on the practice of science and trends toward its marketization. He reminds us that within capitalist society exist many efficient practices, notably science, in which participants are highly motivated and well-informed without reliance on market mechanisms and incentives. Furthermore, incursion of the market threatens the integrity of such practices and ought to be resisted. The extent to which such practices can be generalized to replace market relations altogether is an intriguing question.

40. For a more critical account of China, see Ngo Vinh Long, "China: Ten Years After the Tiananmen Crackdown," *New Political Science* 21, no. 4 (1999): 463–73.

41. An important exception is John Ehrenberg, *The Dictatorship of the Proletariat: Marxism's Theory of Socialist Democracy* (New York: Routledge, 1992).

42. Antonio Gramsci, *Selections from the Prison Notebooks*, ed. Q. Hoare and G. Nowell Smith (New York: International, 1971).

1.

SOCIALIST

RAYMOND WILLIAMS

Socialist emerged as a philosophical and political description in the first third of the nineteenth century. Its linguistic root was the developed sense of *social*. But this could be understood in two ways, which have had profound effects on the use of the term by radically different political tendencies. *Social* in sense (i) was the merely descriptive term for *society* in its now predominant sense of the system of common life; a *social reformer* wished to reform this system. *Social* in sense (ii) was an emphatic and distinguishing term, explicitly contrasted with *individual* and especially *individualist* theories of society. There has of course been much interaction and overlap between these two senses, but their varying effect can be seen from the beginning in the formation of the term. One popular form of sense (i) was in effect a continuation of *liberalism*: reform, including radical reform, of the social order, to develop, extend, and assure the main *liberal* values: political freedom, the ending of privileges and formal inequalities, social justice (conceived as equity between different individuals and groups). A popular form of sense (ii) went in a quite different direction: a competitive, *individualist* form of society—specifically, industrial capitalism and the system of wage-labor—was seen as the enemy of truly *social* forms, which depended on practical cooperation and mutuality, which in turn could not be achieved while there was still *private (individual)* ownership of the means of production. Real freedom could not be achieved, basic inequalities could not be ended, social justice (conceived now as a just social order rather than equity between the different individuals and groups produced by the existing social order) could not be established, unless a society based on *private* property was replaced by one based on *social* ownership and control.

From Raymond Williams, *Keywords: A Vocabulary of Culture and Society* (New York: Oxford University Press, 1976). Reprinted by permission of HarperCollins Publishers Ltd.

The resulting controversy, between many groups and tendencies all calling themselves socialist, has been long, intricate, and bitter. Each main tendency has found alternative, often derogatory terms for the other. But until circa 1850 the word was too new and too general to have any predominant use. It seems to have been first used in the English Owenite *Cooperative Magazine* of November 1827; its first recorded appearance in French is in 1833. On the other hand, *socialisme* seems to have been first used in French in 1831, and in English in 1837 (Owen, *New Moral World: [and Gazette of the Rational Society]*, III, p. 364). (A use of *socialismo* in Italian, in 1803, seems to have no connection with the later development; its meaning was quite different.) Given the intense political climate, in France and in England in the 1820s and 1830s, the exact dates are less important than the sense of a period. Moreover, it could not then have been known which word would come through as decisive. It was a period of very intense and rapid political argument and formation, and until well into the 1840s other terms stood level with *socialist*, or were indeed more common: *cooperative, mutualist, associationist, societarian, phalansterian, agrarianist, radical*. As late as 1848 Webster's *Dictionary* (USA) defined *socialism* as "a new term for agrarianism," although in France and Germany, and to a lesser extent in England, *socialist* and *socialism* were by then common terms. The active verbs, *socialize* and *socialiser*, had been current in English and French from around 1830.

One alternative term, *communist*, had begun to be used in France and England from 1840. The sense of any of these words could vary in particular national contexts. In England in the 1840s *communist* had strong religious attachments, and this was important since *socialist*, as used by Robert Owen, was associated with opposition to religion and was sometimes avoided for that reason. Developments in France and Germany were different: so much so that Engels, in his *Preface* of 1888 looking back to the *Communist Manifesto* which he and Marx had written in 1848, observed:

> We could not have called it a *Socialist* manifesto. In 1847, Socialism was a middle-class movement, Communism a working-class movement. Socialism was, on the continent at least, respectable; Communism was the very opposite.

Communist had French and German senses of a militant movement, at the same time that in England it was being preferred to *socialist* because it did not involve atheism.

Modern usage began to settle from the 1860s, and in spite of the earlier variations and distinctions it was *socialist* and *socialism* which came through as the predominant words. What also came through in this period was a predominance of sense (ii), as the range of associated words—*cooperative, mutualist, associationist,* and the new (from the 1850s) *collectivist*—made natural. Though there was still extensive and intricate internal dispute, *socialist* and *socialism* were, from this period, accepted general terms. *Communist*, in spite of the distinction that had been made in the 1840s, was very much less used, and parties in the

Marxist tradition took some variant of *social* and *socialist* as titles: usually *Social Democratic*, which meant adherence to *socialism*. Even in the renewed and bitter internal disputes of the period 1880–1914, these titles held. *Communism* was in this period most often used either as a description of an early form of society— *primitive communism*—or as a description of an ultimate form, which would be achieved after passing through *socialism*. Yet, also in this period, movements describing themselves as *socialist*, for example the English Fabians, powerfully revived what was really a variant of sense (i), in which *socialism* was seen as necessary to complete *liberalism*, rather than as an alternative and opposed theory of society. To Shaw and others, *socialism* was "the economic side of the democratic ideal" (*Fabian Essays*, p. 33; 1931) and its achievement was an inevitable prolongation of the earlier tendencies which *Liberalism* had represented. It is interesting that opposing this view, and emphasizing the resistance of the capitalist economic system to such an "inevitable" development, William Morris used the word *communism*. The relative militancy of *communist* had also been affected by the example of the Paris Commune, though there was a significant argument whether the correct term to be derived from that was *communist* or *communard*.

The decisive distinction between *socialist* and *communist*, as in one sense these terms are now ordinarily used, came with the renaming, in 1918, of the *Russian Social-Democratic Labor Party (Bolsheviks)* as the *Communist Party of the Soviet Union (Bolsheviks)*. From that time on, a distinction of *socialist* from *communist*, often with supporting definitions such as *social democrat* or *democratic socialist*, became widely current, although it is significant that all *communist* parties, in line with earlier usage, continued to describe themselves as *socialist* and dedicated to *socialism*. Each tendency continues to deny the title to its opponents and competitors, but what has really happened is a resurfacing, in new terms, of the originally variant senses of *social* and thence *socialist*. Those relying on sense (ii) are right to see other kinds of *socialist* as a new stage of *liberalism* (and thus to call them, often contemptuously, *liberals*), while those relying on sense (i), seeing a natural association between *liberal* values and *socialism*, have grounds for opposing *socialists* who in their view are enemies of the *liberal* tradition (where the difficulty, always, is in the alternative interpretations: (a) political freedom understood as an *individual* right and expressed socially in competitive political parties; (b) *individualism* understood as the competitive and antagonistic ethos and practice of capitalism, which *individual* rights and political competition merely qualify).

Some other associated political terms provide further complications. There is the significant development, in mid-nineteenth century, of *anarchy* and its derivatives in new political senses. *Anarchy* had been used in English from the sixteenth century in a broad sense: "this unleful lyberty or lycence of the multytude is called an Anarchie" (1539). But this specific political sense, often interpreted as opposition to a single ruler—"*Anarchism*. . . the being itself of the people without a Prince or Ruler" (1656) (where the sense is close to that of early *democracy*)—was on the whole less common than the more general sense of disorder and chaos. Yet in 1791 Bentham defined the *anarchist* as one who "denies the validity of the law. . . and calls upon all mankind to rise up in a mass, and resist the execution of it," a sense again near that of early *democrat*. What was really new from the mid-nineteenth century was the positive adoption of the term by certain groups, as a statement of their political position; most of the earlier descriptions were by opponents. *Anarchism* and *anarchist*, by the late nineteenth century, represented a specific continuation of earlier senses of *democracy* and *democrat*, but at a time when both *democracy* and, though less widely, *socialism* had acquired new general and positive senses. Anarchists opposed the *statist* tendencies of much of the *socialist* movement, but stressed *mutuality* and *cooperation* as the principles of the self-organization of society. Particular *anarchist* groups opposed particular tyrannies and governments by *militant* and *violent* means, but this was not a necessary or universal result of *anarchist* principles, and there was in any case a complicated overlap between such policies and *socialist* definitions of *revolution*. Yet the persistent general senses of disorder and chaos were relatively easily transferred (often with obvious injustice) to *anarchists*: the variant senses of *lawlessness*—from active criminality to resistance to laws made by others—were in this context critical. *Militant*, meanwhile, had been going through a related development: its early senses in English were stronger in the context of dedicated activity than in the root *military* sense, and the predominant use, to the late nineteenth century, was in religion: *church militant* (from the early fifteenth century); "our condition, whilst we are in this world, is militant" (Wilkins, *Natural Religion*, 251; 1672); "the Church is ever militant" (Newman 1873). The word was effectively transferred from religious to social activity during the nineteenth century: "militant in the endeavour to reason aright" (Coleridge, *The Friend: A Literary, Moral, and Political Weekly Paper, Excluding Personal and Party Politics and the Events of the Day*, 57; 1809); "a normal condition of militancy against social injustice" (Froude [*History of England from the Fall of Wolsey to the Death of Elizabeth*] 1856). The further development from political to industrial *militancy* came in the twentieth century, and much of the earlier history of the word has been forgotten, except in residual uses. There has also been a marked association—as in *anarchism*—with senses of disorder and of *violence*. *Solidarity*, in its sense of unity in industrial or political action, came into English in the mid-nineteenth century, from its immediate forerunner *solidarité* (French, late eighteenth century). *Exploitation* appeared in English from the early nineteenth century, originally in the sense of profitable working of an area or a material, and from the mid-nineteenth century in the sense of using other persons for (selfish) profit; it depended in both senses on its French forerunner, *exploitation* (late eighteenth century).

   Nihilist was invented by [Ivan] Turgenev in *Fathers and Sons* (1862). Its confusion with *anarchist* has been widespread. *Populist* began in the United States, from the People's Party, in the early 1890s; it spread quickly, and is now often used in distinction from *socialist*, to express reliance on popular interests and sentiments rather than on particular (*principled*) theories and movements. *Syndicalist* appeared in French in 1904 and in English in 1907; it has gone through varying combinations with *anarchism* (in its stress on *mutuality*) and with *socialism*.

The widest term of all, the *Left*, is known from the nineteenth century from an accident of parliamentary seating, but it was not common as a general description before the twentieth century, and *leftism* and *leftist* do not seem to have been used in English before the 1920s. The derisive *lefty*, though it has some currency from the 1930s, belongs mainly to the 1950s and after.

PART I.

SOCIALIST CLASSICS

2.

FROM
CRITIQUE OF THE
GOTHA PROGRAM

KARL MARX

"The emancipation of labor demands the promotion of the instruments of labor to the common property of society and the cooperative regulation of the total labor, with a fair distribution of the proceeds of labor."

"Promotion of the instruments of labor to the common property" ought obviously to read their "conversion into the common property"; but this is only passing.

What are the "proceeds of labor"? The product of labor, or its value? And in the latter case, is it the total value of the product or only that part of the value which labor has newly added to the value of the means of production consumed?

"Proceeds of labor" is a loose notion which [Ferdinand] Lassalle has put in the place of definite economic conceptions.

What is "a fair distribution"?

Do not the bourgeois assert that the present-day distribution is "fair"? And is it not, in fact, the only "fair" distribution on the basis of the present-day mode of production? Are economic relations regulated by legal conceptions or do not, on the contrary, legal relations arise from economic ones? Have not also the socialist sectarians the most varied notions about "fair" distribution?

To understand what is implied in this connection by the phrase "fair distribution," we must take the first paragraph and this one together. The latter presupposes a society wherein "the instruments of labor are common property and the total labor is cooperatively regulated," and from the first paragraph we learn that "the proceeds of labor belong undiminished with equal right to all members of society."

"To all members of society"? To those who do not work as well? What remains

From Karl Marx, *Critique of the Gotha Program* (1875) in *Marx/Engels Selected Works*, vol. 3 (Moscow: Progress Publishers, 1970), pp. 13–30, available online at http://www.marxists.org. (The Gotha program was the product of a meeting of the two wings of the German socialist movement in spring 1875.)

then of the "undiminished proceeds of labor"? Only to those members of society who work? What remains then of the "equal right" of all members of society?

But "all members of society" and "equal right" are obviously mere phrases. The kernel consists in this, that in this communist society every worker must receive the "undiminished" Lassallean "proceeds of labor."

Let us take, first of all, the words "proceeds of labor" in the sense of the product of labor; then the cooperative proceeds of labor are the total social product.

From this must now be deducted:

First, cover for replacement of the means of production used up.

Secondly, additional portion for expansion of production.

Thirdly, reserve or insurance funds to provide against accidents, dislocations caused by natural calamities, etc.

These deductions from the "undiminished proceeds of labor" are an economic necessity and their magnitude is to be determined according to available means and forces, and partly by computation of probabilities, but they are in no way calculable by equity.

There remains the other part of the total product, intended to serve as means of consumption.

Before this is divided among the individuals, there has to be deducted again, from it:

First, the general costs of administration not belonging to production.

This part will, from the outset, be very considerably restricted in comparison with present-day society and it diminishes in proportion as the new society develops.

Secondly, that which is intended for the common satisfaction of needs, such as schools, health services, etc.

From the outset, this part grows considerably in comparison with present-day society and it grows in proportion as the new society develops.

Thirdly, funds for those unable to work, etc., in short, for what is included under so-called official poor relief today.

Only now do we come to the "distribution" which the program, under Lassallean influence, alone has in view in its narrow fashion, namely, to that part of the means of consumption which is divided among the individual producers of the cooperative society.

The "undiminished proceeds of labor" have already unnoticeably become converted into the "diminished" proceeds, although what the producer is deprived of in his capacity as a private individual benefits him directly or indirectly in his capacity as a member of society.

Just as the phrase of the "undiminished proceeds of labor" has disappeared, so now does the phrase of the "proceeds of labor" disappear altogether.

Within the cooperative society based on common ownership of the means of production, the producers do not exchange their products; just as little does the labor employed on the products appear here as the value of these products, as a material quality possessed by them, since now, in contrast to capitalist society, individual labor no longer exists in an indirect fashion but directly as a component part of total labor. The phrase "proceeds of labor," objectionable also today on account of its ambiguity, thus loses all meaning.

What we have to deal with here is a communist society, not as it has developed on its own foundations, but, on the contrary, just as it emerges from capitalist society; which is thus in every respect, economically, morally, and intellectually, still stamped with the birthmarks of the old society from whose womb it emerges. Accordingly, the individual producer receives back from society—after the deductions have been made—exactly what he gives to it. What he has given to it is his individual quantum of labor. For example, the social working day consists of the sum of the individual hours of work; the individual labor time of the individual producer is the part of the social working day contributed by him, his share in it. He receives a certificate from society that he has furnished such and such an amount of labor (after deducting his labor for the common funds), and with this certificate, he draws from the social stock of means of consumption as much as the same amount of labor. The same amount of labor which he has given to society in one form he receives back in another.

Here obviously the same principle prevails as that which regulates the exchange of commodities, as far as this is exchange of equal values. Content and form are changed, because under the altered circumstances no one can give anything except his labor, and because, on the other hand, nothing can pass to the ownership of individuals except individual means of consumption. But, as far as the distribution of the latter among the individual producers is concerned, the same principle prevails as in the exchange of commodity-equivalents: a given amount of labor in one form is exchanged for an equal amount of labor in another form.

Hence, equal right here is still in principle—bourgeois right, although principle and practice are no longer at loggerheads, while the exchange of equivalents in commodity exchange exists only on the average and not in the individual case.

In spite of this advance, this equal right is still constantly stigmatized by a bourgeois limitation. The right of the producers is proportional to the labor they supply; the equality consists in the fact that measurement is made with an equal standard, labor.

But one man is superior to another physically or mentally and supplies more labor in the same time, or can labor for a longer time; and labor, to serve as a measure, must be defined by its duration or intensity, otherwise it ceases to be a standard of measurement. This equal right is an unequal right for unequal labor. It recognizes no class differences, because everyone is only a worker like everyone else; but it tacitly recognizes unequal individual endowment and thus productive capacity as a natural privilege. It is, therefore, a right of inequality, in its content, like every right. Right by its very nature can consist only in the application of an equal standard; but unequal individuals (and they would not be different individuals if they were not unequal) are measurable only by an equal standard insofar as they are brought under an equal point of view, are taken from one definite side only, for instance, in the present case, are regarded only as workers and nothing more is seen in them, everything else being ignored. Further, one worker is married, another is not; one has more children than another, and so on and so forth. Thus, with an equal performance of labor, and hence an equal share in the social consumption fund, one will in fact receive more than another, one will be richer than another, and so on. To avoid all these defects, right instead of being equal would have to be unequal.

But these defects are inevitable in the first phase of communist society as it is when it has just emerged after prolonged birth pangs from capitalist society. Right can never be higher than the economic structure of society and its cultural development conditioned thereby.

In a higher phase of communist society, after the enslaving subordination of the individual to the division of labor, and therewith also the antithesis between mental and physical labor, has vanished; after labor has become not only a means of life but life's prime want; after the productive forces have also increased with the all-around development of the individual, and all the springs of cooperative wealth flow more abundantly—only then can the narrow horizon of bourgeois right be crossed in its entirety and society inscribe on its banners: from each according to his ability, to each according to his needs!

I have dealt more at length with the "undiminished proceeds of labor," on the one hand, and with "equal right" and "fair distribution," on the other, in order to show what a crime it is to attempt, on the one hand, to force on our Party again, as dogmas, ideas which in a certain period had some meaning but have now become obsolete verbal rubbish, while again perverting, on the other, the realistic outlook, which it cost so much effort to instill into the Party but which has now taken root in it, by means of ideological nonsense about right and other trash so common among the democrats and French socialists.

Quite apart from the analysis so far given, it was in general a mistake to make a fuss about so-called distribution and put the principal stress on it.

Any distribution whatever of the means of consumption is only a consequence of the distribution of the conditions of production themselves. The latter distribution, however, is a feature of the mode of production itself. The capitalist mode of production, for example, rests on the fact that the material conditions of production are in the hands of nonworkers in the form of property in capital and land, while the masses are only owners of the personal condition of production, of labor power. If the elements of production are so distributed, then the present-day distribution of the means of consumption results automatically. If the material conditions of production are the cooperative property of the workers themselves, then there likewise results a distribution of the means of consumption different from the present one. Vulgar socialism (and from it in turn a section of the democracy) has taken over from the bourgeois economists the consideration and treatment of distribution as independent of the mode of production and hence the presentation of socialism as turning principally on distribution. After the real relation has long been made clear, why retrogress again? . . .

I come now to the democratic section.

A. "THE FREE BASIS OF THE STATE"

First of all, according to II, the German Workers' party strives for "the free state."

Free state—what is this?

It is by no means the aim of the workers, who have got rid of the narrow mentality of humble subjects, to set the state free. In the German Empire the "state" is almost as "free" as in Russia. Freedom consists in converting the state from an organ superimposed upon society into one completely subordinate to it, and today, too, the forms of state are more free or less free to the extent that they restrict the "freedom of the state."

The German Workers' party—at least if it adopts the program—shows that its socialist ideas are not even skin-deep; in that, instead of treating existing society (and this holds good for any future one) as the basis of the existing state (or of the future state in the case of future society), it treats the state rather an independent entity that possesses its own intellectual, ethical, and libertarian bases.

And what of the riotous misuse which the program makes of the words "present-day state," "present-day society," and of the still more riotous misconception it creates in regard to the state to which it addresses its demands?

"Present-day society" is capitalist society, which exists in all civilized countries, more or less free from medieval admixture, more or less modified by the particular historical development of each country, more or less developed. On the other hand, the "present-day state" changes with a country's frontier. It is different in the Prusso-German Empire from what it is in Switzerland, and different in England from what it is in the United States. "The present-day state" is therefore a fiction.

Nevertheless, the different states of the different civilized countries, in spite of their motley diversity of form, all have this in common, that they are based on modern bourgeois society, only one more or less capitalistically developed. They have, therefore, also certain essential characteristics in common. In this sense it is possible to speak of the "present-day states" in contrast with the future, in which its present root, bourgeois society, will have died off.

The question then arises: what transformation will the state undergo in communist society? In other words, what social functions will remain in existence there that are analogous to present state functions? This question can only be answered scientifically, and one does not get a flea-hop nearer to the problem by a thousandfold combination of the word "people" with the word "state."

Between capitalist and communist society there lies the period of the revolutionary transformation of the one into the other. Corresponding to this is also a political transition period in which the state can be nothing but the revolutionary dictatorship of the proletariat.

Now the program does not deal with this nor with the future state of communist society.

Its political demands contain nothing beyond the old democratic litany familiar to all: universal suffrage, direct legislation, popular rights, a people's militia, etc. They are a mere echo of the bourgeois People's Party, of the League of Peace and Freedom. They are all demands which, insofar as they are not exaggerated in fantastic presentation, have already been realized. Only the state to which they belong does not lie within the borders of the German Empire, but in Switzerland, the United States, etc. This sort of "state of the future" is a present-day state, although existing outside the "framework" of the German Empire.

But one thing has been forgotten. Since the German Workers' party expressly declares that it acts within "the present-day national state," hence within its own state, the Prusso-German Empire—its demands would indeed be otherwise largely meaningless, since one only demands what one has not got—it should not have forgotten the chief thing, namely, that all those pretty little gewgaws rest on the recognition of the so-called sovereignty of the people and hence are appropriate only in a democratic republic.

Since one has not the courage—and wisely so, for the circumstances demand caution—to demand the democratic republic, as the French workers' programs under Louis Philippe and under Louis Napoleon did, one should not have resorted, either, to the subterfuge, neither "honest" nor decent, of demanding things which have meaning only in a democratic republic from a state which is nothing but a police-guarded military despotism, embellished with parliamentary forms, alloyed with a feudal admixture, already influenced by the bourgeoisie and bureaucratically carpentered, and then to assure this state into the bargain that one imagines one will be able to force such things upon it "by legal means."

Even vulgar democracy, which sees the millennium in the democratic republic and has no suspicion that it is precisely in this last form of state of bourgeois society that the class struggle has to be fought out to a conclusion—even it towers mountains above this kind of democratism which keeps within the limits of what is permitted by the police and not permitted by logic.

That, in fact, by the word "state" is meant the government machine, or the state insofar as it forms a special organism separated from society through division of labor, is shown by the words "the German Workers' party demands as the economic basis of the state: a single progressive income tax," etc. Taxes are the economic basis of the government machinery and of nothing else. In the state of the future, existing in Switzerland, this demand has been pretty well fulfilled. Income tax presupposes various sources of income of the various social classes, and hence capitalist society. It is, therefore, nothing remarkable that the Liverpool financial reformers, bourgeois headed by [William E.] Gladstone's brother, are putting forward the same demand as the program.

3.

FROM *CAPITAL*

KARL MARX

THE FETISHISM OF COMMODITIES AND THE SECRET THEREOF

A commodity appears, at first sight, a very trivial thing, and easily understood. Its analysis shows that it is, in reality, a very queer thing, abounding in metaphysical subtleties and theological niceties. So far as it is a value in use, there is nothing mysterious about it, whether we consider it from the point of view that by its properties it is capable of satisfying human wants, or from the point that those properties are the product of human labor. It is as clear as noonday, that man, by his industry, changes the forms of the materials furnished by Nature, in such a way as to make them useful to him. The form of wood, for instance, is altered, by making a table out of it. Yet, for all that, the table continues to be that common, everyday thing, wood. But, so soon as it steps forth as a commodity, it is changed into something transcendent. It not only stands with its feet on the ground, but, in relation to all other commodities, it stands on its head, and evolves out of its wooden brain grotesque ideas, far more wonderful than "table-turning" ever was.

The mystical character of commodities does not originate, therefore, in their use-value. Just as little does it proceed from the nature of the determining factors of value. For, in the first place, however varied the useful kinds of labor, or productive activities, may be, it is a physiological fact, that they are functions of the human organism, and that each such function, whatever may be its nature or form, is essentially the expenditure of human brain, nerves, muscles, etc. Secondly, with regard to that which forms the groundwork for the quantitative deter-

From *Capital*, vol. 1 (1867), trans. Samuel Moore and Edward Aveling (1887; reprint, Moscow: Progress Publishers, n.d.); and "The Trinity Formula," in *Capital*, vol. 3 (1863–1883), ed. Friedrich Engels (1894; reprint, New York: International Publishers, n.d.), available on line at http://www.marxists.org.

mination of value, namely, the duration of that expenditure, or the quantity of labor, it is quite clear that there is a palpable difference between its quantity and quality. In all states of society, the labor time that it costs to produce the means of subsistence must necessarily be an object of interest to mankind, though not of equal interest in different stages of development. And lastly, from the moment that men in any way work for one another, their labor assumes a social form.

Whence, then, arises the enigmatical character of the product of labor, so soon as it assumes the form of commodities? Clearly from this form itself. The equality of all sorts of human labor is expressed objectively by their products all being equally values; the measure of the expenditure of labor-power by the duration of that expenditure takes the form of the quantity of value of the products of labor; and finally, the mutual relations of the producers, within which the social character of their labor affirms itself, take the form of a social relation between the products.

A commodity is therefore a mysterious thing, simply because in it the social character of men's labor appears to them as an objective character stamped upon the product of that labor; because the relation of the producers to the sum total of their own labor is presented to them as a social relation, existing not between themselves, but between the products of their labor. This is the reason why the products of labor become commodities, social things whose qualities are at the same time perceptible and imperceptible by the senses. In the same way the light from an object is perceived by us not as the subjective excitation of our optic nerve, but as the objective form of something outside the eye itself. But, in the act of seeing, there is at all events, an actual passage of light from one thing to another, from the external object to the eye. There is a physical relation between physical things. But it is different with commodities. There, the existence of the things qua commodities, and the value relation between the products of labor which stamps them as commodities, have absolutely no connection with their physical properties and with the material relations arising therefrom. There it is a definite social relation between men, that assumes, in their eyes, the fantastic form of a relation between things. In order, therefore, to find an analogy, we must have recourse to the mist-enveloped regions of the religious world. In that world the productions of the human brain appear as independent beings endowed with life, and entering into relation both with one another and the human race. So it is in the world of commodities with the products of men's hands. This I call the Fetishism which attaches itself to the products of labor, so soon as they are produced as commodities, and which is therefore inseparable from the production of commodities.

This Fetishism of commodities has its origin, as the foregoing analysis has already shown, in the peculiar social character of the labor that produces them.

As a general rule, articles of utility become commodities, only because they are products of the labor of private individuals or groups of individuals who carry on their work independently of each other. The sum total of the labor of all these private individuals forms the aggregate labor of society. Since the producers do not come into social contact with each other until they exchange their products, the specific social character of each producer's labor does not show itself except in the act of exchange. In other words, the labor of the individual asserts itself as a part of the labor of society only by means of the relations which the act of exchange establishes directly between the products, and indirectly, through them, between the producers. To the latter, therefore, the relations connecting the labor of one individual with that of the rest appear, not as direct social relations between individuals at work, but as what they really are, material relations between persons and social relations between things. It is only by being exchanged that the products of labor acquire, as values, one uniform social status, distinct from their varied forms of existence as objects of utility. This division of a product into a useful thing and a value becomes practically important, only when exchange has acquired such an extension that useful articles are produced for the purpose of being exchanged, and their character as values has therefore to be taken into account, beforehand, during production. From this moment the labor of the individual producer acquires socially a twofold character. On the one hand, it must, as a definite useful kind of labor, satisfy a definite social want, and thus hold its place as part and parcel of the collective labor of all, as a branch of a social division of labor that has sprung up spontaneously. On the other hand, it can satisfy the manifold wants of the individual producer himself, only insofar as the mutual exchangeability of all kinds of useful private labor is an established social fact, and therefore the private useful labor of each producer ranks on an equality with that of all others. The equalization of the most different kinds of labor can be the result only of an abstraction from their inequalities, or of reducing them to their common denominator, viz., expenditure of human labor power or human labor in the abstract. The twofold social character of the labor of the individual appears to him, when reflected in his brain, only under those forms which are impressed upon that labor in everyday practice by the exchange of products. In this way, the character that his own labor possesses of being socially useful takes the form of the condition that the product must be not only useful, but useful for others, and the social character that his particular labor has of being the equal of all other particular kinds of labor, takes the form that all the physically different articles that are the products of labor have one common quality, viz., that of having value.

Hence, when we bring the products of our labor into relation with each other as values, it is not because we see in these articles the material receptacles of homogeneous human labor. Quite the contrary: whenever, by an exchange, we equate as values our different products, by that very act, we also equate, as human labor, the different kinds of labor expended upon them. We are not aware of this, nevertheless we do it. Value, therefore, does not stalk about with a label describing what it is. It is value, rather, that converts every product into a social hieroglyphic. Later on, we try to decipher the hieroglyphic, to get behind the secret of our own social products; for to stamp an object of utility as a value, is just as much a social product as language. The recent scientific discovery that the products of labor, so far as they are values, are but material expressions of the human labor spent in their production marks, indeed, an epoch in the history of the development of the human race, but by no means dissipates the mist through which the social character of labor appears to us to be an objective character of the products themselves. The fact that in the particular form of production with which we are dealing, viz., the production of commodities, the specific social character of private labor carried on independently, consists in the equality of every kind of that labor, by virtue of its being human labor, which character, therefore, assumes in the product the form of value—this fact appears to the producers, notwithstanding the discovery above referred to, to be just as real and final, as the fact that, after the discovery by science of the component gases of air, the atmosphere itself remained unaltered.

What, first of all, practically concerns producers when they make an exchange, is the question, how much of some other product they get for their own? In what proportions are the products exchangeable? When these proportions have, by custom, attained a certain stability, they appear to result from the nature of the products, so that, for instance, one ton of iron and two ounces of gold appear as naturally to be of equal value as a pound of gold and a pound of iron, in spite of their different physical and chemical qualities, appear to be of equal weight. The character of having value, when once impressed upon products, obtains fixity only by reason of their acting and reacting upon each other as quantities of value. These quantities vary continually, independently of the will, foresight, and action of the producers. To them, their own social action takes the form of the action of objects, which rule the producers instead of being ruled by them. It requires a fully developed production of commodities before, from accumulated experience alone, the scientific conviction springs up that all the different kinds of private labor, which are carried on independently of each other, and yet as spontaneously developed branches of the social division of labor, are continually being reduced to the quantitative proportions in which society requires them. And why? Because, in the midst of all the accidental and ever fluctuating exchange-relations between the products, the labor time socially necessary for their production forcibly asserts itself like an overriding law of Nature. The law of gravity thus asserts itself when a house falls about our ears. The determination of the magnitude of value by labor time is therefore a secret, hidden under the apparent fluctuations in the relative values of commodities. Its discovery, while removing all appearance of mere accidentality from the determination of the magnitude of the values of products, yet in no way alters the mode in which that determination takes place.

Man's reflections on the forms of social life, and consequently, also, his scientific analysis of those forms, take a course directly opposite to that of their actual historical development. He begins, *post festum*, with the results of the process of development ready to hand before him. The characters that stamp products as commodities, and whose establishment is a necessary preliminary to the circulation of commodities, have already acquired the stability of natural, self-understood forms of social life, before man seeks to decipher, not their historical character, for in his eyes they are immutable, but their meaning. Consequently it was the analysis of the prices of commodities that alone led to the determination of the magnitude of value, and it was the common expression of all commodities in money that alone led to the establishment of their characters as values. It is, however, just this ultimate money-form of the world of commodities that actually conceals, instead of disclosing, the social character of private labor, and the social relations between the individual producers. When I state that coats or boots stand in a relation to linen, because it is the universal incarnation of abstract human labor, the absurdity of the statement is self-evident. Nevertheless, when the producers of coats and boots compare those articles with linen, or, what is the same thing, with gold or silver, as the universal equivalent, they express the relation between their own private labor and the collective labor of society in the same absurd form.

The categories of bourgeois economy consist of such like forms. They are forms of thought expressing with social validity the conditions and relations of a definite, historically determined mode of production, viz., the production of commodities. The whole mystery of commodities, all the magic and necromancy that surrounds the products of labor as long as they take the form of commodities, vanishes therefore, so soon as we come to other forms of production.

Since Robinson Crusoe's experiences are a favorite theme with political economists, let us take a look at him on his island. Moderate though he be, yet some few wants he has to satisfy, and must therefore do a little useful work of various sorts, such as making tools and furniture, taming goats, fishing, and hunting. Of his prayers and the like we take no account, since they are a source of pleasure to him, and he looks upon them as so much recreation. In spite of the variety of his work, he knows that his labor, whatever its form, is but the activity of one and the same Robinson, and, consequently, that it consists of nothing but different modes of human labor. Necessity itself compels him to apportion his time accurately between his different kinds of work. Whether one kind occupies a greater space in his general activity than another, depends on the difficulties, greater or less as the case may be, to be overcome in attaining the useful effect aimed at. This our friend Robinson soon learns by experience, and having rescued a watch, ledger, and pen and ink from the wreck, commences, like a true-born Briton, to keep a set of books. His stock-book contains a list of the objects of utility that belong to him, of the operations necessary for their production; and lastly, of the labor-time that definite quantities of those objects have, on an average, cost him. All the relations between Robinson and the objects that form this wealth of his own creation, are here so simple and clear as to be intelligible without exertion, even to Mr. Sedley Taylor. And yet those relations contain all that is essential to the determination of value.

Let us now transport ourselves from Robinson's island bathed in light to the

European Middle Ages shrouded in darkness. Here, instead of the independent man, we find everyone dependent, serfs and lords, vassals and suzerains, laymen and clergy. Personal dependence here characterizes the social relations of production just as much as it does the other spheres of life organized on the basis of that production. But for the very reason that personal dependence forms the groundwork of society, there is no necessity for labor and its products to assume a fantastic form different from their reality. They take the shape, in the transactions of society, of services in kind and payments in kind. Here the particular and natural form of labor, and not, as in a society based on production of commodities, its general abstract form is the immediate social form of labor. Compulsory labor is just as properly measured by time, as commodity-producing labor; but every serf knows that what he expends in the service of his lord is a definite quantity of his own personal labor power. The tithe to be rendered to the priest is more matter of fact than his blessing. No matter, then, what we may think of the parts played by the different classes of people themselves in this society, the social relations between individuals in the performance of their labor appear at all events as their own mutual personal relations, and are not disguised under the shape of social relations between the products of labor.

For an example of labor in common or directly associated labor, we have no occasion to go back to that spontaneously developed form which we find on the threshold of the history of all civilized races. We have one close at hand in the patriarchal industries of a peasant family, that produces corn, cattle, yarn, linen, and clothing for home use. These different articles are, as regards the family, so many products of its labor, but as between themselves, they are not commodities. The different kinds of labor, such as tillage, cattle tending, spinning, weaving, and making clothes, which result in the various products, are in themselves, and such as they are, direct social functions, because functions of the family, which, just as much as a society based on the production of commodities, possesses a spontaneously developed system of division of labor. The distribution of the work within the family, and the regulation of the labor time of the several members, depend as well upon differences of age and sex as upon natural conditions varying with the seasons. The labor power of each individual, by its very nature, operates in this case merely as a definite portion of the whole labor power of the family, and therefore the measure of the expenditure of individual labor power by its duration, appears here by its very nature as a social character of their labor.

Let us now picture to ourselves, by way of change, a community of free individuals, carrying on their work with the means of production in common, in which the labor power of all the different individuals is consciously applied as the combined labor power of the community. All the characteristics of Robinson's labor are here repeated, but with this difference, that they are social, instead of individual. Everything produced by him was exclusively the result of his own personal labor, and therefore simply an object of use for himself. The total product of our community is a social product. One portion serves as fresh means of production and remains social. But another portion is consumed by the members as means of subsistence. A distribution of this portion amongst them is consequently necessary. The mode of this distribution will vary with the productive organization of the community, and the degree of historical development attained by the producers. We will assume, but merely for the sake of a parallel with the production of commodities, that the share of each individual producer in the means of subsistence is determined by his labor time. Labor time would, in that case, play a double part. Its apportionment in accordance with a definite social plan maintains the proper proportion between the different kinds of work to be done and the various wants of the community. On the other hand, it also serves as a measure of the portion of the common labor borne by each individual, and of his share in the part of the total product destined for individual consumption. The social relations of the individual producers, with regard both to their labor and to its products, are in this case perfectly simple and intelligible, and that with regard not only to production but also to distribution.

The religious world is but the reflex of the real world. And for a society based upon the production of commodities, in which the producers in general enter into social relations with one another by treating their products as commodities and values, whereby they reduce their individual private labor to the standard of homogeneous human labor—for such a society, Christianity with its *cultus* of abstract man, more especially in its bourgeois developments, Protestantism, Deism, etc., is the most fitting form of religion. In the ancient Asiatic and other ancient modes of production, we find that the conversion of products into commodities, and therefore the conversion of men into producers of commodities, holds a subordinate place, which, however, increases in importance as the primitive communities approach nearer and nearer to their dissolution. Trading nations, properly so called, exist in the ancient world only in its interstices, like the gods of Epicurus in the Intermundia, or like Jews in the pores of Polish society. Those ancient social organisms of production are, as compared with bourgeois society, extremely simple and transparent. But they are founded either on the immature development of man individually, who has not yet severed the umbilical cord that unites him with his fellowmen in a primitive tribal community, or upon direct relations of subjection. They can arise and exist only when the development of the productive power of labor has not risen beyond a low stage, and when, therefore, the social relations within the sphere of material life, between man and man, and between man and Nature, are correspondingly narrow. This narrowness is reflected in the ancient worship of Nature, and in the other elements of the popular religions. The religious reflex of the real world can, in any case, only then finally vanish, when the practical relations of everyday life offer to man none but perfectly intelligible and reasonable relations with regard to his fellowmen and to Nature.

The life-process of society, which is based on the process of material production, does not strip off its mystical veil until it is treated as production by freely associated men, and is consciously regulated by them in accordance with a settled plan. This, however, demands for society a certain material groundwork or set of conditions of existence which in their turn are the spontaneous product of a long and painful process of development.

Political Economy has indeed analyzed, however incompletely, value and its magnitude, and has discovered what lies beneath these forms. But it has never once asked the question why labor is represented by the value of its product and labor time by the magnitude of that value. These formulas, which bear it stamped upon them in unmistakable letters, that they belong to a state of society in which the process of production has the mastery over man, instead of being controlled by him, such formulas appear to the bourgeois intellect to be as much a self-evident necessity imposed by Nature as productive labor itself. Hence forms of social production that preceded the bourgeois form are treated by the bourgeoisie in much the same way as the Fathers of the Church treated pre-Christian religions.

To what extent some economists are misled by the Fetishism inherent in commodities, or by the objective appearance of the social characteristics of labor, is shown, among other ways, by the dull and tedious quarrel over the part played by Nature in the formation of exchange-value. Since exchange-value is a definite social manner of expressing the amount of labor bestowed upon an object, Nature has no more to do with it, than it has in fixing the course of exchange.

The mode of production in which the product takes the form of a commodity, or is produced directly for exchange, is the most general and most embryonic form of bourgeois production. It therefore makes its appearance at an early date in history, though not in the same predominating and characteristic manner as nowadays. Hence its Fetish character is comparatively easy to be seen through. But when we come to more concrete forms, even this appearance of simplicity vanishes. Whence arose the illusions of the monetary system? To it gold and silver, when serving as money, did not represent a social relation between producers, but were natural objects with strange social properties. And modern economy, which looks down with such disdain on the monetary system, does not its superstition come out as clear as noonday, whenever it treats of capital? How long is it since economy discarded the physiocratic illusion that rents grow out of the soil and not out of society?

But not to anticipate, we will content ourselves with yet another example relating to the commodity-form. Could commodities themselves speak, they would say: Our use-value may be a thing that interests men. It is no part of us as objects. What, however, does belong to us as objects is our value. Our natural intercourse as commodities proves it. In the eyes of each other we are nothing but exchange-values. Now listen how those commodities speak through the mouth of the economist. "Value"—(i.e., exchange-value) "is a property of things, riches"—(i.e., use-value) "of man. Value, in this sense, necessarily implies exchanges, riches do not." "Riches" (use-value) "are the attribute of men, value is the attribute of commodities. A man or a community is rich, a pearl or a diamond is valuable. . . . A pearl or a diamond is valuable" as a pearl or a diamond. So far no chemist has ever discovered exchange-value either in a pearl or a diamond. The economic discoverers of this chemical element, who by the by lay special claim to critical acumen, find however that the use-value of objects belongs to them independently of their material properties, while their value, on the other hand, forms a part of them as objects. What confirms them in this view is the peculiar circumstance that the use-value of objects is realized without exchange, by means of a direct relation between the objects and man, while, on the other hand, their value is realized only by exchange, that is, by means of a social process. Who fails here to call to mind our good friend, Dogberry, who informs neighbor Seacoal, that, "To be a well-favored man is the gift of fortune; but reading and writing comes by nature." . . .

THE REALM OF FREEDOM

The actual wealth of society, and the possibility of constantly expanding its reproduction process, therefore, do not depend upon the duration of surplus labor, but upon its productivity and the more or less copious conditions of production under which it is performed. In fact, the realm of freedom actually begins only where labor which is determined by necessity and mundane considerations ceases; thus in the very nature of things it lies beyond the sphere of actual material production. Just as the savage must wrestle with Nature to satisfy his wants, to maintain and reproduce life, so must civilized man, and he must do so in all social formations and under all possible modes of production. With his development this realm of physical necessity expands as a result of his wants; but, at the same time, the forces of production which satisfy these wants also increase. Freedom in this field can only consist in socialized man, the associated producers, rationally regulating their interchange with Nature, bringing it under their common control, instead of being ruled by it as by the blind forces of Nature; and achieving this with the least expenditure of energy and under conditions most favorable to, and worthy of, their human nature. But it nonetheless still remains a realm of necessity. Beyond it begins that development of human energy which is an end in itself, the true realm of freedom, which, however, can blossom forth only with this realm of necessity as its basis. The shortening of the working day is its basic prerequisite.

4.

SELECTIONS

ROSA LUXEMBURG

SOCIAL REFORM OR REVOLUTION

The Consequences of Social Reformism and General Nature of Reformism

In the first chapter [of *Social Reform or Revolution*] we aimed to show that Bernstein's theory lifted the program of the socialist movement off its material base and tried to place it on an idealist base. How does this theory fare when translated into practice?

Upon the first comparison, the party practice resulting from Bernstein's theory does not seem to differ from the practice followed by the Social Democracy up to now. Formerly, the activity of the Social Democratic Party consisted of trade-union work, of agitation for social reforms and the democratization of existing political institutions. The difference is not in the *what* but in the *how*.

At present, the trade-union struggle and parliamentary practice are considered to be the means of guiding and educating the proletariat in preparation for the task of taking over power. From the revisionist standpoint, this conquest of power is at the same time impossible or useless. And therefore, trade-union and parliamentary activity are to be carried on by the party only for their immediate results, that is, for the purpose of bettering the situation of the workers, for the gradual reduction of capitalist exploitation, for the extension of social control.

From Rosa Luxemburg, *Social Reform or Revolution* (1900) (London: Militant Publications, 1986 [no copyright]), chaps. 5 and 8; *The Mass Strike, the Political Party and the Trade Unions* (1906), trans. Patrick Lavin (Detroit: Marxist Educational Society of Detroit, 1925), chap. 2; *Organizational Questions of the Russian Social Democracy* (1904) (n.p.: Integer Press, 1934), chap. 2; *The Russian Revolution* (1918), trans. Bertram Wolfe (1922; reprint, New York: Workers Age Publishers, 1940), chaps. 6 and 8; all available online at http://www.marxists.org/archive/luxembur/works/.

So that if we do not consider momentarily the immediate amelioration of the workers' condition—an objective common to our party program as well as to revisionism—the difference between the two outlooks is, in brief, the following. According to the present conception of the party, trade-union and parliamentary activity are important for the socialist movement because such activity prepares the proletariat, that is to say, creates the *subjective* factor of the socialist transformation, for the task of realizing socialism. But according to Bernstein, trade unions and parliamentary activity gradually reduce capitalist exploitation itself. They remove from capitalist society its capitalist character. They realize *objectively* the desired social change.

Examining the matter closely, we see that the two conceptions are diametrically opposed. Viewing the situation from the current standpoint of our party, we say that, as a result of its trade-union and parliamentary struggles, the proletariat becomes convinced of the impossibility of accomplishing a fundamental social change through such activity and arrives at the understanding that the conquest of power is unavoidable. Bernstein's theory, however, begins by declaring that this conquest is impossible. It concludes by affirming that socialism can only be introduced as a result of the trade-union struggle and parliamentary activity. For as seen by Bernstein, trade-union and parliamentary action has a socialist character because it exercises a progressively socializing influence on capitalist economy.

We tried to show that this influence is purely imaginary. The relations between capitalist property and the capitalist State develop in entirely opposite directions, so that the daily practical activity of the present Social Democracy loses, in the last analysis, all connection with work for socialism. From the viewpoint of a movement for socialism, the trade-union struggle and our parliamentary practice are vastly important insofar as they make socialistic the *awareness*, the consciousness, of the proletariat and help to organize it as a class. But once they are considered as instruments of the direct socialization of capitalist economy, they lose not only their usual effectiveness but cease being means of preparing the working class for the conquest of power. Eduard Bernstein and Konrad Schmidt suffer from a complete misunderstanding when they console themselves with the belief that even though the program of the party is reduced to work for social reforms and ordinary trade-union work, the final objective of the labor movement is not thereby discarded, for each forward step reaches beyond the given immediate aim and the socialist goal is implied as a tendency in the supposed advance.

That is certainly true about the present procedure of the German Social Democracy. It is true whenever a firm and conscious effort for the conquest of political power impregnates the trade-union struggle and the work for social reforms. But if this effort is separated from the movement itself and social reforms are made an end in themselves, then such activity not only does not lead to the final goal of socialism but moves in a precisely opposite direction.

Konrad Schmidt simply falls back on the idea that an apparently mechanical movement, once started, cannot stop by itself, because "one's appetite grows with eating," and the working class will not supposedly content itself with reforms till the final socialist transformation is realized.

Now the last mentioned condition is quite real. Its effectiveness is guaranteed by the very insufficiency of capitalist reforms. But the conclusion drawn from it could only be true if it were possible to construct an unbroken chain of augmented reforms leading from the capitalism of today to socialism. This is, of course, sheer fantasy. In accordance with the nature of things as they are the chain breaks quickly, and the paths that the supposed forward movement can take from the point on are many and varied.

What will be the immediate result should our party change its general procedure to suit a viewpoint that wants to emphasize the practical results of our struggle, that is, social reforms? As soon as "immediate results" become the principal aim of our activity, the clear-cut, irreconcilable point of view, which has meaning only insofar as it proposes to win power, will be found more and more inconvenient. The direct consequence of this will be the adoption by the party of a "policy of compensation," a policy of political trading, and an attitude of diffident, diplomatic conciliation. But this attitude cannot be continued for a long time. Since the social reforms can only offer an empty promise, the logical consequence of such a program must necessarily be disillusionment.

It is not true that socialism will arise automatically from the daily struggle of the working class. Socialism will be the consequence of (1) the growing contradictions of capitalist economy and (2) of the comprehension by the working class of the unavoidability of the suppression of these contradictions through a social transformation. When, in the manner of revisionism, the first condition is denied and the second rejected, the labor movement finds itself reduced to a simple cooperative and reformist movement. We move here in a straight line toward the total abandonment of the class viewpoint.

This consequence also becomes evident when we investigate the general character of revisionism. It is obvious that revisionism does not wish to concede that its standpoint is that of the capitalist apologist. It does not join the bourgeois economists in denying the existence of the contradictions of capitalism. But, on the other hand, what precisely constitutes the fundamental point of revisionism and distinguishes it from the attitude taken by the Social Democracy up to now, is that it does not base its theory on the belief that the contradictions of capitalism will be suppressed as a result of the logical inner development of the present economic system.

We may say that the theory of revisionism occupies an intermediate place between two extremes. Revisionism does not expect to see the contradictions of capitalism mature. It does not propose to suppress these contradictions through a revolutionary transformation. It wants to lessen, to attenuate, the capitalist contradictions. So that the antagonism existing between production and exchange is to be mollified by the cessation of crises and the formation of capitalist combines. The antagonism between Capital and Labor is to be adjusted by bettering the situation of the workers and by the conservation of the middle classes. And the contradiction between the class State and society is to be liquidated through increased State control and the progress of democracy.

It is true that the present procedure of the Social Democracy does not consist in waiting for the antagonisms of capitalism to develop and in passing on, only then, to the task of suppressing them. On the contrary, the essence of revolutionary procedure is to be guided by the direction of this development, once it is ascertained, and inferring from this direction what consequences are necessary for the political struggle. Thus the Social Democracy has combated tariff wars and militarism without waiting for their reactionary character to become fully evident. Bernstein's procedure is not guided by a consideration of the development of capitalism, by the prospect of the aggravation of its contradictions. It is guided by the prospect of the attenuation of these contradictions. He shows this when he speaks of the "adaptation" of capitalist economy.

Now when can such a conception be correct? If it is true that capitalism will continue to develop in the direction it takes at present, then its contradictions must necessarily become sharper and more aggravated instead of disappearing. The possibility of the attenuation of the contradictions of capitalism presupposes that the capitalist mode of production itself will stop its progress. In short, the general condition of Bernstein's theory is the cessation of capitalist development.

This way, however, his theory condemns itself in a twofold manner.

In the first place, it manifests its *utopian* character in its stand on the establishment of socialism. For it is clear that a defective capitalist development cannot lead to a socialist transformation.

In the second place, Bernstein's theory reveals its *reactionary* character when it refers to the rapid capitalist development that is taking place at present. Given the development of real capitalism, how can we explain, or rather state, Bernstein's position?

We have demonstrated in the first chapter the baselessness of the economic conditions on which Bernstein builds his analysis of existing social relationships. We have seen that neither the credit system nor cartels can be said to be "means of adaptation" of capitalist economy. We have seen that not even the temporary cessation of crises nor the survival of the middle class can be regarded as symptoms of capitalist adaptation. But even though we should fail to take into account the erroneous character of all these details of Bernstein's theory we cannot help but be stopped short by one feature common to all of them. Bernstein's theory does not seize these manifestations of contemporary economic life as they appear in their organic relationship with the whole of capitalist development, with the complete economic mechanism of capitalism. His theory pulls these details out of their living economic context. It treats them as *disjecta membra* (separate parts) of a lifeless machine.

Consider, for example, his conception of the adaptive effect of credit. If we recognize credit as a higher natural stage of the process of exchange and, therefore, of the contradictions inherent in capitalist exchange, we cannot at the same time see it as a mechanical means of adaptation existing outside of the process of exchange. It would be just as impossible to consider money, merchandise, capital as "means of adaptation" of capitalism.

However, credit, like money, commodities, and capital, is an organic link of capitalist economy at a certain stage of its development. Like them, it is an indispensable gear in the mechanism of capitalist economy and, at the same time, an instrument of destruction, since it aggravates the internal contradictions of capitalism.

The same thing is true about cartels and the new, perfected means of communication.

The same mechanical view is presented by Bernstein's attempt to describe the promise of the cessation of crises as a symptom of the "adaptation" of capitalist economy. For him, crises are simply derangements of the economic mechanism. With their cessation, he thinks, the mechanism could function well. But the fact is that crises are not "derangements" in the usual sense of the word. They are "derangements" without which capitalist economy could not develop at all. For if crises constitute the only method possible in capitalism—and therefore the normal method—of solving periodically the conflict existing between the unlimited extension of production and the narrow limits of the world market, then crises are an organic manifestation inseparable from capitalist economy.

In the "unhindered" advance of capitalist production lurks a threat to capitalism that is much graver than crises. It is the threat of the constant fall of the rate of profit, resulting not from the contradiction between production and exchange, but from the growth of the productivity of labor itself. The fall in the rate of profit has the extremely dangerous tendency of rendering impossible any enterprise for small and middle-sized capitals. It thus limits the new formation and therefore the extension of placements of capital.

And it is precisely crises that constitute the other consequence of the same process. As a result of their periodic *depreciation* of capital, crises bring a fall in the prices of means of production, a paralysis of a part of the active capital, and in time the increase of profits. They thus create the possibilities of the renewed advance of production. Crises therefore appear to be the instruments of rekindling the fire of capitalist development. Their cessation—not temporary cessation, but their total disappearance in the world market—would not lead to the further development of capitalist economy. It would destroy capitalism.

True to the mechanical view of his theory of adaptation, Bernstein forgets the necessity of crises as well as the necessity of new placements of small and middle-sized capitals. And that is why the constant reappearance of small capital seems to him to be the sign of the cessation of capitalist development though, it is, in fact, a symptom of normal capitalist development.

It is important to note that there is a viewpoint from which all the above-mentioned phenomena are seen exactly as they have been presented by the theory of "adaptation." It is the viewpoint of the isolated (single) capitalist, who reflects in his mind the economic facts around him just as they appear when refracted by the laws of competition. The isolated capitalist sees each organic part of the whole of our economy as an independent entity. He sees them as they act on him, the single capitalist. He therefore considers these facts to be simple "derangements" of simple "means of adaptation." For the isolated capitalist, it is true, crises are really simple derangements; the cessation of crises accords him a longer existence. As far as he is concerned, credit is only a means of "adapting" his insufficient productive forces to the needs of the market. And it seems to him that the cartel of which he becomes a member really suppresses industrial anarchy.

Revisionism is nothing else than a theoretic generalization made from the angle of the isolated capitalist. Where does this viewpoint belong theoretically if not in vulgar bourgeois economics?

All the errors of this school rest precisely on the conception that mistakes the phenomena of competition, as seen from the angle of the isolated capitalist, for the phenomena of the whole of capitalist economy. Just as Bernstein considers credit to be a means of "adaptation," so vulgar economy considers money to be a judicious means of "adaptation" to the needs of exchange. Vulgar economy, too, tries to find the antidote against the ills of capitalism in the phenomena of capitalism. Like Bernstein, it believes that it is possible to regulate capitalist economy. And in the manner of Bernstein, it arrives in time at the desire to palliate the contradictions of capitalism, that is, at the belief in the possibility of patching up the sores of capitalism. It ends up by subscribing to a program of reaction. It ends up in utopia.

The theory of revisionism can therefore be defined in the following way. It is a theory of standing still in the socialist movement, built, with the aid of vulgar economy, on a theory of a capitalist standstill. . . .

Conquest of Political Power

The fate of democracy is bound up, we have seen, with the fate of the labor movement. But does the development of democracy render superfluous or impossible a proletarian revolution, that is, the conquest of political power by the workers?

Bernstein settles the question by weighing minutely the good and bad sides of social reform and social revolution. He does it almost in the same manner in which cinnamon or pepper is weighed out in a consumers' cooperative store. He sees the legislative course of historic development as the action of "intelligence," while the revolutionary course of historic development is for him the action of "feeling." Reformist activity, he recognizes as a slow method of historic progress, revolution as a rapid method of progress. In legislation he sees a methodical force; in revolution, a spontaneous force.

We have known for a long time that the petty-bourgeois reformer finds "good" and "bad" sides in everything. He nibbles a bit at all grasses. But the real course of events is little affected by such combination. The carefully gathered little pile of the "good sides" of all things possible collapses at the first fillip of history. Historically, legislative reform and the revolutionary method function in accordance with influences that are much more profound than the consideration of the advantages or inconveniences of one method or another.

In the history of bourgeois society, legislative reform served to strengthen progressively the rising class till the latter was sufficiently strong to seize political power, to suppress the existing juridical system, and to construct itself a new one. Bernstein, thundering against the conquest of political power as a theory of Blanquist violence, has the misfortune of labeling as a Blanquist error that which has always been the pivot and the motive force of human history. From the first appearance of class societies having the class struggle as the essential content of their history, the conquest of political power has been the aim of all rising classes. Here is the starting-point and end of every historic period. This can be seen in the long struggle of the Latin peasantry against the financiers and nobility of ancient Rome, in the struggle of the medieval nobility against the bishops, and in the struggle of the artisans against the nobles, in the cities of the Middle Ages. In modern times, we see it in the struggle of the bourgeoisie against feudalism.

Legislative reform and revolution are not different methods of historic development that can be picked out at pleasure from the counter of history, just as one chooses hot or cold sausages. Legislative reform and revolution are different *factors* in the development of class society. They condition and complement each other, and are at the same time reciprocally exclusive, as are the North and South Poles, the bourgeoisie and proletariat.

Every legal constitution is the *product* of a revolution. In the history of classes, revolution is the act of political creation, while legislation is the political expression of the life of a society that has already come into being. Work for reform does not contain its own force, independent from revolution. During every historic period, work for reforms is carried on only in the direction given to it by the impetus of the last revolution, and continues as long as the impulsion from the last revolution continues to make itself felt. Or, to put it more concretely, in each historic period work for reforms is carried on only in the framework of the social form created by the last revolution. Here is the kernel of the problem.

It is contrary to history to represent work for reforms as a long drawn-out revolution and revolution as a condensed series of reforms. A social transformation and a legislative reform do not differ according to their duration but according to their content. The secret of historic change through the utilization of political power resides precisely in the transformation of simple quantitative modification into a new quality, or, to speak more concretely, in the passage of a historic period from one given form of society to another.

That is why people who pronounce themselves in favor of the method of legislative reform *in place of and in contradistinction to* the conquest of political power and social revolution, do not really choose a more tranquil, calmer, and slower road to the *same* goal, but a *different* goal. Instead of taking a stand for the establishment of a new society they take a stand for surface modifications of the old society. If we follow the political conceptions of revisionism, we arrive at the same conclusion that is reached when we follow the economic theories of revisionism. Our program becomes not the realization of *socialism*, but the reform of *capitalism*; not the suppression of the system of wage labor, but the diminution of exploitation, that is, the suppression of the abuses of capitalism instead of suppression of capitalism itself.

Does the reciprocal role of legislative reform and revolution apply only to the class struggles of the past? Is it possible that now, as a result of the development of the bourgeois juridical system, the function of moving society from one historic phase to another belongs to legislative reform, and that the conquest of State power by the proletariat has really become "an empty phrase," as Bernstein puts it?

The very opposite is true. What distinguishes bourgeois society from other class societies—from ancient society and from the social order of the Middle Ages? Precisely the fact that class domination does not rest on "acquired rights" but on *real economic relations*—the fact that wage labor is not a juridical relation, but purely an economic relation. In our juridical system there is not a single legal formula for the class domination of today. The few remaining traces of such formulae of class domination are (as that concerning servants) survivals of feudal society.

How can wage slavery be suppressed the "legislative way," if wage slavery is not expressed in laws? Bernstein, who would do away with capitalism by means of legislative reforms, finds himself in the same situation as Uspensky's Russian policeman who tells: "Quickly I seized the rascal by the collar! But what do I see? The confounded fellow has no collar!" And that is precisely Bernstein's difficulty.

"All previous societies were based on an antagonism between an oppressing class and an oppressed class" (*Communist Manifesto*). But in the preceding phases of modern society, this antagonism was expressed in distinctly determined juridical relations and could, especially because of that, accord, to a certain extent, a place to new relations within the framework of the old. "In the midst of serfdom, the serf raised himself to the rank of a member of the town community" (*Communist Manifesto*). How was that made possible? It was made possible by the progressive suppression of all feudal privileges in the environs of the city: the corvée, the right to special dress, the inheritance tax, the lord's claim to the best cattle, the personal levy, marriage under duress, the right to succession, etc., which all together constituted serfdom.

In the same way, the small bourgeoisie of the Middle Ages succeeded in raising itself, while it was still under the yoke of feudal absolutism, to the rank of bourgeoisie (*Communist Manifesto*). By what means? By means of the formal partial suppression or complete loosening of the corporative bonds, by the progressive transformation of the fiscal administration and of the army.

Consequently, when we consider the question from the abstract viewpoint, not from the historic viewpoint, we can *imagine* (in view of the former class relations) a legal passage, according to the reformist method, from feudal society to bourgeois society. But what do we see in reality? In reality, we see that legal reforms not only do not obviate the seizure of political power by the bourgeoisie, but have, on the contrary, prepared for it and led to it. A formal social-political transformation was indispensable for the abolition of slavery as well as for the complete suppression of feudalism.

But the situation is entirely different now. No law obliges the proletariat to submit itself to the yoke of capitalism. Poverty, the lack of means of production, obliges the proletariat to submit itself to the yoke of capitalism. And no law in the world can give to the proletariat the means of production while it remains in the framework of bourgeois society, for not laws but economic development have torn the means of production from the producers' possession.

And neither is the exploitation inside the system of wage labor based on laws. The level of wages is not fixed by legislation, but by economic factors. The phenomenon of capitalist exploitation does not rest on a legal disposition, but on the purely economic fact that labor power plays in this exploitation the role of a merchandise possessing, among other characteristics, the agreeable quality of producing value—*more* than the value it consumes in the form of the laborer's means of subsistence. In short, the fundamental relations of the domination of the capitalist class cannot be transformed by means of legislative reforms, on the basis of capitalist society, because these relations have not been introduced by bourgeois laws, nor have they received the form of such laws. Apparently Bernstein is not aware of this, for he speaks of "socialist reforms." On the other hand, he seems to express implicit recognition of this when he writes, on page 10 of his book, that "the economic motive acts freely today, while formerly it was masked by all kinds of relations of domination, by all sorts of ideology."[1]

It is one of the peculiarities of the capitalist order that within it all the elements of the future society first assume, in their development, a form not approaching socialism but, on the contrary, a form moving more and more away from socialism. Production takes on a progressively increasing social character. But under what form is the social character of capitalist production expressed? It is expressed in the form of the large enterprise, in the form of the shareholding concern, the cartel, within which the capitalist antagonisms, capitalist exploitation, the oppression of labor-power, are augmented to the extreme.

In the army, capitalist development leads to the extension of obligatory military service, to the reduction of the time of service, and, consequently, to a material approach to a popular militia. But all of this takes place under the form of modern militarism, in which the domination of the people by the militarist State and the class character of the State manifest themselves most clearly.

In the field of political relations, the development of democracy brings—in the measure that it finds a favorable soil—the participation of all popular strata in political life and, consequently, some sort of "people's State." But this participation takes the form of bourgeois parliamentarism, in which class antagonisms and class domination are not done away with, but are, on the contrary, displayed in the open. Exactly because capitalist development moves through these con-tradictions, it is necessary to extract the kernel of socialist society from its capi-talist shell. Exactly for this reason must the proletariat seize political power and suppress completely the capitalist system.

Of course, Bernstein draws other conclusions. If the development of democ-racy leads to the aggravation and not to the lessening of capitalist antagonisms, "the Social Democracy," he answers us, "in order not to render its task more diffi-cult, must by all means try to stop social reforms and the extension of democratic institutions" (p. 71). Indeed, that would be the right thing to do if the Social Democracy found to its taste, in the petty-bourgeois manner, the futile task of picking for itself all the good sides of history and rejecting the bad sides of history. However, in that case, it should at the same time "try to stop" capitalism in gen-eral, for there is not doubt that latter is the rascal placing all these obstacles in the way of socialism. But capitalism furnishes besides the *obstacles* also the only *pos-sibilities* of realizing the socialist program. The same can be said about democracy.

If democracy has become superfluous or annoying to the bourgeoisie, it is on the contrary necessary and indispensable to the working class. It is necessary to the working class because it creates the political forms (autonomous adminis-tration, electoral rights, etc.) which will serve the proletariat as fulcrums in its task of transforming bourgeois society. Democracy is indispensable to the working class, because only through the exercise of its democratic rights, in the struggle for democracy, can the proletariat become aware of its class interests and its historic task.

In a word, democracy is indispensable not because it renders superfluous the conquest of political power by the proletariat, but because it renders this con-quest of power both *necessary* and *possible*. When Engels, in his preface to the *Class Struggles in France*, revised the tactics of the modern labor movement and urged the legal struggle as opposed to the barricades, he did not have in mind—this comes out of every line of the preface—the question of a definite conquest of political power, but the contemporary daily struggle. He did not have in mind the attitude that the proletariat must take toward the capitalist State at the time of the seizure of power, but the attitude of the proletariat while in the bounds of the capitalist State. Engels was giving directions to the proletariat *oppressed*, and not to the proletariat victorious.

On the other hand, Marx's well-known sentence on the agrarian question in England (Bernstein leans on it heavily), in which he says: "We shall probably succeed easier by buying the estates of the landlords," does not refer to the stand of the proletariat *before, but after its victory*. For there evidently can be a ques-tion of buying the property of the old dominant class only when the workers are in power. The possibility envisaged by Marx is not of the *pacific exercise of the dictatorship of the proletariat* and not the replacement of the dictatorship with capitalist social reforms. There was no doubt for Marx and Engels about the necessity of having the proletariat conquer political power. It is left to Bernstein to consider the poultry yard of bourgeois parliamentarism as the organ by means of which we are to realize the most formidable social transformation of history, *the passage from capitalist society to socialism.*

Bernstein introduces his theory by warning the proletariat against the danger of acquiring power too early. That is, according to Bernstein, the proletariat ought to leave the bourgeois society in its present condition and itself suffer a frightful defeat. If the proletariat came to power, it could draw from Bernstein's theory the following "practical" conclusion: to go to sleep. His theory condemns the proletariat, at the most decisive moments of the struggle, to inactivity, to a passive betrayal of its own cause.

Our program would be a miserable scrap of paper if it could not serve us in *all* eventualities, at *all* moments of the struggle, and if it did not serve us by its *application* and not by its nonapplication. If our program contains the formula of the historical development of society from capitalism to socialism, it must also formulate, in all its characteristic fundamentals, all the transitory phases of this development, and it should, consequently, be able to indicate to the proletariat what ought to be its corresponding action at every moment on the road toward socialism. There can be no time for the proletariat when it will be obliged to abandon its program or be abandoned by it.

Practically, this is manifested in the fact that there can be no time when the proletariat, placed in power by the force of events, is not in the condition, or is not morally obliged, to take certain measures for the realization of its program, that is, take transitory measures in the direction of socialism. Behind the belief that the socialist program can collapse completely at any point of the dictatorship of the proletariat lurks the other belief that *the socialist program is, generally and at all times, unrealizable.*

And what if the transitory measures are premature? The question hides a great number of mistaken ideas concerning the real course of a social transformation.

In the first place, the seizure of political power by the proletariat, that is to say by a large popular class, is not produced artificially. It presupposes (with the exception of such cases as the Paris Commune, when the proletariat did not obtain power after a conscious struggle for its goal, but fell into its hands, like a good thing abandoned by everybody else) a definite degree of maturity of economic and political relations. Here we have the essential difference between *coups d'état* along Blanqui's conception, which are accomplished by an "active minority," and burst out like pistol shot, always inopportunely, and the conquest of political power by a great conscious popular mass, which can only be the product of the decomposition of bourgeois society and therefore bears in itself the economic and political legitimization of its opportune appearance.

If, therefore, considered from the angle of political effect, the conquest of political power by the working class cannot materialize itself "too early," then from the angle of conservation of power, the premature revolution, the thought of which keeps Bernstein awake, menaces us like a sword of Damocles. Against that neither prayers nor supplication, neither scares nor any amount of anguish, are of any avail. And this for two very simple reasons.

In the first place, it is impossible to imagine that a transformation as formidable as the passage from capitalist society to socialist society can be realized in one happy act. To consider that as possible is again to lend color to conceptions that are clearly Blanquist. The socialist transformation supposes a long and stubborn struggle, in the course of which, it is quite probable, the proletariat will be repulsed more than once, so that for the first time, from the viewpoint of the final outcome of the struggle, it will have necessarily come to power "too early."

In the second place, it will be impossible to avoid the "premature" conquest of State power by the proletariat precisely because these "premature" attacks of the proletariat constitute a factor, and indeed a very important factor, creating the political conditions of the final victory. In the course of the political crisis accompanying its seizure of power, in the course of the long and stubborn struggles, the proletariat will acquire the degree of political maturity permitting it to obtain in time a definitive victory of the revolution. Thus these "premature" attacks of the proletariat against the State power are in themselves important historic factors helping to provoke and determine the *point* of the definite victory. Considered from this viewpoint, the idea of a "premature" conquest of political power by the laboring class appears to be a political absurdity derived from a mechanical conception of the development of society, and positing for the victory of the class struggle a point fixed *outside* and *independent* of the class struggle.

Since the proletariat is not in the position to seize political power in any other way than "prematurely," since the proletariat is absolutely obliged to seize power once or several times "too early" before it can maintain itself in power for good, the objection to the "premature" conquest of power is at bottom nothing more than a *general opposition to the aspiration of the proletariat to possess itself of State power.* Just as all roads lead to Rome, so too, do we logically arrive at the conclusion that the revisionist proposal to slight the final aim of the socialist movement is really a recommendation to renounce the socialist movement itself. . . .

THE MASS STRIKE, THE POLITICAL PARTY, AND THE TRADE UNIONS

The first revision of the question of the mass strike which results from the experience of Russia relates to the general conception of the problem. Till the present time the zealous advocates of an "attempt with the mass strike" in Germany of the stamp of Bernstein, Eisner, etc., and also the strongest opponents of such an attempt as represented in the trade-union camp by, for example, Bombelburg, stand, when all is said and done, on the same conception, and that the anarchist one. The apparent polar opposites do not mutually exclude each other but, as always, condition and, at the same time, supplement each other. For the anarchist mode of thought is direct speculation on the "great *Kladderadatsch*," on the social revolution merely as an external and inessential characteristic. According to it, what is essential is the whole abstract, unhistorical view of the mass strike and of all the conditions of the proletarian struggle generally. For the anarchist there exist only two things as material suppositions of his "revolutionary" speculations—first imagination, and second goodwill and courage to rescue humanity from the existing capitalist vale of tears. This fanciful mode of reasoning sixty years ago gave the result that the mass strike was the shortest, surest, and easiest means of springing into the better social future. The same mode of reasoning recently gave the result that the trade-union struggle was the only real "direct action of the masses" and also the only real revolutionary struggle—which, as is well known, is the latest notion of the French and Italian "syndicalists." The fatal thing for anarchism has always been that the methods of struggle improvised in the air were not only a reckoning without their host, that is, they were purely utopian, but that they, while not reckoning in the least with the despised evil reality, unexpectedly became in this evil reality, practical helps to the reaction, where previously they had only been, for the most part, revolutionary speculations.

On the same ground of abstract, unhistorical methods of observation stand those today who would, in the manner of a board of directors, put the mass strike in Germany on the calendar on an appointed day, and those who, like the participants in the trade-union congress at Cologne, would by a prohibition of "propaganda" eliminate the problem of the mass strike from the face of the earth. Both tendencies proceed on the common purely anarchistic assumption that the mass strike is a purely technical means of struggle which can be "decided" at the pleasure and strictly according to conscience, or "forbidden"—a kind of pocketknife which can be kept in the pocket clasped "ready for any emergency," and according to the decision, can be unclasped and used. The opponents of the mass strike do indeed claim for themselves the merit of taking into consideration the historical groundwork and the material conditions of the present conditions in Germany in opposition to the "revolutionary romanticists" who hover in the air, and do not at any point reckon with the hard realities and their possibilities and impossibilities. "Facts and figures; figures and facts!" they cry, like Mr. Gradgrind in Dickens's *Hard Times*. What the trade-union opponent of the mass strike understands by the "historical basis" and "material conditions" is two things— on the one hand the weakness of the proletariat, and on the other hand, the strength of Prussian-German militarism. The inadequate organization of the workers and the imposing Prussian bayonet—these are the facts and figures upon which these trade-union leaders base their practical policy in the given case. Now while it is quite true that the trade-union cash box and the Prussian bayonet are material and very historical phenomena, the conception based upon them is not historical materialism in Marx's sense but a policemanlike materialism in the sense of Puttkammer. The representatives of the capitalist police state reckon much, and indeed, exclusively, with the occasional real power of the organized proletariat as well as with the material might of the bayonet, and from the comparative example of these two rows of figures the comforting conclusion is always drawn that the revolutionary labor movement is produced by individual demagogues and agitators; and that therefore there is in the prisons and bayonets an adequate means of subduing the unpleasant "passing phenomena."

The class-conscious German workers have at last grasped the humor of the policemanlike theory that the whole modern labor movement is an artificial, arbitrary product of a handful of conscienceless "demagogues and agitators."

It is exactly the same conception, however, that finds expression when two or three worthy comrades unite in a voluntary column of night watchmen in order to warn the German working class against the dangerous agitation of a few "revolutionary romanticists" and their "propaganda of the mass strike"; or, when, on the other side, a noisy indignation campaign is engineered by those who, by means of "confidential" agreements between the executive of the party and the general commission of the trade unions, believe they can prevent the outbreak of the mass strike in Germany.

If it depended on the inflammatory "propaganda" of revolutionary romanticists or on confidential or public decisions of the party direction, then we should not even yet have had in Russia a single serious mass strike. In no country in the world—as I pointed out in March 1905 in the *Sachische Arbeiterzeitung*—was the mass strike so little "propagated" or even "discussed" as in Russia. And the isolated examples of decisions and agreements of the Russian party executive which really sought to proclaim the mass strike of their own accord—as, for example, the last attempt in August of this year after the dissolution of the Duma—are almost valueless.

If, therefore, the Russian Revolution teaches us anything, it teaches above all that the mass strike is not artificially "made," not "decided" at random, not "propagated," but that it is a historical phenomenon which, at a given moment, results from social conditions with historical inevitability. It is not therefore by abstract speculations on the possibility or impossibility, the utility or the injuriousness of the mass strike, but only by an examination of those factors and social conditions out of which the mass strike grows in the present phase of the class struggle—in other words, it is not by *subjective criticism* of the mass strike from the standpoint of what is desirable, but only by *objective investigation* of the sources of the mass strike from the standpoint of what is historically inevitable, that the problem can be grasped or even discussed.

In the unreal sphere of abstract logical analysis it can be shown with exactly the same force on either side that the mass strike is absolutely impossible and sure to be defeated, and that it is possible and that its triumph cannot be questioned. And therefore the value of the evidence led on each side is exactly the same—and that is nil. Therefore, the fear of the "propagation" of the mass strike, which has even led to formal anathemas against the persons alleged to be guilty of this crime, is solely the product of the droll confusion of persons. It is just as impossible to "propagate" the mass strike as an abstract means of struggle as it is to propagate the "revolution." "Revolution," like "mass strike," signifies nothing but an external form of the class struggle, which can have sense and meaning only in connection with definite political situations.

If anyone were to undertake to make the mass strike generally, as a form of proletarian action, the object of methodical agitation, and to go house-to-house canvassing with this "idea" in order gradually to win the working class to it, it would be as idle and profitless and absurd an occupation as it would be to seek to make the idea of the revolution or of the fight at the barricades the object of a special agitation. The mass strike has now become the center of the lively interest of the German and the international working class because it is a new form of struggle, and as such is the sure symptom of a thoroughgoing internal revolution in the relations of the classes and in the conditions of the class struggle. It is a testimony to the sound revolutionary instinct and to the quick intelligence of the mass of the German proletariat that, in spite of the obstinate resistance of their trade-union leaders, they are applying themselves to this new problem with such keen interest.

But it does not meet the case, in the presence of this interest and of this fine, intellectual thirst and desire for revolutionary deeds on the part of the workers, to treat them to abstract mental gymnastics on the possibility or impossibility of the mass strike; they should be enlightened on the development of the Russian Revolution, the international significance of that revolution, the sharpening of class antagonisms in Western Europe, the wider political perspectives of the class struggle in Germany, and the role and the tasks of the masses in the coming struggles. Only in this form will the discussion on the mass strike lead to the widening of the intellectual horizon of the proletariat, to the sharpening of their way of thinking, and to the steeling of their energy. . . .

ORGANIZATIONAL QUESTIONS OF THE RUSSIAN SOCIAL DEMOCRACY

In general, it is rigorous, despotic centralism that is preferred by opportunist intellectuals at a time when the revolutionary elements among the workers still lack cohesion and the movement is groping its way, as is the case now in Russia. In a later phase, under a parliamentary regime and in connection with a strong labor party, the opportunist tendencies of the intellectuals express themselves in an inclination toward "decentralization."

If we assume the viewpoint claimed as his own by Lenin and we fear the influence of intellectuals in the proletarian movement, we can conceive of no greater danger to the Russian party than Lenin's plan of organization. *Nothing will more surely enslave a young labor movement to an intellectual élite hungry for power than this bureaucratic straightjacket, which will immobilize the movement and turn it into an automaton manipulated by a Central Committee.* On the other hand, there is no more effective guarantee against opportunist intrigue and personal ambition than the independent revolutionary action of the proletariat, as a result of which the workers acquire the sense of political responsibility and self-reliance.

What is today only a phantom haunting Lenin's imagination may become reality tomorrow.

Let us not forget that the revolution soon to break out in Russia will be a bourgeois and not a proletarian revolution. This modifies radically all the conditions of socialist struggle. The Russian intellectuals, too, will rapidly become imbued with bourgeois ideology. The Social Democracy is at present the only guide of the Russian proletariat. But on the day after the revolution, we shall see the bourgeoisie, and above all the bourgeois intellectuals, seek to use the masses as a stepping-stone to their domination.

The game of bourgeois demagogues will be made easier if at the present stage, the spontaneous action, initiative, and political sense of the advanced sections of the working class are hindered in their development and restricted by the protectorate of an authoritarian Central Committee.

More important is the fundamental falseness of the idea underlying the plan of unqualified centralism—the idea that the road to opportunism can be barred by means of clauses in a party constitution.

Impressed by recent happenings in the socialist parties of France, Italy, and Germany, the Russian Social Democrats tend to regard opportunism as an alien ingredient, brought into the labor movement by representatives of bourgeois democracy. If that were so, no penalties provided by a party constitution could stop this intrusion. This afflux of nonproletarian recruits to the party of the proletariat is the effect of profound social causes, such as the economic collapse of the petty bourgeoisie, the bankruptcy of bourgeois liberalism, and the degeneration of bourgeois democracy. It is naïve to hope to stop this current by means of a formula written down in a constitution.

A manual of regulations may master the life of a small sect or a private circle. A historic current, however, will pass through the mesh of the most subtly worded statutory paragraph. It is furthermore untrue that to repel the elements pushed toward the socialist movement by the decomposition of bourgeois society means to defend the interests of the working class. The Social Democracy has always contended that it represents not only the class interests of the proletariat but also the progressive aspirations of the whole of contemporary society. It represents the interests of all who are oppressed by bourgeois domination. This must not be understood merely in the sense that all these interests are ideally contained in the socialist program. Historic evolution translates the given proposition into reality. In its capacity as a political party, the Social Democracy becomes the haven of all discontented elements in our society and thus of the entire people, as contrasted to the tiny minority of capitalist masters.

But socialists must always know how to subordinate the anguish, rancor, and hope of this motley aggregation to the supreme goal of the working class. The Social Democracy must enclose the tumult of the nonproletarian protestants against existing society within bounds of the revolutionary action of the proletariat. It must assimilate the elements that come to it.

This is only possible if the Social Democracy already contains a strong, politically educated proletarian nucleus, class conscious enough to be able, as up to now in Germany, to pull along in its tow the declassed and petty bourgeois elements that join the party. In that case, greater strictness in the application of the principle of centralization and more severe discipline, specifically formulated in party by-laws, may be an effective safeguard against the opportunist danger. That is how the revolutionary socialist movement in France defended itself against the Jaurèsist confusion. A modification of the constitution at the German Social Democracy in that direction would be a very timely measure.

But even here we should not think of the party constitution as a weapon that is, somehow, self-sufficient. It can be at most a coercive instrument enforcing the will of the proletarian majority in the party. If this majority is lacking, then the most dire sanctions on paper will be of no avail.

However, the influx of bourgeois elements into the party is far from being the only cause of the opportunist trends that are now raising their heads in the Social Democracy. Another cause is the very nature of socialist activity and the contradictions inherent in it.

The international movement of the proletariat toward its complete emancipation is a process peculiar in the following respect. For the first time in the history of civilization, the people are expressing their will consciously and in opposition to all ruling classes. But this will can only be satisfied beyond the limits of the existing system.

Now the mass can only acquire and strengthen this will in the course of day-to-day struggle against the existing social order—that is, within the limits of capitalist society.

On the one hand, we have the mass; on the other, its historic goal, located outside of existing society. On one hand, we have the day-to-day struggle; on the other, the social revolution. Such are the terms of the dialectical contradiction through which the socialist movement makes its way.

It follows that this movement can best advance by tacking betwixt and between the two dangers by which it is constantly being threatened. One is the loss of its mass character; the other, the abandonment of its goal. One is the danger of sinking back to the condition of a sect; the other, the danger of becoming a movement of bourgeois social reform.

That is why it is illusory, and contrary to historic experience, to hope to fix, once for always, the direction of the revolutionary socialist struggle with the aid of formal means, which are expected to secure the labor movement against all possibilities of opportunist digression.

Marxist theory offers us a reliable instrument enabling us to recognize and combat typical manifestations of opportunism. But the socialist movement is a mass movement. Its perils are not the product of the insidious machinations of individuals and groups. They arise out of unavoidable social conditions. We cannot secure ourselves in advance against all possibilities of opportunist deviation. Such dangers can be overcome only by the movement itself—certainly with the aid of Marxist theory, but only after the dangers in question have taken tangible form in practice.

Looked at from this angle, opportunism appears to be a product and an inevitable phase of the historic development of the labor movement.

The Russian Social Democracy arose a short while ago. The political conditions under which the proletarian movement is developing in Russia are quite abnormal. In that country, opportunism is to a large extent a by-product of the groping and experimentation of socialist activity seeking to advance over a terrain that resembles no other in Europe.

In view of this, we find most astonishing the claim that it is possible to avoid any possibility of opportunism in the Russian movement by writing down certain words, instead of others, in the party constitution. *Such an attempt to exercise opportunism by means of a scrap of paper may turn out to be extremely harmful—not to opportunism but to the socialist movement.*

Stop the natural pulsation of a living organism, and you weaken it, and you diminish its resistance and combative spirit—in this instance, not only against opportunism but also (and that is certainly of great importance) against the existing social order. The proposed means turn against the end they are supposed to serve.

In Lenin's overanxious desire to establish the guardianship of an omniscient and omnipotent Central Committee in order to protect so promising and vigorous a labor movement against any misstep, we recognize the symptoms of the same subjectivism that has already played more than one trick on socialist thinking in Russia.

It is amusing to note the strange somersaults that the respectable human "ego" has had to perform in recent Russian history. Knocked to the ground, almost reduced to dust, by Russian absolutism, the "ego" takes revenge by turning to revolutionary activity. In the shape of a committee of conspirators, in the name of a nonexistent Will of the People, it seats itself on a kind of throne and proclaims it is all-powerful. [The reference is to the conspiratorial circle which attacked tsarism from 1879 to 1883 by means of terrorist acts and finally assassinated Alexander II.—Marxist Internet Archives Editor] But the "object" proves to be the stronger. The knout is triumphant, for tsarist might seems to be the "legitimate" expression of history.

In time we see appear on the scene an even more "legitimate" child of history—the Russian labor movement. For the first time, bases for the formation of a real "people's will" are laid in Russian soil.

But here is the "ego" of the Russian revolutionary again! Pirouetting on its head, it once more proclaims itself to be the all-powerful director of history—this time with the title of His Excellency the Central Committee of the Social Democratic Party of Russia.

The nimble acrobat fails to perceive that the only "subject" which merits today the role of director is the collective "ego" of the working class. The working class demands the right to make its mistakes and learn the dialectic of history.

Let us speak plainly. Historically, the errors committed by a truly revolutionary movement are infinitely more fruitful than the infallibility of the cleverest Central Committee. . . .

THE RUSSIAN REVOLUTION

The Problem of Dictatorship

Lenin says [in *The State and Revolution*, "The Transition from Capitalism to Communism"]: the bourgeois state is an instrument of oppression of the working class; the socialist state, of the bourgeoisie. To a certain extent, he says, it is only the capitalist state stood on its head. This simplified view misses the most essential thing: bourgeois class rule has no need of the political training and education of the entire mass of the people, at least not beyond certain narrow limits. But for the proletarian dictatorship that is the life element, the very air without which it is not able to exist.

"Thanks to the open and direct struggle for governmental power," writes Trotsky, "the laboring masses accumulate in the shortest time a considerable amount of political experience and advance quickly from one stage to another of their development."

Here Trotsky refutes himself and his own friends. Just because this is so, they have blocked up the fountain of political experience and the source of this rising development by their suppression of public life! Or else we would have to assume that experience and development were necessary up to the seizure of power by the Bolsheviks, and then, having reached their highest peak, become superfluous thereafter. (Lenin's speech: Russia is won for socialism!!!)

In reality, the opposite is true! It is the very giant tasks which the Bolsheviks have undertaken with courage and determination that demand the most intensive political training of the masses and the accumulation of experience.

Freedom only for the supporters of the government, only for the members of one party—however numerous they may be—is no freedom at all. Freedom is always and exclusively freedom for the one who thinks differently. Not because of any fanatical concept of "justice" but because all that is instructive, wholesome, and purifying in political freedom depends on this essential characteristic, and its effectiveness vanishes when "freedom" becomes a special privilege.

The Bolsheviks themselves will not want, with hand on heart, to deny that, step by step, they have to feel out the ground, try out, experiment, test now one way now another, and that a good many of their measures do not represent priceless pearls of wisdom. Thus it must and will be with all of us when we get to the same point—even if the same difficult circumstances may not prevail everywhere.

The tacit assumption underlying the Lenin-Trotsky theory of dictatorship is this: that the socialist transformation is something for which a ready-made formula lies completed in the pocket of the revolutionary party, which needs only to be carried out energetically in practice. This is, unfortunately—or perhaps fortunately—not the case. Far from being a sum of ready-made prescriptions which have only to be applied, the practical realization of socialism as an economic, social, and juridical system is something which lies completely hidden in the mists of the future. What we possess in our program is nothing but a few main signposts which indicate the general direction in which to look for the necessary measures, and the indications are mainly negative in character at that. Thus we know more or less what we must eliminate at the outset in order to free the road for a socialist economy. But when it comes to the nature of the thousand concrete, practical measures, large and small, necessary to introduce socialist principles into economy, law, and all social relationships, there is no key in any socialist party program or textbook. That is not a shortcoming but rather the very thing that makes scientific socialism superior to the utopian varieties.

The socialist system of society should only be, and can only be, a historical product, born out of the school of its own experiences, born in the course of its realization, as a result of the developments of living history, which—just like organic nature of which, in the last analysis, it forms a part—has the fine habit of always producing along with any real social need the means to its satisfaction, along with the task simultaneously the solution. However, if such is the case, then it is clear that socialism by its very nature cannot be decreed or introduced by *ukase*. It has as its prerequisite a number of measures of force—against property, etc. The negative, the tearing down, can be decreed; the building up, the positive, cannot. New territory. A thousand problems. Only experience is capable of correcting and opening new ways. Only unobstructed, effervescing life falls into a thousand new forms and improvisations, brings to light creative force, itself corrects all mistaken attempts. The public life of countries with limited freedom is so poverty-stricken, so miserable, so rigid, so unfruitful, precisely because, through the exclusion of democracy, it cuts off the living sources of all spiritual riches and progress. (Proof: the year 1905 and the months from February to October 1917.) There it was political in character; the same thing applies to economic and social life also. The whole mass of the people must take part in it. Otherwise, socialism will be decreed from behind a few official desks by a dozen intellectuals.

Public control is indispensably necessary. Otherwise the exchange of experiences remains only with the closed circle of the officials of the new regime. Corruption becomes inevitable (Lenin's words, Bulletin No. 29). Socialism in life demands a complete spiritual transformation in the masses degraded by centuries of bourgeois class rule. Social instincts in place of egotistical ones, mass initiative in place of inertia, idealism which conquers all suffering, etc., etc. No one knows this better, describes it more penetratingly; repeats it more stubbornly than Lenin. But he is completely mistaken in the means he employs. Decree, dictatorial force of the factory overseer, Draconic penalties, rule by terror—all these things are but palliatives. The only way to a rebirth is the school of public life itself, the most unlimited, the broadest democracy and public opinion. It is rule by terror which demoralizes.

When all this is eliminated, what really remains? In place of the representative bodies created by general, popular elections, Lenin and Trotsky have laid down the soviets as the only true representation of political life in the land as a whole, life in the soviets must also become more and more crippled. Without general elections, without unrestricted freedom of press and assembly, without a free struggle of opinion, life dies out in every public institution, becomes a mere semblance of life, in which only the bureaucracy remains as the active element. Public life gradually falls asleep, a few dozen party leaders of inexhaustible energy and boundless experience direct and rule. Among them, in reality only a dozen outstanding heads do the leading and an elite of the working class is invited from time to time to meetings where they are to applaud the speeches of the leaders, and to approve proposed resolutions unanimously—at bottom, then, a clique affair—a dictatorship, to be sure, not the dictatorship of the proletariat, however, but only the dictatorship of a handful of politicians, that is a dictatorship in the bourgeois sense, in the sense of the rule of the Jacobins (the postponement of the Soviet Congress from three-month periods to six-month periods!). Yes, we can go even further: such conditions must inevitably cause a brutalization of public life: attempted assassinations, shooting of hostages, etc. (Lenin's speech on discipline and corruption.). . .

Democracy and Dictatorship

The basic error of the Lenin-Trotsky theory is that they too, just like Kautsky, oppose dictatorship to democracy. "Dictatorship *or* democracy" is the way the question is put by Bolsheviks and Kautsky alike. The latter naturally decides in favor of "democracy," that is, of bourgeois democracy, precisely because he opposes it to the alternative of the socialist revolution. Lenin and Trotsky, on the other hand, decide in favor of dictatorship in contradistinction to democracy, and thereby, in favor of the dictatorship of a handful of persons, that is, in favor of dictatorship on the bourgeois model. They are two opposite poles, both alike being far removed from a genuine socialist policy. The proletariat, when it seizes power, can never follow the good advice of Kautsky, given on the pretext of the "unripeness of the country," the advice being to renounce socialist revolution and devote itself to democracy. It cannot follow this advice without betraying thereby itself, the International, and the revolution. It should and must at once undertake socialist measures in the most energetic, unyielding, and unhesitant fashion, in other words, exercise a dictatorship, but a dictatorship of the *class*, not of a party or of a clique—dictatorship of the class, that means in the broadest public form on the basis of the most active, unlimited participation of the mass of the people, of unlimited democracy.

"As Marxists," writes Trotsky, "we have never been idol worshipers of formal democracy." Surely, we have never been idol worshipers of formal democracy. Nor have we ever been idol worshipers of socialism or Marxism either. Does it follow from this that we may also throw socialism on the scrap-heap, à la Cunow, Lensch, and Parvus, if it becomes uncomfortable for us? Trotsky and Lenin are the living refutation of this answer.

"We have never been idol worshipers of formal democracy." All that that really means is: We have always distinguished the social kernel from the polit-ical form of bourgeois democracy; we have always revealed the hard kernel of social inequality and lack of freedom hidden under the sweet shell of formal equality and freedom—not in order to reject the latter but to spur the working class into not being satisfied with the shell, but rather, by conquering political power, to create a socialist democracy to replace bourgeois democracy—not to eliminate democracy altogether.

But socialist democracy is not something which begins only in the promised land after the foundations of socialist economy are created; it does not come as some sort of Christmas present for the worthy people who, in the interim, have loyally supported a handful of socialist dictators. Socialist democracy begins simultaneously with the beginnings of the destruction of class rule and of the construction of socialism. It begins at the very moment of the seizure of power by the socialist party. It is the same thing as the dictatorship of the proletariat.

Yes, dictatorship! But this dictatorship consists in the *manner of applying democracy*, not in its *elimination*, but in energetic, resolute attacks upon the well-entrenched rights and economic relationships of bourgeois society, without which a socialist transformation cannot be accomplished. But this dictatorship must be the work of the *class* and not of a little leading minority in the name of the class—that is, it must proceed step by step out of the active participation of the masses; it must be under their direct influence, subjected to the control of complete public activity; it must arise out of the growing political training of the mass of the people.

Doubtless the Bolsheviks would have proceeded in this very way were it not that they suffered under the frightful compulsion of the World War, the German occupation, and all the abnormal difficulties connected therewith, things which were inevitably bound to distort any socialist policy, however imbued it might be with the best intentions and the finest principles.

A crude proof of this is provided by the use of terror to so wide an extent by the Soviet government, especially in the most recent period just before the col-lapse of German imperialism, and just after the attempt on the life of the German ambassador. The commonplace to the effect that revolutions are not pink teas is in itself pretty inadequate.

Everything that happens in Russia is comprehensible and represents an inevitable chain of causes and effects, the starting point and end term of which are: the failure of the German proletariat and the occupation of Russia by German imperialism. It would be demanding something superhuman from Lenin and his comrades if we should expect of them that under such circumstances they should conjure forth the finest democracy, the most exemplary dictatorship of the proletariat, and a flourishing socialist economy. By their determined revolutionary stand, their exemplary strength in action, and their unbreakable loyalty to international socialism, they have contributed whatever could possibly be contributed under such devilishly hard conditions. The danger begins only when they make a virtue of necessity and want to freeze into a complete theoretical system all the tactics forced upon them by these fatal circumstances, and want to recommend them to the international proletariat as a model of socialist tactics. When they get in their own light in this way, and hide their genuine, unquestionable historical service under the bushel of false steps forced on them by necessity, they render a poor service to international socialism for the sake of which they have fought and suffered; for they want to place in its storehouse as new discoveries all the distortions prescribed in Russia by necessity and compulsion—in the last analysis only by-products of the bankruptcy of international socialism in the present World War.

Let the German government socialists cry that the rule of the Bolsheviks in Russia is a distorted expression of the dictatorship of the proletariat. If it was or is such, that is only because it is a product of the behavior of the German proletariat, in itself a distorted expression of the socialist class struggle. All of us are subject to the laws of history, and it is only internationally that the socialist order of society can be realized. The Bolsheviks have shown that they are capable of everything that a genuine revolutionary party can contribute within the limits of historical possibilities. They are not supposed to perform miracles. For a model and faultless proletarian revolution in an isolated land, exhausted by world war, strangled by imperialism, betrayed by the international proletariat, would be a miracle.

What is in order is to distinguish the essential from the nonessential, the kernel from the accidental excrescences in the policies of the Bolsheviks. In the present period, when we face decisive final struggles in all the world, the most important problem of socialism was and is the burning question of our time. It is not a matter of this or that secondary question of tactics, but of the capacity for action of the proletariat, the strength to act, the will to power of socialism as such. In this, Lenin and Trotsky and their friends were the *first*, those who went ahead as an example to the proletariat of the world; they are still the *only ones* up to now who can cry with Hutten: "I have dared!"

This is the essential and *enduring* in Bolshevik policy. In *this* sense theirs is the immortal historical service of having marched at the head of the international proletariat with the conquest of political power and the practical placing of the problem of the realization of socialism, and of having advanced mightily the settlement of the score between capital and labor in the entire world. In Russia the problem could only be posed. It could not be solved in Russia. And in *this* sense, the future everywhere belongs to "Bolshevism."

NOTE

1. Eduard Bernstein, *Evolutionary Socialism* (New York: Schocken Books, 1961), p. 15; the page references of Luxemburg's citations in the text are to a different edition.—*Ed.*

PART II.

RETROSPECTIVE ASSESSMENTS

5.

SOCIAL DEMOCRACY
AND SOCIALISM

ADAM PRZEWORSKI

Three conclusions do not follow from the arguments developed in [*Capitalism and Social Democracy*]. These arguments do not lead to a rejection of social democracy. They do not assert that reforms are impossible. They do not imply that workers would never opt for socialism. And, since popular wisdom teaches that pessimism is but informed optimism, I do not even consider my views pessimistic, only informed.

This clarification seems necessary because such conclusions tend to be attributed to the analysis developed above by writers who are more sanguine than I am about the transformative potential of the European Left, particularly the Swedish Social Democracy. In fact, I think that social democrats have done about as well as they could have under historical circumstances not of their choosing and I am quite sympathetic to their unenviable predicaments. I only doubt that they would lead their societies to socialism. I am sure that reforms are possible, but that does not mean that reformism is a viable strategy of transition to socialism. I do not know under what conditions workers and other people would prefer socialism over capitalism, but I think I have demonstrated that they are unlikely to opt for socialism in an exclusive pursuit of their economic interests. And since I see the combination of capitalism with political democracy as a form of society that is highly conducive to the pursuit of immediate economic interests, I am skeptical about the possibilities of bringing about socialism by a deliberate action of trade-unions, political parties, or governments.

I do not see my views as implying a rejection of social democracy or, more broadly, reformist socialism because I do not see acceptable historical alterna-

From Adam Przeworski, *Capitalism and Social Democracy* (Cambridge: Cambridge University Press, 1985), pp. 239–48. Reprinted by permission of Cambridge University Press.

tives.[1] In retrospect, the crucial decision was to seek political power. When Marx criticized in 1864 all those who sought to build a socialist society autonomously and independently of the existing institutions, he claimed that their project was unfeasible without first conquering political power. This is why "the great duty" he defined for the working class was to struggle for power. Reformists, specifically Bernstein, eventually translated this task into competition for the control of the existing government institutions, while revolutionaries, notably Lenin, wanted to conquer power in order to destroy these institutions. But in either case the struggle for socialism became politicized; it became a struggle for political power. True, this power was to be used eventually as an instrument for realizing all the goals socialists sought but at the same time all goals which they sought became subordinated to one centralized thrust for political power. Whether at stake were working conditions at the local mill, a neighborhood school, a cultural center, wages, or the situation of women, everything became merged into one big struggle, "the class struggle," that required the conquest of political power. Wanting to improve conditions under which one worked, militating to win equality, forming a consumer cooperative, struggling to free sexuality, or organizing to plant flowers in a local park would be related to socialism by becoming all intertwined into an electoral campaign (or an insurrectionary conspiracy) designed to win control over the government. One could not struggle for socialism in one's personal life, every day; one would not be struggling for it when transforming relations within one's family, work group, or neighborhood. Socialist practice required a unique repository in political parties because they were the institutions that related everything to the "great duty of the working class."

Was the alternative possible? Could the movement for socialism remain independent of the existing political institutions? Could it have developed autonomously, in a decentralized, spontaneous, polymorphous manner? Was it feasible for the cooperatives, unions, and clubs of the 1860s and the 1880s to remain autonomous and to pursue their own goals? Ironically, the first movement in one hundred years which attempted such a "self-limitation" was born under the "communist" rule, in Poland. Yet Arato is right that the limited character of the goals creates a strategic dilemma.[2] This is the same dilemma that socialists and anarchists faced in Western Europe. When confronted with a hostile and repressive state, no movement can stop short of reaching for political power— even if it has most limited objectives; just to protect itself. Socialists had no choice: they had to struggle for political power because any other movement for socialism would have been stamped out by force and they had to utilize the opportunities offered by participation to improve the immediate conditions of workers because otherwise they would not have gained support among them. They had to struggle for power and they were lucky enough to be able to do it under democratic conditions. Everything else was pretty much a consequence.

Once socialists had decided to struggle for political power and once they began to compete within the existing representative institutions, everything that followed was narrowly constrained. Most of the original fears about deleterious effects of participation did materialize: masses could not struggle for socialism but had to delegate this task to leaders—representatives, the movement became bureaucratized, tactics were reduced to electoralism, political discussions were limited to issues that could be resolved as a result of victory in the next elections, any project of society that would not help win elections was denounced as a utopia. Since socialists still could not win elections with majorities necessary to pursue the socialist program—the program with which they originally sought to conquer political power—they had to do what was possible. They became committed to employment, equality, and efficiency. They did do much: socialists strengthened political democracy, introduced a series of reforms in favor of workers, equalized the access to education, provided a minimum of material security for most people. It is moot whether some of the same reforms would not have been introduced by others and the general gist of evidence indicates that social democratic tenure in office does make a difference for efficiency and equality. Where they have been successful, social democrats institutionalized a relatively solid compromise between organizations of workers and of capitalists.

Social democrats brought about a number of reforms: a sufficient proof that reforms are possible. In fact, capitalism was being reformed even before first socialists came to office: there was Disraeli, Bismarck, Giolitti. The issue is not whether reforms are possible but reformism. Those who conclude that reforms are to be expected as the result of the governmental tenure of the Swedish Social Democrats or as an eventual consequence of implementing the Alternative Economic Strategy in Great Britain are most likely correct.[3] But they claim to have demonstrated the possibility of reforms leading to socialism—and that is not the same.

Reforms would lead to socialism if and only if they were (1) irreversible, (2) cumulative in effects, (3) conducive to new reforms, and (4) directed towards socialism. As we have seen, reformist socialists since the 1890s thought that reforms would indeed satisfy all these conditions and thus gradually cumulate in socialism. So far at least they have not.

Reforms are reversible. The recent series of right-wing electoral victories resulted in denationalizations of industries, eliminations of welfare programs, reductions of protection from unemployment, restrictions of civil liberties and of the right to organize, and so forth. Moreover, as Martin has shown, in many cases it is sufficient that the government does nothing for previously introduced reforms to become undone.[4]

Reforms do not necessarily cumulate even if they are not reversed. Reforms would cumulate if each new reform were a step to some state of the world we would recognize as socialism. But life constantly generates new problems that call for resolution, whether these problems result from past reforms or occur independently. Contamination of the environment, proliferation of dangerous products, bureaucratization of the state apparatus, erosion of the private sphere, complication of policy issues beyond the comprehension of most citizens, the growth of administrative control—all these phenomena have arisen since socialists entered the path of reforms. True, many old ills were overcome or at least mitigated, but quite a few new ones emerged. Indeed, lists of problems to be resolved are not any shorter in the socialist programs of today than they were at the turn of the century. The most striking impression one gets from looking at the way in which socialists see their mission today—an exchange of letters among Brandt, Kreisky, and Palme is most revealing—is that they think of themselves as standing ready to cope with whatever problems that are likely to appear, rather than to transform anything.[5] And coping with problems is not reformism.

Not all reforms are conducive to new reforms. This is the thrust of the oldest doubts about the reformist strategy, particularly by Luxemburg. In several situations reforms which satisfy immediate demands of workers undermine future possibilities. "Insofar as trade unions can intervene in the technical department of production," Luxemburg noted, "they can only oppose technical innovation . . . They act here in a reactionary direction."[6] The issue which continues to occupy the center of controversies concerns the effect of reforms upon the working-class movements. Luxemburg was again the most articulate proponent of the view that reforms demobilize—a view for which I find much historical support. Yet several students of the Swedish Social Democracy, notably Korpi,[7] muster empirical evidence to support the argument that each new wave of reforms has had a mobilizing impact upon the Swedish working class. The success of the Swedish Social Democrats is often contrasted to the failure of the British Labour Party to achieve similar reforms and to maintain working-class mobilization.[8] All that can be said at this time is that there is enough evidence on both sides of the argument to call for a more systematic empirical investigation than the issue has received thus far.

What does seem clear is that compressing reforms into a single moment does not resolve but intensifies the difficulties. There are still some writers who believe that the enthusiasm of socialist transition will make everyone so productive that no economic crisis would ensue.[9] Thus far, however, socialist governments which tried to combine nationalizations, redistribution of income, and acceleration of growth invariably discovered that stimulation of demand through redistribution of income does not work when it becomes a part of such a package. Eventually not only investment falls but even capacity utilization; wage gains become eroded; economic constraints become unbearable; and the reform program collapses.

Finally, even if reforms were irreversible, cumulative, and mobilizing, where do they lead? Do they lead to socialism? This is a more controversial issue, since we can no longer avoid saying something about the meaning of "socialism."

If socialism consists of full employment, equality, and efficiency, then the Swedish Social Democrats are reasonably close to the goal and not likely to go too far back from it. If they succeed in addition in socializing a large part of industry under popularly elected public boards of directors and in continuing to run the economy in a fairly efficient manner, many will consider that at least the Swedish ship would have completed the voyage described by Jaures, having floated unnoticeably but unmistakably into socialist waters.[10]

Suppose then that the Swedish strategy does work: industries are socialized without an investment strike, public ownership continues to be supported by voters, workers are disciplined, and the economy enjoys an advantageous position in the international system. Profit is pursued efficiently, an almost full employment is maintained, inequality is reduced to a minimum. Everyone works, everyone works profitably, and everyone is equal. This is certainly an attractive vision.

But one could also describe this society differently. Here is a society in which blind pursuit of profit has become the exclusive principle of rationality, to the point that even the socially owned enterprises are guided by this principle. Wage slavery has become universalized to the point that everyone is subjected to toil. Alienation reigns: individuals are forced to sell their labor power and even the society as a whole cannot control the process of accumulation, which obeys criteria of private profitability. Families and schools are organized and regulated to prepare for production. Young people are forced into molds so that they would fit into places in this system. It would be trivial to go on.

This is not a caricature but a description in terms of the socialist project of one hundred years ago; in terms of that socialist movement that set itself to abolish the pursuit of profit, wage slavery, and the divisions they entail; that was to bring emancipation, liberation. Socialism was to be a society in which people individually would acquire control over their lives because their existence would no longer be an instrument of survival and people would collectively acquire control over shared resources and efforts because their allocation would be a subject of joined deliberation and rational choice. Socialism was not a movement for full employment but for the abolition of wage slavery; it was not a movement for efficiency but for collective rationality; it was not a movement for equality but for freedom.

Socialists gave up these goals when they discovered that they could not realize them in the foreseeable future. Economic conditions were not ripe and political support insufficient. Seeking to advance the immediate interests of their constituents, socialists thus opted for the pursuit of efficiency, employment, and equality—a second-best and the best that was possible.

The simultaneous pursuit of higher wages and full employment placed socialists in a dilemma. The response of profit-maximizing firms to wage pressure is to reduce employment and under capitalism people who are not fully employed are typically much worse off materially. Hence socialists have to struggle to increase employment and to protect those who are not employed, in either case inducing firms to employ more people than they would have otherwise. When socialists push for higher wages, they induce firms to utilize techniques of production which save labor and generate unemployment. When they force firms to employ or to bear the costs of unemployment, they induce firms to utilize techniques which are labor-intensive. Thus either people are unemployed and suffer material deprivation or they labor unnecessarily. Indeed, the struggle for full employment results in retarding the possibilities of liberation of labor.

Since the efforts to secure full employment are becoming increasingly quixotic, socialists are stumbling onto the program of reducing labor time and redistributing work. This program is not popular among fully employed sectors of the working class as well as among socialist politicians and managers who are concerned about efficiency and competitiveness. Yet this program does constitute a way out of the dilemma. Reduction of labor time without a corresponding reduction of wages forces firms to seek labor-saving techniques and thus to create possibilities of subsequent reductions of labor time. These possibilities are constrained by international competition which divides workers in different countries and which prevents governments from legislating reductions of working hours. These possibilities are also limited by the availability of techniques of production. Yet techniques of production are not given. They become available as the "existing" techniques among which firms choose because a society actively seeks the particular kinds of techniques. We all know how many people would have been working today in banks had computers not been invented and introduced. IBM is right: "Machines should work, people should think."

Let us engage in some utopian fantasies. With Marx, imagine first a society where labor in which a human being does what a machine could do has ceased.

All processes of production, maintenance, and distribution are performed by machines unassisted by direct labor. Machines are produced by machines according to instructions of meta-machines, which are programmed to produce a basket of goods while minimizing physical resources. Labor time necessary to produce these goods (including machines and meta-machines) is negligible. Some human activities ("indirect labor") eventually enter this production process but they need not occupy us at the moment.

Secondly, suppose that this process operates in such a way that the output (measured as a vector of physical quantities) can always be strictly larger than it was previously.

Thirdly, all individuals, regardless of their characteristics and contributions, obtain what they need.

These three features—automation, accumulation, and independence of want-satisfaction from labor—constitute the necessary conditions for the liberation of labor, a double liberation simultaneously from toil and from scarcity. A socialist society would be a society organized on two principles. First, production would be organized so as to generate the capacity for an almost instantaneous satisfaction of material wants of everyone while reducing direct labor to a historically feasible minimum. Secondly, besides a historically necessary minimum of mutual claims and guarantees no other institutions would exist. Scarcity, toil, and socially organized repression would be abolished. Free time is a necessary and sufficient condition for socialism because it constitutes freedom from want, labor, and socially induced constraint.

Without going into details, let us see what free time implies. First, note that several problems of capitalism become simply irrelevant. "Unemployment" is no longer the fate of free labor power. Conditions of work lose their importance as work under such conditions disappears. Equality ceases to be a meaningful term: it is an issue only in an unfree society. Freedom from scarcity and labor means that needs become qualitatively heterogeneous, and their satisfaction no longer reducible to a single dimension. Under socialism those people are rich who have rich needs.[11] Even democracy is less problematic: democratic participation in the making of binding decisions loses its urgency when few decisions made by anyone are binding upon others. A democratic family is a family where all members are equal; a socialist family is one in which they are free. The problem is no longer one of extending democracy from the political to the social realm—the quintessence of social democracy under capitalism—but of reducing mutual constraint. Hence, of the needs and problems of capitalism little if anything remains. "Free time—which is both idle time and time for higher activity—has *naturally* transformed its possessor into a different subject."[12]

Time free from labor is free. While certain ways of dividing activities may emerge as a result of freely formulated choices, this division is no longer an institution. Choices are not only freely made: they are freely formulated. When direct labor is not necessary, places-to-be-occupied in the division of labor no longer exist. We are no longer born, as Sartre put it, in the image of our dead grandfather.[13] The choice is no longer "what will I become," where the "what" is prior and given as "a pilot," "a nurse," or "a garbage collector." The "what" itself becomes the object of individual making; it is continually reinvented by each individual for him- or herself.

These choices may result in specialization of activities, as some people push the frontiers of molecular biology while others push those of tennis. Some people may like to teach others while other people may be captivated by watching trees grow. This freedom obviously poses the question upon which Carr reflected in the seclusion of his Oxford study: would labor (indirect, that is, scientific and direct to the extent to which it is still necessary) happen to be performed as a result of free choice?[14] I do not know; we are too far away to speculate.

Free time, from labor and scarcity, also implies that the society, to coin a horror, becomes "defunctionalized." A particular manner of organizing one activity would no longer be necessary for reproducing other activities. Socialist society, to follow Sartre again, would be organized without being institutionalized. "The family" is no longer an institution: people organize cohabitation as and if they cohabit. Since functions of the family are no longer given when labor is no longer necessary, sex, nurture, and maintenance need not be associated according to any prior pattern.[15] Sexual repression loses its social basis.[16]

Needs no longer assume the form of "interests," that is, the limits of their satisfaction are no longer objectifications of human activity. Their dynamic is driven and restricted only by their internal structure. Objectification occurs if and only if it responds to a need for objectification: I paint or split genes because I like to see painting or the truth of hypotheses. No "end of history" occurs here, as is sometimes supposed in the argument that Marx was inconsistent when he posited simultaneously that needs are dynamic and that scarcity can be abolished. We must think dialectically: scarcity is abolished because the capacity to satisfy material needs asymptotically converges to their dynamic path.[17] Whether material needs would continue to grow under socialism I again do not know. As long as the satisfaction of needs is externally constrained, we cannot tell what human needs are.

Speaking of the Paris Commune, Marx emphasized that the working class has no ready-made ideals to realize, it has only to set itself free.[18] This statement should not be taken as an injunction against utopian fantasies and even less as one against utopian analysis. All it asserts is that we cannot tell today what a socialist society would be like precisely because we do not know what human beings would want and what they would do if they were free. Socialism is not yet another social order, it is the end of all social orders: this statement should be taken seriously. "Socialism" in singular is thus a contradiction in terms, for socialism means freedom and thus variety. It means freedom, not democracy, equality, creativity, or happiness. Socialism is not a new form of coercion to make everyone "creative."[19] A free individual may be uncreative; "realization of human potential" may show that it would have been better if this potential remained dormant. Freedom may turn into universal misery; it may bring forth the truly human sources of repression, if indeed the finite nature of life underlies the aggressive and repressive forces.[20] We do not know. Socialism is not a millennium, not a guarantee of happiness. It is a society free of alienation—if this term can still be restored to its meaning rather than be used as a generalized lament—a society in which objective conditions have been abolished, in which people are at every moment free, in which nothing is prior and given, in which life is not an instrument of survival, and things not instruments of power, in which all values are autonomous, in which the relation between a person and oneself is not mediated by things. Abolition of capitalism is a necessity not because such are the laws of history or because socialism is superior to it in any way, neither for reasons of Newton or Kant, but only because capitalism prevents us from becoming whatever we might become when we are free.

Having arrived at an unknown destination we must, unfortunately, return to the very first step. We have seen that capitalism develops the conditions for liberation but it cannot free. We have seen that freedom is necessary and sufficient for socialism. But does capitalism generate the need for freedom, a need that could underlie a political transition toward socialism?

This is not a question to be resolved theoretically. The only way to know is by practice, a political practice in the broadest, Greek, sense of the word "political." Unity of theory and practice does not have a unique repository in political parties. The need for freedom is integral. Socialist democracy is not something to be found in parliaments, factories, or families: it is not simply a democratization of capitalist institutions. Freedom means deinstitutionalization; it means individual autonomy. Socialism may perhaps become possible, but only on the condition that the movement for socialism regains the integral scope that characterized several of its currents outside the dogmas of the Internationals, only on the condition that this movement ceases to make the socialist project conditional upon the continual improvement of material conditions of the working class. It may become possible when socialism once again becomes a social movement and not solely an economic one, when it learns from the women's movement, when it reassimilates cultural issues.

The time is not near. There is every reason to expect that capitalism will continue to offer an opportunity to improve material conditions and that it will be defended by force where and when it does not, while conditions for socialism continue to rot. This is why dreams of a utopia cannot be a substitute for the struggle to make capitalism more efficient and more humane. Poverty and oppression are here, and they will not be alleviated by the possibility of a better future. The struggle for improving capitalism is as essential as ever before. But we should not confuse this struggle with the quest for socialism.

NOTES

1. It takes either an entrenched habit or ill will to interpret my views as an endorsement of Leninism, as does Carmen Sirianni ["Councils and Parliaments: The Problem of Dual Power and Democracy in Comparative Prospective," *Politics and Society* 12, no. 1 (1983): 83–123]. I suspect that the syllogism which leads to this conclusion must be that anyone who is a socialist critical of reformism ergo must be a revolutionary, that is, a Leninist. Personally, I feel free of the mental prison in which this alternative has been perpetuated. I see myself as a follower not of Vladimir Ilyich but of that other great Russian socialist thinker, Georgij Konstantinowich Pessim.

2. Andrew Arato, "The Democratic Theory of the Polish Opposition" (unpublished paper, 1983).

3. For the first, see, for example, John D. Stephens, *The Transition from Capitalism to Socialism* (London: Macmillan, 1979) and Gösta Esping-Anderson, "Comparative Social Policy and Political Conflict in Advanced Welfare States: Denmark and Sweden," *International Journal of Health Services* 9 (1979): 269–93. For the second, see, for example, Geoff Hodgson, "On the Political Economy of Socialist Transition," *New Left Review* 133 (1982): 52–67.

4. Andrew Martin, "Is Democratic Control of Capitalist Economies Possible?" in *Stress and Contradiction in Modern Capitalism*, ed. Leon Lindberg (Lexington, Mass.: Lexington Books, 1975).

5. Willy Brandt, Bruno Kreisky, and Olof Palme, *La Social-democratie et l'avenir* (Paris: Gallimard, 1976).

6. Rosa Luxemburg, *The Russian Revolution and Leninism or Marxism?* (Ann Arbor: University of Michigan Press, 1970), p. 21.

7. Walter Korpi, *The Working Class in Welfare Capitalism: Work, Unions, and Politics in Sweden* (London: Routledge & Kegan Paul, 1978), and *The Democratic Class Struggle* (London: Routledge & Kegan Paul, 1983).

8. Winton Higgins and Nixon Apple, "How Limited Is Reformism? A Critique of Przeworski and Panitch," *Theory and Society* 12 (1983): 603–30.

9. Geoff Hodgson, "On the Political Economy of Socialist Transition," *New Left Review* 133 (1982): 52–67.

10. Jean Jaures, *L'Esprit de socialisme* (Paris: Denoel, 1971).

11. Agnes Heller, *The Theory of Need in Marx* (London: Allison & Busby, 1974).

12. Karl Marx, *Grundrisse*, ed. Martin Nicolaus (New York: International Publishers, 1973).

13. Jean-Paul Sartre, *Critique de la raison dialectique* (Paris: Gallimard, 1960), p. 15.

14. Edward H. Carr, *The New Society* (London: Oxford University Press, 1961), chap. 3.

15. Juliet Mitchell, "Women: The Longest Revolution," *New Left Review* 40 (1966): 11–37.

16. Herbert Marcuse, *Eros and Civilization* (New York: Vintage Books, 1962).

17. Differential calculus is only an application of the dialectical method to mathematics—at least this is what Engels said somewhere in *The Anti-Dühring*.

18. In David McLellan, *The Thought of Karl Marx* (New York: Harper & Row, 1977).

19. See Marcuse's splendid polemic against Fromm in the epilogue to *Eros and Civilization* (New York: Vintage Books, 1962), pp. 216–51.

20. Norman O. Brown, *Life Against Death: The Psychoanalytical Meaning of History* (New York: Vintage Books, 1959).

6.

SOCIALISM, CAPITALISM, AND THE SOVIET EXPERIENCE

ALEC NOVE

What does the Soviet record tell us about the viability, effectiveness, and efficiency of socialism?

There are several questions that arise if one examines the Soviet experience, in addition to the comparative systems aspect (i.e., the comparison between capitalism and socialism). One question relates to the impact of the experience of the Soviet Union on theories of socialism, and also vice versa: the impact and relevance of socialist theory in assessing the Soviet system. Then there is the important issue of the role of specifically *Soviet-Russian* circumstances: traditions, political culture, and work ethic. A poet, Voloshin, wrote, *"Velikii Pyotr bylpervyi bolshevik"* (Peter the Great was the first bolshevik). The eminent philosopher Nikolai Berdyaev also remarked that "Peter's methods were purely bolshevik." Leftists of a Trotskyist persuasion argue that the Soviet Union under Stalin took the wrong turn, that the Soviet Union is not socialist at all, that it is "state capitalist"—run by a "new bourgeoisie," a bureaucratic ruling class—and continue to manufacture other variants on this theme. While official Soviet ideology claims that the USSR is socialist and is following the principles laid down by Marx and Lenin, this can be questioned. One can indeed show that many aspects of the Soviet economic and political scene are at variance with the anticipations of Marx and of Lenin. But from this, one need not draw the conclusion that there was a "revolution betrayed," but rather that some of these anticipations were unreal or unrealizable.

Another approach is to see Soviet historical experience as that of a developing country, and the Stalinist model as a road to rapid industrialization. Com-

From *Socialism*, ed. Ellen Frankel Paul, Fred D. Miller Jr., Jeffrey Paul, and Dan Greenberg (Oxford: Basil Blackwell, 1989), pp. 235–51. Reprinted by permission of Cambridge University Press.

parisons can then be made with other countries at similar levels of development, or with alternative development strategies. This in turn directs our attention to the adequacy of the centralized "crash-program-industrialization" model, with its emphasis on heavy industry (and on the defense-industry sector in particular) to the circumstances of today, with a much more sophisticated economy and population, and so to the urgent need of reform, of which Gorbachev is speaking with great frankness. The "Stalin" model, which Oskar Lange once described as a "war economy *sui generis,*" should be evaluated in terms of its own objectives, which gave high priority to the creation of the basis of a war economy in peacetime, subordinating to this aim its development strategy. A Western war-economy too was centralized (e.g., Great Britain in 1943)—subject to price control, administered allocation of materials, and rationing. It too generated many bureaucratic deformations of the type that we regard as typically "Soviet." Yet even a Chicago economist would hesitate (or would he?) before confidently pronouncing that one wages war more "efficiently" with an untrammelled free market. The question must be asked: efficiency for what?

This is not meant as a defense of Stalin's brutalities or the many crudities of the economic policies and planning mechanism of his time. One simply recalls Hegel: "all that is real is rational." By this I assume he meant that any existing system or institution serves or served some rational purpose (he would certainly have agreed that, through inertia, systems and institutions can become obsolete, or "fetters on the forces of production," as Marx would put it).

But all this presents us with a problem. It is the unanimous view of Soviet "reforming" economists that the economic system inherited from Stalin's day (and little changed since his death) *is* now obsolete, that "radical reform" is very urgently on the agenda. The pages of the Soviet press are daily filled with examples of irrationalities, waste, shortages, poor quality, hoarding, failure to match user requirements, informational distortions, lack of coordination, corruption, and so on. An easy way of writing this paper is to fill it with such quotations, and conclude that this shows the inherent inefficiencies of "socialism." But one must also ask oneself another question, about the system's "reformability." Gorbachev's advisers are engaged in trying to devise a reform package which is intended to overcome these deficiences. Some socialist countries—e.g., Hungary and China—have already made such attempts (with admittedly rather patchy results). Are there not some very different possible models of socialism?

Finally, we must bear in mind the comparative systems aspect. In the introduction to the first edition of my textbook on the Soviet economy,[1] I warned against "comparing model with muddle," comparing the messy reality of Moscow with the *theory* of Chicago (i.e., comparing real Communism with a smoothly functioning perfect or quasi-perfect market). I did once attend a conference at which someone drew on the blackboard a production possibilities frontier, and argued (correctly) that the Soviet planners cannot get to that frontier because their system cannot generate the necessary detailed information. Can ours? Do American or Japanese managers know the dollar-yen exchange rate in six months' time, or the price of oil at that date, or the rate of interest? "Rational expectations" serve well to "close" formal macroeconomic models, but decisions are taken about the future in a state of partial ignorance. It is highly likely that the Soviet economy is further from the (theoretical and invisible) frontier than is the U.S. economy. But the latter is also some distance inside it, given that there is unemployment of human and material resources. General-equilibrium Walrasian models (complete with the nonexistent auctioneer) are totally irrelevant in the context of comparing systems. Our own theories remain deficient in understanding our own economies: "The analysis of the invisible hand in motion is still well beyond us," says Hahn.[2] "The theory of the internal economy of the firm is still in its infancy," says Radner.[3] Radner points out that "with the decentralization of decision making is associated serious imperfections in the monitoring of individuals' information and actions."[4] Clearly, the problems of decentralization in the largest firm of all, USSR Inc., are not unknown to us, either.

Similarly, the Soviet system can legitimately be "accused" of the proliferation of bureaucrats and controllers of all kinds, whose numbers grow fast. I have just been reading Medvedev, who says that "from 1965 to 1982 the gross social product rose 2.5 times, and administrative staffs nearly doubled in number," and this despite "the increased availability of computers, which increase the productivity of administrative labor."[5] He points to the "danger of a very rapid rise in the volume of information circulating within the planning organs. According to cybernetic theory, this volume increases to the square of the number of those employed."[6] But it so happens that on the very same day I read the following—about *our* economies: "Douglas North has argued that the progressive increase in the division of labor has produced an enormous increase in transaction costs, both by itself and because it has increased alienation and hence opportunism. He suggests that the increase has been of such an extent that transaction costs in advanced economies today account for about half of GDP; he interprets the rise in white-collar jobs in this way."[7]

Finally, on a list that could be prolonged, the short time-horizon of Soviet management is indeed worthy of critical comment. But so is the time-horizon of the very mobile American executive, with overconcentration on the short-term bottom line. The contrast here is with the Japanese longer-term commitment and loyalty to the firm. On matters of this sort, the neoclassical paradigm is silent.

Then, of course, we must resist the temptation to attribute measurable statistical differences in factor productivity to the difference between "capitalism" and "socialism." There are also wide differences within the same systems—e.g., between West Germany and Ireland, or East Germany and Romania—due in varying degrees to history, work ethic, and natural endowment, as well as matters organizational and systemic (therefore a comparison between East and West Germany might be more promising). I recall the work of Robert Campbell on the relative productivity of U.S. and Soviet coal mining. The United States is very far ahead, but the most important reason has to do with differences in accessibility and thickness of the coal seams. I would be the first to agree that the collective and state farms are inefficient, but evidently more reliable rainfall, better soil fertility, and a longer growing season are responsible for part of the superior U.S. agricultural performance.

Perhaps the best way of drawing morals from Soviet experience is to examine the deficiencies which the Soviet economics profession itself emphasizes, and which the reforms being introduced or considered by Gorbachev are intended to overcome. We may then see more clearly the link (if any) between these deficiencies and models of socialism (which could help explain why they arose and have not yet been corrected), and whether a modified or reformed socialism could be envisaged in which these sources of weakness and inefficiency could be removed.

I. SCALE AND COMPLEXITY

Contrary to the beliefs of Marxist founding fathers, there is no simple way in which "society" can control the economy and replace the invisible by the visible hand. Nor can computers resolve the problem. As Medvedev has pointed out, no computerized plan-program (and associated input-output tables) can handle more than above a thousand items, yet the disaggregated product mix runs to twelve million and more. To distribute operational task-orders to hundreds of thousands of production units, to ensure the allocation of the needed material supplies, to check on the veracity of information about costs and claims for inputs, and to ensure quality and conformity to the precise requirements of the users: these tasks cannot be efficiently performed. The growth of the economy tends to outpace the improvements in computational capacity. Fedorenko once quipped that a fully balanced, coherent, and disaggregated plan for next year will be ready in roughly thirty thousand years' time! Clearly, next year's plan will be ready next year, but it will not be fully balanced, coherent, and disaggregated. Particularly great strain is placed on the center's coordinating function, since the scale of the task necessarily involves devolution of decision making to sectoral and/or territorial subunits.

There are a number of derivative or associated defects: production for aggregate plan-fulfillment statistics (and not for the customer), concealment of production possibilities (to obtain a plan easy to fulfill), preference for quantity as against quality, risk avoidance, frustration through the unavailability of the desired material inputs, inconsistencies between different elements of the plan, the undesired rewarding of waste in the use and provision of intermediate goods and services (e.g., metal-goods plans in increments of tons encourage unnecessary weight, goods-transport plans in increments of ton-kilometers reward long journeys and penalize economy in the use of lorries, etc.). The emphasis on plan-fulfillment as a predominant success criterion results in a downgrading of profit and causes indifference to (or even inflation of) costs.

All these are consequences of the endeavor to plan centrally, to minimize the influence of what are called "commodity-money relations," i.e., the market. It used to be taken for granted by socialists (especially those of a Marxist persuasion) that the advance of socialism involves—even can be measured by—the gradual reduction of the role of purchase-and-sale and its replacement by planned distribution and allocation. On these assumptions, the defects summarized above are inherent in socialism. This, however, is what Gorbachev is challenging. No, he says, this is an incorrect view; we recognize the impossibility of micro-planning from the center. We recognize too (he and his advisers say) that past efforts to decentralize have ended in failure and in recentralization (e.g., the "reform" of 1979, which was much more centralizing than the abortive reform of 1965[8]). Not much has yet happened, and there is, as yet, no consensus about the alternative model. Some contours are emerging, however, which resemble the Hungarian reform of 1968 in general aspects. Material allocation is to be replaced by freely negotiated contracts, with a choice of supplier. The product mix is to be determined by negotiation with customers. Many or most prices should be subject to negotiation too, instead of being fixed by state authorities for decades. Investment in existing enterprises is to be financed largely out of retained profits and interest-bearing credits. Managerial incentives are to be linked with profits and detached from plan-fulfillment indicators. Instead of imposed output and cost plans, there will be long-term "normatives," linking incomes to performance. This kind of plan should stimulate cost-saving (via an incentive to increase profits); it should remove the perverse incentive to seek easy plans by concealing productive potential.

The center would be relieved of the impossible burden of detailed planning and allocation. However, it is realized that there are sectors of the economy which are centralizable, indeed, sectors where the needed information is best collected and acted upon at the center: electricity generation is an evident example, as there is an interconnected grid for the country as a whole. It is a matter generally neglected in textbooks, but our own experience clearly shows that some activities are dominated by very large firms. Presumably, an optimum decision-making structure in a socialist economy would also be a mixture of large and small units. When one speaks of devolving or decentralizing decision making, the appropriate amount of change will vary.

Will the Soviet leadership in fact adopt a reform on the lines indicated here? It would very seriously affect the power structure in society—the role and privileges of the party "apparatchicki." Skepticism on this question, however, must be separated from the more general question of how a reformed socialist economy *could* operate—if it were reformed. In any country one must distinguish what is impossible on principle (or in theory) from what is politically impracticable in a given short-term situation. Thus the U.S. budget *could* be balanced, but will not be during the present decade. A Soviet-type economy *could* be reformed, if those in power are determined to enforce change. But it may well not be, for reasons which will not be discussed in this paper.

II. SHORTAGES

In capitalist countries, one strives to find customers; in socialist countries, customers strive to find supplies. This tendency was already noted by Bazarov in the twenties,[9] and has been the subject of much attention from Janos Kornai, notably in his *Economics of Shortage*.[10] It is generally agreed that shortage (a sellers' market) adversely affects quality and attention to user needs, engenders take-it-or-leave-it attitudes, and encourages corruption and hoarding by enterprises and households.

No one doubts that the tendency to generate shortage is endemic in Soviet-type socialist economies. But does it have to be? What precisely is its cause? Interestingly, Kornai's analysis has been challenged—in a discussion with some Czech economists (over cups of coffee) and by Soviet critics.

Kornai stresses the role of what he calls a "soft budget constraint." Management knows that, if it overspends, there will be a bailout—a subsidy. Monetary limits are frequently and easily exceeded. So, even if the original plan was supposed to ensure a macro-balance, additional claims on resources will materialize. There is "investment hunger," a demand for more investment which cannot be held in check by a rise in interest rates, since either the needed capital will be granted by the state, or, if the capital is borrowed, the necessary amounts needed to pay interest or repay the principal will be provided. Under conditions of full employment of material and human resources, unforeseen shortages (and errors) cannot be speedily corrected. In addition, price policy for consumers' goods, under conditions of chronic underfulfillment of plans, results in frequent mismatches between effective demand and supply at official prices. One sees the reflection of this inter alia in a wide gap between state prices for food and those ruling in the (legal) free market.

The system also generates imbalances for reasons which are not connected with soft budget constraint. Let me cite two examples. From 1965 to 1975, the output of fertilizer doubled. Serious shortages then emerged: shortages of bags to put the fertilizer in, storage space in which to house it, and machines with which to spread it. This is an imbalance due to uneven growth and to inadequate coordination of investments in complementary sectors. One cannot correct this by hardening budget constraints. An example nearer "home": the University of Glasgow expanded the number of telephones, thereby overloading the switchboard and making it difficult to obtain an outside line. Again, this was a physical imbalance, remediable (and remedied) with a new and larger switchboard which could carry more lines. *Must* the system necessarily engender unbalanced investment plans? The need for conscious coordination is not usually recognized in our textbooks, because—to repeat Hahn's words—"the analysis of the invisible hand in motion is still beyond us." In practice one gets informal lateral communication, or even government-sponsored collusion (e.g., MITI in Japan, or "indicative" planning in France). Unexpected gaps can be plugged by imports. The recent Soviet reform wave does include some liberalization of foreign trade procedures, so this might help. A greater effort to ensure a balanced investment plan would also be helpful; this would have a greater chance of success if the planning organs could concentrate on it, instead of having their primary attention directed to the planning of current output and its allocation between users.

The measures now being taken to harden the budget constraint—to enhance the role of profits—are supposed to eliminate the tendency to overspend in the process of fulfilling plans "at any cost," thereby reducing the excess-demand pressures. As for consumers' goods, excess demand (both macro and for specific goods and services) can be eliminated through a mixture of realistic pricing and a direct link between retail prices and the wholesale prices paid to producing enterprises. It is pointed out that shortages and long lines of customers are rare not only in Hungary, which accepted radical reform, but also in Czechoslovakia and East Germany, which did not. So it could be argued that they are not an objective necessity even in a centralized socialist economy. Indeed, it was much easier to buy meat in the USSR in 1965 than it is today; incomes have doubled since then, while official prices have been unaltered. It is this price policy, rather than "socialism," that can be blamed for the shortage of meat.

III. MONOPOLY

"Why are capitalist monopolies more efficient than socialist monopolies?" asked a Czech economist after a visit to the United States. He answered his own question as follows: "There is nothing so monopolistic as a socialist monopoly." If you are tied to one supplier and not allowed to go elsewhere, then the supplier can afford to ignore your needs and you do not dare use the legal remedies that are nominally available. A capitalist monopolist is always aware that poor service or excessive profits could attract a competitor.

The harm is minimal in such a sector as electricity, where the product is homogenous and performance (and price) can easily be monitored. It is very serious indeed in all those instances where quality and product mix matter.

Must socialism involve monopoly? Not necessarily. Thus in Moscow there are about thirty theaters, all publicly owned, which compete for spectators. This is because the spectators have a choice. If shortages can be overcome, state shops compete for customers. In some countries (e.g., Hungary and Poland), there are competing cooperative and sometimes private providers of some goods and many services. Something along these lines is envisaged for the Soviet Union, too. The trouble in Soviet industry and agriculture is the system of administered material allocation: managers are tied to *one* supplier, cannot exercise choice, and cannot go elsewhere. Many reforming economists therefore publicly advocate "trade in means of production," which, as already noted, must involve choice and therefore competition between suppliers. Once again, this may not in fact occur in the

USSR for a number of reasons. But it entitles us to question the proposition that socialism is necessarily associated with monopoly and its attendant abuses, even while the Soviet experience abundantly demonstrates what these abuses are.

IV. FULL EMPLOYMENT

Most socialist countries do ensure that virtually everyone has a job. This can be said to be a clear advantage over capitalism. It can be pointed out that, for example, if three million are workless in Great Britain, the loss in output (and the human tragedies) must be set against the waste and inefficiencies of the Soviet centralized system. In fact, the opponents of reform in Moscow point to the dangers of unemployment which could grow swiftly if profit became the dominant criterion for management: unprofitable activities would cease, many workers would be declared redundant, and so security of employment, regarded as a major achievement of socialism, would come to an end.

On the other hand, full employment is associated with under- or misemployment. Labor is often hoarded by enterprises for the same reason they hoard materials. Labor discipline suffers when the manager does not dare to dismiss a worker; it may be impossible to find a replacement, and it is easy to get another job.

A Soviet author, commenting on the poor performance of the farm labor force, remarked that "at one time they reasoned: why should we work, we will not be paid. Now they reason: why should we work, we will be paid anyway."[11] Incentives are weakened by a pervasive egalitarianism and by the too-frequent fact that extra earnings cannot be spent on what the wage earner particularly wants to buy (a consequence of chronic shortages).

Full employment is also connected with the soft budget constraint: money to pay wages will be provided, even if the enterprise lacks funds. So, all in all, the student of comparative economic systems may find it difficult to identify the balance of advantage.

V. PRICES

Marx had nothing to say about prices under socialism, since he imagined that, in a true socialist society, there would be no purchase-and-sale. All Soviet reforming economists agree that the price system that now exists is inefficient. Being (supposedly) cost-based, and altered at infrequent intervals, prices reflect cost and effort, not result. Many critical remarks refer to the *Zatratnaya kontseptsiya tseny,* the cost-based notion of price, which fails to reflect use-value, demand, or the alternative uses (opportunity-cost) of inputs. Any allocation decisions based on such prices, whatever the level of the decision, are necessarily unsound and lead to avoidable inefficiencies and misallocation. Of course the real prices of the real capitalist world do not conform to textbook standards of perfection. In particular, there can be no all-embracing futures market. However, most of our prices do not mislead decision makers most of the time.

Must their prices be misleading? One recalls old debates: Mises, Hayek, Lange, and Lerner.[12] Can there be a rational "socialist" price system in the absence of private ownership of the means of production? Soviet experience certainly shows that the USSR has so far failed to develop a price system which could be described as rational. Indeed, the system was based on the supposition that producer prices played a largely passive role, and that plans were, as far as possible, expressed in quantities. In practice, many plans (and investment choices too) inevitably used prices, e.g., output plans were expressed in gross values, or rates of return on investments were compared.

Suppose the reformers get their way, and prices are altered to reflect supply and demand, with most of them freely negotiable. Would this be effective, and would it be socialist? Of course, there are other questions too: if profitability is to serve as a guide to decision making, who is to keep what share of the profits? What of the need for a capital market—a subject much discussed in both Hungary and China? Should enterprises be allowed to invest in other enterprises? But in legitimately criticizing the investment problems faced by reformed and unreformed socialist economies, we should not overlook the weaknesses of our own investment theories. (Hahn wrote that the whole question of investment "is deeply mysterious under perfect competition."[13]) Also, while the absence of bankruptcy in socialist economies can be seen as an institutional weakness (part of the "soft budget constraint"), it should not be forgotten that bankruptcy, like divorce, is not itself a "good"; it is evidence of business or marital failure.

VI. INNOVATION

The Soviet record in the field of innovation is modest. While suitable for imposing innovation from above, the system has unintentionally discouraged initiative from below. This is due to two mutually reinforcing reasons: one is risk-aversion (risk, as such, is not rewarded; priority in performance evaluation is given to the fulfillment of current plans); the other is the strict control over material allocation and finance, so that the would-be innovator is often frustrated when trying to acquire the needed resources. Various devices to counter this have hitherto been ineffective. It remains to be seen whether the proposed much greater incentive to make profits, and their freer use to finance decentralized investments, plus "trade in means of production," will be a remedy. There is no doubt as to the desire of the party leadership to modernize, to reequip, and to encourage initiative. The unanswered question is whether, in the end, public ownership of the underlying capital assets is, in itself, a bar to innovation. Perhaps greater flexibility in prices and material rewards, plus the goad of competition, could have some positive results. After all, subunits within large privately owned corporations do innovate, even though the individuals who initiate action are not themselves owners of the means of production.

VII. COLLECTIVE/STATE AGRICULTURE

Soviet agriculture has been the subject of many jests, both in and out of the Soviet Union. "If we collectivize the Sahara, soon we will be importing sand," is one example of many. The negative lessons are all too visible. Let us try to classify them.

One is the "original sin" of *forcible* collectivization—the act of depriving the direct producers of their land, their control over means of production, and the product, with all its consequences in terms of alienation. The process of forcing the peasants into pseudocooperatives in the early thirties cost millions of lives and embittered relations with the peasants.

Another is the overestimation of the economies of scale and disregard for diseconomies of scale. Farms are too big and diverse, and have too large a labor force, for efficient management. Lack of effective labor incentives does much damage.

Then there is the habit, still encountered, of ordering farm management about. Party or state interference with routine operations (e.g., imposition of investments or crop pattern or livestock numbers) can be engineered by bureaucrats who sometimes ignore local conditions and fail to overcome the handicaps of soil and climate.

Recent attempts to modernize and to introduce new technology (as well as the increased use of fertilizers and other chemicals) has increased management's dependence on industrial inputs. Many are the complaints about poor quality of machinery, the failure to supply spare parts, and the existence of monopolist supply and service agencies which have their own plans to fulfill. The net effect has been a substantial rise in costs. The attempt to solve the problem by bureaucratic restructuring—the creation of a hierarchical "agro-industrial complex"—has done little or nothing to improve matters.

Finally, there is a notorious lack of infrastructure (roads, storage space, specialized transport, rural amenities), which causes severe losses and results in the loss of skilled workers through out-migration.

All these defects are well known and publicly debated in the USSR. Again, the question is not whether the record is negative, but whether, within a basically "socialist" structure, agriculture could function efficiently. The Hungarian model is here a guide to possibilities. Its essential features, contrasting with the Soviet model, are:

a) No compulsory delivery quotas or (as a rule) any other imposed production plans. Prices are subject to negotiation, with producers free not to sell, or to sell in the free market.

b) Freedom to purchase material inputs (no material allocation bureaucracy), subject only to import restrictions due to currency shortage.

c) Freedom to use or not to use service agencies—to participate or not in "agro-industrial complexes," and freedom to undertake a variety of non-agricultural activities.

d) Flexible arrangements to provide incentives for collective labor, combined with greater freedom to undertake private activities, independently or as subcontractors. (Unlike Poland, there are hardly any purely private farms, but there is a lively private sector within the collectives.)

Hungary's agriculture has been carefully studied in the USSR and some lessons are being partially applied, such as the extension of small-group and family contract. Large sums are being expended on infrastructure. There are still many difficulties with the supply system (they will persist unless and until they shift to "trade in means of production" with customer choice), and party officials and the "agro-industrial" bureaucracy still interfere in management. This is not the place to discuss the current problems of agricultural reform. The only point to make is that the Hungarian example does suggest that a reform could work with reasonable efficiency without decollectivization—if the Soviet variety is radically altered in the context of a wider economic reform.

VIII. THE NEGATIVE EFFECT OF OUTLAWING PRIVATE ENTERPRISE

Private, small-scale workshops providing such items as paper clips, toothbrushes, tools, and such services as cafés, repairs, and travel agencies would fill the many gaps left by official provision. The sheer scale of the planning process ensures that small items get overlooked. Private and cooperative enterprises can be very effective, and conversely the ban on such enterprises, and on private traders, imposes a cost on society. Some countries (e.g., Hungary, Poland, and China) have recognized this and have legalized such activities, subject to certain limits (e.g., on numbers of employees). The USSR has resisted such ideas until very recently; only now is encouragement being given to cooperative enterprise, and limited private activities are being tolerated (but without the right to *employ* anyone). It appears to me that some private and cooperative enterprise could—should—be part of an effective model of socialism. It is a matter of controversy in the Soviet Union.

IX. PARTY RULE, ARBITRARINESS, AND THE ROLE OF CONTRACT

There is an inherent contradiction between economic reform, which rests upon contractual obligations, and the arbitrary powers of party officialdom. This extends far beyond the economy. Much is now being written about local officials dictating decisions to the supposedly independent judiciary (see, for example, the devastating critique by Vaksberg).[14] In an odd way, one is reminded of the neo- (or pseudo-) Marxist views of the legal philosopher Pashukanis in the early thirties. He had argued that law and legal norms generally derive from commercial contract, and that when these are replaced by conscious planning, law will wither away. As Marx had foretold, under full socialism there will be no need for laws. Pashukanis's insight into the connection between the observance of commercial contract and the legal order as a whole has a point. Arbitrariness replaced contract, and arbitrariness also spread into the judicial process itself, with elementary human rights a casualty. Bureaucrats ignored the procedural rights which form part of the Soviet legal code, just as interenterprise contracts were too often not respected: "what mattered was 'orders from above.'"[15]

Now, Gorbachev (a lawyer by training) is insisting on *both* the observance of contracts in the economy *and* the need for a legal order in society as a whole. Obviously, contrary to Pashukanis's view, an efficient and ethically tolerable socialism requires law: commercial, civil, and criminal. Its absence means not some unrealizable folk self-rule, but arbitrariness, unpredictability, and oppression. One of the key problems facing today's Soviet reformers is to find a way to limit the powers of *the* party and its full-time officials in what is still a one-party state. It is too soon to tell if they will find a way.

X. RANK-BASED PRIVILEGE, *NOMENKLATURA*, AND CORRUPTION

Despite some Western literature to the contrary, the USSR is not a society as unequal as ours. The pay of quite senior officials of party and state is a fraction of that of leading executives of even a medium-sized American corporation— though many times higher than the legal minimum wage. However, a very important element of inequality exists in access to scarce goods and services. Rank in the official hierarchy, *nomenklatura* status, provides material privileges, and, of course, also power—power that can be abused. Reference to the existence of such privileges was strictly banned and did not appear in any publication for fifty years or so until an issue of *Pravda* in February 1986 raised it directly. The value of such privileges is also a function of the degree of unavailability of particular goods and services to ordinary citizens without influence. To this extent, prices which balance supply and demand have the effect of reducing the value of privileged access to scarce goods and services. Power to allocate resources has resulted in power to allocate to the allocators. This would not surprise Trotsky, who duly noted that whoever had such power "would never forget themselves." There is a lively controversy about whether the rulers, the *nomenklatura* officials, constitute a "new class." It should be noted that privilege is rank-based and is lost on retirement or dismissal from office. One hundred and fifty years ago, the great poet Pushkin remarked that overdependence for status on rank (and so on the tsar) made for slavishness towards authority. A person who owes his position to personal wealth, or to aristocratic birth, can afford a greater degree of independence. Lower down the social scale, a source of income not dependent on the state sets in itself some limits on state power: thus the poet Mandelshtam, in exile in Voronezh, dreamt of owning a cow, so that it would be possible to live even if the local literary bureaucrats refused to publish any of his works.

Rank-based privilege is itself subject to rules. In the absence of a free press or an opposition party, however, these rules can be neglected, and recent publicity about corruption and abuse of power in the Soviet hierarchy shows what the consequences can be. However, we cannot ignore the fact that corruption is a disease from which any system can suffer (we need only refer to recent scandals in Wall Street and the City of London).

XI. ECOLOGY, EXTERNALITIES, THE PUBLIC GOOD— AND METHODOLOGICAL INDIVIDUALISM

Soviet *theory* emphasizes the general interest, and has been "guilty" of ignoring the individual while extolling the "collective." Western mainstream theory, by contrast, tends to concentrate on the individual, and to regard the whole as no more than the sum of its parts. Yet there are circumstances in which the pursuit of self-interest, or a deal profitable for those making it, has a positive or negative impact which is not "caught" by the profit-and-loss account. Men (and women) can sometimes worsen their position by the pursuit of individual self-interest, as compared with collaboration and collusion. If everyone tried to get to work by car in London, Paris, or New York, paralysis would ensue. The provision of a public-transport alternative (e.g., metros) everywhere requires public action, plus a subsidy. Infrastructure is usually externality-prone, yielding profits to third parties, which is why much of it is seen logically to "belong" in the public sector. Ecological considerations call for regulation, for reasons too obvious to require discussion. In my own work on "feasible socialism,"[16] I tried to identify those areas in which a decentralized profit-oriented market can be expected to yield the desired result, and those where divergence between private profit and the more general interest is likely to be large enough to warrant action by public bodies. A role for public authorities, and a recognition of the existence of a *common* weal, would seem to require recognition, or so socialists would argue. This said, it must be admitted that the Soviet record in these matters is unsatisfactory. While much publicity has recently been given to ecological problems and new laws have been passed, the USSR continues to stand high in the pollution league, as do most of her East European allies. While cheap public transport is usually provided, local town-planning authorities have had little power to deal with economic vested interests in the shape of economic ministries, and the press frequently mentions abuses in public housing allocations. It is apparent from Soviet experience that one cannot internalize *all* externalities, i.e., consider everything in the context of everything, because of informational and administrative overload. Tasks must be subdivided. The center itself becomes a loose federation of semiautonomous ministries and departments, presenting not only major burdens of coordination but also creating administrative boundary lines. These in turn reproduce the externality problem: anything that is not within the purview of a given official or department is, for him or her, an externality. A Soviet chemical factory is just as likely to pollute a river as any capitalist factory unless forcibly prevented, since its manager is not responsible for the damage to fishing or bathing. Examples of so-called *vedomstvennost* ("departmentalism") are legion. The effect on regional and industrial location policies is notorious: while the center may desire a move towards less developed areas, ministries strive to plan their investments in the more developed regions to save on infrastructure. The "free" medical service has been seriously underfunded and is the subject of much public criticism, not least for the bribes that have to be paid. Passing to a more general point, Soviet would-be reformers have often spoken of the need to devise a scheme by which enterprises' interests are in line with the general interest, and (not surprisingly) have not been successful. In fact there is some danger that, in reacting against excessive centralization, they could well overlook informational and technological economies of scale, and fragmentize excessively. This has surely been the case in Yugoslavia.

Should one therefore conclude that Soviet experience proves that the socialist agenda is, in these respects, irrelevant or negative? It seems reasonable to note that in *any* large economy or large firm there are questions of centralization and decentralization, and organizational dividing lines can affect what the decision maker might find it rational to do. Externalities exist as a problem in some form everywhere. One can argue that it is the endeavor to overcentralize that led (paradoxically) to the division of the bureaucratic apparatus and so to administrative overload, which manifests itself in neglecting the very externalities which socialist theorists had expected to be better handled when the state owns the means of production. The strengthening of the market mechanism could then leave more time for the planners to cope with their coordinating and "internalizing" task, confining attention to sectors and decisions where important external effects can be anticipated. Socialists are not wrong in stressing that the profitability criterion *can* mislead, but it must be recognized that the Soviet record in coping with externalities has seldom been impressive. Similarly, the heavy burden of current operational planning has left the center with insufficient time to devote to longer-term considerations.

CONCLUSION

One can only repeatedly stress that the Soviet experience must be seen in its historical and national context. It must be reiterated that the economic performance (and political culture) of a country is deeply influenced by its past. Thus, it would hardly be possible to assess the remarkable achievements of the Japanese economy without taking into account factors specific to the Japanese people. No explanation of Stalinism would be complete without consideration of Russia's autocratic tradition—the very large role played by the state in its economic development in past centuries. And it is only now that a serious attempt is being made to modify the centralized economic structure inherited from the Stalinist period. It is also worth recalling that the Russians have not been noted through the ages for possessing a great deal of discipline or work ethic. Not only are some institutions and practices partly explicable by "Russian" traditions and circumstances, but these same institutions can be made to work better in a more "efficient" environment, such as East Germany. The Soviet path to so-called modernization was ruthless, despotic, and centralizing. These methods were costly in human terms, and also in micro-economic allocational inefficiency. These methods came, in many people's minds in and out of the USSR, to be equated with "socialism." *The* question, not yet answered, is whether the USSR and other Communist-ruled countries will find it possible to achieve a modernization based upon a substantial enhancement of the role of markets and prices, with competition (albeit between state-owned enterprises plus some cooperative ones), user choice, and plans based on negotiation and contract. If the answer is positive, a very different paper may have to be written in (say) five years' time. The attempt may founder. However, we may have a few problems too: mass Third World default and a collapse of the dollar could have disastrous consequences for the world economy.

Suppose the Gorbachev reforms succeed—and I again stress that it is early yet. Would such a system still qualify as "socialist"? It is a matter of definition. If by "socialism" we mean the dominance of public or cooperative ownership of the means of production, then a species of "market socialism" would not be a contradiction in terms. Soviet economists (and Gorbachev himself) have been stressing that markets are not, as such, capitalistic. Nontheless, it is true that the Marxian vision of socialism did foresee the replacement of the market by conscious allocation—by production directly for use by so-called associated producers. The founding fathers of Marxism thought that this would be a simple matter. They could not have been more wrong. So now we are in the presence of a search for feasible combinations of plan and market. Let us not write this off in advance. Let us wait and see.

NOTES

1. Alec Nove, *The Soviet Economy* (London: Allen & Unwin, 1961), p. 22.

2. Frank Hahn, "On Involuntary Unemployment," *Conference Papers:* supplement to *Economic Journal* 97 (1987): 14.

3. Roy Radner, "The Internal Economy of Large Firms," *Conference Papers:* Supplement to *Economic Journal* 96 (1986): 3.

4. Ibid., p. 17.

5. Pavel Medvedev, "Ekonomiko-matematicheskie Metody v Plamrovanii," *Voprosy Ekonomiki* 12 (1986): 49.

6. Ibid., p. 49.

7. R. C. O. Matthews, "The Economics of Institutions and the Sources of Growth," *Economic Journal* 96 (December 1986): 907.

8. The so-called Kosygin reform of 1965 had as its declared objective the strengthening of enterprise autonomy and of the profit motive. However, Soviet economists now agree that it was halfhearted and inconsistent, and had little or no effect. The "reform" of 1979 stressed quantitative planning from above and tended to downgrade profits as a success indicator.

9. Bazarov wrote, "The tendency to relative underproduction should be recognized as inherent for our social structure, just as a tendency to overproduction is for capitalism." Vladimir Bazarov, *Kapitalisticheskiye Tsikly i Vosstanovitel'nyi Protsess Khozyaistua SSSR* (Capitalist Cycles and the Reconstruction Process in the USSR) (Moscow: GIZ, 1927), p. 99.

10. J. Kornai, *The Economics of Shortage* (Amsterdam: North Holland, 1980).

11. Vikulov, "Chto Zavisit ot Rukovodibelya," *Pravda*, 4 February 1987.

12. See Israel M. Kirzner, "Some Ethical Implications for Capitalism of the Socialist Calculation Debate," *Social Philosophy and Policy* 6, no. 1 (autumn 1988): 165–82.

13. F. Hahn, "Of Marx and Keynes and Many Things," *Oxford Economic Papers* 38 (July 1986): 360.

14. Arkadi Vaksberg, "Pravda v glaza," *Literaturnaya Gazeta,* no. 51 (December 1986): 13.

15. V. Skvorrsova, "Dogovor . . . ," *Selskaya Zhizn* (2 January 1987): 3.

16. Alec Nove, *The Economics of Feasible Socialism* (London: Allen & Unwin, 1983).

PART III.

MODELS OF SOCIALISM

7.

MARKET SOCIALISM

A Defense

DAVID SCHWEICKART

It is not à la mode these days to advocate socialism of any sort. The pundits have stopped repeating the mantra that socialism is dead and that liberal capitalism is the telos of history. This is no longer news. It is an accepted "fact." Socialism is dead.

The death certificate has been signed not only for classical command socialism but for all versions of market socialism as well, with or without worker self-management. Hungarian economist Janos Kornai, once an advocate of market socialism, now confidently asserts:

> Classical socialism is a coherent system. . . . Capitalism is a coherent system.
> . . . The attempt to realize market socialism, on the other hand, produces an incoherent system, in which there are elements that repel each other: the dominance of public ownership and the operation of the market are not compatible.[1]

As for self-management, "it is one of the dead-ends of the reform process."[2]

There are at least two good reasons, one theoretical, the other empirical, to dissent from Kornai's fashionable wisdom. First of all, there has developed over the last twenty years a large body of theoretical literature concerned with market alternatives to capitalism that reaches a different conclusion.[3] Secondly, the most dynamic economy in the world right now, encompassing some 1.2 billion people, is market socialist.

CHINA

If it is not fashionable to defend socialism these days, it is even less so to defend China. At least on the left there remain some stalwart defenders of socialism, but left, right, or center, no one likes China. In China there are executions, human rights violations, lack of democracy, workers working under exploitative conditions, misogyny, environmental degradation, and political corruption. Moreover, China projects no compelling internationalist vision that might rally workers of the world or the wretched of the earth.

China is not inspirational now the way Russia was in the aftermath of the Bolshevik Revolution, or as China was for many on the Left in the 1960s or as Vietnam or Nicaragua or Cuba have been. One wishes that the defects of Chinese society were not so glaring.[4] There is a role for utopian imagery in a political project such as socialism. We need stirring visions. We need to be able to imagine what is, as yet, "nowhere." Yet there is also a need for realism in assessing the accomplishments and failures of actual historical experiments. Since there are few experiments more momentous than what is now transpiring in China, we need to think carefully about what can and cannot be deduced from the Chinese experience.

If by "socialism" we mean a modern economy without the major means of production in private hands, then China is clearly a socialist economy. Not only does China describe itself as "market socialist," but the self-description is empirically well-grounded. As of 1990, only 5.1 percent of China GNP was generated by the "private" sector.[5] And despite considerable quantities of foreign capital flowing into the country (mostly from Hong Kong and Taiwan, mostly into joint ventures), that portion of Chinese investment in fixed assets utilizing funds from abroad is only 13 percent (as of 1993), and employs barely 4 percent of the nonagricultural workforce, some five or six million workers. By way of contrast, there were, as of 1991, some 2.4 million cooperative firms in China, employing 36 million workers, and another 100 million workers employed in state-owned enterprises.

This "incoherent" market socialist economy has been strikingly successful, averaging an astonishing 10 percent per year annual growth rate over the past fifteen years, during which time real per capita consumption has more than doubled, housing space has doubled, the infant mortality rate has been cut by more than 50 percent, the number of doctors has increased by 50 percent, and life expectancy has gone from sixty-seven to seventy. And on top of all this, inequality, as measured by the Gini coefficient, has actually *declined* substantially—due to the lowering of the income differential between town and country.[6] Even so skeptical an observer as Robert Weil, who taught at Jihin University of Technology in Changchun in 1993, concedes:

> Changchun university students, who come even from poorer peasant backgrounds, speak of the transformation of their villages, with investments in modern farm implements and new consumer goods. For the working people in

the city who until a year or so ago had to live through the winter on cabbage and root crops and buy what few other vegetables and fruits were available off the frozen sidewalks, the plethora of bananas, oranges, strawberries, greens, and meats of all kinds that can now be purchased in indoor markets year round has changed their lives and their diet. Across the nation meat consumption per capita has increased some two and a half times since 1980. Millions of workers have gained new housing during "reforms," [the scare quotes are Weil's] built by their enterprises, so that the two or three families that used to share a single apartment now each have their own homes. Within the last few months, the work week in state-owned firms has been lowered from forty-eight hours to forty-four, a major and widely welcomed improvement.[7]

The empirical evidence does not suggest that China is Utopia. It is far from that. Critics are not wrong to be concerned about human rights violations, the lack of genuine democracy, worker exploitation (evidenced by, among other things, a horrendous rate of industrial accidents), the markedly higher infant mortality rates for girls than for boys, environmental degradation, and widespread corruption. Nevertheless, China's real accomplishments have been stunning. If socialism is an emancipatory project concerned with improving the real material conditions of real people, and not an all-or-nothing Utopianism, then socialists of good will (particularly those of us who have regular access to bananas, strawberries, greens, and meat) should not be too quick to dismiss these accomplishments.

Moreover, China's developmental trajectory remains unclear. It is possible that the contradictions of Chinese socialism will intensify to the point of social explosion. It is also possible that China will one day enter the ranks of capitalism. But those who maintain the inevitability of one *or* both of these eventualities are, it seems to me, reading tea leaves. We do not yet know how the Chinese experiment will come out. China may remain master of the productivity energies it has unleashed, and may move to democratize itself and to address its other grave deficiencies. This too is possible.

In any event, to maintain in the face of such powerful evidence to the *contrary* that market socialism is *unworkable* is surely problematic. The Eastern European economists who so confidently made such assertions and who so wholeheartedly embraced the privatization and free-marketization of their own economies would do well to compare the wreckage induced by *their* reforms to what a market socialism has wrought.

WHAT IS MARKET SOCIALISM?

China demonstrates that a form of market socialism is compatible with a dynamic economy that spreads its material benefits broadly. But China is too complex a phenomenon, too much shaped by historical and cultural contingencies, too much in flux, for one to draw many firm conclusions. In order to go beyond the mere assertion of possibility it is more fruitful to engage the market socialism debate at a more theoretical level.

I wish to defend a two-part thesis: (a) market socialism, at least in some of its versions, is a viable economic system vastly superior, as measured by norms widely held by socialists and nonsocialists alike, to capitalism, and (b) it is the *only* form of socialism that is, at the present stage of human development, both viable and desirable. Nonmarket forms of socialism are either economically non-viable or normatively undesirable, often both at once.

Let us be more precise about the meaning of "market socialism." Capitalism has three defining institutions. It is a market economy, featuring private owner-ship of the means of production and wage labor. That is to say, most of the eco-nomic transactions of society are governed by the invisible hand of supply and demand; most of the productive assets of society belong to private individuals either directly or by virtue of individual ownership of shares in private corpora-tions; most people work for salaries or wages paid directly or indirectly by the owners of the enterprises for which they work. A market socialist economy elim-inates or greatly restricts private ownership of the means of production, substi-tuting for private ownership some form of state or worker ownership. It retains the market as the mechanism for coordinating most of the economy, although there are usually restrictions placed on the market in excess of what is typical under capitalism. It may or may not replace wage labor with workplace democracy, wherein workers get, not a contracted wage, but specified shares of an enterprise's net proceeds. If it does, the system is a "worker-self-managed" market socialism.

Various theoretical models of market socialism have been proposed in recent years, but all advocates of market socialism agree on four points.

1. The market should not be identified with capitalism.
2. Central planning is deeply flawed as an economic mechanism.
3. There exists no viable, desirable socialist alternative to market socialism; that is to say, the market is an essential (if imperfect) mechanism for organizing a viable economy under conditions of scarcity.
4. Some forms of market socialism are *economically* viable and vastly preferable to capitalism.

Let us examine each of these contentions.

THE "MARKET = CAPITALISM" IDENTIFICATION

The identification of capitalism with the market is a pernicious error of both con-servative defenders of laissez-faire and most left opponents of market reforms. If one looks at the works of the major apologists for capitalism, Milton Friedman, for example, or F. A. Hayek, one finds the focus of the apology always on the virtues of the market and on the vices of central planning.[8] Rhetorically this is an effective strategy, for it is much easier to defend the market than to defend the other two defining institutions of capitalism. Proponents of capitalism know well that it is better to keep attention directed toward the market and away from wage labor or private ownership of the means of production.

The left critique of market socialism tends to be the mirror image of the conservative defense of capitalism. The focus remains on the market, but now on its evils and irrationalities. In point of fact, it is as easy to attack the abstract market as it is to defend it, for the market has both virtues and vices. Defenders of capitalism (identifying it as simply "a market economy") concentrate on the virtues of the market, and dismiss all criticisms by suggesting that the only alternative is central planning. Critics of market socialism concentrate on the vices and dismiss all defenses by suggesting that models of market socialism are really models of quasi-capitalism. Such strategies are convenient, since they obviate the need for looking closely at how the market might work when embedded in networks of property relationships different from capitalist relationships—convenient, but too facile.

THE CRITIQUE OF CENTRAL PLANNING

It must be said that conservative critics have been proven more right than wrong concerning what was relatively recently *the* reigning paradigm of socialism: a nonmarket, centrally planned economy. They have usually been dishonest in disregarding the positive accomplishments of the experiments in central planning, and in downplaying the negative consequences of the market, but they have not been wrong in identifying central weaknesses of a system of central planning, nor have they been wrong in arguing that "democratizing" the system would not in itself resolve these problems.

The critique of central planning is well known, but a summary of the main points is worth repeating. A centrally planned economy is one in which a central planning body decides what the economy should produce, then directs enterprises to produce the goods in specified quantities and qualities. Such an economy faces four distinct sets of problems: information problems, incentive problems, authoritarian tendencies, and entrepreneurial problems.[9]

As for the first: a modern industrial economy is simply too complicated to plan in detail. It is too difficult to determine, if we do not let consumers "vote with their dollars," what people want, how badly, and in what quantities and qualities. *Moreover*, even if planners were able to surmount the problem of deciding what to produce, they must then decide, *for* each item, how to produce it. Production involves inputs as well as outputs, and since the inputs into one enterprise are the outputs of many others, quantities and qualities of these inputs must also be planned. But since inputs cannot be determined until technologies are given, technologies too must be specified. To have a maximally coherent plan, all of these determinations must be made by the center, but such calculations, interdependent as they are, are far too complicated for even our most sophisticated computational technologies. Star Wars, by comparison, is child's play.

This critique is somewhat overstated. In fact planners *can* plan an entire economy. Planners in the Soviet Union, in Eastern Europe, in China and elsewhere did exactly that for decades. By concentrating the production of specific products into relatively few (often huge) enterprises and by issuing production targets in aggregate form, allowing enterprise managers flexibility in disaggregation, goods and services were produced, and in sufficient quantity to generate often impressive economic growth. It is absurd to say, as many commentators now do, that Ludwig von Mises and Friedrich Hayek have been proven right by events, that a centrally planned socialism is "impossible." To cite only the Soviet Union: an economic order that endured for three-quarters of a century in the face of relentless international hostility and a German invasion, and that managed to industrialize a huge, quasi-feudal country; to feed, clothe, house, and educate its citizenry; and to create a world-class scientific establishment should not be called "impossible."

However, the opposite of "impossible" is not "optimal." The Soviet economy and those economies modeled on Soviet economy always suffered from efficiency problems, and these became steadily worse as the economies developed. Information problems that were tractable when relatively few goods were being produced, and when quantity was more important than quality, became intractable when more and better goods were required. It is not without reason that *every* centrally planned economy has felt compelled to introduce market reforms once reaching a certain level of development.[10]

In theory a nonmarket socialism can surmount its information problems. In theory markets can be simulated. Planners can track the sale of goods, adjust prices *as if* supply and demand were dictating them, and convey this information to producers, instructing them to act *as if* they were in competition with each other to maximize profits. But market simulation and central planning generally founders on the second set of problems, those concerning *incentives*. There are many incentive problems inherent in central planning. Among the theoretically predicted and commonly observed:

- If output quotas are set by the planning board, enterprises have little incentive to expend resources or effort to determine and to provide what consumers really want.
- If both inputs and outputs are set by the planning board, enterprises will be inclined to understate their capabilities and overstate their needs, so as to make it easier to fulfill their part of the plan. They also have a large incentive to lobby the planning board for lower production quotas and for ample supplies of raw materials.
- If employment is guaranteed, but incomes are not tied to enterprise needs, workers have little incentive to work.

- If the planning board is responsible for the entire economy, it has little incentive to close inefficient units, since that will either contribute to unemployment or necessitate finding new jobs for the displaced workers.

There are also political problems associated with central planning. Planners have enormous power. Decisions as to production quotes (or prices) have major impact on enterprises, so the danger of corruption is large. A well-placed bribe that allows for a quota reduction or price rise can do a company far more immediate good than careful attention to product quality or the development of a new product line, or the introduction of a new production process.

Moreover, even if planners are scrupulously honest, they can be expected to centralize production into ever larger units, even when excessive size is inefficient, since it is easier to plan when there are fewer units with which to deal. They can also be expected to set up as many *barriers* as possible between themselves and workers or consumers. Planning a large economy is an enormously complex task, made infinitely more difficult when the plan is being constantly criticized, modified, or even rejected by an empowered citizenry. To be effective, planning must be coherent, so the modification of one part of the plan necessitates adjustments elsewhere. Adjustments that satisfy one group of angry constituents may impact adversely on other groups, causing them to clamor for change. Whatever public statements planners may make in support of participatory democracy, they cannot really be expected to like it. This problem, which is inherent in any democratic institution, is tractable when the number of options and variables are limited. But when everything in the economy is subject to political debate—every price, every product, every technology—the expected outcome is either anarchy, or, more likely, the subtle or not so subtle shutting down of democratic input.

Finally, there is the entrepreneurial problem. However much credit one wants to give to the accomplishments of centrally planned economies (and more credit should be given than is commonly given today), one cannot credit them with being highly innovative economically. Very few new products or new production techniques can be traced to these economies. Structural reasons are not difficult to locate. If enterprises do not compete, they have little need to innovate. They do not have to worry that if they do not keep abreast of the new technologies, their rivals will capture their markets, so the negative threat of failure is not there. Nor is there much in the way of positive incentive. An individual with an innovative idea cannot set up an enterprise, gambling that her great idea will pay off big. At best she can try to convince her superiors that a new product or a new technology will be worth the time, effort, and risk involved. Not surprisingly, managers and planners in a centrally planned economy tend to be "conservative." Mistakes are more easily recognized, and hence career-threatening, than innovative successes. Risks are generally avoided—unless the high-risk ventures originate at the top, in which case one is reluctant to criticize even a bad idea, since one is absolved of responsibility if the project fails.

WHY NOT A NONMARKET, DECENTRALIZED ECONOMY?

Many nonmarket socialists are inclined to object at this point in the argument that market socialists seem to think that the only alternative to the market is central planning. But why should that be the only alternative? Why not advocate and struggle for a nonmarket, democratic, *decentralized* economy?

The market socialists' reply is that such an economy, at the present state of economic development, is neither viable *nor* desirable. To be sure, if an economy were decentralized into small, semi-agrarian, autarchic communities, then, yes, a democratic, nonmarket economy might be possible. But given the complexities of modern technologies and given the range of goods that modern consumers (socialists-included) may legitimately expect from their economy, the dream of small, self-sufficient communities is a dream without a constituency, a wholly Utopian fantasy.[11]

If instead of decentralized autarchy, one wants decentralized, participatory bottom-up planning that results in a unified plan for a large industrial economy, it can't be done. I can think of no better proof than to invite the reader to look carefully at Michael Albert and Robin Hahnel's recent, detailed proposal for just such an economy, a participatory economy that utilizes personal computers, large data banks, and an array of neighborhood, regional, and national councils. It is unworkable. Utterly. Moreover, even it were workable, it would not be desirable. Too many hours on the computer. Too many meetings.[12]

MODELS OF MARKET SOCIALISM: JOHN ROEMER'S

Thus far my argument has been negative. I have argued that there cannot be a viable, desirable socialism without a market. It must be further demonstrated that market socialism *is* a viable, desirable option. There are in fact many different proposals for market socialism now under discussion. Let us consider two, John Roemer's and my own.[13]

In essence Roemer's market socialism looks much like contemporary capitalism, but with five fundamental differences:

1. All the stocks of all the corporations in the country have been redistributed, so as to give each citizen, initially, a per-capita share. Each citizen at birth receives a stock portfolio, and hence an entitlement to a share of the dividends generated by the companies whose stocks she holds. When she dies, the stocks return to the government. These stocks, once acquired, may be traded for other stocks, *but they may not be sold for cash.* (Hence it is impossible for the rich to buy out the poor and obtain controlling interest in the economy.)
2. All banks are nationalized. These banks collect funds from private savers

and make loans to businesses, using substantially the same criteria as capitalist banks.

3. The management of a corporation is determined by the corporation's board of directors, which is comprised of delegates of the main commercial bank from which it gets its funding, representatives of the firm's workers, and representatives of the stockholders.

4. The government undertakes significant investment planning, using differential interest rates to encourage or discourage certain kinds of specific investment.

5. Capitalist firms are permitted, if started by an entrepreneur, but a firm is nationalized (with compensation) when it reaches a certain size, or on the death of the founder, and shares of its stock redistributed to the general public.

Roemer argues cogently that this model is economically viable. The basic problems of the central-planning model have been alleviated. Firms in this economy compete with each other (and also with foreign firms) in a market setting, so the information and incentive problems disappear. There is no authoritarian tendency to this model, since firms are independent of the political process, and, since, moreover, there is no central planning agency on whose good will all firms depend. The entrepreneurial problem is addressed in two ways. Competition forces public firms to be alert to develop and implement new products and technologies. Secondly, there is a place in the economy for capitalist entrepreneurs, although not so large a place that they can come to dominate.

This model also addresses two of the most fundamental problems with capitalism: economic inequality and investment irrationality. Economic inequality is sharply curtailed (although not eliminated) by drastically reducing the basic source of capitalist income, the income arising from ownership of the means of production. All citizens have roughly equal shares of the collective assets of society, and so all benefit to a roughly equal degree from the surplus generated. What inequalities of asset ownership that do develop as citizens trade their shares are not allowed to persist beyond a person's lifetime, and so they do not accumulate and concentrate as they do under capitalism.[14]

Investment irrationalities are also addressed. Roemer's model recognizes explicitly what all economists know but do not much talk about in public. The market is *not* an efficient mechanism for making the investment decisions that determine the long-range health of an economy. The visible hand of the government must supplement Adam Smith's invisible hand. Virtually all the economies of the world today touted as miracles— Japan, Germany, South Korea, Taiwan—have learned to guide the investment process. Experience suggests, however, that the visible hand should not be too heavy a hand—hence Roemer's reliance on interest-rate manipulation.

MODELS OF MARKET SOCIALISM: ECONOMIC DEMOCRACY

My own model of market socialism, designated Economic Democracy, is different from Roemer's, in that it puts worker self-management at the heart of the system, as opposed to egalitarian ownership of the means of production. As in Roemer's model, all enterprises compete. As in Roemer's model, funds for new investment come primarily from banks, which are public, not private, institutions.

In Economic Democracy there is no stock market, for there are no stocks. The capital assets of the country are thought of as collective property, but they are controlled by the workforces that utilize them. That is to say, each enterprise is run democratically, with workers legally empowered, one person, one vote, to elect the enterprise's management. The model for an enterprise under Economic Democracy is political community, not private property. An enterprise is not a *thing* that is *owned* by its workers; rather, it is an *association* that is *governed* by them. Ultimate authority resides with the workers of an enterprise, although, in all but small firms, workers will elect representatives to a worker council that will select and oversee the firm's management.

Worker self-management is the first defining feature of Economic Democracy. The second feature that sets it apart from capitalism (and from Roemer's model of socialism) is its mechanism for generating and dispensing funds for new investment. Both capitalism and Roemer's market socialism rely on private savings as the source of investment funding. Economic Democracy relies on taxation. Each enterprise must pay a tax on the capital assets under its control. (This tax may be thought of as rent paid society for access to the collective property of society.) Economically this tax functions as an interest rate on capital—and thus obviates the necessity of paying interest to private savers. Generating the investment fund by taxing enterprises rather than by "bribing" individuals to save not only shuts down a major source of capitalist inequality, namely interest payments to private individuals, but it frees an economy from its dependence on the "animal spirits" of savers and investors.

The proceeds of the capital-assets tax constitute society's investment fund, all of which are plowed back into the economy. The plow-back mechanism here is also different from what it is under capitalism. The market does *not* dictate investment flows. Under Economic Democracy on a per capita basis (as a prima facie entitlement). Thus capital flows to where the people are. People are not forced to follow the flow of capital. Once in communities, the investment funds are then "loaned" to the enterprises in the community, or to collectives wanting to set up new concerns, via a network of public banks, according to a double criteria: projected profitability and employment creation. Only at this stage are market criteria invoked, and even at this stage they are not the only criteria.[15]

In sum, Economic Democracy may be thought of as an economic system with three basic structures, worker self-management of enterprises, social control of investment, and a market for goods and services. These contrast with the defining elements of capitalism: wage labor, private ownership of the means of production, and a market for goods, services, capital, and labor.

I argue at length in *Against Capitalism* that this model is economically viable. The essential moves are these: At the enterprise level, the cooperative nature of the firm insures an efficient internal organization. (The empirical evidence is overwhelming that cooperative enterprises are almost always as efficient as comparable capitalist enterprises, often much more so.) At the level of enterprise interactions with each other and with consumers, the competitive nature of the economy insures that the informational and incentive problems associated with central planning do not arise. At the level of economic development over time, the investment mechanism allows for the kind of market-conforming planning that most economists agree is superior to unrestrained market forces. The entrepreneurial problem is addressed, much as it is in Mondragon, by having local banks set up an entrepreneurial division to seek out new investment opportunities, and to provide technical assistance and start-up capital to groups of individuals interested in developing a new enterprise. Competitive pressures compel existing firms to stay abreast of technical developments in their areas. The possibility of workers in an enterprise reaping either monetary gains, shorter working hours, or better working conditions supplies a positive incentive to innovate.

I also argue at length in *Against Capitalism* that Economic Democracy is superior to capitalism over a whole range of issues. It is vastly more egalitarian, since it eliminates property income. It is vastly more democratic, since it extends democracy downward into the workplace, and upward into the determination of macroeconomic developmental policies. It also confronts squarely what may be the single most destructive feature of contemporary capitalism: the hypermobility of capital. Given recent technological and political developments, capital now has a greater capability and a freer hand than ever before in history to move rapidly to whatever part of [the] globe promises the highest return. The resulting job insecurities, destruction of communities, and mass migrations are now everywhere to be seen.

Economic Democracy radically alters this pattern. Worker-run enterprises do not vote to relocate to lower wage regions of the country or the world. Publicly generated capital does not cross borders in search of higher returns; the tax-generated investment fund is mandated by law to be returned to communities. Consequently, communities do not have to compete for capital (by offering lower wages, or fewer environmental restrictions). Moreover, they are assured a regular flow of new investment capital, and hence have far more control over their own economic destinies than do communities under capitalism.

BUT IS IT SOCIALISM?

Hillel Ticktin has written that for an anti-Stalinist Marxist, socialism would be defined by the degree to which the society was planned.[16] By this definition neither Roemer's market socialism nor Economic Democracy is very socialist. Indeed, by this definition "market socialism" becomes a sort of oxymoron, since it is precisely the point of a market to remove a large part of a society's economic activity from the arena of conscious, society-wide planning.

But I (who am also an anti-Stalinist Marxist) would dissent from a definition that equates socialism to ever-more-extensive social planning. There is an important normative-conceptual issue that needs to be addressed here. It is certainly central to the socialist project that human beings be able to control, rather than be controlled by, economic forces. But control has both a positive and a negative sense. I control my dog when I train him to do tricks and obey my commands. I also control him when I teach him not to bite the neighbors or urinate on the carpet. In the first case, I am bending him to my will in a positive sense. In the second, I am trying to ward off unpleasant surprises.

I would contend that a socialist economy should aim more for negative control than positive control, particularly if a reasonably high level of development has been reached. We do not need an economy that will allow us to storm the heavens. There is a hubris in such a conception that has been given historical form in some of the worst excesses of Stalinism and Maoism. We need an economy that will allow us to get on with our lives without having to worry so much about economic matters. To be sure, at the workplace we may want to try to develop new products or new technologies, and in our communities we may want to try new ways of organizing our collective well-being. Occasionally we might want to give scope to a larger vision, a material project affecting the whole nation, but by and large the focus of our attention is more properly concerned with local matters. But this means *local* planning at the workplace and community level, not *national* planning. Certainly there are problems that must be addressed at the national and international level, environmental damage, for example, or the terrifying poverty that exists in so many places. But to be able to focus on the large issues that require national and global attention, we need an economic environment where most of what goes on is relatively automatic. Indeed, even to concentrate on locally large issues, we need an environment where we, as citizens, need not think about most of what goes on in the economy.

The market has long been touted by apologists *for* capital as the automatic regulator that frees us from unnecessary complexity. Unfortunately, as we can now so clearly see, when the market extends beyond goods and services to capital and labor, it begins biting the neighbors, urinating on the carpet, and worse. And it does so automatically. The point of market socialism is to reign in these negative consequences without subjecting the economy to the massive discipline that maximal planning implies.

Is this really socialism? There is, after all, still competition, still inequality, still advertising, still potential unemployment. It is important here to invoke a Marxian distinction. Socialism is not to be identified with the highest form of communism. Socialism emerges from the womb of capitalism, and is marked by its origin. It is not a perfect society. It is a noncapitalist economic order that *preserves* the best that capitalism has attained, while overcoming its worst evils.

Advocates of market socialism often find themselves being urged by people without a Left background who find the ideas persuasive not to call the position "socialist," since "socialism," it is said, has such negative connotations. I have never been tempted by that suggestion. The fact of the matter is, market socialism *is* socialism, and whether or not antimarket Leftists will call it that, every supporter of capitalism will, regardless of what label we give it. For market socialism is resolutely anticapitalist, resting on the fundamental insight that the capitalist qua capitalist is, in the modern world, functionally obsolete. Capitalists are no longer needed to raise capital, manage industries, or create new products or technologies. There are other, better, ways of performing these functions.

Not only is market socialism resolutely anticapitalist, but it also embodies the best ideals and values of the socialist tradition, and it is faithful to the vision of an economy controlled by, rather than controlling the producers. Market socialism is not a "utopian" socialism. It recognizes that at least at this stage of our development, none of our values will be perfectly realized, and there will indeed have to be trade-offs. But this is simply good (Marxian) common sense.

NOTES

1. Janos Kornai, *The Socialist System: The Political Economy of Communism* (Princeton: Princeton University Press, 1992), p. 500.

2. Kornai, p. 469. 1 cannot resist pointing out that Kornai's long, learned, sad book was underwritten, as he acknowledges in the preface, by the Sloan Foundation, the Ford Foundation, the McDonnell Foundation, and the Hungarian National Scientific Research Foundation. He composed much of the book at Harvard, where he taught regularly a course in political economy to, among others, "naive members of the 'New Left,' quite unaware of the grave absurdities of the socialist systems" (p. xxvi).

3. My own book, *Against Capitalism* (Cambridge: Cambridge University Press, 1993), draws heavily on this literature, and includes an extensive bibliography. See also, John Roemer, *A Future for Socialism* (Cambridge: Harvard University Press, 1994).

4. More appealing for many is the success of the Mondragon cooperative experiment, a network of some 100 cooperatives, employing 25,000 workers, in the Basque region of Spain. This network of worker-owned cooperatives is the leading economic actor in the Basque region, with sales in 1993 of 8 billion dollars. Its member enterprises are often capital intensive, and employ the most sophisticated technology available, some of it generated by its own internationally well-regarded research center. (For more details, see William Foote Whyte and Kathleen King White, *Making Mondragon: The Growth and Dynamics of the Worker Cooperative Complex* [Ithaca, N.Y.: Cornell University Press, 1988] and Roy Morrison, *We Build the Road as We Travel* [Philadelphia: New Society Publishers, 1991].)

My own model of market socialism draws heavily on the lessons of Mondragon, so I do not want to belittle its significance. Still and all, the Chinese experiment must be regarded as vastly more important.

5. This figure and subsequent data are drawn from Peter Nolan, "The Chinese Puzzle," *Challenge* 37 (January–February 1994): 25–31, and from Robert Weil, "China at the Brink: Class Contradictions of 'Market Socialism'—Part 1," *Monthly Review* 4 (December 1994): 10–35.

6. See Nolan and also M. J. Gordon, "China's Path to Market Socialism," *Challenge* 35 (January–February 1992): 53–56.

7. Weil, "China at the Brink," pp. 22–23.

8. Cf. Milton Friedman, *Capitalism and Freedom* (Chicago: University of Chicago Press, 1962), Milton Friedman and Rose Friedman, *Free to Choose* (New York: Harcourt, 1980); F. A. Hayek, *The Road to Serfdom* (Chicago: University of Chicago Press, 1944), F. A. Hayek, *The Constitution of Liberty* (Chicago: University of Chicago Press, 1960).

9. This latter problem is essentially an incentive problem, but it is so important that it is worth treating separately.

10. Marxists should not find it surprising that at a certain point the productive forces of societies came into conflict with the relations of production, thus requiring a radical readjustment of the latter.

11. This is not to say that communities cannot become *more* self-sufficient, and hence more in control of their own destinies than they are now. Indeed, one of the structural consequences of the model of market socialism I advocate is that communities have considerably more economic autonomy than they do under capitalism.

12. See Michael Albert and Robin Hahnel, *The Political Economy of Participatory Economics* (Princeton: Princeton University Press, 1991), and their less technical companion volume, *Looking Forward: Participatory Economics for the Twenty-First Century* (Boston: South End Press, 1991). I offer an extended critique of the Albert-Hahnel [model] in *Against Capitalism,* pp. 329–34.

13. For seven distinct models, see John Roemer and Pranab Bardhan, eds., *Market Socialism: The Current Debate* (Oxford: Oxford University Press, 1993). See also James Yunker, *Socialism Revised and Modernized: The Case for Pragmatized Market Socialism* (New York: Praeger, 1992), and Leland Stauber, *A New Program for Democratic Socialism* (Carbondale, Ill.: Four Willows Press, 1987).

In what follows I will provide only an outline of one of Roemer's models and my own, so as to give the reader a sense of the range of structures that are compatible with a (socialist) market. What I am calling "the Roemer model" draws on his *A Future for Socialism.* For more details concerning my model, see *Against Capitalism.*

14. Frank Thompson, "Would Roemer's Socialism Equalize Income from Surplus?" prepared for the "A Future for Socialism Conference," University of Wisconsin, Madison, Wisconsin, 13–15 May 1994, has argued that substantial inequalities of a capitalist sort can still develop, since Roemer relies on private savings paid a market-determined rate of interest for his investment fund. This critique seems right to me. Roemer, however, could respond that this sort of inequality is relatively harmless, since it cannot be transformed into control over enterprises, and since a confiscatory inheritance tax can keep it from accumulating over generations.

15. At this stage differential tax rates can also be employed as in the Roemer model, to encourage or discourage certain types of production, thus giving society more direct control over its developmental trajectory.

16. Hillel Ticktin, "The Problem of Market Socialism" (unpublished manuscript, 1993), p. 2.

8

PARTICIPATORY PLANNING

MICHAEL ALBERT AND ROBIN HAHNEL

Since we have long agreed with Marx that allocation via markets must eventually be abolished if we are to achieve a desirable economy, we find the recent rush among many self-declared Marxists to champion models of "market socialism" somewhat ironic. After all, Marx and Engels could hardly have been clearer on this subject. In his *Critique of the Gotha Program* Marx wrote: "Within the cooperative society based on common ownership of the means of production, the producers do not exchange their products." And Engels echoed this view in *Anti- Dühring*: "The seizure of the means of production by society puts an end to commodity production . . . which is replaced by conscious organization on a planned basis." Marx and Engels's idea was clear, even if the appropriate procedures for implementing it were left vague. In socialism the "associated producers" would finally seize control of their destinies by consciously and democratically planning their interconnected labors.

But the results of replacing markets with planning by self-proclaimed Marxist regimes proved disappointing. The Soviet and East European economies that defined "socialism" in the public eye proved less flexible and dynamic in some respects than their capitalist rivals; more importantly, they sprouted new kinds of inequities and class divisions and failed to incorporate the "direct producers" in economic decision making. As a result, even before the recent collapse of authoritarian planning, many erstwhile Marxists were abandoning Marx's "abolitionist" position on markets and commitment to comprehensive planning. While we have always been critical of authoritarian planning,[1] in this article we would like to respond to three claims voiced by supporters of market socialism:

From Michael Albert and Robin Hahnel, "Participatory Planning," *Science & Society* 56, no. 1 (spring 1992): 39–59. Reprinted with permission.

1. Public ownership market economies are a far cry better than capitalism.
2. Left critics misunderstand and falsely accuse markets.
3. There is no other possibility. Allocation can be done via markets or authoritarian planning, but the vision of a third alternative, of some kind of democratic and participatory planning, is a dangerous pipe dream.

On this last point, Alec Nove has thrown down the gauntlet in no uncertain terms:

> I feel increasingly ill-disposed towards those who. . . substitute for hard thinking an image of a world in which there would be no economic problems at all (or where any problems that might arise would be handled smoothly by the "associated producers." . . . In a complex industrial economy the interrelation between its parts can be based in principle either on freely chosen negotiated contracts [i.e., markets], or on a system of binding instructions from planning offices [i.e., authoritarian planning]. *There is no third way.* What can exist, of course, is some *combination* of the two.[2]

While Allen Buchanan poses the challenge in a more agnostic vein:

> It is impossible to show that a feasible nonmarket system at least approaches the productivity of the market unless (1) a rather well-developed theoretical model of the nonmarket system is available, and (2) it is demonstrated that a sufficiently productive approximation of the ideal socialist system described in the theoretical model is practically possible. Unfortunately, [no one] has achieved even the first step—that of providing a theoretical model for a nonmarket system.[3]

Our major purpose in this article is to rebut the claim that there is no alternative to markets and authoritarian planning. In the main body we describe our model of participatory planning and explain why there is every reason to believe it is both feasible and desirable.[4] But before presenting and discussing our model, we briefly review the case against markets.

THE SIMPLE CASE AGAINST MARKETS

The distributive maxim implicit in private enterprise market economies is payment according to personal contribution and the contribution of property owned. The distributive maxim implicit in public enterprise market economies is payment according to personal contribution. The distributive maxim that guides our model of participatory planning is payment according to effort interpreted as personal sacrifice in work and training toward the public benefit.

While redistributive policies could be deployed in any of the three economies to skew results slightly, the fact remains that powerful political, psychological, and ideological forces limit the degree to which any real-world version of these economies could deviate from its implicit maxim. So the issues are: Which distributive maxim is morally justifiable, or equitable? And, are there other considerations, such as efficiency, that might lead us to abandon a more equitable economy for a less equitable one? We will address the second question after the section on participatory planning, and take up the first issue here.

Ironically, the same argument used to rebut the claim that property income is justifiable applies to the claim that all the income that results from payment according to the value of one's personal contribution is justifiable. Socialists have never had trouble seeing that to the extent that differential ownership of productive property is the result of the inheritance lottery, rather than any personal sacrifice, it is unjustifiable. But many fail to recognize that to the extent that differences in people's marginal revenue products are the result of the genetic lottery, rather than any personal sacrifice, payment according to the value of one's personal contribution is equally unjustified. To put it differently, and more precisely, a good case can be made that those who make greater personal sacrifices for the common good have a correspondingly greater claim on the social product. One might add that greater need may also justify a greater claim. But if my greater than average property ownership is not the result of *my* greater sacrifice, and if my higher than average marginal revenue product is not the result of *my* greater sacrifice, then I have no moral claim on more of the social product than anyone else.

To our credit, socialists have never suffered from the illusion that greater personal sacrifice is the major cause of differential ownership of productive property in real-world capitalist economies. But many socialists conveniently forget that inherited talent, training at public expense, and just plain luck have much to do with differential labor productivities in real-world economies. This is not to say that greater productivity should not merit greater reward if it is the result of greater effort. But material reward according to effort is the maxim that guides participatory planning, not market systems. In any case, the first argument against all forms of public enterprise market economies is they are inequitable because they fail to reward participants in accord with the personal sacrifices they undertake for the social benefit.

The second argument against market allocation is that it is inefficient. Even if we ignore inefficiencies caused by market disequilibrium, it is a well-known result from traditional public finance that markets are biased against provision of goods with greater than average positive external effects and biased in favor of goods with greater than average negative external effects. But what is not readily admitted is that external effects are the *rule,* not the exception, because this implies that market prices generally *mis*estimate social benefits and costs, and that markets generally *mis*allocate resources. And what is also not admitted is that because social structures affect the way people develop, the bias in market structures will have a deleterious effect on people's development trajectories which will further aggravate the misallocation of resources.[5]

So while we cannot spell it all out here, we believe it is the proponents of market "socialism" who misunderstand and misconstrue the properties of markets. It is their naivete, not ours, that leads them to unwittingly accept a grossly misleading view of the mixture of private and public goods that directly contradicts the complex social nature of the human condition. For only by assuming that the great preponderance of human economic activities have individually isolated effects could a competent economist conclude that markets yield efficient allocations. Moreover, it is they who respond with silence to the charge that even if markets could generate "efficiency prices and wages," and even if "efficiency wages" were equitable wages, market competition would still systematically destroy community values and social solidarity. In market environments competitive pressures make cooperation individually irrational. Neither buyers nor sellers can afford to consider the interests of the other, as it would be self-defeating to do so. Polluters must try to hide their transgressions, since paying a pollution tax or buying environmentally sound equipment lowers profits. Even if one producer in an industry does not behave egocentrically, others will, and if the altruists persist in their socially responsible behavior they will ultimately be driven out of business for their trouble. All of which holds regardless of ownership relations.

Finally, the information, incentive, and role characteristics of markets subvert the rationale for workers to take initiative in workplace decisions *even if* they have the legal right to do so. We happily admit that employee-managed market economies are preferable to market economies managed by state-appointed managers. But even if employees have the right to manage themselves, market competition generates powerful incentives not to do so. Competition forces decision makers to maximize a bottom line. Any human effects unrepresented in costs and revenues are ignored on pain of competitive failure. Workers' councils motivated by qualitative, human considerations ultimately fail, and since competitive pressures militate against criteria such as work satisfaction, it is perfectly sensible for workers' councils in a market environment to hire others to make their decisions for them. The pattern is simple. First, under market constraints, worker's desire for self-management erodes. Next, workers hire managers who hire engineers and administrators who transform job roles according to competitive dictates. Even in the absence of private ownership, a process that begins with workers choosing to delegate technical and alienated decisions to experts ends by increasing the fragmentation of work, bloating managerial prerogatives, and substituting managers' goals for those of workers. It is not too long before a burgeoning managerial class of "coordinators" begins to maximize the surplus earmarked for themselves and to search for ways to preserve their power. That this can lead to popular apathy, egocentric perspectives, and a new ruling class is clear. Certainly nothing in the historical experience of Yugoslavia, Hungary, or experiments such as Mondragon suggest otherwise.

We also readily concede that public enterprise market economies are preferable to capitalism. Despite all their deficiencies, which provide more than enough reasons to search for a more desirable alternative, elimination of the obscene inequalities inherent in private ownership, especially if applied on a world scale, is compelling. But in addition to their own inadequacies, there is increasing evidence that public enterprise market economies may lead back to capitalism more easily than forward to a truly equitable and participatory economy. Psychological and ideological dynamics of public enterprise market economies clearly "grease the skids" toward full blown capitalism. And the degree of inequality inherent in public enterprise market economies certainly provides a fertile breeding ground for political initiatives to restore private ownership as an easier tool for accumulating still greater privilege and passing it on more easily to one's progeny.

THE UNTRIED ALTERNATIVE: PARTICIPATORY PLANNING

Why can't workers in different enterprises and industries, and consumers in different neighborhoods and regions, coordinate their joint endeavors themselves—consciously, democratically, equitably, and efficiently? Why can't councils of consumers and workers propose what they would like to do, and revise their proposals in light of increasingly accurate information about the impact of their desires on others? If councils must win approval for their proposals from other councils where none enjoys advantage in pressing its claims, why won't consumers' councils find they must modify requests so as not to place a greater burden on workers and resources than others do? And why won't workplace councils be compelled to submit proposals where the social benefits of the outputs they supply outweigh the social costs of the inputs they use? What is impossible about a social, iterative, planning procedure in which workers and consumers propose and revise their own activities in light of increasingly accurate information about what is efficient and what is fair? The answer is that there is nothing impossible about such an economy, no matter what skeptics say.

Consumers' and Workers' Councils

Every individual, family, or living unit would belong to a neighborhood consumption council. Each neighborhood council would belong to a federation of neighborhood councils the size of a city ward or rural county. Each ward would belong to a city consumption council, each city and county council would belong to a state council, and each state council would belong to the national consumption council.

One reason for the nesting of the consumers' councils is to allow for the fact that different kinds of consumption affect different numbers of people. The color of my underwear concerns only me and my most intimate acquaintances. The shrubbery on my block concerns all who live on the block. The quality of play equipment in a park affects all in the neighborhood. The number of volumes in the library and teachers in the high school affect all in a ward. The frequency and punctuality of buses and subways affect all in a city. The disposition of waste affects all States in a watershed. "Real" national security affects all citizens in a country, and protection of the ozone layer affects all humanity—which means that my choice of deodorant, unlike my choice of underwear, concerns more than me and my intimates!

Failure to arrange for all those affected by consumption activities to participate in choosing them not only implies an absence of self-management, but, if the preferences of some are disregarded or misrepresented, a loss of efficiency as well. It is to accommodate the range of consumption activities from the most private to the most public that we organize different "levels" of consumption councils, all of which participate in the planning procedure. This is an important feature that permits participatory planning to offer more meaningful opportunities for citizen participation in economic decision making than market economies and yields efficiency advantages as well.

Similarly, every workplace would be governed by a workers' council in which each worker has one vote. There would be smaller councils for divisions, units, and work teams as circumstances dictate. And while majority vote of the workplace council would be the ultimate arbiter, leaving matters that affect only a subgroup of workers for them to decide, assigning initiative for proposals to those most affected, and weighing voting to reflect differential impacts would be some of the ways workers' councils would approximate the goal of self-management.

Beside workplace councils there would be industry councils and regional federations of workers' councils. Among other functions, regional federations of workers' councils would handle production externalities, and industry councils would handle economies of scale. By having regional, industry, and consumer federations participate in the social, iterative planning procedure described below, we eliminate incentives to misrepresent preferences and ignore what in market economies become external effects, thereby improving efficiency and better approximating collective self-management.

Planning by Associated Producers and Consumers

Others before us have described "council" models of socialism. Democratic workers' councils are common to syndicalism and employee self-managed market models alike. And consumer and citizen councils were featured in Guild Socialism. But what distinguishes our model of a participatory economy from earlier contributions is the careful elaboration of a planning procedure that allows the various councils and federations to propose and revise their own activities efficiently and fairly.

How Consumers Participate. In each iteration of the planning procedure living units propose consumption requests to neighborhood councils; neighborhood councils propose the individual requests of members as well as neighborhood consumption requests; ward councils ask for inputs required to carry out consumption activities affecting all in the ward, and so on. Every council must eventually win approval for its proposal from other councils. This means a neighborhood council must win approval for its consumption request from the other neighborhood councils in its ward; ward councils must win approval from the other wards in a city, etc. Moreover, consumers' councils must win approval of their proposals from workers' councils and vice versa. As we explain below, to win approval consumption councils must demonstrate that their requests do not entail greater social costs per member than the requests of other consumption councils. Or, if a request does have a higher social cost than average, the council will have to provide an explanation others find compelling.

The idea is that consumers' councils will make proposals that maximize their well-being subject to the constraint that all other consumers are to have equal opportunity to do so. In other words, each consumers' council, *CC(h)*, will try to maximize its well-being subject to the constraint that it should not presume to use more of society's scarce productive resources, per member, than other councils. The following heuristic model helps define the situation consumers' councils face in participatory planning.

Let *U(h)* represent the well-being of *CC(h)*. Let x be a vector of activity levels for the economy, *A* be the input matrix of produced goods for those activities (intermediate products), *K* be the capital input coefficient matrix for the activities (machines, plant, and capacity that must be on hand in order to produce output), *R* be the input matrix of nonproducible scarce resources for the activities, and *L* the direct labor input matrix of different kinds of labor for the activities. [A,K,R,L] constitute the technical relations of production in the economy and include multiple techniques. Defining *p(k)* as the vector of shadow prices for scarce capital goods, *p(r)* as the vector of shadow prices for scarce nonproducible resources, and *p(l)* as the vector of shadow prices for different types of labor, [p(k),p(r),p(l)] is the solution to the dual of the primal programming problem for the economy.[6]

Now, suppose *y(h)* is a column vector of consumption requests by *CC(h)*, that is, a vector of particular quantities of all the different kinds of produced goods. Consider the sum:

$$p(k)K(I-A)^{-1}y(h) + p(r)R(I-A)^{-1}y(h) + p(l)L(I-A)^{-1}y(h).$$

This reads: the (shadow) value of the direct plus indirect capital stocks, plus the value of the direct plus indirect nonreproducible resources, plus the value of the direct plus indirect labor inputs into the consumption bundle, all summed together. This sum, in other words, is the social cost of consumption proposal *y(h)*. So consumers' councils propose bundles they like, that is, they seek to maximize *U(h)*. But in participatory planning these proposals will be judged by other consumers' councils with an eye to whether or not the proposal, *y(h)*, implies a greater than per capita use of society's scarce productive resources. In other words, those in other councils will want to know whether:

$$\{[p(k)K + p(r)R + p(l)L][(I - A)^{-1}]\}[\ y(h)\ -y(a)] \le\ 0,$$

where y(a) is the average consumption council request. In words: they will want to know that the social cost of the particular consumption request is not larger than (and hopefully smaller than) the average request.

Participatory planning invites consumers to critically assess each others' proposals. But for proposals that do not exceed average social cost per consumer, other councils are limited to friendly rather than parental advice: parents can veto, friends can only cajole. On the other hand, for proposals in excess of average social cost per consumer, other consumer councils are permitted parent-like veto powers.

All this is straightforward, *assuming we have accurate shadow prices for scarce productive resources.* We explain below how prices "indicative" of social costs and benefits emerge from the planning procedure.

How Workers Participate. In each iteration, workplace councils propose their own production plan. That is, they propose a list of outputs and inputs. Regional federations calculate associated external effects, and industry federations search for economies and diseconomies of scale. We assume every workers' council would like its work to be pleasant and fulfilling, and they will propose inputs and outputs with this in mind. But like consumers' councils, they must win approval for their proposals from other councils. In the case of workplace councils approval hinges on demonstrating that the outputs they will provide generate greater social benefits than the social costs of the inputs they will use.

Unconventionally, we view workers' councils like consumer councils, as centers of human activity which affect not only the well-being of members, but also the prospects of others in the economy. Seen in this way, the issue is whether the human consequences for the workers in a council are as desirable as possible given the fact that there are workers and consumers in other councils desirous of the same. We use the same heuristic model to clarify how workers' councils could be expected to behave under the conditions of participatory planning.

We assume each workers' council, $WC(j)$, will make proposals that maximize the well-being of its members as they see it, $U(j)$, just as we assumed consumers' councils would. But workers' councils must do so subject to the constraint that their workplace be as useful to the rest of society in the work it performs as any equally endowed workplace. A workers' council is defined by its members' particular training and skills, and by the physical productive assets (plant and machinery) at its disposal. But some workplaces will have greater productive capabilities than others. Output proposals that might represent generous work efforts and sacrifices for a council with a small productive endowment might represent insufficient effort for a workplace with a large productive endowment. In formulating their own proposals and judging the proposals of others, workers' councils must have some way of measuring productive capabilities. Once again, shadow prices play a critical role in comparing the productive endowments of different workplaces, whether they produce the same or different products. If we have a vector of shadow prices, we can measure the human and physical productive capabilities of any WC, as well as the social costs of intermediate inputs and natural resources requested, and the social usefulness of the outputs the WC will supply.

Let $K(j)$ be the vector of physical capital stocks (plants and machinery) and $L(j)$ be the vector of different categories of labor $WC(j)$ begins with. The value of the productive resources $WC(j)$ will be "charged" for, initially is

$$p(k)K(j) + p(l)L(j)$$

since this represents the degree to which $WC(j)$ can be expected to contribute to society's benefit. If $WC(j)$ is willing to be "charged" for more productive labor, or wishes to be charged for less, it can submit as part of its proposal $l(ij) > 0$ (demanding more labor type i) or $l(ij) < 0$ (releasing labor type i). And if $WC(j)$ wants to request more or release some of its physical capital stock, it can submit as part of its proposal $k(ij) > 0$ (demanding more capital good i) or $k(ij) < 0$ (releasing capital type i). We let $l(j)$ and $k(j)$ represent the vectors of changes in labor and capital requested, respectively, and let $a(j)$ represent the vector of produced inputs requested, $r(j)$ the vector of primary resources requested, and $y(j)$ the vector of outputs $WC(j)$ offers to produce with all these inputs. In which case

$$p(k)[K(j) + k(j)] + p(l)[L(j) + l(j)] + pa(j) + p(r)r(j)$$

represents the social value of the inputs $WC(j)$ requests, plus the social value of the part of its productive endowment it proposes to retain. And $py(j)$ represents the social value of the outputs $WC(j)$ proposes to supply.

As long as the value of inputs requested is not greater than the value of outputs supplied, or in symbols

$$p(k)[K(j) + k(j)] + p(l)[L(j) + l(j)] + pa(j) + p(r)r(j) \leq py(j),$$

$WC(j)$'s proposal is not what we might call "socially abusive," and should be approved by other councils participating in the planning procedure.

Summarizing, the problem for a typical Consumers' Council, $CC(h)$, is:

max: $U(h)$ subject to:

$$\{[(\,p(k)K + p(r)R + p(l)L][1-A)^{-1}]\}[y(h)-y(a)] \leq 0.$$

And the problem for a typical Workers' Council, $WC(j)$, is:

max: $U(j)$ subject to:

$$p(k)[\ K(j) + k(j)] + p(l)[\ L(j) + 1(j)] + pa(j) + p(r)r(j) \leq py(j).$$

As readers might suspect, the convergence and optimality properties of our planning procedures when studied in a formal model hinge on the convexity properties of council well-being functions. If the well-being functions of consumers' councils have the convexity properties traditionally assumed for individual consumer's preferences, then our consumer council constraint, read as an equality, is a separating hyperplane between $CC(h)$'s "at least as preferred consumption set" and what we might call the "socially nonabusive," or "not-too-greedy" consumption set. And if the well-being functions of our worker councils have similar convexity properties, and production possibility sets have the convexity properties traditionally assumed, then our workers' council constraint, read as an equality, is a separating hyperplane between $WC(j)$'s "at least as preferred production set" and what we might call $WC(j)$'s "socially nonabusive," or "not-too-lazy" production set. Under these assumptions our planning procedure will converge to an efficient plan. We return to the likelihood of convexity after describing the planning procedure.

The Planning Procedure. The actors in participatory planning are consumers' and workers' councils and federations, and a planning bureau we call an Iteration Facilitation Board (IFB). The IFB plays an entirely mechanical function in our formal model. It neither accumulates nor recalls information from previous iterations, and makes no discretionary decisions. As a matter of fact, since we can describe its functions completely, the IFB need not exist in our theoretical model. But in real-world participatory planning the IFB would play a role, and could engage in a range of discretionary decisions.[7]

In formal terms the procedure is quite simple. The IFB announces "indicative prices" for all goods, resources, categories of labor, and capital stocks. Each consumer council (and federation) responds with a consumption proposal, and each worker council (and federation) responds with a production proposal. The IFB calculates the excess demand or supply for each good and adjusts the indicative price for the good up, or down, in light of the excess demand or supply. Using the new prices as more accurate indications of social costs and benefits, consumer and worker councils (and federations) revise and resubmit their proposals. The IFB recalculates excess demands and supplies, readjusts prices, and consumer and worker councils respond again. Iterations continue until excess demands and supplies are eliminated, yielding a feasible plan that will be equitable and efficient as well.

In our other works, cited above, we develop the formal model in detail and analyze the planning procedure's convergence and efficiency properties; and explore ways in which participatory planning in real-world settings would necessarily diverge from the procedures implied by the formal model. Here we can only summarize a few key points.

1. Participatory planning is a social, iterative procedure. Consumers and

workers are responsible for preparing their own initial proposals. And they alone are responsible for revising these proposals in light of updated information on social costs and benefits, and in response to pressure from others not to ask for more than others can have or work less than others will have to. Workers and consumers are free to apply for work and residence wherever they wish, and may form new workers' and consumers' councils as well. The only restriction is that all must participate in the planning procedure and win approval for their final proposal.

2. Essentially the procedure "whittles" overly optimistic, infeasible proposals down to a feasible plan in two different ways. (a) Unjustifiable consumer greediness is reduced by the refusal of other consumer councils' to approve requests that require a greater than per capita use of society's scarce productive resources. Unjustifiable worker laziness is reduced by the refusal of other workers to approve proposals that entail less than average work effort. (b) At the same time, excess demands for particularly scarce inputs and socially costly outputs are whittled down by raising the prices units requesting them are charged. And excess supplies of plentiful inputs and socially inexpensive outputs are reduced by lowering the prices units requesting them are charged. These relative price changes will induce "shifting" behavior on the part of optimizing consumers' and workers' councils who will seek to "shift" rather than "reduce" wherever possible. For this reason efficiency and equity are generated simultaneously.

3. Under strict convexity assumptions our formal procedure will converge to a feasible and optimal plan, and generate "efficiency" prices for labor, natural resources, plant, and equipment. While very different in substance, technically our model is a variation of a well-known procedure developed by Arrow and Hurwicz.[8]

4. Our consumer councils differ from the consumers of traditional theory because they consist of a number of people, whose individual preferences presumably differ. Our treatment of workers' councils is even farther from traditional treatments of production. In addition to treating groups rather than individuals, we have framed workers' choice in exactly the same terms as consumer choice. Since all this is novel, there is no discussion in the literature of what the convexity properties of such preference orderings might be like.

But in our opinion convexity assumptions have long been an assumption of convenience rather than conviction for most economists. The reasons for doubting the plausibility of convexity assumptions in traditional treatments of market economies have long been numerous and compelling. But the necessity of ignoring these doubts in order to proceed has been more compelling still. In this vein, we do not see working through the logic of our economic model under what are in all likelihood dubious convexity assumptions as any different than traditional analysis of more familiar economic systems.

What distinguishes us from traditional theorists in this regard is that since we do *not* expect convexity assumptions to hold in real-world settings, we take the trouble to discuss practical procedures that can be deployed to prevent time-consuming loops in the iterative planning procedure when they inevitably arise. There are several automatic and discretionary procedures IFBs might use to facilitate convergence when troublesome real-world nonconvexities inevitably arise.

5. About a half century ago, Oskar Lange, Abba Lerner, and Frederick Taylor responded to an erroneous consensus that public enterprise economies could not operate efficiently by elaborating a model of such an economy they argued was capable of yielding Pareto optimal outcomes.[9] While not an end to the "socialist calculation debate," their model served as a powerful challenge to what had become a firmly held "impossibility" conviction among economists regarding the supposed inability of public enterprise systems to yield efficient results. Interestingly, their model derived rather directly from propositions well known to microeconomic theorists of their day.

Our formal model of participatory planning also relies heavily on work well known to microeconomic theorists familiar with the literature on iterative planning mechanisms that flourished in the late 1960s and early 1970s. Hopefully our model will also serve to challenge an unwarranted pessimism among economists about public enterprise economies, namely, the erroneous consensus that in such economies there is no alternative allocative mechanism to markets or authoritarian planning.

EQUITY, EFFICIENCY, AND INCENTIVES

In participatory planning payment is according to effort, or personal sacrifice for the social benefit. As discussed above, we consider this a major virtue because we find less egalitarian outcomes such as payment according to the value of one's personal contribution morally indefensible. But payment according to effort will yield considerably more egalitarian outcomes than usual. Even among those who find this equitable, many fear it is incompatible with efficient incentives. We challenge this widely held belief.

Differences in the value of people's contributions are due to differences in talent, training, job placement, luck, and effort. Once we clarify that "effort" includes personal sacrifices incurred in training, the only factor influencing performance over which an individual has any discretion is effort. By definition, neither talent nor luck can be induced by reward. Rewarding the occupant of a job for the contribution inherent in the job itself does not enhance performance. And provided that training is undertaken at public rather than private expense, no reward is required to induce people to seek training. In sum, if we include an effort component of training in our definition of effort, the only discretionary factor influencing performance is effort, and the only factor we should reward to enhance performance is effort—which certainly turns common wisdom on its head! Not only is rewarding effort consistent with efficiency, but rewarding the combined effects of talent, training incurred at public not private expense, job placement, luck, and effort, is not.

Having explained this, we should clarify something we said earlier that might be misleading. In explaining the logic of participatory planning we said other consumers would keep an eye on whether or not a consumer's proposal had a higher social cost than average, and in our heuristic model we formulated the consumer council's constraint in this way. In fact participatory planning has procedures for consumer borrowing and saving, and special provisions that encourage granting exceptions based on need, all of which can lead to individual and council deviations from average consumption requests. But, in addition, our formulation was based on an assumption of equal effort. Any disparities in consumers' efforts in their roles as workers would be reflected in disparate consumption allowances during the planning process. The idea is "equal consumption right for equal personal sacrifice" not "equal consumption right for unequal sacrifice"—which is neither equitable nor efficient. But let there be no doubt, participatory planning would be considerably more egalitarian than either capitalism or public enterprise market economies.

So while participatory planning is designed to make maximum use of the incentive to accomplish what you, yourself have proposed, the incentive to do one's fair share, and the incentive to win the respect and esteem of one's peers, participatory planning *does* have material incentives. People receiving higher effort ratings from co-workers will consume more than people with lower ratings. However, there are two senses in which the degree of material incentives is flexible. Individual consumers' councils can decide how much weight to give to effort versus need when they review members' consumption proposals and the qualitative information people submit. This means that the reliance on material incentives can vary from one part of the economy to another. But the question of the degree to which productive innovation of individuals and/or groups will be materially rewarded is more complicated. For example, how would the individual inventor of something like the Lotus spread sheet and her workers' council be treated in participatory planning?

First, let's be clear why this matters. It matters because we want to know if she would have bothered to invent a new spread sheet, and if her workers' council would have bothered to implement and develop it. But it also matters whether the innovation would have spread to other workplaces in the economy as quickly as possible, since this determines to what extent and how quickly the net social product will be increased by the innovation.

If the only means of stimulating innovation were material reward, the only way to maximize socially desirable innovative effort would be to give the innovator 100 percent of the potential social benefits from the innovation *over all time!* Anything less would understimulate socially beneficial innovation. (Anything more would be irrational for the rest of us to agree to.) Once this reward is paid, the innovation must be implemented throughout the economy as quickly as possible in order to turn the potential benefits of the innovation into actual benefits. Contrary to popular opinion, capitalism and patent systems do neither, nor would any variant of a public enterprise market system. In other words, *no* economy would ever treat innovation in the way modern principal-agent theory implies it should be treated. If innovation were treated this way, Einstein's heirs would be consuming half of world GNP by now!

In our model the woman who invented the spread sheet gets rated by her co-workers. Since performance is *usually* at least *partially* a reflection of effort, and since this is a human discretionary judgment in any case, she would presumably get a very high rating. Since no system is going to award her the full material social benefits to all future generations of her invention, a system that enhances the motivational power of social appreciation by basing fame directly on social serviceability would have important advantages in stimulating innovation over a system in which fame is only earned through fortune.

But how would the innovator's workplace be treated in our system? Assuming she was sufficiently motivated to invent the new spread sheet, what are the incentives for her workplace to begin to use it, and how rapidly will the innovation diffuse to other workplaces? If her workplace could use the new spread sheet and keep other workplaces from using it they would be able to meet the national social benefit to cost ratio with less effort than before, and therefore less effort than other workplaces where nothing would have changed. The result would be plenty of incentive for her workplace to implement her idea, but little benefit to the economy since only one workplace would be using the more pro-ductive technique. It is also obvious that keeping other workplaces from using the new technique breeds inequities as well as inefficiency. On the other hand, if the new technique is immediately made available to all other workplaces, the benefit of the innovation to the economy is maximized, and no inequities arise, but it would appear the innovating workplace would gain no more in material terms than every other workplace.

Our proposal is that all innovations be made available to all workplaces immediately to avoid inefficiency. But the degree to which an innovating work-place is awarded extra material benefit beyond what others gain, and the period of time over which this material bonus is paid can be flexible. Innovating work-places could be granted material rewards in the form of either more desirable working conditions or greater consumption allowances over a period of time. Clearly what is at stake is equity vs. stimulation of productive innovation. And the best way to improve the equity vs. stimulation "tradeoff" would be to strengthen the motivational power of nonmaterial rewards and create work units whose *product* is innovation. But the extent and duration of material rewards for innovating workplaces would be determined by open and democratic debate among the participants in the economy, providing flexibility in the use of mate-rial incentives to reward innovating units.

CONCLUSION

The simple truth is that socialism as originally conceived has never been tested. Which is not to say that private ownership of the means of production was not eliminated in a number of economies, or that this is not necessary to eradicate capitalist exploitation and replace production for profit with planning for social use. But it wasn't nearly enough. Producers have never planned their activities with one another and with the consumers of their goods and services. In many cases where capitalism was temporarily shelved, impulses for popular participation in economic decision making were belittled rather than encouraged in the process of imposing authoritarian planning, and as new elites consolidated power, inequities in pay and work conditions increased rather than diminished.

The answer to the question *why* democratic planning has yet to be tried is complicated. It was not our purpose to review the debate over internal and external "objective" constraints, ideological confusions, and political betrayals that have been favorite culprits of the Left. However, recently economists such as Alec Nove and Robert Heilbroner have added their voices to the longtime conservative answer that participatory planning has never been tried because it is impossible, and more than a few on the left have switched from criticizing to defending markets. Our intent in this article was simply to restate Marx's reasons for rejecting market systems, and summarize our rebuttal to the claim that participatory planning is impossible. Markets look no better at the end of the twentieth century than they did from Marx's vantage point in the late nineteenth century. And a participatory, equitable economy in which workers and consumers propose, revise, and coordinate their own activities efficiently *is* feasible, and *is* as inspiring as always.

Admittedly, such an economy is harder to achieve than abandoning all attempts to decide our own fates, which is the market "solution" to the economic "problem." And it is harder to organize than turning our lives over to a tiny, professional elite, which was the unfortunate "solution" of authoritarian planning. But the "price" of our collective mental and political laziness has been the systematic abuse and misuse of the productive capabilities of the planet and its inhabitants. It is time to take up the challenge of forging a desirable economy rather than abandon the project, offering as an excuse the opinion of some dismal economists and ex-socialists that the project was always, and has now proven, impossible.

NOTES

1. For our most comprehensive critique of authoritarian planning, including our criticisms of its practice in the Soviet Union, China, and Cuba, see *Socialism Today and Tomorrow* (Boston: South End Press, 1981).

2. Alec Nove, *The Economics of Feasible Socialism* (London: George Allen and Unwin, 1983), pp. ix–x, 44.

3. Allen Buchanan, *Ethics, Efficiency, and Market* (Totowa, N.J.: Rowman and Littlefield, 1985), p. 29.

4. The description here is an abbreviated discussion of arguments and results presented in two books on participatory planning. In *The Political Economy of Participatory Economics* (Princeton, N.J.: Princeton University Press, 1991) we present a theoretical model of participatory planning, carry out a rigorous welfare-theoretic analysis of its properties, and outline simulation experiments that could substantiate its feasibility. In *Looking Forward: Participatory Economics for the Twenty-First Century* (Boston: South End Press, 1991) we examine the intricacies of participatory decision making in a variety of realistic settings, describe day-to-day behavior, and treat a number of practical issues conveniently ignored by theoretical models.

5. We refer readers to chapter 7 of Robin Hahnel and Michael Albert, *Quiet Revolution in Welfare Economics* (Princeton, N.J.: Princeton University Press, 1990) for a full statement of our argument that a reasonable view of human economies leads to the opposite conclusion from the one suggested by the traditional economic paradigm, and that the consequences of pervasive external effects are much more damaging than usually assumed.

6. The primal programming problem for the economy is:

$$\text{max: } v(I\text{-}A)x \text{ subject to:}$$

$$Kx \leq k^*; Rx \leq r^*; Lx \leq l^*; x \geq 0$$

where v is the (row) vector of relative social values of produced goods, k^* is the vector of available capital goods, r^* is the vector of scarce nonproducible resources, and l^* is the vector of different kinds of labor available. The associated dual programming problem is:

$$\text{min: } p(k)k^* + p(r)r^* + p(l)l^* \text{ subject to:}$$

$$p(k)K + p(r)R + p(l)L \geq v(I\text{-}A); \ p(k) \geq 0; \ p(r) \geq 0; \ p(l) \geq 0$$

7. In *Looking Forward*, chapter 9, we examine practical considerations that make a working IFB advisable, and procedures that could prevent its staff from biasing outcomes should it be authorized to exercise discretionary powers.

8. See K. Arrow, L. Hurwicz, and H. Uzawa, *Studies in Linear and Non-Linear Programming* (Stanford: Stanford University Press, 1958). A proof that such procedures converge to Pareto optimal allocations and efficiency prices under strict convexity assumptions is conveniently outlined in G. M. Heal, *The Theory of Economic Planning* (Amsterdam: North Holland, 1973), chap. 4. ["Convexity" is "a characteristic of tastes or technology that a combination of commodities is preferable to any one on its own. If someone prefers a (half) slice of bread and half a gram of butter to either a whole slice of bread or a whole gram of butter, they have convex preferences. If it is easier to make one car using ten men and ten machines than to make it using twenty men and no machines or using twenty machines and no men, the production technology is convex. Convexity implies that combinations of products are more desirable than extremes." Graham Bannock, R. E. Baxter, and Evan Davis, *The Penguin Dictionary of Economics*, 5th ed. (London: Penguin Books, 1992), pp. 88–89.—*Editor*]

9. For an accessible, modern rendition of their work see Oskar Lange and Frederick Taylor, *On the Economic Theory of Socialism* (New York: Monthly Review Press, 1964).

PART IV.

FREEDOM AND EQUALITY

9.

ELEGANT TOMBSTONES
A Note on Friedman's Freedom

C. B. MACPHERSON

Academic political scientists who want their students to think about the problem of liberty in the modern state are properly anxious to have them confront at first-hand various contemporary theoretical positions on the relation between freedom and capitalism. The range of positions is wide: at one extreme freedom is held to be incompatible with capitalism; at the other freedom is held to be impossible except in a capitalist society; in between, all sorts of necessary or possible relations are asserted. Different concepts of freedom are involved in some of these positions, similar concepts in others; and different models of capitalism (and of socialism) are sometimes being used. It is clearly important to sort them out. But there is some difficulty in finding adequate theoretical expositions of the second extreme position, which might be called the pure market theory of liberalism. There are very few of them. Probably the most effective, and the one most often cast in this role, is Milton Friedman's *Capitalism and Freedom* which is now apt to be treated by political scientists as the classic defence of free-market liberalism. As such it deserves more notice from the political theorists' standpoint than it got on publication, when its technical arguments about the possibility of returning to laissez-faire attracted most attention.[1] Whether or not *Capitalism and Freedom* is now properly treated as the classic defense of the pure market theory of liberalism, it is at least a classic example of the difficulty of moving from the level of controversy about laissez-faire to the level of fundamental concepts of freedom and the market.

The first thing that strikes the political scientist about *Capitalism and Freedom* is the uncanny resemblance between Friedman's approach and Herbert

Reprinted by permission of the *Canadian Journal of Political Science* 1 (March 1968): 95–106; reprinted in C. B. Macpherson, *Democratic Theory: Essays in Retrieval* (Oxford: Clarendon, 1973).

Spencer's. Eighty years ago Spencer opened his *The Man versus the State* by drawing attention to a reversal which he believed had taken place recently in the meaning of liberalism: it had, he said, originally meant individual market freedom as opposed to state coercion, but it had come to mean more state coercion in the supposed interest of individual welfare. Spencer assigned a reason: earlier liberalism had in fact abolished grievances or mitigated evils suffered by the many, and so had contributed to their welfare; the welfare of the many then easily came to be taken by liberals not as a by-product of the real end, the relaxation of restraints, but as the end itself. Spencer regretted this, without offering any evidence that market freedom ever was more basic, or more desired, than the maximization of wealth or of individual welfare. Professor Friedman does the same. *Capitalism and Freedom* opens by drawing attention to the same reversal of meaning, and rejecting it out of hand. "Freedom of the individual, or perhaps of the family" is for him the liberal's "ultimate goal in judging social arrangements." His case is that "a free private enterprise exchange economy," or "competitive capitalism" is both a direct component of freedom, and a necessary though not a sufficient condition of political freedom, which he defines as "the absence of coercion of a man by his fellow men."[2]

To maximize this freedom, he argues, governments should be allowed to handle only those matters "which cannot be handled through the market at all, or can be handled only at so great a cost that the use of political channels may be preferable."[3] This would mean government moving out of almost all its welfare and regulatory functions. Controls on, or support of, any prices, wages, interest rates, rents, exports, imports, and amounts produced, would all have to go; so would present social security programs, housing subsidy programs, and the like. The functions properly left to governments because the market cannot perform them at all, or perform them well, are summarized:

> A government which maintained law and order, defined property rights, served as a means whereby we could modify property rights and other rules of the economic game, adjudicated disputes about the interpretation of the rules, enforced contracts, promoted competition, provided a monetary framework, engaged in activities to counter technical monopolies and to overcome neighborhood effects widely regarded as sufficiently important to justify government intervention, and which supplemented private charity and the private family in protecting the irresponsible, whether madman or child—such a government would clearly have important functions to perform. The consistent liberal is not an anarchist.[4]

No one ever thought that laissez-faire was anarchism; Spencer would scarcely have objected to this list of allowable government functions. But what is this economic game which is supposed to maximize individual freedom? The argument is that competitive capitalism can resolve "the basic problem of social organization," which is "how to coordinate the economic activities of large numbers of people,"[5] by voluntary cooperation of individuals as opposed to central direction by state coercion.

In addition to arguing that competitive capitalism is a system of economic freedom and so an important component of freedom broadly understood, Professor Friedman argues that capitalism is a necessary condition of political freedom (and that socialism is incompatible with political freedom). And although he is more concerned with freedom than with equity, he does argue also that the capitalist principle of distribution of the whole product is not only preferable to a socialist principle but is in fact accepted by socialists.

This essay deals with (I) an error which vitiates Friedman's demonstration that competitive capitalism coordinates men's economic activities without coercion; (II) the inadequacy of his arguments that capitalism is a necessary condition of political freedom and that socialism is inconsistent with political freedom; and (III) the fallacy of his case for the ethical adequacy of the capitalist principle of distribution.

I

Professor Friedman's demonstration that the capitalist market economy can coordinate economic activities without coercion rests on an elementary conceptual error. His argument runs as follows. He shows first that in a simple market model, where each individual or household controls resources enabling it to produce goods and services either directly for itself or for exchange, there will be production for exchange because of the increased product made possible by specialization. But "since the household always has the alternative of producing directly for itself, it need not enter into any exchange unless it benefits from it. Hence no exchange will take place unless both parties do benefit from it. Cooperation is thereby achieved without coercion."[6] So far, so good. It is indeed clear that in this simple exchange model, assuming rational maximizing behavior by all hands, every exchange will benefit both parties, and hence that no coercion is involved in the decision to produce for exchange or in any act of exchange.

Professor Friedman then moves on to our actual complex economy, or rather to his own curious model of it:

> As in [the] simple model, so in the complex enterprise and money-exchange economy, co-operation is strictly individual and voluntary *provided*: (a) that enterprises are private, so that the ultimate contracting parties are individuals and (b) that individuals are effectively free to enter or not to enter into any particular exchange, so that every transaction is strictly voluntary.[7]

One cannot take exception to proviso (a): it is clearly required in the model to produce a cooperation that is "strictly individual." One might, of course, suggest that a model containing this stipulation is far from corresponding to our actual complex economy, since in the latter the ultimate contracting parties who have the most effect on the market are not individuals but corporations, and moreover, corporations which in one way or another manage to opt out of the fully competitive market. This criticism, however, would not be accepted by all economists as self-evident: some would say that the question who has most effect on the market is still an open question (or is a wrongly posed question). More investigation and analysis of this aspect of the economy would be valuable. But political scientists need not await its results before passing judgment on Friedman's position, nor should they be tempted to concentrate their attention on proviso (a). If they do so they are apt to miss the fault in proviso (b), which is more fundamental, and of a different kind. It is not a question of the correspondence of the model to the actual: it is a matter of the inadequacy of the proviso to produce the model.

Proviso (b) is "that individuals are effectively free to enter or not to enter into any particular exchange," and it is held that with this proviso "every transaction is strictly voluntary." A moment's thought will show that this is not so. The proviso that is required to make every transaction strictly voluntary is *not* freedom not to enter into any *particular* exchange, but freedom not to enter into any exchange *at all*. This, and only this, was the proviso that proved the simple model to be voluntary and noncoercive; and nothing less than this would prove the complex model to be voluntary and noncoercive. But Professor Friedman is clearly claiming that freedom not to enter into any *particular* exchange is enough: "The consumer is protected from coercion by the seller because of the presence of other sellers with whom he can deal. . . . The employee is protected from coercion by the employer because of other employers for whom he can work. . . ."[8]

One almost despairs of logic, and of the use of models. It is easy to see what Professor Friedman has done, but it is less easy to excuse it. He has moved from the simple economy of exchange between independent producers, to the capitalist economy, without mentioning the most important thing that distinguishes them. He mentions money instead of barter, and "enterprises which are intermediaries between individuals in their capacities as suppliers of services and as purchasers of goods,"[9] as if money and merchants were what distinguished a capitalist economy from an economy of independent producers. What distinguishes the capitalist economy from the simple exchange economy is the separation of labor and capital, that is, the existence of a labor force without its own sufficient capital and therefore without a choice as to whether to put its labor in the market or not. Professor Friedman would agree that where there is no choice there is coercion. His attempted demonstration that capitalism coordinates without coercion therefore fails.

Since all his specific arguments against the welfare and regulatory state depend on his case that the market economy is not coercive, the reader may spare himself the pains (or, if an economist, the pleasure) of attending to the careful and persuasive reasoning by which he seeks to establish the minimum to which coercion could be reduced by reducing or discarding each of the main regulatory and welfare activities of the state. None of this takes into account the coercion involved in the separation of capital from labor, or the possible mitigation of this coercion by the regulatory and welfare state. Yet it is because this coercion can in principle be reduced by the regulatory and welfare state, and thereby the amount of effective individual liberty be increased, that liberals have been justified in pressing, in the name of liberty, for infringements on the pure operation of competitive capitalism.

II

While the bulk of *Capitalism and Freedom* is concerned with the regulatory and welfare state, Friedman's deepest concern is with socialism. He undertakes to demonstrate that socialism is inconsistent with political freedom. He argues this in two ways: (1) that competitive capitalism, which is of course negated by socialism, is a necessary (although not a sufficient) condition of political freedom; (2) that a socialist society is so constructed that it cannot guarantee political freedom. Let us look at the two arguments in turn.

1. The argument that competitive capitalism is necessary to political freedom is itself conducted on two levels, neither of which shows a necessary relation.

(a) The first, on which Friedman properly does not place very much weight, is a historical correlation. No society that has had a large measure of political freedom "has not also used something comparable to a free market to organize the bulk of economic activity." Professor Friedman rightly emphasizes "how limited is the span of time and the part of the globe for which there has ever been anything like political freedom"; he believes that the exceptions to the general rule of "tyranny, servitude, and misery" are so few that the relation between them and certain economic arrangements can easily be spotted. "The nineteenth century and early twentieth century in the Western world stand out as striking exceptions to the general trend of historical development. Political freedom in this instance clearly came along with the free market and the development of capitalist institutions." Thus, for Professor Friedman, "history suggests. . . that capitalism is a necessary condition for political freedom."[10]

The broad historical correlation is fairly clear, though in cutting off the period of substantial political freedom in the West at the "early twentieth century" Friedman seems to be slipping into thinking of economic freedom and begging the question of the relation of political freedom to economic freedom. But granting the correlation between the emergence of capitalism and the emergence of political freedom, what it may suggest to the student of history is the converse of what it suggests to Professor Friedman: i.e., it may suggest that political freedom was a necessary condition for the development of capitalism. Capitalist institutions could not be fully established until political freedom (ensured by a competitive party system with effective civil liberties) had been won by those who wanted capitalism to have a clear run: a liberal state (political freedom) was needed to permit and facilitate a capitalist market society.

If this is the direction in which the causal relation runs, what follows (assuming the same relation to continue to hold) is that freedom, or rather specific kinds and degrees of freedom, will be or not be maintained according as those who have a stake in the maintenance of capitalism think them useful or necessary. In fact, there has been a complication in this relation. The liberal state which had, by the mid-nineteenth century in England, established the political freedoms needed to facilitate capitalism, was not democratic: that is, it had not extended political freedom to the bulk of the people. When, later, it did so, it began to abridge market freedom. The more extensive the political freedom, the less extensive the economic freedom became. At any rate, the historical correlation scarcely suggests that capitalism is a necessary condition for political freedom.

(b) Passing from historical correlation, which "by itself can never be convincing," Professor Friedman looks for "logical links between economic and political freedom." The link he finds is that "the kind of economic organization that provides economic freedom directly, namely, competitive capitalism, also promotes political freedom because it separates economic power from political power and in this way enables the one to offset the other." The point is developed a few pages later. The greater the concentration of coercive power in the same hands, the greater the threat to political freedom (defined as "the absence of coercion of a man by his fellow men"). The market removes the organization of economic activity from the control of the political authority. It thus reduces the concentration of power and "enables economic strength to be a check to political power rather than a reinforcement."[11]

Granted the validity of these generalizations, they tell us only that the market enables economic power to offset rather than reinforce political power. They do not show any necessity or inherent probability that the market *leads to* the offsetting of political power by economic power. We may doubt that there is any such inherent probability. What can be shown is an inherent probability in the other direction, i.e., that the market leads to political power being used not to offset but to reinforce economic power. For the more completely the market takes over the organization of economic activity, that is, the more nearly the society approximates Friedman's ideal of a competitive capitalist market society, where the state establishes and enforces the individual right of appropriation and the rules of the market but does not interfere in the operation of the market, the more completely is political power being used to reinforce economic power.

Professor Friedman does not see this as any threat to political freedom because he does not see that the capitalist market necessarily gives coercive power to those who succeed in amassing capital. He knows that the coercion whose absence he equates with political freedom is not just the physical coercion of police and prisons, but extends to many forms of economic coercion, e.g., the power some men may have over others' terms of employment. He sees the coercion possible (he thinks probable) in a socialist society where the political authority can enforce certain terms of employment. He does not see the coercion in a capitalist society where the holders of capital can enforce certain terms of employment. He does not see this because of his error about freedom not to enter into any particular exchange being enough to prove the uncoercive nature of entering into exchange at all.

The placing of economic coercive power and political coercive power in the hands of different sets of people, as in the fully competitive capitalist economy, does not lead to the first checking the second but to the second reinforcing the first. It is only in the welfare-state variety of capitalism, which Friedman would like to have dismantled, that there is a certain amount of checking of economic power by political power.

The logical link between competitive capitalism and political freedom has not been established.

2. Professor Friedman argues also that a socialist society is so constructed that it cannot guarantee political freedom. He takes as the test of political freedom the freedom of individuals to propagandize openly for a radical change in the structure of society: in a socialist society the test is freedom to advocate the introduction of capitalism. He might have seemed to be on more realistic ground had he taken the test to be freedom to advocate different policies within the framework of socialism, e.g., a faster or slower rate of socialization, of industrialization, etc.: it is on these matters that the record of actual socialist states has been conspicuously unfree. However, since the denial of freedom of such advocacy has generally been on the ground that such courses would lead to or encourage the reintroduction of capitalism, such advocacy may all be subsumed under his test.

We may grant at once that in the present socialist states (by which is meant those dominated by communist parties) such freedom is not only not guaranteed but is actively denied. Professor Friedman does not ask us to grant this, since he is talking not about particular socialist states but about any possible socialist state, about the socialist state as such; nevertheless the actual ones are not far from his mind, and we shall have to refer to them again. His case that a socialist state as such cannot guarantee political freedom depends on what he puts in his model of the socialist state. He uses in fact two models. In one, the government is the sole employer and the sole source from which necessary instruments of effective political advocacy (paper, use of printing presses, halls) can be had. In the other, the second stipulation is dropped.

It is obvious that in either model a government which wished to prevent political advocacy could use its economic monopoly position to do so. But what Professor Friedman is trying to establish is something different, namely, that its economic monopoly position would render any socialist government, whatever its intentions, incapable of guaranteeing this political freedom. It may be granted that in the first model this would be so. It would be virtually impossible, for a government which desired to guarantee freedom of political advocacy, to provide paper, presses, halls, etc., to all comers in the quantities they thought necessary.

But in the second model this would not apply. The second model appears when Professor Friedman is urging a further argument, namely, that a government which desired to guarantee free political advocacy could not effectively make it possible because, in the absence of capitalism and hence of many and widely dispersed private fortunes, there would be no sufficient source of private funds with which to finance propaganda activities, and the government itself could not feasibly provide such funds. Here there is assumed to be a market in paper, presses, and halls: the trouble is merely shortage of funds which advocates can use in these markets.

This second argument need not detain us, resting as it does on the unhistorical assumption that radical minority movements are necessarily unable to operate without millionaire angels or comparably few sources of large funds. Nor, since the second argument assumes that paper, presses, and halls can be purchased or hired, need we challenge the assumption put in the first model, that these means of advocacy are unobtainable in the socialist state except by asking the government for them.

We have still to consider the effect of the other stipulation, which is made in both models: that the government is the sole employer. Accepting this as a proper stipulation for a socialist model, the question to be answered is: does the monopoly of employment itself render the government incapable (or even less capable than it otherwise would be) of safeguarding political freedom? Friedman expects us to answer yes, but the answer is surely no. A socialist government which wished to guarantee political freedom would not be prevented from doing so by its having a monopoly of employment. Nor need it even be tempted to curtail political freedom by virtue of that monopoly. A government monopoly of employment can only mean (as Friedman allows) that the government and all its agencies are, together, the only employers. A socialist government can, by devolution of the management of industries, provide effective alternative employment opportunities. True, a government which wished to curtail or deny the freedom of radical political advocacy could use its monopoly of employment to do so. But such a government has so many other ways of doing it that the presence or absence of this way is not decisive.

It is not the absence of a fully competitive labor market that may disable a socialist government from guaranteeing political freedom; it is the absence of a firm will to do so. Where there's a will there's a way, and, for all that Friedman has argued to the contrary, the way need have nothing to do with a fully competitive labor market. The real problem of political freedom in socialism has to do with the will, not the way. The real problem is whether a socialist state could ever have the will to guarantee political freedom. This depends on factors Friedman does not consider, and until they have been assessed, questions about means have an air of unreality, as has his complaint that Western socialists have not faced up to the question of means. We shall return to both of these matters after looking briefly at the factors which are likely to affect such a will to political freedom.

On the question of the will, we cannot say (nor indeed does Professor Friedman suggest) that a will to guarantee political freedom is impossible, or even improbable, in a socialist state. True, if one were to judge by existing socialist states controlled by communist parties, the improbability would be high. (We are speaking here of day-to-day political freedom, which is the question Friedman has set, and not with the will to achieve some higher level of freedom in an ultimately transformed society.) But if we are to consider, as Professor Friedman is doing, socialist states that might emerge in the West, we should notice the differences between the forces in the existing ones and those inherent in possible future Western ones.

There are some notable differences. First, the existing socialist states were virtually all established in underdeveloped societies, in which the bulk of the people did not have the work habits and other cultural attributes needed by a modern industrial state. They have had to change an illiterate, largely unpolitical, peasant population into a literate, politicized, industrially oriented people. While doing this they have had to raise productivity to levels which would afford a decent human minimum, and even meet a rising level of material expectations. The pressures against political freedom that are set up by these factors are obvious. In the few instances, e.g., Czechoslovakia, where socialism did not start from such an underdeveloped base, it started under an external domination that produced equal though different pressures against political freedom. None of these pressures would be present in a socialist state which emerged independently in an already highly developed Western society.

Secondly, in the existing socialist states the effort to establish socialism has been made in the face of the hostility of the Western powers, whether manifested in their support of counterrevolution or in "encirclement" or "cold war." The ways in which this fact has compounded the pressures against political freedom due to the underdeveloped base are obvious. Presumably the force of this hostility would be less in the case of future socialist takeovers in Western countries.

Thirdly, the existing socialist states were all born in revolution or civil war, with the inevitable aftermath that "deviations" from the line established from time to time by the leadership (after however much or little consultation) tend to be treated as treason against the socialist revolution and the socialist state. We may at least entertain the possibility of a socialist takeover in an advanced Western nation without revolution or civil war (as Professor Friedman presumably does, or he would not be so concerned about the "creeping socialism" of the welfare state). A socialist state established without civil war would not be subject to this third kind of pressure against political freedom. Thus of the three forces that have made the pressures against political freedom generally predominate in socialist states so far, the first will be absent, the second reduced or absent, and the third possibly absent, in a future Western socialist state that emerged without external domination.

When these projections are borne in mind, Professor Friedman's complaint about Western socialists appears somewhat impertinent. He complains that "none of the people who have been in favor of socialism and also in favor of freedom have really faced up to this issue [of means], or made even a respectable start at developing the institutional arrangements that would permit freedom under socialism."[12] Perhaps the reason is that they think it more important, in the interests of freedom, to examine and even try to influence the circumstances in which socialism might arrive, than to begin planning institutional arrangements. Western socialists who believe in political freedom are, or should be, more concerned with seeking ways to minimize the cold war (so as to minimize the chances that the second of the projected forces against political freedom will be present in the socialist transformation they hope to achieve in their country), and seeking ways to minimize the likelihood of civil war (so as to minimize the third of the forces against political freedom), than with developing "institutional arrangements that would permit freedom under socialism."

But although, in a socialist state, the existence of a predominant will for political freedom may be more important than institutional arrangements, the latter should not be neglected. For even where there is, on the whole, a will to guarantee political freedom, there are likely always to be some pressures against it, so that it is desirable to have institutions which will make infringements difficult rather than easy. What institutional arrangements, beyond the obvious ones of constitutional guarantees of civil liberties and a legal system able to enforce them, are required? Let us accept Professor Friedman's statement of additional minimum institutional requirements. Advocates of radical change opposed to the government's policies must be able to obtain the indispensable means of advocacy—paper, presses, halls, etc. And they must be able to propagandize without endangering their means of livelihood.

As we have already seen, there is no difficulty inherent in socialism in meeting the first of these requirements, once it is granted (as Professor Friedman's second model grants) that the absence of a complete capitalist market economy does not entail the absence of markets in paper, presses, and halls.

The second requirement seems more difficult to meet. If the government (including all its agencies) is the sole employer, the standing danger that the monopoly of employment would be used to inhibit or prevent certain uses of political freedom is obvious. The difficulty is not entirely met by pointing out that a socialist state can have any amount of devolution of industry or management, so that there can be any number of employers, or by stipulating as an institutional arrangement that this devolution must be practiced. For it is evident that if there is a ubiquitous single or dominant political party operating in all industries and all plants (and all trade unions), it can make this multiplicity of employment opportunities wholly ineffective, if or insofar as it wishes to do so. The problem is not the absence of a labor market but the possible presence of another institution, a ubiquitous party which puts other things ahead of political freedom.

The stipulation that would be required to safeguard political freedom from the dangers of employment monopoly is not merely that there be devolution of management, and hence employment alternatives (which could be considered an institutional arrangement), but also that there be no ubiquitous party or that, if there is, such a party should consistently put a very high value on political freedom (which stipulation can scarcely be set out as an institutional arrangement). We are back at the question of will rather than way, and of the circumstantial forces which are going to shape that will, for the presence or absence of such a party is clearly going to depend largely on the circumstances in which a socialist state is established. There is, however, one factor (which might be institutionalized) which may, in any socialist state established in the West, reduce even the possibility of such intimidation through employment monopoly. This is the decreasing necessity, in highly developed societies whose economic systems are undergoing still further and rapid technological development, of relating income to employment. One need not be as sanguine as some exponents of the guaranteed income[13] to think it possible, even probable, that before any advanced Western nation chooses socialism it will have seen the logic of using its affluence and averting difficulties both political and economic by introducing a guaranteed minimum annual income to everyone regardless of employment. In this event, the technical problem that worries Professor Friedman—how to ensure that a threat to employment and hence to livelihood could not be used to deny political freedom—would no longer be a problem. A threat to employment would no longer be a threat to livelihood. It would indeed be a cost, but as Professor Friedman says, "what is essential is that the cost of advocating unpopular causes be tolerable and not prohibitive."[14]

But even without such a separation of employment from income, the technical problem of securing political freedom from being denied by the withholding of employment can be met by such devolution of management as would constitute a set of alternative employments *provided* that this is not offset by a ubiquitous party hostile to political freedom. If there is such a party, no institutional arrangements for safeguarding political freedom are reliable; if there is not, the institutional arrangements do not seem to be difficult.

III

We noticed (at the end of section I above) that Professor Friedman, in arguing that freedom would be increased if most of the regulatory and welfare activities of contemporary Western states were abandoned, did not take into account the coercion involved in the separation of capital from labor or the possible mitigation of this coercion by the regulatory and welfare state. But in chapter 10, on the distribution of income, he does deal with a closely related problem. Here he sets out the ethical case for distribution according to product, as compared with "another [principle] that seems ethically appealing, namely, equality of treatment." Distribution according to product he describes, accurately enough, as the principle "To each according to what he and the instruments he owns produces": to be strictly accurate this should read "resources" or "capital and land" instead of "instruments," but the sense is clear. This is offered as "the ethical principle that would directly justify the distribution of income in a free market society."[15] We can agree that this is the only principle that can be offered to justify it. We may also observe that this principle is not only different from the principle "to each according to his work," but is also inconsistent with it (except on the fanciful assumption that ownership of resources is always directly proportional to work). Professor Friedman does not seem to see this. His case for the ethical principle of payment according to product is that it is unthinkingly accepted as a basic value judgment by almost everybody in our society; and his demonstration of this is that the severest internal critics of capitalism, i.e., the Marxists, have implicitly accepted it.

Of course they have not. There is a double confusion here, even if we accept Friedman's paraphrase of Marx. Marx did not argue quite, as Friedman puts it, "that labor was exploited. . . because labor produced the whole of the product but got only part of it"—the argument was rather that labor is exploited because labor produces the whole of the value that is added in any process of production but gets only part of it—but Friedman's paraphrase is close enough for his purpose. Certainly the implication of Marx's position is that labor (though not necessarily each individual laborer) is entitled to the whole of the value it creates. But in the first place, this is, at most, the principle "to each according to his work," not "to each according to what he and the instruments he owns produces" or "to each according to his product." In the second place, Marx accepted "to each according to his work" only as a transitionally valid principle, to be replaced by the ultimately desirable principle "to each according to his need." Professor Friedman, unaccountably, only refers to this latter principle as "Ruskinian."[16]

Having so far misread Marx, Professor Friedman gives him a final fling.

> Of course, the Marxist argument is invalid on other grounds as well. . . [most] striking, there is an unstated change in the meaning of "labor" in passing from the premise to conclusion. Marx recognized the role of capital in producing the product but regarded capital as embodied labor. Hence, written out in full, the premises of the Marxist syllogism would run: "Present and past labor produce the whole of the product." The logical conclusion is presumably "Past labor is exploited," and the inference for action is that past labor should get more of the product, though it is by no means clear how, unless it be in elegant tombstones.[17]

This nonsense is unworthy of Professor Friedman's talents. The Marxist premises are: present labor, and the accumulation of surplus value created by past labor and extracted from the past laborers, produce the whole value of the product. Present labor gets only a part of the part of the value which it creates, and gets no part of that part of the value which is transferred to the product from the accumulated surplus value created by past labor. The logical conclusion is presumably that present labor is exploited and past labor was exploited, and the inference for action is that a system which requires constant exploitation should be abandoned.

Ignorance of Marxism is no sin in an economist, though cleverness in scoring off a travesty of it may be thought a scholarly lapse. What is more disturbing is that Professor Friedman seems to be satisfied that this treatment of the ethical justification of different principles of distribution is sufficient. Given his own first postulate, perhaps it is. For in asserting at the beginning of the book that freedom of the individual, or perhaps of the family, is the liberal's "ultimate goal in judging social arrangements," he has said in effect that the liberal is not required seriously to weigh the ethical claims of equality (or any other principle of distribution), let alone the claims of any principle of individual human development such as was given first place by liberals like Mill and Green, against the claims of freedom (which to Friedman of course means market freedom). The humanist liberal in the tradition of Mill and Green will quite properly reject Friedman's postulate. The logical liberal will reject his fallacious proof that the freedom of the capitalist market is individual economic freedom, his undemonstrated case that political freedom requires capitalism, and his fallacious defense of the ethical adequacy of capitalism. The logical humanist liberal will regret that the postulate and the fallacies make *Capitalism and Freedom* not a defense but an elegant tombstone of liberalism.

NOTES

1. Milton Friedman, *Capitalism and Freedom* (Chicago: University of Chicago Press, 1962).

2. Ibid., pp. 12, 13, 15.

3. Ibid., p. 25.

4. Ibid., p. 34.

5. Ibid., p. 12.

6. Ibid., p. 13.

7. Ibid., p. 14.

8. Ibid., pp. 14–15.

9. Ibid., pp. 13–14.

10. Ibid., pp. 9–10.

11. Ibid., pp. 11–12, 9, 15.

12. Ibid., p. 19.

13. Robert Theobald, ed., *The Guaranteed Income: Next Step in Economic Evolution?* (Garden City, N. Y.: Anchor, 1967).

14. Friedman, *Capitalism and Freedom*, p. 18.

15. Ibid., pp. 161–62.

16. Ibid., p. 167.

17. Ibid., pp. 167–68.

10.

SOCIALISM AND EQUALITY

STEVEN LUKES

There is now, with the existence of a large amount of sociological research on inequality of opportunity and inequality of result, and with the resurgence of interest among moral philosophers in inequality, as manifested in John Rawls's work, the possibility of serious examination of social ideals and social reality in this area.

—James S. Coleman[1]

Professor Coleman's remarks raise three questions. First, what are the "social ideals" of equality? What forms of inequality are undesirable and what forms of equality desirable, and on what grounds? Second, what are the "social realities" of inequality? What is the upshot of all the research into inequality in contemporary societies? And third, what bearing does the answer to the second question have on that to the first? How does social reality affect social ideals? What is desirable, in the light of the actual and what appears possible? The relevance of these questions to the subject of [the socialist idea] needs no explanation. The ideal of equality has always been central to the socialist tradition: thus Professor Taylor specifies "greater equality in the conditions of life" as the first goal of "any socialist in a Western country today."[2] In assessing the contemporary viability of the socialist idea, then, the three questions raised above demand to be faced: first, why is "greater equality in the conditions of life" desirable?[3] Second, how unequal are such conditions in contemporary industrial societies, capitalist and state socialist, and what explains these inequalities? And third, are these inequalities ineradicable, or eradicable only at an unacceptable cost?

Clearly, I cannot begin to answer these momentous questions here. What I shall try to do is to offer some suggestions as to how they might be answered. Concerning the first (philosophical) question, I shall seek to suggest a modified Kantian ethical basis for the social, political, and economic equalities that socialists have traditionally sought to establish. As for the second (sociological) question, I shall briefly sketch some of the evidence about actual inequalities and the range of explanations for them. And with regard to the third question I shall briefly consider a number of arguments for the inevitability of inequality. Having done these things, it will be clear to even the most sympathetic reader that everything remains to be done.

THE SOCIAL IDEALS OF EQUALITY

The ideal of equality has been made to seem absurd in either of two opposing ways. It has been interpreted as based either on the principle of absolute and unconditional equality "treat everyone equally in every respect"—or else on the empty formal principle, "treat people equally unless there are relevant or sufficient reasons for treating them unequally." In fact, few serious thinkers, let alone socialists, have advocated the former,[4] and all the interesting forms of egalitarianism have put content into the latter in two ways: negatively, by ruling out certain sorts of reasons as justifications for treating people unequally; and positively, by advancing, or presupposing, a set of reasons for treating them equally.

Historically, the fight for equality has taken the form of attacking specific inequalities and their alleged justifications: inequalities of privilege and power—legal and political, then social and economic—have been attacked as unjustifiable, because arbitrary, capricious, or irrational. For example, it has been suggested that inequalities are unjustifiable unless they can be shown to satisfy one or more of the following criteria: (1) merit or deserts; (2) need; (3) social benefit (and on such a basis it would be hard to justify the present extreme inequality of inherited wealth in Britain).[5] But, quite apart from the difficulty of interpreting these criteria, especially the last, such an approach always presupposes a view of what is justifiable, that is, what are relevant and sufficient sorts of reasons for unequal treatment, and over this individuals, classes, and cultures conflict. What, then, of the positive way?

One influential argument for treating people equally—and in particular for according them equal income and wealth—is the utilitarian argument for attaining the maximum aggregate satisfaction, on the assumption of diminishing marginal utility: as Dalton put it, an "unequal distribution of a given amount of purchasing power among a given number of people is likely to be a wasteful distribution from the point of view of economic welfare."[6] In their recent important study of inequality, Christopher Jencks and his associates state their position as follows:

We begin with the premise that every individual's happiness is of equal value. From this it is a short step to Bentham's dictum that society should be organized so as to provide the greatest good for the greatest number. In addition, we assume that the law of diminishing returns applies to most of the good things in life. In economic terms this means that people with low incomes value extra income more than people with high incomes. It follows that if we want to maximize the satisfaction of the population, the best way to divide any given amount of money is to make everyone's income the same. Income disparities (except those based on variations in "need") will always reduce overall satisfaction, because individuals with low incomes will lose more than individuals with high incomes gain.[7]

But this assumption is questionable. Why assume that a given amount of purchasing power yields equal utility for everyone (assuming one could make the interpersonal comparison), and why assume that it diminishes as income or wealth increases?

In any case, egalitarians and socialists have not rested their case on this precarious basis alone: there is an alternative tradition of thought on the subject, of which Rousseau is the classical figure and Rawls the major contemporary exponent, which offers an alternative interpretation of equality and which appeals to deeper values than the utilitarian. This interpretation may be called the principle of equality of consideration or respect. On this view, all human beings have certain basic features which entitle them to be considered or respected as equals, and this is seen as implying practical policies for implementing substantial political, social, and economic equality.[8]

What, then, are the basic features of human beings which command equal consideration or respect? For Christians the answer is that they are all children of God, for Kant that they are rational wills and thus members of the Kingdom of Ends, for classical liberals that they share "common rights to which they are called by nature,"[9] for many socialists and anarchists that they share a "common humanity." These are all transcendental answers, whether religious or secular. Others speak of man's "inherent dignity," "intrinsic or infinite value," or "human worth." But in all these cases, no independent reasons are given for respecting people equally—or at least none that would convince a skeptic disposed to do so unequally, according to, say, birth or merit. But it is arguable that there are a number of empirical features which could provide such reasons, to which, throughout their history, egalitarian doctrines have, implicitly or explicitly, appealed. On the one hand, there are basic human needs—minimally, the means to life and health—without which they could not function in a recognizably human manner. On the other hand, there are certain basic capacities (of which more below), characteristic of human beings, whose realization is essential to their enjoyment of freedom. It may be objected that, since people have these needs and capacities to different degrees, they are therefore worthy of unequal respect. But to this it may be replied that it is the existence of the needs and capacities, not the degree to which the former are met and the latter realized or realizable, that elicits the respect, and that respecting persons precisely consists in doing all that is necessary and possible to satisfy their basic needs and to maintain and enhance their basic capacities (and to discriminate between them in this regard is to fail to show them equal respect).

The principle of equal respect for needs tells against all humanly alterable economic and social arrangements which discriminate between individuals' access to the means of sustenance and health (and it is not irrelevant in contemporary Britain, where there are still marked class differences in the risks of death and infant mortality). But "need" is a concept to which appeal cannot be made beyond this basic (if rising) minimum level: beyond that point, it becomes a question of individuals' entitlement to the means of realizing certain basic capacities. Three such capacities appear to be of particular significance.

There is, first, the capacity of human beings to form intentions and purposes, to become aware of alternatives and choose between them, and to acquire control over their own behavior by becoming conscious of the forces determining it, both internally, as with unconscious desires and motives, and externally, as with the pressures exerted by the norms they follow or the roles they fill. In other words, human beings have the capacity to act with relative autonomy and to be or become relatively self-determining, to become conscious of the forces determining or affecting them, and either consciously to submit to them or become independent of them. Obviously, not all exercise this capacity to an equal degree, but all, except the mentally defective or deranged, possess it.

Secondly, human beings have the capacity to think thoughts, perform actions, develop involvements, and engage in relationships to which they attach value but which require a certain area of noninterference in order to have that value. Enjoyments and delights of all kinds, intellectual and artistic activities, love and friendship are examples: all these require a space free and secure from external invasion or surveillance in order to flourish. There is, of course, considerable room for differences about which of these activities and relationships are of most value and about what kind of value they have, and indeed about which of them people should be left alone to engage in. But what seems indisputable is that there is a range of such activities and relationships in some of which all persons have the capacity to engage and to which they attach value.

Thirdly, human beings have the capacity for self-development. By this I mean that everyone has the capacity to develop in himself some characteristic human excellence or excellences—whether intellectual, aesthetic or moral, theoretical or practical, personal or public, and so on. Obviously, not everyone will be able to develop any given excellence to the same degree—and perhaps, pace Marx, not all will be able to develop them in a many-sided, all-round fashion. But all human beings share the capacity to realize potentialities that are worthy of admiration. What counts as worthy of admiration will be subject to moral disagreement and cultural variation, but it is arguable that there is a delimited range of human excellences which are intrinsically admirable, though the forms they take differ from society to society, and that all human beings are capable of achieving some of them to some degree.

I have argued that these three characteristics of persons are at least part of the ground on which we accord them respect. What, then, does that respect consist in? The unsurprising answer is that, whatever else it involves, respecting them involves treating them as (actually or potentially) autonomous, as requiring a free and secure space for the pursuit of valued activities and relationships, and as capable of self-development. That answer has, given certain further assumptions, far-reaching social, economic, and political implications, and points towards a society with substantially reduced inequalities, both of material and symbolic rewards and of political power.

What, we may ask, constitutes a denial of such respect? We fail to respect someone by denying his autonomy not only when we control or dominate his will, but also when we unreasonably restrict the range of alternatives between which he can choose. Such control and restriction is as likely to be social and economic as political, and as typical of the work situation and the family and of opportunities for education and employment as of the relation between the state and the citizen. In this sense, Tawney saw a central aim of "measures correcting inequalities or neutralizing their effects" as increasing "the range of alternatives open to ordinary men, and the capacity of the latter to follow their own preferences in choosing between them."[10] But we also cease to respect someone when we fail to treat him as an agent and a chooser, as a self from which actions and choices emanate, when we see him and consequently treat him not as a person but as merely the bearer of a title or the occupant of a role, or as merely a means to securing a certain end, or, worst of all, as merely an object. We deny his status as an autonomous person to the extent that we allow our attitudes to him to be dictated solely by some contingent and socially defined attribute of him, such as his "merit" or success or occupational role or place in the social order—or what Tawney called "the tedious vulgarities of income and social position."[11] This denial of autonomy was what William Godwin had in mind when he urged universal and equal political participation on the grounds that "each man will thus be inspired with a consciousness of his own importance, and the slavish feelings that shrink up the soul in the presence of an imagined superior, will be unknown."[12] It is what William Morris meant when he wrote of socialism as a "condition of equality" in which a man "would no longer take his position as the dweller in such and such a place, or the filler of such and such an office, or (as now) the owner of such and such property, but as being such and such a man."[13] It is what Tawney intended when he wrote of an egalitarian society as one in which "money and position count for less, and the quality of human personalities for more"[14] and what George Orwell was thinking of when he wrote of "breathing the air of equality" in revolutionary Spain, with "no boss-class, no menial-class, no beggars, no prostitutes, no lawyers, no priests, no boot-licking, no cap-touching."[15] Respecting persons in this way, as Bernard Williams has well put it, implies that they be "abstracted from certain conspicuous structures of inequality" in which they are found and seen, "not merely under professional, social, or technical titles, but with consideration of their own views and purposes," as "conscious beings who necessarily have intentions and purposes and see what they are doing in a certain light."[16] But more is involved in respecting autonomy than looking behind the surface of socially defined titles or labels and seeing the world (and the labels) from the agent's point of view. Social existence in part determines consciousness; and the most insidious and decisive way of denying the autonomy of persons is to diminish, or restrict their opportunity to increase, their consciousness of their situation and activities. It is for this reason that respecting autonomy points towards a "single status society" and away from the ideal of a stable hierarchy, since

> what keeps stable hierarchies together is the idea of necessity, that it is somehow foreordained or inevitable that there should be these orders; and this idea of necessity must be eventually undermined by the growth of people's reflective consciousness about their role, still more when it is combined with the thought that what they and others have always thought about their roles in the social system was the product of the social system itself.[17]

Secondly, one manifestly fails to respect someone if one invades his private space and interferes, without good reason, with his valued activities and relationships (and above all with his inner self). Examples of where it can be justifiable so to interfere are in cases, say, of imprisonment or conscription during wartime—where it may be claimed that there is "'good reason' for interference and thus no denial of respect insofar as they are necessary infringements of a person's freedom, either to preserve the freedom of others, or his own and others" in the long run, or as the only way of realizing other cherished values. But, in the absence of these justifications, such an invasion or interference is clearly a denial of human respect. It is easy to think of extreme forms of such a denial, as in the prison camps described by Solzhenitsyn or total institutions described by Erving Goffman. But less extreme forms result from inequalities of power and privilege in all contemporary societies. Liberals characteristically attack such invasions of liberty, especially in nonliberal societies, when they take the form of political authoritarianism, bureaucratic tyranny, social pressures to conformity, religious and racial discrimination. But interference with valued activities and relationships occurs in other ways to which liberals are less sensitive—through class discrimination, remediable economic deprivation and insecurity, and what Hayek has called the "hard discipline of the market,"[18] where nominally equal economic and social rights are unequally operative because of unequal but equalizable conditions and opportunities.

Finally, one also importantly fails to respect someone if one limits or restricts his opportunities to realize his capacities of self-development. It is the systematic and cumulative denial of such opportunities to the less-favored citizens of stratified societies, both capitalist and state socialist, that constitutes perhaps the strongest argument against the structured inequalities they exhibit. That argument really has two parts. The first part is simply an argument against discrimination, against the failure to "bring the means of a good life within the reach of all."[19] Thus the principal argument against a discriminatory educational system is not that it creates social inequality (which, as Jencks shows, it scarcely does, serving "primarily to legitimize inequality, not to create it"),[20] but rather that it blocks the self-development of the less favored and thereby fails to respect them. Again, where it is possible to make certain types of work more challenging and require a greater development of skill or talent or responsibility, it is a denial of human respect to confine workers within menial, one-sided, and tedious tasks. Furthermore, workers—and citizens in political society as a whole—are denied respect to the degree to which they are denied possibilities of real participation in the formulation and taking of major decisions affecting them, for they are thereby denied the opportunity to develop the human excellence of active self-government celebrated by Rousseau and John Stuart Mill and central to the various forms of classical democratic theory. The second part of this argument against structured inequalities is that they provide an unfavorable climate for the self-development of ordinary people. The assumption that this is so was well expressed by Matthew Arnold, who claimed that for "the common bulk of mankind," "to live in a society of equals tends in general to make a man's spirits expand, and his faculties work easily and actively; while, to live in a society of superiors, although it may occasionally be a very good discipline, yet in general tends to tame the spirits and to make the play of the faculties less secure and active."[21] Tawney made the same assumption, arguing that "individual differences, which are a source of social energy, are more likely to ripen and find expression if social inequalities are, as far as practicable, diminished."[22] Individuals, Tawney argued, "differ profoundly. . . in capacity and character" but "they are equally entitled as human beings to consideration and respect, and. . . the well-being of a society is likely to be increased if it so plans its organization that, whether their powers are great or small, all its members may be equally enabled to make the best of such powers as they possess."[23] His case was that establishing "the largest possible measure of equality of environment, and circumstance, and opportunity" was a precondition for ensuring "that these diversities of gifts may come to fruition."[24]

I have argued, then, that certain basic human needs and capacities provide at least part of the ground for equality of respect, and give some content to that notion of "respect," and I have further suggested that a society practicing equal respect would be one in which there were no barriers to reciprocal relations between relatively autonomous persons, who see each other and themselves as such, who are equally free from political control, social pressure, and economic deprivation and insecurity to engage in valued pursuits, and who have equal access to the means of self-development. Such a society would not be marked by inequalities of power and privilege (which is not to say that a society without such inequalities would necessarily practice equal respect).

However, I should conclude this section by noting an important tension between the notion of equality of respect, as discussed here, and that of "equality of opportunity," as normally understood. In the context of public debate, especially about education, this latter principle is *not* generally taken to refer to equality of opportunity to develop individual powers or gifts, but rather equality of opportunity to achieve scarce social rewards. Thus understood, it comes into conflict with equal respect, since it focuses attention upon forms of differentiation and grading which carry status and prestige. It endorses and serves to perpetuate those very structures of inequality, characterized by competition and emulation, of which equality of respect makes light—and, practiced seriously, would abolish. This distinction was well drawn by Tawney when he contrasted "the claim for an open road to individual advancement" with the desire "to narrow the space between valley and peak."[25] The former aspiration has, of course, a central place in the history of socialism: it represents the meritocratic policy of widening the social base of recruitment to privileged positions, which has always been the central plank of social democracy. Thus C. A. R. Crosland wrote:

> The essential thing is that every citizen should have an equal chance—that is his basic democratic right; but provided the start is fair, let there be the maximum scope for individual self-advancement. There would then be nothing improper in either a high continuous status ladder. . . or even a distinct class stratification. . . since opportunities for attaining the highest status or the topmost stratum would be genuinely equal. Indeed the continuous traffic up and down would inevitably make society more mobile and dynamic, and so less classbound.[26]

By contrast, the egalitarian socialist focuses on equalizing the rewards and privileges attached to different positions, not on widening the competition for them. In fact, of course, these two strands are often intertwined in socialist theory and practice. But, although there are well-known arguments (an example of which we shall consider) to the effect that unequal rewards, together with equal opportunity to reap them, have essential economic and social functions, they are in tension with the social, political, and economic implications of the principle of equal respect, which, as we have seen, points towards greater equality in the conditions of life, that is, of wealth, income, status, and power.

THE REALITIES OF INEQUALITY

Contemporary industrial societies manifest structured inequalities of such conditions, and of much else besides, such as access to education, social services, and other public benefits, economic security, promotion prospects, etc. Some patterns of inequality appear to be common to all such societies, both capitalist and state socialist, others to the one system or the other, yet others to particular countries. But three myths, prevalent in recent times, are belied by the evidence. The first is that of "convergence," according to "the logic of industrialism." This is misleading insofar as it suggests a continuing trend in the development of industrial societies towards greater overall economic equality, towards an ever-increasing consistency of stratification systems around the occupational order (e.g., towards the congruence of middle incomes and middle-class lifestyle and status), and towards a uniform pattern of social mobility.[27] The second is that "affluence" in capitalist societies has eroded inequalities of income, wealth, and security of life and that the power of private capital has been tamed, from within by the "managerial revolution" and the divorce between ownership and control, and from without by the growth of the state and/or a pluralistic diffusion of power among competing interest groups. The third myth is the official communist (especially Soviet) interpretation of state socialist societies, which, while acknowledging the existence of nonantagonistic classes (working class and peasantry) and the stratum of the intelligentsia, and the existence of inequalities of income, consumption goods, education, etc., between rural and urban population and between occupational strata, maintains that these inequalities are in process of continuing decline (the so-called process of *sblizhenie*, or "drawing together") denies that there is a hierarchy of status and is silent about the hierarchy of power.

Of the patterns of inequality common to industrial societies, it appears broadly true to say that, in contrast with traditional or nonindustrial societies, "the occupational order comes increasingly to be the primary source of symbolic as well as material advantages:"[28] thus

> The occupational structure in modern industrial society not only constitutes an important foundation for the main dimensions of social stratification, but also serves as the connecting link between different institutions and spheres of social life, and therein lies its great significance. The hierarchy of prestige strata and the hierarchy of economic classes have their roots in the occupational structure; so does the hierarchy of political power and authority, for political authority in modern society is largely exercised as a full-time occupation. . . .[29]

As for income, there appears to be a remarkable similarity in capitalist and communist societies in the structure of earnings—more precisely, in the distribution of pre-tax money wages or salaries of fully employed male adult workers in all industries but farming.[30] There is a broad relationship between the hierarchy of skills and knowledge demanded by occupations on the one hand, and the hierarchy of material rewards on the other (though there is a narrower range of differentials under command than market economies), and, related to this, there are certain more specific trends: high rewards accruing to those in management and to the technically highly qualified and skilled, and a relative decline in the rewards of clerical work. As for status inequality (allowing for the "softness" of the data and their paucity for socialist systems, except Poland), various studies suggest a common structure of occupational prestige. For example, according to Sarapata, the correlation between the occupational prestige hierarchies of Poland and the USA is 0.882, Poland and England 0.862, and Poland and West Germany 0.879.[31] As for inequalities of power, apart from the obvious differences, parallels can be seen in the differential distribution of power and authority (whether in the form of legal ownership or directive control) within "imperatively coordinated associations," such as the industrial enterprise; conversely, a tendency towards political pluralism, albeit of a highly restricted and managed type, has been observed in communist systems.[32]

Of the inequalities characteristic of capitalism, the most obvious is that of wealth. It has been justly said that "capitalism produces extremely rich people with a great deal of capital, and this is the most striking difference between the two systems."[33] Moreover, such capital "means so much more than the income it provides: security, diminished pressure to save, and (in very large quantities) political power."[34] The most recent study of the subject in Britain[35] estimates that the top 5 percent of wealth holders own between one-half and three-quarters of the total personal wealth. There has, it is true, been a long-term trend towards a greater spread of such wealth, but this has mainly been from the top 1 percent to the next 2–5 percent (i.e., to relatives and others), as a defense against taxation.[36] It has been estimated that, equally divided, the yield from private property would substantially change the overall income distribution, providing a married couple with something over £9.00 a week.[37] Similar (though less extreme) concentrations of property ownership are found in other capitalist countries. Its impact is considerable because it "leads to unequal incomes, and concentrates control over the economy in a few hands":[38] this is

> accentuated by the fact that the very rich tend to hold their wealth in the form of company shares and real property yielding a higher return than the assets typically owned by small savers. The concentration of share ownership is even greater than that in the distribution of wealth as a whole, which is important since shares convey not only income but also rights of control, and even allowing for the increasing power of corporation managers these still remain of considerable significance.[39]

As for income inequality, after a temporary narrowing in the 1940s, it has remained relatively fixed and in some cases somewhat widened—both before direct taxation and (as far as one can estimate) after it. Overall taxation appears to be almost neutral in relation to income and in certain cases (the USA, West Germany) directly regressive, while redistribution through the Welfare State, although it obviously aids the poor more than the rich in relative terms, is paid for by wage-earners themselves, and is mainly "horizontal" rather than "vertical"—i.e., it takes the form of a "life-cycle" transfer within social classes; moreover, these welfare facilities often tend to favor more privileged groups.[40] In general, the social democratic "welfare approach" brings about little disturbance of the stratification system[41]—and some have claimed that there is increasing inequality at its base, with the growth of an underclass of unemployed and unemployables.[42] In capitalist societies that stratification system exhibits a cleavage between the manual and nonmanual categories of occupation—not merely with respect to income (here, indeed, there is substantial overlap) but with respect to a whole range of privileges and advantages: white-collar workers have strikingly better sick pay and pension schemes, holidays and other fringe benefits, life-cycle promotion and career opportunities, long-term economic stability (including for many guaranteed salary increases), working environment, freedom of movement and from supervision, etc. Nonmanual workers "even when they diverge are more like one another than they are like manual workers" and "the big divide still comes between manual workers on the one hand and nonmanual grades on the other."[43] As for status inequality, such evidence as exists appears to point away from the thesis of an accommodative *embourgeoisement* of affluent workers and increasingly towards different forms of polarization between what Kerr terms "the managers" and the "managed."[44] Inequalities of political power in capitalist societies are of course manifest in the inequalities already considered, since these represent the power of the dominant class to command a disproportionate share of rewards and privileges vis-à-vis the subordinate class. A full consideration of this topic would also involve an examination of all the means available to the former to preserve its rewards and privileges, not only within governmental institutions, but within the administrative service, the educational system, industry, the law, mass communications, etc., not only through coercive power but also through "the mobilization of bias," operating anonymously through the structure of institutions (especially private property and the market), the rituals of social and political life, and ideological assumptions.[45]

The inequalities typical of state socialist societies display a different pattern. Property, in the sense of legal ownership, is, of course, largely absent: as Lane writes, "the really significant difference in the system of social stratification compared to Western industrial societies is the absence of a private propertied class possessing great concentrations of wealth."[46] On the other hand, following Djilas, one can argue that the white-collar intelligentsia, and the *appuratchiki* above all, exercise rights of control over the use and products of collective property and expropriate surplus value from the subordinate class. On the other hand, there is no direct inheritance of such rights, as with private property, although there is evidence of de facto inheritance of educational privileges. The analogy between "legal" and "sociological" ownership cannot be taken too far, but clearly there is a considerable hierarchy of monetary privilege and power based upon such authority roles and above all upon party membership. With respect to income inequality, this has gone through a number of phases in all socialist regimes. The general pattern is this: a highly egalitarian stage of "socialist reconstruction," followed by a substantial widening of differentials (most pronounced in the USSR with Stalin's attacks on "equality mongering") in order to increase material incentives, followed by a subsequent move towards greater equality.[47] The current picture is one of a substantially narrower range of money incomes in socialist than in capitalist societies: thus, for example, the ratio of the lowest wage to the average in the USSR is 60:112.6 and even the most extreme estimate of the total range is substantially less than what is widely accepted as true of the USA.[48] Moreover, apart from Yugoslavia, there is no structural unemployment. The stratification system has a different pattern from that in capitalist systems: social strata are distinguished by money incomes, consumption patterns, styles of life, education, use of the social services, housing, "cultural level," but there appears to be no major "break" or "big divide," as under capitalism, between the manual and the nonmanual strata. As Parkin suggests, in many state socialist societies highly skilled or craft manual workers enjoy a higher position in the scale of material and status rewards, and promotion prospects, than do lower white-collar employees.[49] Thus, for example, in both Poland and Yugoslavia skilled manual positions have higher occupational prestige than do lower routine white-collar positions. Parkin suggests that the overall reward hierarchy is as follows: "(1) White-collar intelligentsia (i.e., professional, managerial, and administrative positions), (2) Skilled manual positions, (3) Lower or unqualified white-collar positions, (4) Unskilled manual positions," and that the major break lies between the skilled and the unskilled.[50] Thus "the most obvious break in the reward hierarchy occurs along the line separating the qualified professional, managerial, and technical positions from the rest of the occupational order."[51] Thus the status hierarchy does not appear to reflect and reinforce a dichotomous class structure on the Western capitalist model (though Machonin provides conflicting evidence on this point from Czechoslovakia).[52] Clearly, however, the most significant contrast between the systems lies in the hierarchy of political power. Here, despite the pluralistic tendencies identified by certain Western observers, the explicitly hierarchical, monistic, and all-pervasive structure of party control, increasingly manned by the white-collar intelligentsia, is altogether distinctive.

Finally, brief mention should be made of inequalities characteristic of particular societies within these two broad systems. Thus, with respect to income inequality, the UK is more equal than the USA[53] and Norway is substantially more equal still, while the USSR has carried income equalization very far within the socialist bloc, especially through the redistributive effects of collective consumption,[54] whereas Yugoslavia has seen a marked widening of the span of incomes and life-chances, with the introduction of "market socialism," as to a lesser extent did Czechoslovakia in the later 1960s. Other peculiarities relate to racial, religious, and linguistic factors (USA, Northern Ireland, Canada), where inconsistencies between income and status hierarchies are to be seen, and long-range historical factors, as for example in Britain, where the stratification takes a distinctive form and the concentration of wealth is especially high.[55]

The explanation of inequality can be approached in either of two ways. On the one hand, one may seek to explain why individuals attain different positions, rewards, and privileges; on the other hand, one may seek to account for the allocation of rewards and privileges to different social positions. The first approach implies a focus upon inequality of opportunity among persons; the second upon inequality of reward among occupational positions. In the foregoing, I have implicitly concentrated on the second question and I have also implicitly suggested a range of explanations for inequality at different levels. Some such explanations will be historically and geographically specific. Examples are, say, the particular circumstances explaining the exceptionally high status of Poland's intelligentsia,[56] or the cultural factors in ethnically or religiously divided communities or the long-range historical factors referred to above. Other factors explaining the differences between income distributions in different countries, and in the same country over time, are the activities of the central government and local authorities in allocating taxes and distributing benefits, the control of entry into occupations by professional associations and unions, national rates of economic growth, level of unemployment, etc. Other explanations will be at the level of the economic system, and will focus primarily on the institution of private property, and all that protects and legitimates it, under capitalism; and on political intervention, allocating rewards and privileges, in accordance with the ruling elite's policy objectives, under state socialism. However, at the next level, the constraints operating on both systems come into view: the division of labor under advanced industrialism, it has been argued, creates a certain role structure inevitably accompanied by differentials of material reward, status, and power, which are in turn perpetuated by the nuclear family.[57] Some writers have sought explanations of inequality at a higher level still: according to them social inequalities arise from the functional prerequisites or basic features of all human societies, or, more universally still, from the genetic, biological, or psychological differentiation of human nature itself.

THE REALIZABILITY OF EQUALITY

This leads us naturally to the question of the alleged inevitability of inequality. There are a number of such arguments (of which I shall cite some typical contemporary examples), ranging from the "hard" to the "soft." The hardest are those which appeal to biological and psychological data which, it is argued, set sharp limits to the possibility of implementing egalitarian social ideals: "Biology," writes Eysenck, "sets an absolute barrier to egalitarianism."[58] Then there are sociological arguments which maintain that inequalities are functional to, or inherent in, all possible social systems—or less strongly, in all industrial societies. And finally, there are arguments of a different order, which seek to show that the cost of implementing equality in contemporary societies are unacceptably high, because they conflict with other values.

The hard-line approach to the realizability of equality is currently taken by various participants in the contemporary debate about genetics, environment, and intelligence. Professors Jensen, Herrnstein, and Eysenck assert that "intelligence" is mainly determined by heredity specifically that about 80 percent of the variance in IQ scores is genetically determined. Eysenck urges "recognition of man's biological nature, and the genetically determined inequality inevitably associated with his derivation."[59] Social class is "determined quite strongly by IQ," and educational attainment depends "closely" on IQ: "talent, merit, ability" are "largely innate factors."[60] Eysenck maintains that "regression to the mean" through social mobility and the redistribution of genes prevents social classes from calcifying into hereditary castes, and he concludes that a "society which would come as near to our egalitarian desires as is biologically attainable would give the greatest scope possible to this social mobility."[61] Herrnstein,[62] by contrast, ignores "regression to the mean" and stresses the process of "assortative mating" between partners of similar IQ levels, and foresees a future in which, as the environment becomes more favorable to the development of intelligence, social mobility increases, and technological advance sets a higher premium on intelligence, social classes will become ever more castelike, stratifying society into a hereditary meritocracy. Finally, Jensen, observing that some racial groups, especially American whites and blacks, differ markedly in their distribution of IQ scores (the mean IQ differing from 10 to 15 points), concludes that, since no known environmental factors can explain such differences, their explanation must be largely genetic. In his latest book, he affirms the hypothesis that "something between one-half and three-fourths of the average IQ difference between American Negroes and Whites is attributable to genetic factors, and the remainder to environmental factors and their interaction with the genetic differences."[63] He attaches much importance to this conclusion, since he believes that IQ is a major determinant of success in our society.

These claims obviously cannot be adequately considered here, but a few remarks are worth making. First the estimate of 80 percent genetic determination of IQ is controversial. Others suggest a substantially lower figure. According to Jencks it is something like 45 percent: Jencks and his colleagues estimate that "genotype explains about 45 percent of the variance in IQ scores, that environment explains about 35 percent, and that the correlation between genotype and environment explains the remaining 20 percent."[64] Moreover the evidence with respect to genetic determination is far less univocal than these writers imply: "different methods of estimating the heritability of test scores yield drastically different results" and "studies of different populations yield somewhat different results."[65] Again, children's test scores are not immune to considerable improvement by effecting changes in their environment. Eysenck suggests that "clearly the whole course of development of a child's intellectual capabilities is largely laid down genetically,"[66] yet this is strikingly contradicted by a number of twin and adoption studies.[67] Secondly, psychologists notoriously differ about what IQ tests measure: some, such as Jensen, Herrnstein, and Eysenck, believe it measures some basic property of the intellect; others believe that intelligence is multidimensional, that it cannot be measured by a single number, and (according to many authorities) that that number in any case measures educationally and culturally specific aptitudes with limited wider applicability. Thirdly, and related to this last point, it has been established (at least for the United States) that (1) social class is not, pace Eysenck, "determined strongly" by IQ; (2) educational attainment depends less on IQ than on family background; and (3) IQ is not a major determinant of economic and social success.[68] Fourthly, the difference in average IQ test performance between blacks and whites is consistent with all three of the following hypotheses: that it is explained by genes, by environment, and by both.[69] Moreover it appears indisputable that present data and techniques cannot resolve this issue. It certainly has not been established that one can extrapolate from genetic determinants of differences within a population to explain mean differences between populations. And it is worth observing that, in any case, genetic differences within races are far greater than those between them, accounting for 60–70 percent of all human genetic variation. In general, it appears entirely reasonable to conclude with Jencks that it is "wrong to argue that genetic inequality dictates a hierarchical society."[70] This is so even if Jensen should turn out to be nearer the truth than Jencks, and heredity does substantially constrain the maximum achievable by different individuals in the best of all possible environments. For, as we have argued, the principle of equal respect requires, in Tawney's words, that society's organization be planned so that "whether their powers are great or small, all its members may be equally enabled to make the best of such powers as they possess." Since this requires the equalization of rewards and privileges, biological differences would correlate with social positions but not with unequal rewards and privileges attaching to those positions.

Sociological arguments for the inevitability of inequality are of two broad types. One is that inequalities are functionally necessary for any society, the other that they are inherent in the very nature of social life. A much-discussed example of the former is the so-called functionalist theory of stratification; an interesting instance of the latter is furnished by Ralf Dahrendorf.

Davis and Moore's "functionalist theory of stratification" seeks to demonstrate "the universal necessity which calls forth stratification in any social system."[71] It advances the following propositions:

1. Certain positions in any society are functionally more important than others.
2. Adequate performance in these positions requires appropriate talents and training.
3. Some such talents are scarce in any population.
4. It is necessary (a) to induce those with the requisite talents to undergo the sacrifice of acquiring the appropriate training; (b) to attract them to the functionally important positions; and (c) to motivate them to perform in these positions adequately.
5. To achieve these objectives, differential incentives must be attached to the posts in question—and these may be classified into those things which contribute to (i) "sustenance and comfort"; (ii) "humor and diversion"; and (iii) "self-respect and ego expansion."[72]
6. These differential incentives (unequal rewards) constitute social inequality, which, in securing that the most talented individuals occupy and adequately perform in the functionally important positions, fulfils a necessary function in any society: "Social inequality is thus an unconsciously evolved device by which societies insure that the most important positions are conscientiously filled by the most qualified persons."[73]

Controversy over this theory has raged for well over two decades,[74] and it is fair to say that the balance of the argument has largely lain with the theory's critics. There is the evident difficulty of identifying the "functionally important" positions, as distinct from those which a given society values as important (bankers or miners? elementary or university teachers?) and the dubious assumption that training for these positions is sacrificial (especially since there would, presumably, be no material loss in an egalitarian society). Also, it ignores the point that a stratified society itself restricts the availability of talent and the further point that an advanced industrial society is in principle able substantially to increase the availability of talent and training. A further weakness of the theory is its assumption that unequal rewards (defined in a most culture-specific way) are the only possible means of mobilizing qualified individuals into adequately performing important jobs. It leaves out of account the intrinsic benefits of different positions, in relation to the expectations, aptitudes, and aspirations of different individuals (potential surgeons being anyway attracted by practicing surgery and potential carpenters by carpentry); and it fails in general to consider functional alternatives to a system of unequal rewards—such as intrinsic job satisfaction, the desire for knowledge, skills, and authority, an ethos of social or public service and a diminution of acquisitiveness and status-seeking, the use of negotiation, persuasion, or direct planning, changes in the organization of work and decision making, and so on. Finally, to the extent to which the thesis does remain valid, at least for contemporary industrial societies—that is, insofar as unequal rewards are needed so that certain jobs are adequately filled—this in no way implies a society-wide system of structured social inequality, linking wealth, income, status, and power (indeed, it would probably imply the reverse); nor is it plausible to suggest that the range and scope of actual inequalities, such as those surveyed in the previous section of this essay, can be explained in this beneficently functional manner. It is, incidentally, noteworthy that liberal reformers in East European countries have used arguments analogous to Davis and Moore's to justify the widening of income differentials (as did Stalin in the 1930s). But the Davis-Moore theory does not specify any particular range of inequality as functionally necessary—or rather, it all too easily serves to justify any such range which its proponents may seek to defend or establish.

Dahrendorf's theory seeks to demonstrate that "inequalities among men follow from the very concept of societies as moral communities. . . the idea of a society in which all distinctions of rank between men are abolished transcends what is sociologically possible and has its place in the sphere of poetic imagination alone."[75] The thesis is essentially this: that "(1) every society is a moral community, and therefore recognizes norms which regulate the conduct of its members; and (2) there have to be sanctions connected with these norms which guarantee their obligatory character by acting as rewards for conformism and penalties for deviance,"[76] from which Dahrendorf concludes that "the sanctioning of human behavior in terms of social norms necessarily creates a system of inequality of rank and that social stratification is therefore an immediate result of the control of social behavior by positive and negative sanctions."[77] But the conclusion does not follow from the premises. It does not follow from the mere existence of social norms and the fact that their enforcement discriminates against those who do not or cannot (because of their social position) conform to them that a society-wide system of inequality and "rank order of social status" are "bound to emerge."[78] Dahrendorf slides unaccountably from the undoubted truth that within groups norms are enforced which discriminate against certain persons and positions (he cites the example of gossiping neighbors making the professional woman an outsider) to the unsupported claim that, within society as a whole, a system of inequality between groups and positions is inevitable. To support that claim he would need to show the necessity of society-wide norms whose enforcement necessarily discriminates between persons and social positions, and this he fails to do. Nothing he says rules out the empirical possibility of a society containing a plurality of norms, each conferring and withholding status and prestige (so that gossiping neighbors look down on professional women, and vice versa), without themselves being ranked within a single system of inequality or stratification.

Finally, I turn to the argument that inequality is eradicable only at an unacceptable cost. This argument has been voiced in many forms, by those both friendly and hostile to socialism. A forceful contemporary formulation is that of Frank Parkin, who argues that

A political system which guarantees constitutional rights for groups to organize in defense of their interests is almost bound to favor the privileged at the expense of the disprivileged. The former will always have greater organizing capacities and facilities than the latter, such that the competition for rewards between different classes is never an equal contest. This is not merely because the dominant class can more easily be mobilized in defense of its interests, but also because it has access to the all-important means of social control, both coercive and normative. Given this fundamental class inequality in the social and economic order, a pluralist or democratic political structure works to the advantage of the dominant class.[79]

What this argument perhaps suggests, Parkin writes, is that

> socialist egalitarianism is not readily compatible with a pluralist political order of the classic Western type. Egalitarianism seems to require a political system in which the state is able continually to hold in check those social and occupational groups which, by virtue of their skills or education or personal attributes, might otherwise attempt to stake claims to a disproportionate share of society's rewards. The most effective way of holding such groups in check is by denying them the right to organize politically or in other ways to undermine social equality.[80]

But historical experience of this approach has been pretty uniform: gross abuses of constitutional rights, terrorism and coercion, and, even when these latter are relaxed, the continuance of party control over all areas of social life, including literature and the arts. As Parkin observes,

> The fact that the humanistic ideals central to the socialist tradition have found little, if any, expression in the European socialist states highlights an unresolved dilemma; namely, whether it is possible to establish the political conditions for egalitarianism while also guaranteeing civil rights to all citizens within a system of "socialist legality."[81]

CONCLUSIONS

Fortunately, this is not the place to enter into the whole question of the "socialist transition." I merely wish to conclude this essay with three brief observations. The first is that the massive inequalities of power and privilege outlined in the second part are, for many socialists, intolerable mainly because they violate something like the principle of equal respect delineated in the first part—a principle which derives from liberal premises, but which takes them seriously. The second is that the arguments for the unrealizability of equality considered in the third part all fail to show that these inequalities are ineradicable, whether on psychological or sociological grounds. And the third is that the argument that the costs of implementing equality are too high is the most crucial facing any socialist today. And it is perhaps the inclination to see the accumulated weight of historical evidence for the apparent need to pay such costs—from the rise of Stalin to the fall of Allende—as a challenge rather than as a source of despair that is, in the end, the distinguishing mark of an egalitarian socialist.

NOTES

1. James S. Coleman, "Equality of Opportunity and Equality of Results," *Harvard Educational Review* 43 (February 1973): 137.

2. See p. 56.

3. Though equality is an objective central to socialism, socialists have not, in general, been very explicit about its content or the values on which it rests. I have (perhaps surprisingly) found the ideas of certain English egalitarians and socialists (Arnold, Morris, Tawney, Cole, Orwell) especially helpful.

4. [Gracchus] Babeuf came perhaps the nearest to doing so, proclaiming, "Let there be no other difference between people than that of age or sex. Since all have the same needs and the same faculties, let them henceforth have the same education and the same diet. They are content with the same sun and the same air for all; why should not the same portion and the same quality of nourishment not suffice for each of them?" *Manifeste des égaux* [1796], in *Les Précurseurs français du socialisme de Condorcet à Proudhon*, ed. M. Leroy (Paris: *Editions du temps présent*, 1948), pp. 67–68 (trans. S. Lukes).

5. See A. B. Atkinson, *Unequal Shares: Wealth in Britain* (London: Allen Lane, Penguin Press, 1972), pp. 80ff.

6. H. Dalton, *Some Aspects of Inequality of Incomes in Modern Communities* (London: Routledge, 1925), cited in ibid., p. 84.

7. Christopher Jencks et al., *Inequality: A Reassessment of the Effects of Family and Schooling in America* (London: Allen Lane, Penguin Press, 1974), pp. 9–10.

8. The argument which follows, spelling out the principle of equal respect, is taken from the present author's *Individualism* (Oxford: Blackwell, 1973), pt. 3.

9. Jean-Antoine-Nicolas de Caritat, Marquis de Condorcet, *Sketch for the Progress of the Human Mind* [1793], trans. June Barraclough (London: Weidenfeld and Nicolson, 1955), p. 184.

10. R. H. Tawney, *Equality*, 4th ed. (London: Allen and Unwin, 1952), p. 260.

11. Ibid., p. 153.

12. William Godwin, *Enquiry Concerning Political Justice and Its Influence on Morals and Happiness* [1793], 3d ed., vol. 1 (London: G. G. and J. Robinson, 1798), pp. 214–15.

13. William Morris, *Letters on Socialism* [1888] (London: privately printed, 1894), Letter 1, p. 5.

14. Tawney, *Equality*, p. 254.

15. George Orwell, *Homage to Catalonia* (London: Secker and Warburg, 1938; Penguin edition, 1962), p. 66.

16. Bernard Williams, "The Idea of Equality," in *Philosophy, Politics and Society: Second Series*, ed. P. Laslett and W. G. Runciman (Oxford: Blackwell, 1962), pp. 117, 118.

17. Ibid., pp. 119–20.

18. Friedrich A. Hayek, *Individualism, True and False* (Dublin: Hodges, Figgis & Co and Oxford: Blackwell, 1946), p. 24.

19. Tawney, *Equality*, p. 87.

20. Jencks, *Inequality*, p. 135.

21. Matthew Arnold, "Democracy"[1861], in *The Portable Matthew Arnold*, ed. Lionel Trilling (New York: Viking Press, 1949), pp. 442–43.

22. Tawney, *Equality*, p. 49.

23. Ibid., pp. 35–36.

24. Ibid., p. 47.

25. Ibid., p. 108.

26. C. A. R. Crosland, *The Future of Socialism* (London: Cape, 1956), pp. 150–51.

27. See J. H. Goldthorpe, "Social Stratification in Industrial Society," reprinted in *Class, Status and Power: Social Stratification in Comparative Perspective*, ed. R. Bendix and S. M. Lipset, 2d ed. (London: Routledge, 1967).

28. Frank Parkin, *Class, Inequality and Political Order* (London: MacGibbon and Kee, 1971), p. 39.

29. P. M. Blau and O. D. Duncan, *The American Occupational Structure* (New York: John Wiley, 1967), p. 7.

30. See H. F. Lydall, *The Structure of Earnings* (Oxford: Oxford University Press, 1968).

31. Cited in David Lane, *The End of Inequality? Stratification under State Socialism* (Harmondsworth: Penguin Education, 1971), p. 81.

32. See, e.g., H. Gordon Skilling and Franklyn Griffiths, eds., *Interest Groups in Soviet Politics* (Princeton: Princeton University Press, 1971).

33. P. J. D. Wiles and S. Markowski, "Income Distribution under Communism and Capitalism: Some Facts about Poland, the UK, the USA, and the USSR," *Soviet Studies* 22 (1971): 344.

34. Ibid., p. 353.

35. Atkinson, *Unequal Shares*.

36. See John Westergaard and Henrietta Resler, *Class in Contemporary Britain* (London: Heinemann, 1975). I am grateful to the authors for their permission to read the text of this extremely valuable study in advance of publication.

37. Atkinson, Unequal Shares, pp. 37–38.

38. Ibid., p. 251.

39. Ibid., p. 77.

40. See Westergaard and Resler, *Class in Contemporary Britain*; and Parkin, *Class, Inequality*, pp. 125–26.

41. Parkin, *Class, Inequality*, p. 127.

42. See Goldthorpe, "Social Stratification in Industrial Society," p. 653.

43. D. Wedderburn and C. Craig, "Relative Deprivation in Work," paper presented at the British Association for the Advancement of Science (Exeter, 1969), cited in Parkin, *Class, Inequality*, p. 26.

44. C. Kerr et al., *Industrialism and Industrial Man* (Cambridge, Mass.: Harvard University Press, 1960).

45. See Westergaard and Resler, *Class in Contemporary Britain*, and the present

author's *Power: A Radical View* (London: Macmillan, 1974), and "Political Ritual and Social Integration," *Sociology* 9, no. 2 (May 1975): 289–308.

46. Lane, *The End of Inequality*, p. 69.

47. See Parkin, *Class, Inequality*, p. 144, and his article, "Class Stratification in Socialist Societies," *British Journal of Sociology* (December 1969): 355–74.

48. Lane, *The End of Inequality*, pp. 72–74.

49. Parkin, *Class, Inequality*, p. 146.

50. Parkin, ibid., p. 147; cf. Lane, *The End of Inequality*, p. 78.

51. Parkin, *Class, Inequality*, p. 149.

52. P. Machonin, "Social Stratification in Contemporary Czechoslovakia," *American Journal of Sociology* 75 (1970): 725–41. For an English summary of Machonin and his associates' full-scale study of this subject, see Ernest Gellner, "The Pluralist Anti-levelers of Prague," *European Journal of Sociology* tome XII (1971): 312–25.

53. Wiles and Markowski, "Income Distribution," p. 344.

54. Ibid.

55. See Atkinson, *Unequal Shares*, p. 77; and Lydall, *Structure*.

56. See Michalina Vaughan, "Poland," in *Contemporary Europe: Class, Status and Power*, ed. Margaret Scotford Archer and Salvador Giner (London: Weidenfeld and Nicolson, 1971).

57. Lane, *The End of Inequality*, pp. 129–37.

58. H. J. Eysenck, *The Inequality of Man* (London: Temple Smith, 1973), p. 224.

59. Ibid., p. 270.

60. Ibid., pp. 159, 224.

61. Ibid., p. 224.

62. R. Herrnstein, *IQ in the Meritocracy* (London: Allen Lane, Penguin Press, 1973).

63. Arthur R. Jensen, *Educability and Group Differences* (London: Methuen, 1973), p. 363.

64. Jencks, *Inequality*, p. 315.

65. Ibid., p. 71.

66. Eysenck, *The Inequality of Man*, p. 111.

67. See Jencks, *Inequality*, Appendix A.

68. See Jencks, *Inequality*.

69. Ibid., chap. 3, pt. 2.

70. Ibid., p. 72.

71. K. Davis and W. E. Moore, "Some Principles of Stratification," in Bendix and Lipset, *Class Status and Power* (see n. 27), p. 47.

72. Ibid., p. 48.

73. Ibid.

74. See G. A. Huaco, "The Functionalist Theory of Stratification: Two Decades of Controversy," *Inquiry* 9 (autumn 1966): 215–40.

75. Ralf Dahrendorf, "On the Origin of Social Inequality," in *Philosophy, Politics and Society: Second Series*, ed. P. Laslett and W. G. Runciman (Oxford: Blackwell, 1962), p. 107.

76. Ibid., p. 103.

77. Ibid.

78. Ibid., p. 102.

79. Parkin, *Class, Inequality*, pp. 181–82.
80. Ibid., p. 183.
81. Ibid., p. 184.

11.

WHY BLACK AMERICANS ARE NOT SOCIALISTS

MANNING MARABLE

> *The chief hope lies in the gradual but inevitable spread of the knowledge that the denial of democracy in Asia and Africa hinders its complete realization in Europe. It is this that makes the Color Problem and the Labor Problem to so great an extent two sides of the same human tangle. How far does white labor see this? Not far, as yet.*
> —W. E. B. Du Bois, *The Negro Mind Reaches Out*, 1925

Marxists have always been conscious of the symbiotic relationship between racism and capitalism. Marx himself made the point succinctly in *Capital*: "Labor cannot emancipate itself in the white skin where in the black it is branded." A half century later, W. E. B. Du Bois, radical black scholar and founder of the NAACP, observed that "more and more the problem of the modern workingman is merging with the problem of the color line." For Du Bois, socialism was an impossible goal unless antiracist politics dominated labor organizations. "So long as black laborers are slaves," he concluded, "white laborers cannot be free."[1] Thus, the relationship between race and class and the political link between racial equality and the emancipation of the working class were clearly stated a long time ago.

Although objectively, as the most oppressed section of the working class, blacks should be in the forefront of a class-conscious movement for a socialist America, actually relatively few black workers, activists, or intellectuals have joined socialist organizations.

From *Socialist Perspectives*, ed. Phyllis Jacobson and Julius Jacobson (Princeton: Karz- Cohl Publishing, Inc., 1983), pp. 63–95. Copyright © 1983 by the editors. Reprinted with permission. This essay was reprinted in *Speaking Truth to Power: Essays on Race, Resistance, and Radicalism* by Manning Marable (New York: Westview Press, 1996).

The first part of this essay explores some of the reasons for the failure of socialism within black America, taking up the legacy of racism on the left, examining the political development of black socialists and the path they took to Marxism as differentiated from the one followed by white leftists, and noting some of the sociological factors which have retarded the development of a broad-based socialist consciousness in the black community from 1865 to the present. In the second section, there is a discussion of the current black struggle and the continued gap between major black organizations and the American Left.

THE RACIST LEGACY

The history of the relationship between blacks and American white radicals is filled with broken promises, ethnocentrism, and outright contempt. Racism has blunted the critical faculties of white progressives from the colonial period to the present. Any proper understanding of black historic reluctance to support calls for socialism by radical intellectuals and white workers must begin with this twisted heritage of racism.[2]

Blacks have seen an endless series of prominent white liberal and progressive allies betray their trust and embrace the politics of white supremacy. Populist Tom Watson, the Georgia lawyer in the early 1890s, became the fiercest proponent of lynching and racist hatred the South had ever known.[3] Elizabeth Cady Stanton's call for women's right to vote at Seneca Falls, New York, in 1848 was seconded by black abolitionist Frederick Douglass. As Angela Davis notes, "Douglass was responsible for officially introducing the issue of women's rights to the Black Liberation movement, where it was enthusiastically welcomed."[4] Stanton repaid black supporters with this racist diatribe:

> As long as [the Negro] was lowest in the scale of being, we [white women] were willing to press his claims; but now, as the celestial gate to civil rights is slowly moving on its hinges, it becomes a serious question whether we had better stand aside and see "Sambo" walk into the kingdom first. . . . Are we sure that he, once entrenched in all his inalienable rights, may not be an added power to hold us at bay? Why should the African prove more just and generous than his Saxon peers? . . . It is better to be the slave of an educated white man, than of a degraded, ignorant black one.[5]

Birth-control advocate Margaret Sanger championed black and white workers' rights, and for a time maintained close ties to the Socialist Party. By 1919, however, Sanger defended birth control as "more children from the fit, less from the unfit." In a letter to one associate, Sanger confided, "We do not want word to get out that we want to exterminate the Negro population."[6] Such was the profound racism that has underscored American politics, right to left.

An early socialist whose career parallels Watson's, Stanton's, and others was Orestes A. Brownson. Two decades before the 1848 revolutions and the publication of the *Communist Manifesto*, Brownson pursued a radical labor organizing career. A Universalist minister, Brownson was a supporter of the Robert Owen-Frances Wright faction of the Workingmen's Party. In the 1830s, he was a strong advocate of black emancipation. "We can legitimate our own right to freedom," Brownson wrote in 1838, "only by arguments which prove also the negro's right to be free." After 1840, Brownson had begun to believe that laborers "are neither numerous nor strong enough to get or to wield the political power of the State." With his renunciation of radicalism, Brownson also abandoned any support for black liberation. By 1844, he supported South Carolina senator and slaveholder John C. Calhoun for the Democratic Party's presidential nomination. After the Civil War, he protested black suffrage, warning that black voters "will always vote with the wealthy landowning class, and aid them in resisting socialistic tendencies." He applauded Jim Crow laws, taunting his abolitionist opponents, "You will never make the mass of the white people look upon the blacks as their equals."[7]

Marxists have always insisted that the flow of social history is determined by the relationship between the subjective and objective factors—the superstructure or ideological, cultural, and political apparatuses and the base, or forces of production. But what most American socialists and Marxists adhered to was a philosophy not of Marxism—which also suggests that the relations between superstructure and base are reciprocal, one affecting the other—but of economic determinism, not unlike that of American historian Charles Beard.[8] The left economic determinists held that the base, the means of production, strictly determines the character of all other human institutions and thought. Racism was, therefore, only part of the larger class question. The rights of Negroes, per se, were no different in any decisive respect than those of Polish-American factory workers in Chicago or white miners and lumberjacks in the Great Northwest. This is not to suggest that all white socialists who held this view were racist or insensitive to racism. Eugene V. Debs made it a point of principle never to address any racially segregated audience. The Socialist Party would "deny its philosophy and repudiate its own teaching," Debs said, "if, on account of race consideration, it sought to exclude any human being from political and economic freedom." Socialist historian Albert Fried applauds Debs's enlightened views, but adds that Debs "and probably most socialists" during the early 1900s "reduced the Negro problem to a class problem. They assumed that equality would prevail in America the moment capitalism ceased to exist. Until that day they preferred to keep the race issue as far out of sight and hearing as possible."[9]

This theoretical rigidity produced two political by-products. First, militant socialists like Curaçao-born Daniel De Leon who were sympathetic to black demands for civil rights nevertheless "regarded the plight of the Negro as essentially a class issue," according to historian David Herreshoff. De Leon did not take seriously the loss of black voting rights in the 1890s, because in his own words, "the tanglefoot Suffrage legislation while aimed at the Negro ostensibly as a Negro, in fact aims at him as a wage slave." De Leon personally opposed racist legislation, but he believed "it was a waste of time for socialists to explore the differences between whites and blacks" as to their relative degrees of race/class exploitation.[10] The second and more devastating result was that white American socialists never made the issue of racism a basic point of struggle either internally or propagandistically. Thus, socialist John Sandgren was not censured for expressing the view in the Party's newspaper that blacks, women, and migrant workers "can in no manner be directly interested in politics." No one pressed for the expulsions of centrist leader Morris Hillquit and newspaper editor Hermann Schlueter for championing the exclusion of immigration of "workingmen of inferior races—Chinese, Negroes, etc."[11]

White social democrats repeatedly disappointed black leftists in their tolerance, and sometimes outright approval, of racism. In a 1911 speech before the New York City Socialist Party, Du Bois publicly attacked white leftists for refusing to combat racism.[12] In 1913, he urged the American Socialist Party to redouble its efforts to recruit blacks. "There is a group of ten million persons in the United States toward whom socialists would better turn serious attention," he declared.[13] Du Bois's campaign to force white leftists into the struggle for racial justice was effective, in certain respects. Moderate socialist/social worker Jane Addams supported Du Bois's research activities at Atlanta University. Addams and more militant intellectuals in the Socialist Party, like Mary White Ovington, William English Walling, and Charles Edward Russell, were founding members of the NAACP.[14] However, other white socialists either ignored Du Bois's call or simply restated the popular racist bigotry of the age. A typical example was Victor Berger, powerful leader of the Milwaukee socialists and head of the Wisconsin AFL, who said that "the negroes and mulattoes constitute a lower race," and were a menace to white labor. The "free contact with the whites has led to the further degradation of the negroes."[15] The Socialist Party in the South was for "whites only," and some party theoreticians expounded the view that "socialism would bring complete segregation: blacks and whites should not live in the same areas or even work in the same factories."[16]

Even some of the most "progressive" white socialists who were actively involved in antiracist work could harbor a private hatred for blacks. For example, in December 1928, Molders Union leader John P. Frey was the AFL speaker at a large interracial meeting in Washington, D.C. Publicly, Frey supported black civil rights; privately, he was "a notorious racist." Despite the AFL's long record of racist exclusion, Frey claimed that the Federation "not only organized the negro, but brought him into the white man's unions." He added that racial prejudice against African Americans in unions was not greater than that experienced by Italians, Jews, or Poles. Du Bois and NAACP assistant secretary Walter White denounced Frey's speech. Seeking to resolve the dispute, William English Walling counseled White to halt public attacks on Frey. As a leading Socialist

Party theoretician and a member of the NAACP executive board, Walling openly fought the "color line" but privately condemned his black coworkers. In a letter to Frey, Walling described Du Bois and other black NAACP critics of the AFL as "nasty reds. Labor's attitude on the color question is 100 percent OK and it has nothing to be ashamed of." Frey's response to Walling charged that blacks themselves were to blame for their "low" representation in all-white unions![17]

From its origins, the Communist Party always maintained better relations with the black movement than the socialists. Initial black recruitment efforts were unsuccessful. During the 1920s only 200 black Americans joined the Party, but among them were some of the most gifted writers and organizers of the "Harlem Renaissance," like Cyril Briggs, founder of the revolutionary black nationalist organization the African Blood Brotherhood. The Party's real growth did not occur until the Great Depression. Communists established integrated Unemployment Councils and led "hunger marches" in dozens of state capitals and in Washington, D.C. Two black Communists organized a sharecroppers' union at Camp Hill, Alabama, in 1931 that quickly mushroomed into a mass movement among black rural farmers in the state. The Party launched the National Miners' Union, which promptly elected a black Indiana miner, William Boyce, as its national vice president. Thousands of blacks supported NMU strikes and organizing activities because, in Boyce's words, "it fights discrimination, segregation, Jim Crowism, and disenfranchisement." Black Party leader James W. Ford, secretary of the Harlem Section, was instrumental in organizing tenant and worker protests reaching tens of thousands of poor blacks.[18] During those years of astronomically high unemployment, vast numbers of poor blacks acquired a deep respect for the Communist Party, the first socialist organization in their experience to emphasize racial egalitarianism in theory and practice.

But subsequent Communist activity lost the Party black support. When black social democrat A. Philip Randolph organized the Negro March on Washington Movement in 1941 to pressure the Roosevelt administration to desegregate defense plants, Communists opposed the mobilization. After Nazi Germany's attack on the Soviet Union, the Party "frowned upon any struggles that might interfere with the war effort," writes historian Philip S. Foner. Thus, black Communist spokesperson Ben Davis urged blacks to put aside "all questions of discrimination" and to "sacrifice" for the war effort. The Party's newspaper, the *Daily Worker*, told blacks to sign "no-strike pledges," and charged that black protesters involved in the August 1943 Harlem riot were "fifth columnists and pro-fascists." The Party was silent about the immoral internment of thousands of Japanese-Americans in West Coast camps, and applauded the use of the atomic bomb on Hiroshima. "It was to be exceedingly difficult for the Communists to overcome the resentment among blacks created by the Party's wartime policies," Foner observes. "The Communists never completely erased the feeling in sections of the black community that they had placed the Soviet Union's survival above the battle for black equality."[19]

Since 1945, American Marxists have generally supported the struggle for equal rights, but their contributions to the black movement have not been decisive. White social democrats provided financial support for Martin Luther King's Montgomery bus boycott in 1955–56. Many "red diapers babies" of the New Left generation joined the Student Nonviolent Coordinating Committee (SNCC) in the early 1960s. Most white social democrats, however, were bewildered when the civil rights cause turned into a struggle for "Black Power." They thought that Malcolm X was a racist or a madman; they could not comprehend Stokely Carmichael or H. Rap Brown. Conversely, some of the younger white radicals applauded any angry black spokesperson—Eldridge Cleaver is a sorry example—without any serious analysis of the dynamics of race and class in American society. Small wonder, then, that by the 1980s, no socialist or communist organization, Old Left or New, had won over any significant number of black activists, intellectuals, or workers.

At the core of the Left's legacy, therefore, is the ongoing burden of racism. In the 1920s, Du Bois characterized American social democracy and the white working class as "autocratic and at heart capitalistic, believing in profit-making industry and wishing only to secure a larger share of profits for particular guilds." After World War I and the successful revolution in Russia, however, there existed the faint possibility for a democratic movement for socialism which was antiracist. For Du Bois the logical question was: "Will the new labor parties welcome the darker race to this industrial democracy?" Reflecting critically on the United States, Du Bois had to admit that the long-term prospects were decidedly bleak:

> White laborers can read and write, but beyond this their education and experience are limited and they live in a world of color prejudice. The propaganda, the terrible, ceaseless propaganda that buttresses [white racism] . . . has built a wall which for many centuries will not break down. Born into such a spiritual world, the average white worker is absolutely at the mercy of its beliefs and prejudices. Color hate easily assumes the form of religion and the laborer becomes the blind executive of the decrees of the "punitive" expeditions; he sends his sons as soldiers and sailors; he composes the Negro-hating mob, demands Japanese exclusion, and lynches untried prisoners. What hope is there that such a mass of dimly thinking and misled men will ever demand universal democracy for men?[20]

The overwhelming majority of white American socialists have yet to confront this question seriously.

THE BLACK PATH TO SOCIALISM

A few black workers and intellectuals were attracted to socialist ideas as early as the 1870s. One of the nation's most prominent black trade unionists, New York engineer John Ferrell, was a socialist and a leader of the Knights of Labor. Peter H. Clark, the principal of the Colored High School of Cincinnati, Ohio, was "probably the first American Negro Socialist," according to Foner. During the 1877 railroad strike, Clark publicly hailed black-white unity and "called for socialism as the solution for labor's grievances." Probably the most effective black leftist before 1900 was the militant editor of the *New York Age*, Timothy Thomas Fortune. In a series of newspaper and periodical articles, Fortune demanded that "Southern capitalists give their wage workers a fair percentage of the results of their labor. If there is any power on earth which can make the white Southern employers of labor face the music," he wrote, "it is organized white and black labor."[21] Fortune called for a class struggle to liberate black Americans. "What are millionaires, anyway, but the most dangerous enemies of society?" he asked his readers. Fortune was convinced that black people had to adopt a socialist analysis to comprehend the economic forces that exploited them. "Their revolution is upon us, and since we are largely of the laboring population, it is very natural that we should take sides with the labor forces in their fight for a juster distribution of the results of labor."[22]

Lucy Parsons was one of a number of black women socialists who have been buried in the pages of history. Born in 1853, Parsons joined the Socialist Labor Party in her mid-twenties. She married a radical Southerner, Albert R. Parsons, who had served briefly in the Confederate army. Even before her husband was indicted for complicity in the deaths of seven policemen during the Haymarket Square riot of May 4, 1886, and executed in November 1887, Lucy Parsons traveled the country in support of anarchism. Most socialist historians have ignored her writings and activities against sexism and lynching. A few have even questioned her racial identity.[23] Her contemporaries knew her as a militant supporter of the Industrial Workers of the World, and a defender of the Scottsboro Nine in 1931. Parsons joined the Communist Party in 1939, and died three years later.[24]

Some black leaders advanced socialist ideas after 1900, but relatively few joined the Socialist Party. J. Milton Waldron, a Jacksonville, Florida, Baptist minister, was a supporter of cooperatives and black-white labor unity. In 1901, he organized the Afro-American Industrial Insurance Society, and four years later joined Du Bois's Niagara Movement, the black political opposition to accommodationist educator Booker T. Washington. Politically, however, Waldron aligned himself with the Democratic Party through an all-black organization, the National Independent Political League. J. Max Barber, assistant editor of the *Voice of the Negro*, was another Niagara Movement activist who sympathized with socialist reforms.[25] In Harlem, street propagandist and black nationalist organizer Hubert Harrison had, by 1914, begun to combine the issues of race and class into a unique political program. Younger Harlem black radicals involved in union organizing, A. Philip Randolph and Chandler Owen, joined the Socialist Party. Randolph's subsequent career as the leader of the Brotherhood of Sleeping Car Porters and founder of the National Negro Congress in 1935 is, of course, well known. But for our purposes, it has relatively little relationship to Marxism. By 1920, Randolph had broken with militant socialism, and by the end of his life had become an apologist for crude anticommunism and white racism inside the AFL-CIO.[26]

Among the thousands of blacks who joined the Communist Party during the Great Depression, Angelo Herndon is, perhaps, the best known. Born in 1913, Herndon was a construction laborer and worked in the Kentucky coal mines. In 1930, he joined the Party-led Unemployment Council of Birmingham. Two years later, he was arrested and jailed for possession of Marxist literature, provoking labor violence, and trying "to establish a group and combination of persons, colored and white." The case of Angelo Herndon became a national cause for the Left and many white liberals. Randolph drafted a resolution to free Herndon which was presented to the 1936 AFL Convention. NAACP attorney Thurgood Marshall supported the Herndon defense. In 1937, the Supreme Court narrowly reversed Herndon's conviction in a five to four vote. Of interest here is not Herndon's subsequent career—he broke with the Party after World War II—but the political evolution that led him to socialism. In his youthful autobiography, *Let Me Live*, Herndon explained that his "conversion" to Communism was virtually a religious awakening:

> The Negro leaders tell us that the poor white workers are responsible for our sufferings. But who controls the powerful weapons with which to spread anti-Negro propaganda? . . . Decidedly, it could not be the poor white workers who had all they could to keep themselves alive. Therefore, it could only be the rich white people who were our oppressors, for they controlled the churches and the schools and the newspapers and the radio. . . . [To] secure their profits from human sweat and brawn they fall back upon these wicked methods of "divide and rule," divide the white workers from their Negro brothers.[27]

For Herndon and other unemployed black workers, Marxism manifested itself first in racial terms as a theory of human equality and social justice.

The most significant national black leader won to socialism during the first half of the twentieth century and who remained a militant leftist throughout his public career was W. E. B. Du Bois. As a radical journalist, he stood above De Leon, Fortune, and Randolph; as a pioneering social scientist, his voluminous writings, from *The Soul of Black Folks* (1903) to *Black Reconstruction* (1935), influenced scholars worldwide. For decades his name was the personification of the black freedom struggle in the United States, the West Indies, and Africa. For these reasons his evolution as a Marxist merits considerable attention.

Du Bois viewed himself as a socialist by 1904. In his early journal, *Horizon*, and later in the NAACP publication *Crisis*, he "advised the socialists that their movement could not succeed unless it included Negro workers, and wrote that it was simply a matter of time before white and black workers would see their common economic cause against the exploiting capitalists."[28] Like Parsons, Randolph, and Herndon, Du Bois was impressed with the nonracist personal behavior of many white socialists, and probably gravitated to leftist politics because they seemed to share his burning commitment to racial equality. As early as 1908, Du Bois made this point quite clearly: "The only party today which treats Negroes as men, North and South, are the Socialists."[29] Thus, he vigorously applauded Los Angeles socialists for nominating a black man for city council in 1911.[30] African Americans view society through the prism of race, and when they come to radicalism it is as a response to and rejection of racism and the inherent irrationality of capitalism. In August 1927, for example, Du Bois noted in *Crisis* that several blacks in Louisville, Mississippi, had been "burned alive" because of the widespread indignation at the "refusal of Negroes traveling in slow, secondhand Fords to give the road to faster cars." Small wonder, Du Bois exclaimed, that some black Americans were turning to "bolshevism." Given the level of racist atrocities, he thought larger numbers of blacks would turn to Marxism.[31]

However, Du Bois's conversion to Marxism did not begin until well after the Bolshevik Revolution. Although in September 1916 he predicted that the war would create "the greater emancipation of European women, the downfall of monarchies. . . and the advance of true Socialism,"[32] when the autocracy fell in St. Petersburg six months later, Du Bois worried "whether the German menace is to be followed by a Russian menace."[33] In the summer of 1921, the black editor was criticized by novelist Claude McKay for neglecting to mention the accomplishments of the Soviet Union. Du Bois tartly rejected the slogan "dictatorship of the proletariat," and informed McKay, "[I am] not prepared to dogmatize with Marx and Lenin." He urged blacks not to join a revolution "which we do not at present understand."[34] Du Bois's leap toward the left only began in earnest with a two-month visit to the Soviet Union in 1926. He was not surprised to see so many poor people, food lines, and "orphan children, ragged and dirty, [crawling] in and out of sewers." What impressed Du Bois was the Soviet government's commitment to "the abolition of poverty. . . . Schools were multiplying; workers were being protected with a living wage, nurseries for children, night schools, trade unions, and wide discussion." Ever the puritan, Du Bois noted that "there were no signs of prostitution or unusual crime. . . some drunkenness, but little gambling."[35] Summarizing his experience in *Crisis*, Du Bois declared with enthusiasm:

> I stand in astonishment and wonder at the revelation of Russia that has come to me. I may be partially deceived and half-informed. But if what I have seen with my eyes and heard with my ears in Russia is Bolshevism, I am a Bolshevik.[36]

Even earlier, Du Bois believed that the essence of the socialist revolution and the most important product of Bolshevism "is the vision of great dreamers that only those who work shall vote and rule."[37] By 1931, he urged *Crisis* readers to study *Capital*.[38]

During the Depression, Du Bois's affection for the Soviet model of socialism grew. Visiting Russia again in late 1936, he was pleased with what he felt to be the nation's progress: "There were no unemployed, all children were in schools, factories, shops and libraries had multiplied, and there was evidence of law and order everywhere. The peasant was in close cooperation with, and not in revolt against, the factory worker."[39]

In retrospect, though, Du Bois's silence on the massive Soviet political upheavals during those years is difficult to explain. The "liberals" in the Politburo, particularly Leningrad chief Sergei Kirov, Vice Premier Rudzutak, Kalinin, and Voroshilov, were being displaced (or in Kirov's case assassinated on Stalin's orders). The "trial of the sixteen," which included former Comintern leader Grigori Zinoviev, occurred in August 1936. Former Soviet leaders Piatakov, Radek, and fifteen others were "tried" for committing crimes against the state in January 1937. One of Marxism's greatest theoreticians, Nikolai Bukharin, would be executed on false charges the following year.[40] By 1939, one-quarter of the entire Soviet officer's corps was imprisoned; 1 million party members were expelled. "The Great Purge destroyed a generation not simply of Old Bolshevik veterans of the antitsarist struggle but of very many of their juniors who had joined the movement after 1917 and served as active implementers of Stalinism in its first phase," political scientist Robert Tucker writes. "It virtually transformed the composition of the Soviet regime and the managerial elite in all fields."[41] . . .

[Du Bois's] support for Communism increased with the beginning of the Cold War. Persecuted by the federal government, his passport revoked, and his books banned from public libraries and universities, Du Bois concluded that Russia was the only hope for liberating the oppressed peoples of color across the world. He later acknowledged the crimes of Stalinism but argued that the Soviet state deserved praise for what he believed to be its positive influence on the national liberation movements in Africa, Asia, and the Americas.[42]

Since his death in 1963, no single African American leader has emerged to articulate the socialist vision with anything approaching Du Bois's skill and power. Congressperson Ronald V. Dellums and Georgia State Senator Julian Bond are members of the Democratic Socialists of America, but neither is known particularly as a socialist among blacks. Angela Davis, the Communist Party's vice presidential candidate in 1980, known for her work in black and feminist history, is a prominent activist in struggles which involve poor and working-class blacks, but it is certainly questionable whether her activities are helped by her identification with the Party. Since 1968, a number of black scholar/activists, including Adolph Reed, Robert L. Allen, Damu Imara Smith, William W. Sales, William Strickland, James Foreman, and Earl Ofari, have become socialists of various ideological hues, but none has the means that were available to Du Bois to reach millions of black workers.[43]

From Timothy Thomas Fortune to W. E. B. Du Bois and those mentioned above, blacks have become radicals, socialists, and Marxists as a result of their commitment to black liberation, which usually involved protest activities and organizing in the black community. White socialists could express solidarity with the black struggle, but precious few actually incorporated militantly antiracist politics into the core of their own writings and activities; for them, the race question has always been secondary to the class question. On the other hand, for black socialists race and class have been an interdependent dynamic. They discovered Marx on the road to black liberation.

HISTORICAL IMPEDIMENTS TO BLACK SOCIALIST CONSCIOUSNESS

The basic theme of black U.S. history is the schism between protest and accommodation, struggle and compromise, radicalism and conservatism. Most leftists accept as given the proud heritage of black resistance—Nat Turner, Frederick Douglass, W. E. B. Du Bois, Sojourner Truth, Fannie Lou Hamer, Malcolm X, Martin Luther King Jr., Paul Robeson. Yet for each of these gifted women and men, there were many African American leaders who did not openly fight racism, Jim Crow laws, and economic exploitation. Most black Reconstruction politicians were cautious and pragmatic, ready to campaign for voting rights and civil liberties, but unwilling to call for armed self-defense of the black community and a radical divestment of the white planters' property. From 1865 until the eve of the Great Depression, over 80 percent of all black people were Southern farmers and sharecroppers. Today, we fail to appreciate the fact that, historically, blacks' sense of nationality, racial pride, and culture are essentially rural in origin. Rural attitudes toward life and labor tended to be fairly orthodox and were reinforced by the rigid code of racial segregation. Any strict caste system retards the internal social/cultural/economic dynamics of the oppressed group. New ideological and cultural currents expressed by a subgroup are repressed; the race/class interests of those in authority are often infused into the worldview or "common sense" of the oppressed. Protest in any racist, totalitarian order like the U.S. South between 1877–1960 was difficult even under the best of conditions. It should not surprise us, therefore, that the majority of black leaders emerging from such a racist society would not propose a socialist program.

Historically, the central political demand of any oppressed peasant class is the redistribution of the land. In this country, that was translated into the call for "forty acres and a mule." Those black leaders closest to the agricultural production process called for small proprietary holdings which would free blacks from the yoke of tenancy. With the migration of blacks to the Northern cities into the 1930s, this demand found its Northern echo in programs with the slogan "Don't buy where you can't work." Such policies, which it was hoped would lead to greater black employment, were supported by both the Garveyites and the NAACP, but they did not attack the root of black joblessness—capitalism. Those who migrated to the cities took their rural ideological limitations with them in the form of "black Capitalist" programs for the African American ghetto.

The role of religion in the black community provided yet another barrier to socialism. The language of black politics has always been conditioned by the idiom of the church. Opposition to Marxism and socialism often comes from black preachers and those most heavily influenced by them. Atheism could never be popular among a peasant and working-class people whose nationality and identify were forged in part through faith in their churches and in a just God. For example, on Herndon's admission into the Party's Unemployment Councils, he "bubbled over with enthusiasm" and talked to his relatives and friends "about Negroes and whites fighting together against their bosses so they might live like human beings." Without exception, his friends were aghast and warned Herndon "that I had better stay away from those Reds who were wicked people blaspheming against God." Older religious blacks lamented that the young man had fallen into the atheist movement.[44]

Hosea Hudson's experiences with the black church were even more bitter. Born in 1898, in rural Wilkes County, Georgia, Hudson had attended church since childhood. For years, his ambition was to become a minister like his brother. When he joined the Communist Party in September 1931, he says, "I lost sight of that preaching, I lost sight of the Bible." Churchgoing blacks had little interest in Hudson's concern about the Scottsboro Nine case. Black ministers urged black Communists to "quit talking about" Scottsboro, and demanded that Hudson "keep that devilment out of the church." Devout friends denounced him as "a terrible something, and infidel." In his later years Hudson wrote, "We turned a lot of people away. . . . That's the way they looked upon Reds, Reds didn't believe in no God. They's dangerous." He blamed the capitalist ruling class for "whipping up the minds of people" to oppose socialism on religious grounds. But even after a half century in the Communist Party, Hudson did not escape his social and cultural origins. "I never did finally stop believing in God," he admits. "I haven't stopped believing yet today. I don't argue about it. I don't discuss it, because it's something I can't explain."[45]

Another factor responsible for the black community's indifference, even hostility to socialism was the negative influence of the small African American petty bourgeoisie. From the 1870s to the present, the overwhelming majority of middle-class black intellectuals, political leaders, and entrepreneurs have opposed socialism. Black Reconstruction politician John R. Lynch, Speaker of the Mississippi legislature in 1872 and a three-term Republican congressperson, had no sympathy for "socialism" or "anarchism." Blacks, he felt, should strive to join interracial unions, but should repudiate violence.[46] Booker T. Washington made headlines with his caustic criticism of socialism, radicalism, and Negro participation in the trade union movement. Even Washington's liberal black critics were committed to his "black capitalism" program.

John Edward Bruce, a founder of the first black academic society, the American Negro Academy, was decidedly antisocialist. After inviting A. Philip Randolph to speak before the academy on December 30, 1919, Bruce judged the address "a bitter attack on all things not socialist." Bruce wrote in his diary, "I have no faith in socialism and its propagandists. It has occupied the attention of thinkers for centuries past and no three of them seem to agree as to its efficacy as a solvent for the ills of the body politic. Socialists are themselves divided and there can never be unity in division."[47] On the crucial point of a strategy for black economic development, black nationalists who supported Marcus Garvey and the staunchest of racial integrationists in the NAACP could agree: American capitalism was not structurally racist, and the desperate material condition of blacks could be alleviated through the accumulation of capital in the pockets of black entrepreneurs.[48]

Many prominent leaders of the contemporary black movement continue to "exhibit a simplistic fixation on racism and are unable (or unwilling) to delve any deeper into the American social structure."[49] Although he has since moved to a variety of socialism (Kwame Nkrumahist thought), Stokely Carmichael best represented this "fixation" in the black movement during the late 1960s. At an anti-Vietnam War conference in April 1968, for instance, the former SNCC leader claimed that Marxism was "irrelevant to the black struggle because it dealt only with economic questions, not racism." As for Karl Marx, Carmichael said that he refused to "bow down to any white man." On the question of black-white working-class coalitions, Carmichael declared, "Poor white people are not fighting for their humanity, they're fighting for more money. There are a lot of poor white people in this country, you ain't seen none of them rebel yet, have you?"[50]

In the 1970s, many cultural nationalists surpassed John E. Bruce in their hostility to Marxism. "Our struggle cannot be defined as class struggle in the traditional Marxist manner," wrote *Black Books Bulletin* publisher Haki Madhubuti. "As far as skin color is concerned in the United States, if you are black, you are a slave." Cultural nationalist author Shawna Maglangbayan denounced Marxism as a "reactionary and white supremacist ideology whose chief aim is to maintain Aryan world hegemony once capitalism is overthrown. The idea of an 'alliance' with left-wing white supremacy is a stillborn infant which black Marxists fanatics resuscitate each time they muster enough force to rear their heads in the black community."[51] In fairness, it is most accurate to describe the majority of black elected officials as moderate to liberal social democrats. They do not take the anticommunist polemics of either the Reagan administration or black cultural nationalists too seriously. However, few could be viewed historically as socialist, and in only rare instances would they be considered Marxist. The economic programs of Congressional Black Caucus members range from liberal Keynesianism to laissez-faire capitalism. On balance, most tend to agree with Du Bois's 1940 statement, "The split between white and black workers was greater than that between white workers and capitalists; and this split depended not simply on economic exploitation but on a racial folklore grounded on centuries of instinct, habit, and thought."[52]

Finally, black civil society had been so conditioned by capitalism that it is difficult to find major institutions owned or run by blacks which to any degree advocate socialism. This is particularly true in the area of higher education. Historically, black colleges and universities furnish little valuable information critical of the "free enterprise system." Indeed, what is usually taught in the social sciences could be termed "noneconomics": a total lack of any economic analysis critical of capitalism. Reflecting on his own education at Fisk University in Nashville, Tennessee, Du Bois wrote that "my formal education had touched on politics and religion, but on the whole had avoided economics." Courses on African American slavery discussed the institution's "moral aspects" but never its economic dynamics. "In class I do not remember ever hearing Karl Marx mentioned nor socialism discussed. We talked about wages and poverty, but little was said of trade unions and that little was unfavorable."[53]

The inevitable result of this process of economic miseducation has been a general tendency among black intellectuals in the social sciences to relegate "class issues" to oblivion. Du Bois's series of landmark sociological studies on the Negro in America, published at Atlanta University between 1896 and 1914, illustrates this problem. The annual reports covered widely divergent topics: "The College-Bred Negro," "Notes on Negro Crime," "The American Negro Family." In only two brief volumes, published in 1899 and 1907, did Du Bois concentrate on black economic activities, and even then the works espoused no serious criticism of capitalism. A half century later, Du Bois would write that his entire "program was weak on its economic side. It did not stress enough the philosophy of Marx and Engels."[54] His scholarship on race relations, without equal at the turn of the century, was seriously flawed. "I [did not know] Marx well enough," Du Bois said, "to appreciate the economic foundations of human history."[55] Today, for most black Americans, "class" is perceived purely as a function of personal income. The notions of a "proletariat" and a "capitalist ruling class" are abstractions which have little meaning in everyday language.

THE FAILURE OF LEADERSHIP

The absence of a viable socialist presence within black America has become a critical problem in the 1980s. The election of Ronald Reagan and the electoral successes of conservative Republicans across the United States in 1980 threw the black movement into disarray. Black nationalist political organizations on the left were increasingly victimized by federal and local harassment; black elected officials in Congress and in state legislatures fought desperately to maintain the number of black majority districts; civil rights groups endeavored to reverse hundreds of Reagan-sponsored initiatives reducing job-training programs, public housing, welfare benefits, and health care. This political assault in the wake of the victory of the right is not limited to black concerns. The early 1980s witnessed the defeat of the Equal Rights Amendment; attacks on affirmative action for women and all minorities; a rapidly expanding federal defense budget at the expense of social programs; more overt restriction of the rights of gays and lesbians, etc. In some respects, at least for blacks, the socioeconomic and political terrain of the early 1980s parallels the situation in the mid- to late 1890s, an era dominated by a severe economic depression, the passage of strict Jim Crow legislation, the loss of black male suffrage in the South, and the growth of white vigilante violence. The movement for racial equality which characterized the period of Reconstruction, from 1865 to 1877, succumbed to the control of capital and a conservative Republican-dominated federal government. Similarly, the optimism and activism that were part of the "Second Reconstruction," 1954 to 1966, have been replaced within the black community by frustration and self-doubt.

During the earlier period, the major black figure was Booker T. Washington, founder of Tuskegee Institute, political boss of the "Tuskegee Machine," and leader of the first association of black entrepreneurs, the Negro Business League. Washington counseled public submission to Jim Crow laws and urged blacks to enter into a "historical compromise" with Northern capital and former Southern slaveholders against white workers. The personification of the tendency toward accommodation within the black community at that time, he believed that no real political gains could be achieved through alignment with the trade unions, Populists, or socialists. He accepted the American capitalist system as it existed and urged blacks to take an active role in it. Black capital accumulation was the key element of his program.

Seventy years later, during the Black Power upsurge of the late 1960s, many young nationalists simply revived the Washington strategy and cloaked it in militantly antiwhite rhetoric. Speaking for this Black Power tendency, black social critic Harold Cruse debated Marxists in 1967, in the following manner:

> When we speak of Negro social disabilities under capitalism, however, we refer to the fact that he does not own anything—even what is ownable in his own community. Thus to fight for black liberation is to fight for his right to own. The Negro is politically compromised today because he owns nothing. He has little voice in the affairs of state because he owns nothing. . . . Inside his own communities, he does not own the houses he lives in, the property he lives on, nor the wholesale and retail sources from which he buys his commodities. He does not own the edifices in which he enjoys culture and entertainment.[56]

Washington would have embraced Cruse enthusiastically. "The opportunity to earn a dollar in a factory is worth infinitely more than the opportunity to spend a dollar in an opera house," he told his followers. "No race that has anything to contribute to the markets of the world is long in any degree ostracized."[57]

The coming of Reaganism has given Booker T. Washington's "black capitalism" new relevance for national black political leaders. Suffering from historical amnesia, they do not usually attribute their own political and economic agendas to the Tuskegee accommodationist, but since they lack political ties with the socialist movement, past or present, most have uncritically readopted the Tuskegee "self-help" philosophy as their modus operandi. Rejecting socialism, and even European-style social democracy, many now espouse a "bootstraps" program to counter high black unemployment, plant closings, and social-service reductions. The failure of socialism to develop ties to the black movement has opened the door to the right in the 1980s.

Across the country, interest in black private enterprise strategy increased as the 1982 recession deepened. In Buffalo, New York, for example, a group of blacks formed the Ferguson and Rhodes American Business Careers Institute to train blacks in entrepreneurial skills. The institute's motto, "to help those who want to help themselves," clearly evokes the spirit of Tuskegee and the old Negro Business League.[58] The Reverend Jesse Jackson's Operation PUSH (People United to Save Humanity) pressured the Seven-Up Corporation to sign a $61 million commitment to invest capital in black-owned businesses in June 1982. The Seven-Up agreement called for $10 million for the creation of black-owned Seven-Up beverage wholesalerships, $5 million invested in black-owned life insurance companies, and another $4.35 million in advertisements in black-owned newspapers and radio stations. PUSH purchased 100 shares of stock in Chrysler, General Motors, Ford, and American Motors, in order to "assure us the right and the platform to voice our concern," according to Jackson.[59] Other black political leaders joined PUSH in proposing black alliances with capitalists.

In June 1982, New Orleans Mayor Dutch Morial told a U.S. Black Chamber of Commerce meeting in San Francisco that "a strong line of communications with bankers [is] essential for the success of black businesses." Former aide to Martin Luther King Jr. and currently mayor of Atlanta, Andrew Young suggested that the decisive integration battle of the 1980s would be "the desegregation of the money markets." Jesse Jackson, however, remained unsurpassed in his "evangelical advocacy" of black capitalism. At a gathering of the New Orleans Business League in July 1982, Jackson proclaimed, "We must move from Civil Rights to Silver Rights and from aid to trade." He urged black clergy to promote the development of small businesses among their congregations, declaring that "churches are financial institutions as well as soul-saving institutions." Jackson said, "Black America does more business with corporate America than Russia, China, and Japan combined. Therefore, we want our share of opportunities for risks and rewards! There's something tricky and vicious about the way we're locked out of the private sector. . . . The marketplace is the arena for our development."[60]

Various civil rights organizations applauded Jackson's initiatives, and also emphasized the necessity for aggressive black economic programs. At the seventy-third national convention of the NAACP in Boston, *Black Enterprise* publisher Earl Graves warned the organization:

> We must learn to be more dependent on ourselves, economically and politically. We know by now that as black Americans we cannot depend solely on govern-

ment. We cannot depend on anyone or anything outside ourselves to provide real economic opportunity or justice. We have been standing in the same station waiting for economic opportunity, watching train after train pass us by.[61]

Following Graves's address, NAACP delegates endorsed "Operation Fair Share," a campaign of nationwide boycotts against businesses that resist affirmative action efforts.

With the recessions of 1981 and 1982, NAACP leader Benjamin Hooks authorized the creation of an economics analysis unit and a task force to assist local branches to help black small entrepreneurs and unemployed black workers. In Kokomo, Indiana, NAACP members responded to Reagan cutbacks in food stamps by organizing a food cooperative, and in Galloway Township, New Jersey, they pressured local officials to set aside half of all new municipal jobs for blacks, women, and handicapped people. In Memphis, NAACP leaders persuaded the Nissan Corporation to buy supplies for its local automobile plant from black vendors.[62]

Even with its new "economic agenda," the NAACP is reluctant to develop a militant black capitalist program. When William Perry, the NAACP president of Miami, Florida, introduced a proposal for a "Black Monday"—a plan to have blacks and whites buy exclusively from black businesses on June 28, 1982—national officers were furious. Local whites in the NAACP strongly opposed the idea, and Earl Shinhoster, Southeastern Regional Director of the NAACP, sent a testy mailgram to Perry on June 23, suspending him "immediately and indefinitely." Perry's explanation that the Black Monday "was not intended to be a boycott, just a campaign to support black businesses" did not satisfy his organizational superiors. Shinhoster argued that "any unit of the NAACP is a subordinate unit to the national organization. Autonomy [of the local branch] only extends to issues that are within the scope of the organization." Hooks gave Perry "five days to explain what happened and why his suspension should not be made permanent." Meanwhile, Perry resigned as president and promptly organized an Operation PUSH chapter in Miami. Perry informed the *Miami Times* that Jesse Jackson and PUSH "provide its local units with more autonomy than the NAACP gives its branches."[63]

The Urban League continued in its role as the right wing of the black movement. When Reagan was elected, former league director Vernon Jordan made the most pathetic concessions to the conservative trend. Reagan deserved "the benefit of the doubt," and it was "dangerous," in Jordan's words, to criticize him. Jordan was willing to wait and see whether "equality can be achieved by conservative means, to look at conservative approaches to see if they will help black people." Jordan's successor, John E. Jacob, moved the organization only slightly to the left. Jacob denounced the recent draft report of the Department of Housing and Urban Development which called for an end to federal aid to inner cities. He revived a twenty-year-old proposal developed by former league director Whitney Young which called for "massive federal efforts" combined with "local public-private sector efforts" to retard unemployment and urban decay. Jacob called for joint Democratic and Republican Party efforts to encourage "investments in human capital, urban infrastructure, and economic resources needed to get the national economy moving again."[64]

In Philadelphia, on June 9, 1982, the "Hire One Youth" program was launched by the Reverend Leon Sullivan, chairperson of the Opportunities Industrialization Centers (OICs). The stated goal of "Hire One Youth" was to encourage the private sector to hire 300,000 "disadvantaged young people" during the summer and an additional 700,000 youths by the middle of 1983. "I am appealing to the patriotism of American companies, large and small, in this critical and urgent time of need to put the youth of America back to work," Sullivan explained to the press. "Immediate bipartisan action on the part of President Reagan, the Congress, and the private sector is necessary." Behind Sullivan's appeal for jobs was an omnipresent threat of urban rebellion. "America must act now to put the unemployed youth in jobs before chaos and disorder erupt in our cities," Sullivan said bluntly. "The unemployed youth problem is social dynamite and it is about to explode." Sullivan reminded corporations that a $3,000 tax credit was available to all employers who hired Vietnam-era veterans, cooperative education students, involuntarily terminated CETA workers, and teenagers from "economically disadvantaged" areas. "If every American corporation, business, school. . . puts just one [youth] to work, we can get idle youth off the streets and into the productive mainstream of the American workforce."

Sullivan's program instantly won the support of a broad segment of both political parties and corporations. A number of urban mayors, including Andrew Young of Atlanta, Bill Green of Philadelphia, Jane Byrne of Chicago, Coleman Young of Detroit, Marion Barry of Washington, D.C., and Tom Bradley of Los Angeles, endorsed "Hire One Youth." Conservative political forces, including the U.S. Chamber of Commerce, Reagan's "Task Force for Private Sector Initiatives," and Republican Governor James Thompson of Illinois, publicly supported the effort. The Seven-Up Corporation agreed to pay for Sullivan's advertising and public relations costs. For all the media hype and political support, it seems unlikely that the effort will generate more than one-fifth of the number of permanent jobs it seeks. Sullivan's OIC was a product of Lyndon Johnson's Great Society programs. From 1964–1980, the OIC network of job training and industrial education programs received more than $500 million in federal funds. According to one source, only 13 percent of those trained in the Philadelphia OIC were working in training-related jobs. Many of the OICs nationwide "suffer from mismanagement and poor program performance." Under heavy criticism since the mid-1970s, Reverend Sullivan authored the so-called Sullivan Principles, which provide loose guidelines to justify continued U.S. corporate investment in apartheid South Africa. Like the Tuskegee accommodationist, Sullivan has been a useful tool for both the Republican Party and U.S. corporate interests in a number of ways. For example, in early 1981, Sullivan testified before the Senate Foreign Relations Committee in support of former Secretary of State

Alexander Haig. The anticommunist general was "necessary for America," Sullivan declared. Since the mid-1970s, Gulf Oil and other major corporations have funneled tens of thousands of dollars to Sullivan. It would appear, given Sullivan's checkered history, that "Hire One Youth" was less a strategy to end black joblessness than a program to pacify the black ghetto while maintaining the process of capital accumulation within black America.[65]

In October 1980, two important aides to the late Martin Luther King Jr. endorsed Reagan—the Reverend Ralph David Abernathy and Georgia State Representative (D) Hosea Williams. Williams said his support for Reagan was justified because "the mounting KKK's violent activities against blacks all across the country" were indirectly a product of the Carter administration. Appearing with South Carolina segregationist Strom Thurmond, in December 1980, Williams and Abernathy announced that they were "for the Republican platform" and supported the bizarre suggestion that Thurmond, once a presidential candidate of the Dixiecrat Party, serve as "a liaison officer between Republicans on behalf of minorities." As loyal members of what one journalist termed "Strom Thurmond's Black Kitchen Cabinet," Williams and Abernathy received a "letter of introduction" from Reagan for a black trade mission to Japan in June 1982. They met with Prime Minster Zenko Suzuki and Japanese business leaders "to promote Japanese investments in the United States by offering tax incentives to businesses that invest in joint Japanese-Afro-American ventures." The seventeen-day trade mission sparked some "interest and curiosity" among Japanese corporations, which admitted that they had "never considered establishing a joint-venture factory in the United States with either black or white businessmen." The entire effort may have been futile, however, because on Williams's return he was sentenced to serve one year in a Georgia penitentiary for numerous traffic violations and for fleeing the scene of an accident in 1981.[66]

The pro-capitalist economic initiatives of black managers in the private sector have ranged from "conservative" to simply absurd. A good representative of their tendency is Joe Black, a vice president of the Greyhound Corporation. In July 1982, Black condemned unemployed black youth for not understanding the "thrust of the civil rights movement." "Too many of them have chosen to be guided by emotion and want to believe that it was to prove that black can beat white or mistakenly think that we were to receive something just because we're black." In Black's opinion, it was time for "black adults" to "have the intestinal fortitude to tell youthful blacks that they are spending too much time worrying about the word—'racism.' When we were young, we called it 'prejudice,' 'segregation,' and 'jim crow,' but we did not spend our time worrying about it." Racism was not the reason that black unemployment was at an all-time high: "Too often black college students select 'sop' courses rather than those studies that will make them competitive in today's labor market." Like Hoover Institution Professor Thomas Sowell and other black conservative economists, Black suggested that blacks' ignorance and inadequate training were to blame for their lack of employment opportunities.[67]

What almost no civil rights leader, corporate manager, or black politician comprehends is that the current economic plight of African Americans is an integral part of a worldwide crisis of capitalism. Reaganism, its British counterpart, Thatcherism, and the conservative fiscal policies of Japan, West Germany, and other capitalist countries have escalated unemployment throughout the West. Total unemployment in all Western countries has soared from 10 million in 1971–72 to a projected 31 million by the end of 1982. Reagan's July 1, 1982, "tax cut" did not increase U.S. corporate investment or consumer spending. Conversely, European basic industries, such as shipbuilding, steel, and petrochemicals, are "all in deep trouble," according to the *Wall Street Journal*. British unemployment exceeds 13 percent, and even Japanese unemployment is at a post–World War II record. The Western crisis in capital accumulation has forced pay cuts in workers' salaries in virtually every nation. In 1980, the average West German worker, for example, received $12.26 an hour; last year, the average salary was $10.47. In the United States a similar process of capitalist austerity has occurred. Average wage increases in the first contract year for settlements made by unions covering plants of at least 1,000 workers declined from 11.8 percent in April–June 1981 to 2.2 percent in January–March 1982. The result for U.S. black workers was entirely predictable: official adult unemployment above 18 percent; black youth unemployment, 58 percent; the projected failure of over 20 percent of all black-owned businesses *in 1982 alone*.[68]

The recession of 1982 illustrates with painful clarity the essential political bankruptcy of black middle-class "leaders" and organizations. Unable and unwilling to advance a socialist reorganization of America's political economy, they rely on corporate paternalism and "self-help efforts," which have all been tried previously without success. Responding to the economic desperation of the black working class and poor, they offer rhetoric more suitable to the age of Washington. Without a coherent anti-capitalist alternative, it appears likely that no meaningful solution to the long-term crisis of black underdevelopment will be achieved. The distance between the black movement and the socialist vision has actually widened and may continue to do so for the next period.

[CONCLUSION]

None of the political problems posed here can be resolved quickly. White democratic socialists still seldom respect or even comprehend the African American's legitimate claim to a unique national identity, culture, and tradition of struggle. White Marxists often tend to idealize the black community, ignoring tendencies toward compromise and accommodation found not only among the black elite but also within the working class. White social democrats seem to ignore racism entirely, or simply reduce it solely to a question of class. On the other side of the color line, many blacks from different classes and for various reasons of self-

interest oppose socialist politics within the black community. Narrow nationalists hate Marxism because they don't trust radical whites; black entrepreneurs
hate Marxism because it threatens black private capital accumulation; black
politicians hate Marxism because they are committed to some form of liberal
Keynesianism to conservative capitalism; and black preachers hate Marxism
because it's atheistic. All of these antisocialist sentiments are reinforced by conservative tendencies within black civil society and by the continued manifestations of racism by white workers, labor unions, and white "progressives."

We need to understand the theoretical and practical relationship between race
and class. The place to begin, I believe, is with black revolutionary socialist C. L. R.
James. In his truly wonderful account of the Haitian Revolution, *The Black Jacobins*,
James make a comment which strikes me as the initial step toward resolving the
paradox: "The race question is subsidiary to the class question in politics, and to
think of imperialism in terms of race is disastrous. But to neglect the racial factor as
merely incidental is an error only less grave than to make it fundamental."[69]

NOTES

1. W. E. B. Du Bois, "Problem Literature," *Crisis* 8 (August 1914): 195–96.

2. Part of the rationale for some black nationalists' fears that Marxism is a form of
"left-wing racism" must be attributed to the writings of Marx himself. Marx's vicious
statements about German socialist leader Ferdinand Lassalle were both racist and anti-
Semitic: "It is now quite clear to me that, as shown by the shape of [Lassalle's] head and
. . . hair, that he is descended from the negroes who joined the flight of Moses from Egypt
(unless his mother or grandmother . . . were crossed with a nigger). This union of Jew and
German on a negro foundation was bound to produce something out of the ordinary. The
importunity of the fellow is also negroid." David McLellan, *Karl Marx: His Life and
Thought* (New York: Harper and Row, 1973), p. 322.

In Marx's letter to Friedrich Engels, dated June 14, 1853, he argued, in a comparison
between black Jamaicans and slaves in the United States, that the former "always consisted of newly imported barbarians," whereas Afro-Americans are "becoming a native
product, more or less Yankeefied, English speaking, etc., and there *fit for emancipation*."
See Marx-Engels correspondence reprinted in Shlomo Avineri, ed., *Karl Marx on Colonialism and Modernization* (Garden City, N.Y.: Anchor Books, 1969), p. 454.

At one point, Marx described Mexicans as "*les derniers des hommes*" [the last of the
men]. Engels was even worse. In one work he asserted that "the Germans were a highly gifted
Aryan branch" of humanity, an "energetic stock" who have the "physical and intellectual
power to subdue, absorb, and assimilate its ancient eastern neighbors." Obviously, it may be
unfair to judge the founders of historical materialism by the standards of the late twentieth
century. But these and many other blatantly racist statements by the early proponents of
socialism must give pause to many contemporary would-be black leftists. See M. M. Bober,
Karl Marx's Interpretation of History (New York: W. W. Norton, 1965), pp. 69–70.

3. In the election of 1892, Watson drafted the Populist Party's platform on a united front
between black and white farmers. "You are kept apart that you may be separately fleeced of

your earnings. You are made to hate each other," Watson declared, "because upon that hatred is rested the keystone of the arch of financial despotism which enslaves you both." Biographer C. Vann Woodward declares that "Watson was perhaps the first native white Southern leader of importance to treat the Negro's aspirations with the seriousness that human strivings deserve." With the collapse of Populism, Watson turned to racism and anti-Semitism with gusto. By 1904 he favored the abandonment of the Fifteenth Amendment. In 1910 he bragged that he would no more hesitate to lynch a "nigger" than to shoot a mad dog. Even Booker T. Washington, the model of Negro accommodation, was too radical for Watson. He closed a racist diatribe against the black educator with the statement: "What does Civilization owe the negro? Nothing! Nothing! NOTHING!!!" See C. Vann Woodward, *Tom Watson: Agrarian Rebel* (New York: Oxford University Press, 1970), pp. 220–21, 374, 380, 432–33.

4. Angela Davis, *Women, Race, and Class* (New York: Random House, 1981), p. 51.

5. Ibid., pp. 70–71.

6. Ibid., pp. 212–15.

7. David Herreshoff, *The Origins of American Marxism: From the Transcendentalists to De Leon* (New York: Monad, 1973), pp. 17–18, 31–32, 39–47. Also see Arthur M. Schlesinger, "Orestes Brownson, American Marxist Before Marx," *Sewanee Review* 47 (July–September 1939): 317–23.

8. The classical statement of American economic determinist thought is Charles A. Beard's *An Economic Interpretation of the Constitution of the United States* (New York: Macmillan, 1913). Of some interest is Beard's introduction to the 1935 edition of his seminal study. Beard admitted that he was "interested in Marx when I discovered in his works the ideas which had been cogently expressed by outstanding thinkers and statesmen." However, he denounced the widely held view that his writing was influenced by Marx. Of Marxist views, he declared, "have I the least concern. I have never believed that 'all history' can or must be 'explained' in economic terms, or any other terms."

9. Albert Fried, ed., *Socialism in America* (Garden City, N.Y.: Anchor, 1970), p. 387.

10. Herreshoff, *The Origins of American Marxism,* pp. 159, 168–69.

11. Ibid., pp. 127, 148, 159, 169.

12. Du Bois, "The Socialists," *Crisis* 1 (March 1911): 15.

13. Du Bois, "A Field for Socialists," *New Review* (January 11, 1913): 54–57. Also see Du Bois, "Socialism and the Negro Problem," *New Review* 1 (February 1, 1913): 138–41.

14. Du Bois, *The Autobiography of W. E. B. Du Bois* (New York: International Publishers, 1968), pp. 218, 260. Mary White Ovington was among the few white socialists in the early 1900s to make the cause of racial equity central to their vision of a socialist society. See Ovington, "Vacation Days on San Juan Hill—A New York Negro Colony," *Southern Workman* 38 (November 1909): 627–34; Ovington, "The Negro in the Trade Unions in New York," *Annals of the American Academy of Political and Social Science* 27 (June 1906): 551–58; Ovington, "The National Association for the Advancement of Colored People," *Journal of Negro History* 9 (April 1924): 107–16.

15. Fried, *Socialism in America,* p. 386.

16. Milton Cantor, *The Divided Left: America Radicalism, 1900–1975* (New York: Hill and Wang, 1978), p. 14.

17. Philip S. Foner, *Organized Labor and the Black Worker, 1619–1973* (New York: International Publishers, 1974), pp. 175–76. Du Bois denounced Frey's "awkward and insincere defense of the color line in the A. F. of L." in "Postscript," *Crisis* 36 (July 1929): 242.

18. Ibid., pp. 162, 191–95, 209; and Cantor, *The Divided Left,* pp. 15, 122. A valuable source on the rise of black participation in the U.S. Communist Party is Mark I. Solomon, "Red and Black: Negroes and Communism, 1929–1932" (Ph.D. dissertation, Harvard University, 1972).

19. Foner, *Organized Labor and the Black Worker,* pp. 278–80.

20. Du Bois, "The Negro Mind Reaches Out," in *The New Negro,* ed. Alain Locke (1925; reprint, New York: Atheneum, 1977), p. 407.

21. Foner, *Organized Labor and the Black Worker,* pp. 52, 53, 103.

22. August Meier, *Negro Thought in America, 1880–1915* (Ann Arbor: University of Michigan Press, 1963), pp. 46–47; Seth M. Scheiner, "Early Career of T. Thomas Fortune, 1879–1890," *Negro History Bulletin* 28 (April 1964): 170–72. Fortune eventually came under the hegemony of Booker T. Washington's "Tuskegee Machine," renounced many of his leftist views, and quietly receded into political oblivion. See Emma Lou Thornbrough, "More Light on Booker T. Washington and the *New York Age,"* *Journal of Negro History* 43 (January 1958): 34–49; and August Meier, "Booker T. Washington and the Negro Press," *Journal of Negro History* 38 (January 1953): 68–82.

23. Albert Fried describes Lucy Parsons as "a dark-skinned Mexican" in the collection he edited, *Socialism in America,* p. 187.

24. See Carolyn Asbaugh, *Lucy Parsons: American Revolutionary* (Chicago: Charles H. Kerr, 1976).

25. Meier, *Negro Thought in America, 1880–1915,* pp. 203–204.

26. Wilfred D. Samuels, "Hubert H. Harrison and 'The New Negro Manhood Movement,'" *Afro-Americans in New York Life and History* 5 (January 1981): 29–41; Manning Marable, *From the Grassroots: Social and Political Essays Towards Afro-American Liberation* (Boston: South End Press, 1980), pp. 59–85.

27. Angelo Herndon, *Let Me Live* (1937; reprint, New York: Arno Press, 1969), pp. iii–x, 77, 80, 82–83, 186–87.

28. Meier, *Negro Thought in America, 1880–1915,* pp. 142, 180, 186–87.

29. Du Bois, "To Black Voters," *Horizon* 3 (February 1908): 17–18. Also see Du Bois's 1911 editorial "Gift," *Crisis* 3 (December 1911): 68. Du Bois repeats the assertion that the Socialist Party "is the only party which openly recognizes Negro manhood. Is it not time for black voters to carefully consider the claims of this party?"

30. Du Bois, "Along the Color Line" *Crisis* 2 (October 1911): 227–33.

31. Du Bois, "Postscript," *Crisis* 34 (August 1927): 203–204.

32. Du Bois, "The Battle of Europe," *Crisis* 12 (September 1916): 216–18.

33. Du Bois, "The World Last Month," *Crisis* 13 (March 1917): 215.

34. Du Bois, "The Negro and Radical Thought," *Crisis* 22 (July 1921): 204.

35. Du Bois, *Autobiography,* pp. 29–30.

36. Du Bois, "Russia, 1926," *Crisis* 33 (November 1926): 8.

37. Du Bois, "Forward," *Crisis* 18 (September 1919): 235.

38. Du Bois, "Postscript," *Crisis* 39 (June 1932): 191.

39. Du Bois, *Autobiography,* pp. 31–32.

40. Isaac Deutscher, *Stalin: A Political Biography* (New York: Oxford University Press, 1949), pp. 345–85.

41. See Robert C. Tucker, ed., *Stalinism: Essays in Historical Interpretation* (New York: W. W. Norton, 1977).

42. W. E. B. Du Bois, "Colonialism and the Russian Revolution," *New World Review* (November 1956): 18–22; Du Bois, "The Stalin Era," *Masses and Mainstream* 10 (January 1957): 1–5; Du Bois, "The Dream of Socialism," *New World Review* (November 1959): 14–17.

43. A representative sample of literature by recent black revolutionary nationalists, Marxist-Leninists, and democratic socialists includes Angela Davis, *Angela Davis: An Autobiography* (New York: Random House, 1974); Davis, *Women, Race, and Class*; Robert Allen, *Black Awakening in Capitalist America: An Analytic History* (Garden City, N.Y.: Anchor, 1969); James Foreman, *The Making of Black Revolutionaries* (New York: Macmillan, 1972); William Sales, "New York City: Prototype of the Urban Crisis," *Black Scholar* 7 (November 1975): 20–39; William Strickland, "Whatever Happened to the Politics of Black Liberation?" *Black Scholar* 7 (October 1975): 20–26; Damu I. Smith, "The Upsurge of Police Repression: An Analysis," *Black Scholar* 12 (January–February 1981): 35–37; John Conyers, "The Economy Is the Issue, Planning for Full Employment," *Freedomways* 17 (spring 1977): 71–78; Ronald Dellums, "Black Leadership: For Change or for Status Quo?" *Black Scholar* 8 (January–February 1977): 2–5; Julian Bond, *A Time to Speak, a Time to Act* (New York: Simon and Schuster, 1972).

44. Herndon, *Let Me Live*, pp. 80, 114–15. Herndon's own writing is also filled with religious symbols and overtones. On pages 82–83, he denounces Du Bois, who was not yet a Communist, and black Chicago Congressperson Oscar De Priest as "the tools and the lickspittles of the white ruling class. They speak with the voice of Jacob, but they extend the hairy hand of Esau."

45. Nell Irvin Painter, *The Narrative of Hosea Hudson: His Life as a Negro Communist in the South* (Cambridge: Harvard University Press, 1979), pp. xiii, 24, 133–35. Also see Hosea Hudson, *Black Worker in the Deep South* (New York: International Publishers, 1972).

46. John Hope Franklin, *From Slavery to Freedom* (New York: Random House, 1969), pp. 318–21; Meier, *Negro Thought in America, 1880–1915*, p. 46.

47. Alfred A. Moss Jr., *The American Negro Academy: Voice of the Talented Tenth* (Baton Rouge: Louisiana State University Press, 1981), pp. 145–46.

48. Allen, *Black Awakening in Capitalist America*, pp. 100–101. As Allen puts it, "Garvey took Washington's economic program, clothed it in militant nationalist rhetoric, and built an organization which in its heyday enjoyed the active support of millions of black people."

49. Ibid., p. 250.

50. Ibid., pp. 250–51.

51. Manning Marable, *Blackwater: Historical Studies in Race, Class Consciousness, and Revolution* (Dayton: Black Praxis Press, 1981), p. 110.

52. Du Bois, *Dusk of Dawn*, p. 205.

53. Du Bois, *Autobiography*, p. 126.

54. Ibid., pp. 215–17.

55. Ibid., p. 228.

56. Harold Cruse, *Rebellion or Revolution* (New York: William Morrow, 1968), pp. 238–39.

57. Meier, *Negro Thought in America, 1880–1915*, p. 101.

58. "Area's First Minority-Owned Business Institute Established," *Buffalo Challenger*, 28 July 1982.

59. "PUSH Scores Again: 7-Up Agrees to Invest Money in 'Black Business': Auto Industries Next!" *Buffalo Challenger*, 21 July 1982. The major corporations are, of course, eager to provide token amounts of capital to the black middle class, if in doing so they increase their representative shares of the $125 billion black-consumer market. In June 1982, Anheuser-Busch announced that it would spend $1 million in black-owned newspaper advertising. A black vice president of Anheuser-Busch made the pledge before a meeting of black publishers in Baltimore. "We are committed to the economic development of those companies which are owned and operated by minorities. [We] will expand the number of minority suppliers and contractors with whom we do business. Blacks support our products," he stated, "and [we] need to communicate to [black] consumers how much we appreciate their support." "Anheuser-Busch to Spend $1 Million with Black Newspapers," *San Antonio Register,* 1 July 1982.

60. "PUSH Leader Says We Must Move to Silver Rights and to Trade," *Omaha Star,* 22 July 1982.

61. Tony Brown, "Kennedy: Trumped-Up White Liberal," *Buffalo Challenger,* 21 July 1982.

62. Diane E. Lewis, "Is the NAACP in Step or Out?" *Boston Globe,* 28 June 1982; "NAACP Attacks Reagan, Backs Liberal Democrats," *Guardian,* 21 July 1982.

63. "William Perry Suspended from NAACP," *Miami Times*, 15 July 1982; Marable, *Blackwater*, p. 160.

64. John E. Jacob, "Formulating Urban Policy," *Fort Lauderdale Westside Gazette*, 8 July 1982; Sheila Rule, "Urban League Asks for U.S. Jobs Plan," *New York Times,* 2 August 1982.

65. Marable, *Blackwater*, pp. 154, 165; "OIC Announces Youth Hiring Program," *Fort Lauderdale Westside Gazette*, 8 July 1982.

66. Marable, *Blackwater*, pp. 156–57, 160; "Black Trade Mission to Japan Successful," *Pensacola Voice*, 19–25 July 1982.

67. Joe Black, "By the Way. . . ," *Buffalo Challenger,* 14 July 1982.

68. "Unemployment on the Rise Across the Western World," *San Francisco Chronicle*, 11 May 1982; Anthony Mazzocchi, "It's Time for Management Concessions," *New York Times*, 27 June 1982; Daniel Yergin, "Umemployment: The Outlook Is Grim," *New York Times*, 13 July 1982; Lauri McGinley, "Joblessness Rise Shows Economy Is Getting Worse," *Wall Street Journal*, 10 May 1982; Art Pine, "Europeans Pessimistic as Recession Appears Deep, Hard to Reverse," *Wall Street Journal*, 10 May 1982.

69. C. L. R. James, *The Black Jacobins: Toussaint L'Ouverture and the San Domingo Revolution* (New York: Vintage, 1963), p. 283.

12

WHY FEMINISM AND SOCIALISM NEED EACH OTHER

ANN FERGUSON

In [*Sexual Democracy*] I have argued that male dominance is based in systems of sex/affective production that, together with economic systems, create different organizations of human sexuality, parenting, and social bonding. Patriarchal systems of sex/affective production perpetuate unequal sexual and parenting arrangements that have been embedded in class-, race-, and ethnic-divided societies.

How does this socialist-feminist analysis of male dominance help us to understand the relation of the goals of feminism to socialism? Is a gender-egalitarian society a necessary condition for achieving a class-egalitarian (or classless) society, the goal of socialism? Conversely, is a socialist reorganization of the economy a necessary condition for gender equality?

There are at least two ways to go about answering these questions. One is the abstract philosophical discussion of values and definitions: What counts as gender egalitarianism? Does this require that all women have the same material opportunities as all men? If so, this would seem to imply that social classes based on control or lack of control of material goods have been eliminated, which implies socialism.[1] Conversely, if socialism is defined as common ownership and control of production, the implicit egalitarianism of this formula seems to imply that no one social group (such as men or whites) should have more control or benefits than others over and from the organization of production.[2]

Aside from such theoretical issues, however, there are also empirical questions about the connections between feminism and socialism. Does the achievement of public ownership of production, socialism in the narrow sense of the term, automatically cause male dominance to be overthrown? Even if there is no automatic connection of this sort, is the elimination of capitalism at least causally necessary for women's liberation? If so, that suggests that fighting for socialism should be a strategic priority for feminists. But what are the strategic links between social movements advocating women's liberation and those advocating socialism? Should feminists accept the "unite and fight" strategy, advocated by many socialist groups, of joining with men to fight for socialism (the "class first" position)? Or, realizing that men as a sex class have an interest in maintaining male domination, should women insist on if not a separatist, then at least an autonomous, women's movement with its own goals and priorities?

In addition to the empirical question whether socialist transformation is a necessary means to women's liberation, there is the converse empirical question whether feminist goals, processes, and means are necessary means for the achievement of full socialism. Unfortunately, as we shall see, past socialist struggles have not ultimately centered on the necessity of feminism for socialism. Perhaps because the leaders of such struggles have been men, they have focused more on what the socialist struggle had to offer women than what the feminist struggle had to offer socialists.

A historical perspective must be taken to answer the definitional questions about the connections between feminism and socialism as well as the empirical questions of ends and means. Definitional questions always involve values, and the defense of values assumes a historical context. Western socialist feminism defines itself in a historical political culture where both individual freedom and democratic rule are assumed to be intrinsic ends. Thus my understanding of socialism implies both formal civil rights for individuals (freedom of speech, religion, sexual preference) and formal and substantial democracy for groups of individuals. Formal democracy for groups amounts to political pluralism, that is, that social groups having common interests (women; racial, sexual, religious, and ethnic minorities; workers; consumers) have the legal right to form political organizations, factions, and parties. Substantial democracy has been ignored or downplayed in Western capitalist democracies. This is because it refers to material structures that allow everyone as far as possible an equal weight in political decisions that affect their lives, and this requires state restraints on the power of capital to privilege the options of the owning elite at the expense of the few. Substantial democracy involves two components, social democracy and economic democracy. Social democracy requires that the state ensure social services such as education, health, childcare, and transportation that equalize everyone's material opportunity to meet their material needs as well as to participate in political decisions. Economic democracy requires workers' control of decisions concerning production.[3]

If this version of democratic socialism is accepted, it clearly requires feminism's goal of gender equality. Women as individuals should have the same civil rights as men, and as a group should not be formally or materially disadvantaged compared to men. I have maintained above that feminism's goal of gender egalitarianism must by definition include the goals of socialism (cf. note 1). Thus I have concluded that, on the abstract level, in the Western cultural context at least, socialism and feminism are interconnected goals.[4]

Settling the definitional issue, however, doesn't really answer an equally important question, the historical and empirical question whether and under what conditions socialism and feminism are jointly achievable. Western feminists have argued that existing state socialist societies, such as the Soviet Union, China, Cuba, and Eastern Europe, and historical socialist movements have in fact never succeeded in placing an equal weight on eliminating sexism as they have put on eliminating capitalism. Consequently, though important initial steps were taken toward gender equalization in socialist revolutions, patriarchal aspects still remain. Furthermore, classical Marxist theory on the "woman question," as it has been applied in practice, has tended to downplay the importance of women's liberation in the international workers' struggle for socialist liberation. Why, then, should feminists struggle for socialism as an important strategic step toward women's liberation?

In my view, it is a mistake to emphasize, as some Western feminists do, only the ways in which socialist revolutions have failed to do away with sexism. After all, socialist transformations have occurred both in underdeveloped, peasant societies (Russia, China, Cuba, Vietnam, Mozambique, Nicaragua) and in industrial societies (Eastern Europe). Even though patriarchal aspects remain in all existing socialist societies, in order to assess how successful socialist revolutions have been in achieving feminist goals, we must contrast such societies with other nonsocialist societies at a similar economic stage of development. Thus Western feminists ought to compare the gains of socialist revolutions in other industrialized countries with their own capitalist industrial societies when considering whether struggling for socialism is necessary to achieve feminist goals in their countries.

There are two general problems that socialist regimes in nonindustrialized societies have had with achieving gender equality. First, peasant cultures have historically been more patriarchal than industrial societies. This is not only because of the greater weight of patriarchal religions in those societies but also because family patriarchies, that is, those in which male dominance is reproduced primarily by the power of male kin rather than the state, are stronger systems than state or public patriarchies.

Second, in most socialist revolutions in nonindustrialized countries the degree of material scarcity and the low level of productive forces[5] have seriously limited the available resources for socializing domestic work (building childcare centers, canteens, socialized medicine, etc.). It can thus be argued that such societies lack the material resources to free women from the patriarchal mode of sex/affective production based in the family domestic economy.

The situation in industrial countries is different. Here the problem has been not so much the lack of material resources to fund public projects benefiting women, although this has been a major problem for some.[6] Rather, a combination of historical and political priorities has led to a failure to focus attention on such projects. Furthermore, in Eastern European countries the possibilities of autonomous women's movements and other social movements have been restricted by the lack of formal democratic rights in totalitarian socialist societies.

The recent shake-up in Eastern European countries is a welcome sign that previously totalitarian socialist societies can reform from within. But the reorganization of these societies has just begun. Thus it is not clear at this point whether their interest in reestablishing some aspects of market economies will lead in the end to capitalism proper or to some type of market socialism.[7]

One issue of key importance with respect to women's liberation is whether these social upheavals will lead to a continuation or a cessation of the state-supported social programs that have benefited women in many of these countries. For example, if we compare the material situation of East German women before autumn 1989 to women in the United States, a much larger and wealthier country, we find some striking ways in which East German women were comparatively better off because of certain socialist programs. This suggests that socialism, though not by itself sufficient to bring about women's liberation, may well be a necessary step for gender equality.

In spite of the success of East German socialism for gender equality, until the 1989 upheavals there was a lack of a visible women's movement or the kind of cultural and psychological empowerment that Western women's movements have offered women. This stemmed from a general weakness in the classical Marxist strategy of dealing with the woman question. I argue that Western feminism's emphasis on the personal as political is a key precept that must be incorporated into an expanded feminist-materialist perspective on women's liberation. Though both classical liberalism (the emphasis on formal legal rights for individuals: the need for choice) and classical Marxism (the need for material social equality for oppressed groups) must be part of a strategy to challenge male domination, even together they are not enough. They need to be supplemented by a socialist-feminist analysis that stresses not only choice and equality but also self-determination as a process goal for those oppressed by patriarchy, capitalism, and other forms of social domination such as racism and ethnicism. Neither liberalism nor Marxism has acknowledged the independent weight of the social organization of sexuality, parenting, and nurturance in the reproduction of systems of social domination. Consequently, the importance of a revolutionary process of redirecting desires toward egalitarian relationships must be an important aspect of a socialist-feminist strategy.

SOCIALISM AS A NECESSARY CONDITION
FOR WOMEN'S LIBERATION

Alternative Models for Underdeveloped Countries

Existing socialist governments in the Soviet Union and the Third World have vastly improved the lot of women, even though the historical contexts in which they took power, as well as failures in theory, have not yet allowed for the full development of social equality for women. But given the intensely patriarchal peasant cultures in which these social revolutions took place, women in these countries could only have attained the degree of social equality they have because of the gender reforms set in place by these revolutions. Among the changes are marriage reforms (including the right to divorce); women's right to property; public access to safe, affordable abortions and birth control; state-supported public childcare; and national health care. Thus previous socialist revolutions, though they have not in themselves been *sufficient* to eliminate patriarchy, were absolutely *necessary* first steps for women's liberation.

The dependence of women's liberation on socialist revolutions can be highlighted by considering the records of alternative social structures. For the so-called underdeveloped countries of the world, there seem to be only three: (1) "modernization," that is, a dependent neocolonial relation with a capitalist state; (2) religious theocratic regimes, such as that in Iran: or (3) some type of socialist economy, often requiring smaller nations (like Cuba) to enter into a client-state relationship with a larger socialist state (such as the Soviet Union). Given these possibilities, the record is clear that the third option has reduced male dominance whereas the other two options tend to worsen conditions for women. Modernization, a euphemism for the development of capitalist imperialist relations of poor producer countries to rich buyer countries, has most often meant the insertion of the cash/use crops dynamic into the sexual division of labor.[8] This has just increased women's workload and economic dependence on men. On the other hand, revolutionary theocracies have compounded male dominance by bringing the power of the state to bear in enforcing patriarchal religious edicts on women.

Capitalism and Feminism

It is not only in the poor countries of the world that socialist development is a necessary condition for the liberation of women. Institutionalized racism and classism in advanced industrial societies and the development of public patriarchy and welfare state racism in the United States make it clear that here, too, the elimination of the social oppression of women requires a radical transition to a democratic socialist society. There is no other way to do away with the feminization and racialization of poverty structurally implicated in advanced capitalist societies. For capitalist societies cannot support full employment, state-guaranteed minimum family incomes, and national health care and childcare without jeopardizing the conditions of reproducing the capitalist system itself, that is, a malleable and needy workforce that will accept nondemocratic work structures. And without full national health care, available and affordable child-care, and a feminist reproductive-rights national policy, including free abortions on demand, an end to sterilization abuse, and effective sex education in the public schools, women and racial minorities will continue disproportionally to constitute an underprivileged underclass of poor. Capitalism will remain resistant to instituting such radical reforms because it structurally requires unemployment, hence reserve armies of labor—historically made up of women and minority men—in order to avoid major cycles of depression and recession. For this reason, status quo forces will continue to perpetuate sexism and racism by supporting a continued racial and sexual division of wage and home labor that allows women and minorities to be used as reserve armies of labor. Thus the classic socialist-feminist principle that capitalism must be challenged in order to promote sisterhood across race, class, and cultural differences remains true: None of us can be free until all of us are free.

CONFLICTING IDEOLOGIES ON THE WOMAN QUESTION

Classical Liberalism and the Choice Paradigm

In spite of the structural inability of a capitalist economy to create gender equality, the classical liberal ideology that arose in the transition to a market society is one important ideological grounding for feminist movements around the world.

Classical liberals like John Locke, Mary Wollstonecraft, Thomas Jefferson, and J. S. Mill[9] rejected the organic worldview typical of feudal societies and patriarchal religions such as Judaism, Christianity, and Islam. The organic world-view holds that the role of individuals in society is analogous to organs in a living organism: They are designed to serve the purpose of the whole and get their value from satisfactorily performing their role. Human individuals are created with natural variations—gender, race, inborn abilities—in order to perform different functions within the community, ensuring its harmonious operation. The organic world views of Plato and Aristotle and theologies based on such philosophies justified slavery, male dominance, human dominance over animals, and social hierarchies as part of the purposes of Nature and God.[10]

In contrast to the organic worldview, classical liberal ideology developed a theory of the relationship between individuals and community on the one hand and the state on the other that emphasized the right for individuals to make their own choices with respect to life goals: jobs, marriages, citizenship. Individuals' ability to use reason to make their own decisions and the possibility of self-determination (freedom) for personal development were the ultimate values. Thus community practices and state laws should protect individual rights to freedom and self-development.

Classical liberal feminists analyzed the woman question using the ideology of individual rights and advocating the value of freedom and self-development.[11] From this perspective, which we can label the choice paradigm,[12] patriarchal arrangements in the family, the state, and society that assumed women should be legally and economically dependent on fathers and husbands were wrong. These arrangements interfered with women's natural rights to make their own contracts, choose marriages, divorce, work for wages and control their own income, and own property independently of their husbands and male kin.

According to classical liberal feminists, the legal and economic inequalities of women are due both to traditional attitudes based in patriarchal religions and to remnants of feudal economic arrangements. Therefore, the liberal strategy for gender equalization involves education to challenge traditional patriarchal attitudes, at the same time initiating legal reforms to make women equal citizens under the law. Classical liberal feminism, exemplified in the first-wave women's movements in the United States and Great Britain in the nineteenth and early twentieth centuries, argued that these reforms, in combination with a capitalist economy, would guarantee that a gender egalitarian culture could gradually supplant old patriarchal attitudes.

Utopian Versus Scientific Socialism

Socialist movements in Britain, France, and the United States in the early nineteenth century challenged the classical liberal feminists' choice paradigm and consequent strategy for achieving gender equality. These movements, based on the ideas of Robert Owen and Comte de Saint-Simon, criticized not only patriarchal attitudes based on the organic worldview but also the capitalist system. According to these socialists, simple reform in marriage law is not sufficient to liberate women, for the whole institution of marriage is based on the concept of private property. As long as the economy and the family is based on the concept of private property, men will continue to believe that they can own women and both men and women will consider children their private property to do with as they wish. Thus the only way to liberate women is to reform the whole system in which some own private property, whether in goods or in people, that allows them to exploit others. There should be communal ownership of productive property (socialism), love unions should be entered into and dissolved at will, and children should be a collective rather than an individual responsibility of biological parents.[13]

The Owenist emphasis on the whole system of private property and how it reinforces the patriarchal nuclear family suggests the embryo of what Marxist theory would later develop into the equality paradigm of women's liberation: It is not until the whole system of economic arrangements of society is reorganized so as to allow women material social equality with men that women will be fully liberated. But before we develop the implications of the equality paradigm for socialist strategies on the woman question, we must consider the split within socialist ranks that hindered the development of theory and practice on this issue.

Owenist ideas had spawned a number of socialist experiments, ranging from Owen's attempt at cooperative management of his factories by workers to workers' cooperatives and communal living. Unfortunately, the producer cooperative movement in Britain was smashed when the workers' major strikes failed in 1833–1834, and the communes disintegrated because of bad management. The failure of the practice of Saint-Simonism and Owenism led Marx and Engels to label these movements "utopian socialisms" and to distinguish their own view as "scientific socialism." Engels argued that the attempt to establish workers' cooperatives and communal living arrangements as a way to reform capitalism from within was impractical.[14] Although his criticism may have been accurate, the resulting split in the socialist movements was unfortunate from a feminist perspective.

With respect to the woman question, Marx, Engels, and the socialist parties based on their theories espoused the view that any egalitarian reorganization of marriage and the family could only take place *after* a socialist revolution had occurred. They therefore dismissed socialist feminists who placed equal priority on the fight for gender equality and for socialism as either "utopian" or else "bourgeois feminists." Ironically, then, the so-called scientific socialists ended up refusing to consider coalition strategies with feminist groups, which might have expanded the socialist movement and helped develop a more sophisticated socialist-feminist theory of women's liberation.[15] For example, Marx went so far as to recommend excluding the U.S. section from the First International on the grounds that their organizers preferred the woman question over the labor question, although the U.S. members insisted that they ranked them equally. Engels attacked the political demand of feminists for equal pay for equal work on the grounds that it, too, was utopian, even though *The Communist Manifesto* had argued that the proletarianization of women and children was an inevitable development of capitalism.[16] And Lenin criticized socialist Klara Zetkin for trying to organize German women around the "minor" feminist issues of marriage and sexuality that should be left until after the socialist revolution.

The classic Marxist theory on the woman question is found in Engels's *Origin of the Family, Private Property and the State*.[17] From this brilliant, promising, but ultimately flawed work come both the Marxist equality paradigm for women's liberation and a theory of origins of male dominance. Because my theory of sex/affective production has points both of agreement and disagreement with Engels's approach, it is helpful to consider his argument in some detail.

Marxist Theory of the Origins of Male Dominance

Engels sketches a history of the human family as it transformed from matriarchal to patriarchal organization. Like classical liberalism, Marxism refuses to accept the conservative organic worldview that biological differences between men and women make male domination inevitable, natural, and right. Unlike liberalists, however, Engels argues that it is not merely patriarchal attitudes or ideology but the structural economic arrangements of the human family that determine whether women are equal or subordinate to men. Engels posits that early human societies were organized by a natural sexual division of labor based on women's childbearing and child-rearing functions. But this division did not automatically create male dominance. Rather, early societies were matriarchal in terms of the matrilineal kinship structures and inheritance practices and involved communal ownership rather than class divisions based on private property.

Even though Engels somewhat confusingly labels them "matriarchal," early societies were more or less gender egalitarian because property was communally owned by the gens, or tribe, and distributed according to need. It was only when a new economic development threatened the matrilineal family that male dominance developed: The domestication of animals and the creation of herding allowed for a surplus in the productive sphere controlled by men. This gave them an interest in changing inheritance rights from matrilineal to patrilineal, in order better to control their wealth by passing it on to their sons rather than to their sister's children. At the same time herding created a use for extra labor to generate more wealth, so slaves began to be taken in battles with other tribes. Thus class society, and private property in both persons and goods, arose at the same time as the patriarchal family. Women were owned and exchanged by men in marriage,[18] a situation characterized by a double standard of monogamy: Prostitution allowed a man to satisfy his sexual lusts outside of marriage, but a woman had to remain monogamous in order to guarantee that her offspring were from her husband's seed, avoiding possible disputes about inheritance rights.

Having posited that patriarchal marriage is the economic base for the oppression of women, one that persists through different class-divided modes of economic production (slavery, feudalism, capitalism), Engels views the development of industrial capitalism as the beginning of the process of women's liberation. Because capitalists seek the cheapest wage labor in order to increase their profits, women will inevitably be drawn into wage labor, at first as part-time, temporary workers (as a reserve army of labor) and finally full time as an underpaid group competing with male workers. Although this process will compound the misery of the working class, it will also destroy the patriarchal family, as women will have some base for economic independence from men.

The classical Marxist strategy for liberation of women has three components: (1) socialize the means of production (socialism); (2) get women into production (wage labor); and (3) get service production out of the household. After the means of production are socialized by a revolution, goods production is removed from the household. But service production, or housework, child care, and other domestic labor for consumption of goods,[19] tends to remain in the household after goods production exits. This creates a contradiction for the wife, for "if she carries out her duties in the private service of her family, she remains excluded from social production and unable to earn; and if she wants to take part in public production and earn independently, she cannot carry out her family duties."[20] The solution to this is to bring women into public industry, and because no one will be left to perform privatized services in the household, this will require the socialization of service production. Housework and child care will become public services offered by the state rather than private services offered by wives to husbands and children. With no economic motive to sustain sexism, it will wither away, and women will come to be paid the same wages for their work as men.

Engels's origins theory and the equality paradigm for women's liberation have many important insights. His emphasis on the economic motives for the perseverance of the patriarchal family and its connection to class society is an important corrective to the shallowness of the liberal choice paradigm's target (traditional attitudes) and its inadequate palliative (legal reform to guarantee women's rights). Furthermore, his origins theory has the merit of suggesting that patriarchy is social and historical, thus changeable, rather than biological and inevitable.

Nonetheless, Engels's theories of origins need to be expanded and corrected in the light of subsequent research.[21] His too facile assumption that male dominance is based in the patriarchal family, which will "wither away" in socialism, ignores other sites and economic motives for the persistence of patriarchy that are quite compatible with public ownership of production. For example, I and other writers have argued that advanced capitalism has shifted the site of male control of women from family patriarchy to the state and the sexual division of wage labor, a type of system we call "public patriarchy." Marilyn Young has used the same term to refer to both advanced capitalist and state socialist societies. Thus, even though male control of women in the family may weaken, male control could persevere through male bonding in the state political sphere and in public production.[22]

To say that patriarchal power is centered in the state and public spheres does not imply that the family has no role in public patriarchies. Public patriarchies often emphasize the importance of the family in society. Indeed, most state socialist societies have developed an ideology of the family that makes it central to the socialist state. This has tended to create a sex/affective culture that is still sexist and heterosexist. For in a context where there is a continued second-shift problem for wives and mothers because of the persistence of privatized domestic labor, privileging the heterosexual nuclear family directs sex/affective energy to a masculinity that takes male privilege for granted and a femininity that eroticizes a nonreciprocal service of others.[23] Wilhelm Reich, radical Marxist and Freudian therapist, critiqued the Russian Revolution because the Communist Party lacked a theory of how sexual repression worked to perpetuate classism and authoritarian regimes.[24] Many feminist analyses of existing state socialist societies point out that sexually repressive cultures persist in these countries. Discussing violence against women and outlawed homosexuality is taboo, and the Communist Party leadership has no theory of the connection between sexual liberation and human liberation.

How do we explain the persistence of patriarchy in socialist revolutions? Put another way, how do we explain the apparent tendency of socialist revolutions to renege on their initial promise of feminist reforms? Various writers have argued that socialist revolutions have involved an initial period of challenging the patri- archal family followed by periods of reaction when state policy seeks to strengthen the patriarchal family.[25] Explanations for this pattern include psycho- analytic theories of gendered sexual conflicts,[26] inability due to material scarcity,[27] failures of Marxist theories and strategies for challenging patriarchy,[28] political alliances with patriarchs,[29] economic benefits to the socialist state of con- tinuing the unequal sexual division of labor,[30] and economic benefits to men for continuing patriarchal arrangements in socialism.[31] Let us explore the plausibility of these theories by examining some particular socialist revolutions to see what factors may have been involved in their social policies on the woman question.

REVOLUTIONS IN PEASANT CULTURES AND THE WOMAN QUESTION

The Russian Revolution, as the first socialist revolution, has exercised undue influence on subsequent revolutionary strategy, not merely through the force of its example but also through the Russian Communist Party's control of the Third International's (Comintern's) official theories and policies on socialist revolu- tion. There are various explanations why the initial promising reforms of the Soviet Union on the woman question in the 1920s were overturned or rolled back in a reactionary manner in the 1930s.

Wendy Goldman's analysis of the 1920s and 1930s in the Soviet Union gives material scarcity and the need for political accommodation with entrenched patriarchal interests as the reason for the shift.[32] She points out that the 1918 Family Law was the most progressive in the world at the time. It created legal equality for women, eliminated the religious base for marriage, allowed divorce at will for either party, awarded alimony to either partner based on need rather than gender, did away with the concept of common family property in favor of reserving property to each of the partners, and eliminated the concept of illegiti- macy. Because the Soviet Union was still a primarily agricultural society where the predominant mode of production was production for use, adoption was out- lawed for fear that children would be taken in simply for their economic benefit to peasants. The state, it was felt, should exercise the collective responsibility for children by taking care of orphans.

The Land Code of 1922 was an attempt to give women property rights they had not previously had. Unfortunately, it was a compromise between the previous patriarchal peasant law and a complete guarantee of women's legal equality to men with respect to property and divorce rights. Though it allowed women a right to a share of the household property and a right to leave the household on divorce, it left in place the communal property aspects of the household for those who stayed. Thus husbands couldn't withdraw money legally owed to divorced wives from the communal *dvor* (property-income pool). Consequently, divorced peasant wives were not paid alimony, putting them at a severe disadvantage to men.

The Family Code of 1922 was undermined by the problem of *besprizormiki*, or homeless children. Material scarcity made it impossible for the state to care for these orphans of war in an adequate fashion, and funds put out for their care drained the state coffers for other social services (childcare centers, etc.) relevant to socializing women's home service production. A compromise was reached by the revised Family Code of 1926, which reestablished adoption rights as an incentive to get peasants to adopt homeless children, thus taking them off the hands of the impoverished state. In the process, however, the state reneged on an important feminist demand: that responsibility for child-rearing be collectivized. Instead, it reaffirmed the importance of unpaid work in the family to bring up children at minimal social cost. The right of housewives to a claim on their husband's wage, given in the second code, weakened the concept of no common family property of the first family code.

Unfortunately, the alimony and child support provisions of the family code turned out to be unenforceable, as divorced men simply couldn't pay alimony when they were often unemployed, underemployed, or supporting another family. Because women's wages were only 65 percent of those of men, divorce often left women destitute. No wonder that peasant women were opposed to easy divorce on the grounds that women were the ones economically harmed thereby. Feminist leader Alexandra Kollontai's advocacy of free-love unions was certainly not shared by the masses of peasant women![33] In any case, the influence that leftist feminists *could* have had on the masses or state policy disappeared in 1930 when Stalin abolished the Zhenotel, the Women's Department of the Soviet state that had pioneered in fashioning the family codes and in advocating for women.

Sheila Rowbotham documents the resistance of patriarchal peasant culture to the Bolsheviks' attempts to institutionalize civil rights for women and material social equality.[34] As in China, initial feminist reforms on the part of the Communist Party and subsequent attempts by women to claim these rights were met by massive patriarchal backlash. Women who refused arranged marriages, bobbed their hair as a symbolic gesture, or insisted on their right to divorce were often murdered by their husbands, fathers, or brothers. Thus it is a mistake to place the blame for takebacks of initial gains for women solely on material scarcity or on theoretical failures of the Communist Party leadership without noting the political problem of the fierce resistance of the peasant masses to feminist ideas.

In any case, Stalin's decision to forcibly collectivize agriculture in the late 1920s in Russia, though opposed, was eventually successful and did abolish the patriarchal household as the material base of women's oppression. Under Stalin's leadership in the 1930s, however, many of the legal gains for women's civil and sexual rights were reversed. Abortion, which had been legalized in the 1920s, was again made illegal, as Stalinism valorized motherhood as a way to increase the birthrate endangered by World War I and the civil war. Homosexuality was also outlawed, and divorce was made difficult to obtain. The goal of this legislation was to strengthen the nuclear family, which was seen as central to the efficient reproduction of the future labor force. This in turn was to ensure the existence of an important productive force for the building of socialism.

Articles by Christina Gilmartin and Marilyn Young[35] argue that in the Soviet Union and China the consolidated socialist state becomes a public patriarchy for both economic and political reasons. In both, the initial feminist phases of revolution undermine the patriarchal family by instituting legal reforms that provide women with civil, property, and reproductive rights. Thereafter, however, women act as a reserve army of labor, their choices and their material equality with men eroded by patriarchal backlash by party cadres and peasant masses and by party ideological shifts. This reversion comes not merely to pacify patriarchal political allies,[36] but also as part of defining the economic interests of the socialist state in the use of women's reproductive capacity and a reorganization of their role in the family household so as to more cheaply and efficiently aid in socialist accumulation.[37]

But are there real economic advantages, as opposed to patriarchal rationalizations, for socialist states to restrict women's control over their productive and reproductive possibilities? Batya Weinbaum argues that patriarchy has persisted in the transition to a socialist economy because the socialist state has an interest in maintaining an unequal sexual division of labor in order to further socialist accumulation. Weinbaum claims that the socialist state in China had an interest in continuing the reorganization of the household sphere started by capitalism[38] but for different reasons. We can generalize her theory as follows: Although capitalists want only individual profit, the managers of socialist states want socialist accumulation in the interest of the whole community. Unfortunately, for agricultural economies that hope to industrialize rapidly, the cheapest and fastest way to achieve this goal is to foster an unequal sexual division of labor that perpetuates patriarchal relations between men and women.

Weinbaum argues that as socialism developed in China, women were pushed *out* of the industrial sector into which capitalists had initially drawn them, and *into* the service sectors (health, education, culture, neighborhood collective factories).[39] Workers in these sectors were underpaid compared to industrial workers. Further, urban collectives, which were 80 to 90 percent women, were not financed by state investment and thus saved the state money.

State policy that perpetuated an unequal sexual division of wage labor and encouraged women's privatized service in the household was motivated by several considerations. First, the state wanted as fast a rate as possible of capital development. So, for example, between 1953 and 1957 the state investment of capital in heavy industry was 86.2 percent and in consumer goods only 9.3 percent. This led to demands for higher wages, inflation in consumer goods prices, and black markets in such goods.

The rise of illegal nonstate production of consumer goods created a crisis for state production, solved by the organization of legal housewives' collectives outside the state sector, as well as increased production for use of consumer goods in the homes.[40] This allowed the state to continue its primary investment in heavy industry to speed socialist accumulation yet meet the need for consumer goods and let households acquire supplemental incomes. Unfortunately, it also solidified an unequal sexual division of labor and thus perpetuated patriarchy.[41]

Generalizing from Weinbaum's case study of China, feminists can challenge the classical Marxist argument that women's status will improve as growing productivity raises the economic level in underdeveloped socialist countries. Rather, as one of the ways to increase productivity and speed socialist accumulation depends on the reproduction of women's inequality, socialist revolutions in underdeveloped countries are faced with a trade-off: Either speed socialist accumulation at the expense of continuing short-run women's material inequality or choose a slower route to socialist accumulation in order to provide conditions for material equality for women sooner. Thus, to take an example, arguments defending the absence of sufficient childcare facilities in Cuba, on the grounds that material scarcity does not allow the state to fully socialize home service production, ignore the way socialist accumulation in underdeveloped countries benefits from having women not fully incorporated into production.[42]

If our generalization of Weinbaum's views about the economic advantages for Chinese socialist accumulation of an unequal sexual division of labor and household income pooling is accepted, it provides feminists with an important reason to challenge the automatic connection between rapid economic development and feminist goals. In a transition to socialism, the *political process* of comparing costs and benefits of different economic strategies of development must become a central arena for feminist input. In this process, the values of gender justice must be weighed against a facile utilitarian argument that would favor faster economic development, ostensibly in the common interest of all, over the material and social equality of women to men.

From a feminist point of view, there are three general problems that have been involved with the political process in existing socialist revolutions. First, because socialist revolutions have occurred in agricultural rather than industrial economies, Engels's strategy for women's liberation—getting women into public industry and socializing domestic labor—is inappropriate in many contexts. For example, Sonya Kruks and Ben Wisner note that in Mozambique most peasant families are supported by the woman's production for use, whereas the men do occasional wage labor or produce cash crops that supplement the family income. Nonetheless, Engels's classical theory of women's liberation is mechanically applied by the Organizacão da Mulher Moçambicana (Mozambican Women's Organization, or OMM), the women's branch of the Mozambique Liberation Front (FRELIMO). According to a 1984 conference document, 58 percent of women are not "economically active" (read: are not in wage labor or producing cash crops), and the OMM must find ways to get more women into industry! Not only is women's productive work downgraded by this analysis, but strategies to include more women in producer cooperatives are hampered by a lack of a contextualized economic analysis of what would empower women in work.[43]

A second problem of politics in existing socialisms is the use of the Leninist "vanguard party" model as a way of organizing socialist struggles.[44] Marxist-Leninist parties, particularly those that have had to engage in guerrilla struggles for years before coming to power, have adopted a democratic centralist model of political process. Mass organizations for particular interests, such as women's, youth, and trade union organizations, have been subsumed to the vanguard party's leadership. Independent organizations claiming to represent particular interests have been repressed, as they are said to lead to "factionalism" and are adverse to the common interest of socialist struggle against the reactionary forces of national and international capitalism.

Though a vanguard party organization may be a necessity in protracted wars for national liberation, its continued use after the seizure of state power is problematic. As recent popular protests in state socialist countries have shown (Solidarity in Poland, student demands for democratic rights in China), a more pluralist democratic political structure is required to ensure that entrenched party elites do not preempt power. This is particularly true for women's interests, for, as we have seen, patriarchal backlash and economic shortcuts to speedy industrialization can impede a gender egalitarian socialist process that defies male privilege and brings about women's material equality with men. Thus women require autonomous political organizations to struggle for their interests, and these must have more autonomy than has typically been the case in the relation between Marxist-Leninist vanguard parties and mass organizations for women.[45] Racism, ethnicism, and the oppression of national minorities might also be alleviated by ensuring the rights of racial and ethnic groups to organize autonomous political organizations to press for their own interests.[46]

The final problem with existing socialist revolutions' political processes has to do with the excessively rationalist approach taken by socialist leaderships that adhere to the classical Enlightenment worldview, a view also held by Marxists. The assumption that social classes and privileged groups generally act to promote their own rational self-interests, unsupplemented by any political theory of the human unconscious and the way that its workings may impede movements for social change, does not help us understand either the success of fascism in Germany and Italy or the force of patriarchal backlash against advances by women.

To better analyze the persistence of patriarchy in socialist revolutions we should adapt Freudianism, expunging its conservative and ahistorical elements to understand how sexual repression and the patriarchal coding of sexual desire interfere with the egalitarian aims of socialist movements. Reich sketched an expanded Marxist theory of social domination incorporating a Freudian perspective.[47] His view was that sexual repression in patriarchal family upbringings created children who unconsciously desired to be dominated by a patriarchal authoritarian leader. He was concerned that the Bolshevik Party after the Russian Revolution had no adequate theory or strategy to radicalize sexual mores. This was necessary not only to free women from the patriarchal family but also to challenge what he called "sex negative" culture, which kept desires for domination alive and undermined the achievement of democratic workers' control of economic and political decisions. In *Blood at the Root*, I agree with this aspect of Reich's analysis and argue that patriarchal modes of sex/affective production eroticize desires for domination and submission that impede the feminist goal of reciprocal exchanges of sex/affective energy, whether this be in sexual and love relationships, friendships, work relationships, or political structures.[48]

Weinbaum develops a Freudian-Marxist theory that supplements Reich's perspectives and explains the initial feminist advances and subsequent patriarchal reactionary periods in socialist revolutions.[49] She argues that resistance to the father figures of the bourgeois and feudal political leadership fuels the unconscious motivations of the revolutionary cadres. Thus in the first revolutionary phase, radical men make alliances with radical women in the symbolic role of "brothers" and "sisters" challenging the patriarchal power of the "fathers." Once the revolution is successful, however, and radical men gain power as leaders, they then want to achieve the symbolic role of fathers and to relegate their women comrades to mere "wife" status. That is, they see it as in their interests as men to institute a husband patriarchy after having successfully challenged father patriarchy. Whether or not we accept Weinbaum's general theory, we still need a theory of sex/affective production to explain the insistence of the pattern of initial advance and subsequent retrenchment in socialist revolutions in very different contexts.

One important aspect of sex/affective production in advanced industrial societies, neglected by both Reich's and Weinbaum's theories of unconscious desire, is the existence of unconscious gender identities and sexual desires that undercut patriarchal desires. As I argue in *Blood at the Root*, capitalist public patriarchies create a set of contradictory desires, one aspect of which eroticizes equal sexual and love relationships and the other of which eroticizes patriarchal domination and submission. Presumably, a similar process is at work in industrial state socialisms where egalitarian and patriarchal aspects of economic, political, and sex/affective processes conflict with one another.

What this demonstrates is that women's liberation has a social base from which to develop in both capitalist and socialist countries. To see why feminists in industrial capitalist countries ought to put socialism on our agenda, we need to take a brief look at the situation of women in East Germany. This will make clear both the advances socialism has brought to women and the need for further consciousness-raising there of the sort advocated by current Western feminist movements.

GENDER EQUALITY IN INDUSTRIAL COUNTRIES:
THE UNITED STATES VERSUS EAST GERMANY

Women in East Germany have been in a more powerful situation vis-à-vis men than they have in Russia, China, or the other industrialized Eastern European socialist countries. They have also been better off than U.S. women with respect to many aspects of their lives, notably their political representation, services that partially socialize domestic labor (public childcare, national health care), and measures that reduce the conflict between wage work and mothering (maternity grants and leave). On the other hand, there has been a taboo on public discussion of such topics as rape and domestic violence against women, male sharing of housework, and issues of sexual autonomy, most notably homosexuality. What accounts for this mixture of empowerment and repression?

Barbara Einhorn argues that one reason there have been more political and economic structures supporting women's social and material equality in Germany than in other state socialist countries is that the East German Democratic Women's Federation, the DFD, existed as an independent group prior to the socialist transformation of 1949 and maintained relative autonomy from the East German Communist Party.[50] Equal pay for equal work was won in 1946.

Further evidence of the power of feminism in East Germany is that women there escaped the cutbacks in social services and reproductive rights of other Eastern European countries. Though Soviet strictures on East German development, involving World War II reparations, forced a concentration on heavy industry over light industry and consumer goods, this direction was never used, as it was in other Eastern European countries, as a rationale to cut back on childcare facilities and on women's wage work.[51]

In 1950 the strong Act for the Protection of Mother and Child and the Rights of Women was passed, which set up state responsibility for public childcare centers, mandated generous one-year paid maternity leaves, revised marriage and family law, and initiated measures to gain women access to male-dominated occupations.

Abortion rights were never restricted to increase the birthrate, as happened in other Eastern European countries. In fact, the abortion rights law, passed belatedly in 1972, is the only state socialist law of its kind that incorporates the liberal choice paradigm into its position, acknowledging that individual women should have the right to make their own decisions on reproduction.

East German women have had much stronger political representation than women in any of the capitalist countries and more than other state socialist societies. In the Volkskammer, the national congress, 161 of 500 seats were held by women. (Compare the United States, with only 5 percent female representation in the House of Representatives and 2 percent in the Senate!) In general, many more women in the GDR have been in public political life than have women in the Western industrial states. For example, 25 percent of local mayors and 47 percent of the members of local arbitration commissions were women; county, district, and borough representation averaged 40 percent. In spite of such good showing in most political arenas, however, women were still only 35 percent of the SED (the Socialist Unity Party, East Germany's Communist Party), made up just 13 percent of its Central Committee, and had no members in the Politburo.[52]

Women have had much more economic independence vis-à-vis men than their industrial capitalist counterparts. This is in part because 80 percent were in wage labor, facilitated by the nearly universal childcare available. Between 80 and 90 percent of children were in infant school daycare, and 84 percent of six- to ten-year-olds were in after-school programs. East German women have also made greater inroads into former male-dominated occupations. In 1977–1979 women were 45 percent of all judges, 35 percent of lawyers, and, in 1983, 57 percent of dentists and 52 percent of doctors. Compare this to the United States, where in 1987 women were 8 percent of lawyers, 6 percent of dentists, and 17 percent of doctors; to the UK, where women were 4 percent of lawyers and 16 percent of doctors; and to West Germany, where women were 15 percent of judges and 14 percent of lawyers. From a feminist perspective East Germany has clearly been doing something better.

The downside of these encouraging statistics is that there has been no effort to challenge gender stereotypes in the universal daycare programs for children. Certain professional sectors continue to resist gender equalization, particularly those of very high status, such as university teachers and professors (only 7 percent of college lecturers and many fewer professors are women) and those jobs involving authority over other workers. There is also a continued second-shift problem for women, as they do 80 percent of the domestic labor. Indeed, women are estimated to put in a second day for every day worked: forty hours a week of domestic work in addition to a forty-hour wage-work week.

The lack of gender sharing of housework connects to the standard Marxist-Leninist political practice to achieve the equality paradigm, emphasizing the socialization of domestic labor but ignoring the personal aspects of the political struggle for women's liberation. Hence the official party and women's organization did not create a consciousness-raising culture that would politicize the unequal exchange of domestic labor between men and women. As there was no official theory of how unequal sexual and nurturance exchange in marriage and parenting, sexual repression, and the eroticization of domination and submission in sex contribute to male dominance, there has been until lately no theoretical base from which to launch a feminist initiative in these areas.

Einhorn has argued that in recent years feminist literature has begun to play an important consciousness-raising function in East Germany. The writer Christa Wolf has suggested that women in the GDR are in a unique situation to reach a new level of self-expression.[53] Because women have been forced to shoulder multiple responsibilities, they are able both to see the limitations of male-identified career hierarchies and to retain a broader socialist-feminist vision of a future society in which mutual respect, nurturance, and cooperation would replace domination and subordination. The development of the East German women's peace movement is one sign that a new feminist movement there may adopt the Western radical feminist notion that the personal is political and use this insight to supplement the classical liberal choice and the Marxist equality paradigms for women's liberation.

This movement has been given much greater impetus since the recent upheavals that have brought reunification with capitalist West Germany. Although more freedom of expression is now allowed to feminist artists and writers, the lack of state funds and subsidies due to the development of a market economy has forced a cutback in a number of the social programs that working mothers have relied on. Many nursery schools have already closed, and other social programs especially benefiting women, such as maternity leaves, job guarantees, and abortion clinics, have been placed in jeopardy. Even the right to abortion is likely to be severely restricted to bring the East German legal code in line with that of West Germany. East German feminist writer Daniela Dahn argued in a recent trip to the States that this means many working women will be forced into the home and many younger women will not be able to enter the workforce. Thus the movement is faced with having to fight for programs for material equality that they had under socialism but that are being lost in the transition to capitalism.

The new women's movement is also politically naive. Before the recent overthrow of the government, the independent women's movement allied with the Green Party in expectations of congressional representation in return for their support. But of the eight seats the Green Party won in the ensuing free elections, none was given to women. At least now East German women recognize their political power and are determined not to let such betrayal occur again.[54]

CONCLUSION

I have argued that socialism and feminism are necessary conditions for each other, both conceptually and practically. A democratic socialist vision requires full gender equality, and an ideal feminist society requires the elimination of other social domination structures such as classism and racism, as well as the elimination of sexism. Socialist revolutions in nonindustrialized peasant economies have been hampered in theory, material resources, and political practice from achieving full gender equality for women, but they have still created a better situation for women than have nonsocialist countries with comparable economies and material resources. A comparison of the Western capitalist industrial nations such as the United States and the UK with the socialist industrial state of East Germany shows that state socialism has made women better off in political representation, economic independence, and social services than in the former countries. East Germany, however, has lacked the theory and practice of the personal as political pioneered in Western feminism as a way to continue the

230 FREEDOM AND EQUALITY

struggle for women's liberation. I hope I have shown how the theory of sex/affective production . . . is able to supplement both the choice and equality paradigms for women's liberation by adding a personal political paradigm. Only a socialist-feminist theory that incorporates choice, equality, and personal/political paradigms into its practice can hope to be successful in the struggle for a socialist-feminist revolution. . . .

NOTES

1. It is possible to define gender egalitarianism in a way that does not imply a classless or nonhierarchical society. For example, one could define it as the situation where women of any economic class, race, ethnic, or other social grouping have the same material opportunities and benefits as the men of that group. By this definition, striving for feminism is not creating a sisterhood to challenge social privilege between women. Such a characterization of feminism, though consistent, is not likely to allow for the coalitions across class, race, and other social boundaries necessary to achieve gender egalitarianism in either sense. Thus I shall assume that a viable feminist politics requires a gender egalitarianism that implies the elimination of other social dominations as well.

2. Such a spelling out of the concept of socialism implies that none of the existing state socialist societies has completely attained the socialist ideal, as none has completely abolished gender, class, and ethnic or racial inequalities. Marxist-Leninist theory of the transition to a classless society acknowledged that full social equality was a process that would not automatically occur after the takeover of state power by the proletariat and the public ownership of production.

In *State and Revolution* Lenin posits three stages of postcapitalist development: socialist revolution, state socialism, and communism. Only in the last stage is it possible to erase classes and other social inequalities. In the second stage there will still be classes because people will be paid by the standard "from each according to their ability, to each according to their work." Only after everyone has been resocialized to think cooperatively and not individualistically can communism develop, which will allow pay by the standard "from each according to their ability, to each according to their need."

The development of the Stalinist theory of "socialism in one country" as a stage to world socialist revolution has meant that existing state socialist societies following Marxist-Leninism think of themselves as in the second phase of state socialism, not having achieved the final utopian stage of communism. For them, thus, communism and not socialism is the ideal model of society. Because Western ideology treats all state socialist societies that espouse Marxist-Leninism as communist, it would be misleading to use the terminology of socialism and communism in this theoretical way. Thus I have chosen to develop a concept of democratic socialism as the model of an ideal society, and I am using the concept of socialism in a different manner than it is used in Marxist-Leninist thought.

3. In my view, social and economic democracy will eventually engender the sort of resocialization that Marx, Engels, and Lenin expected could yield a transition from an individualistic "equal pay for equal work" standard (from each according to their ability, to each according to their work/merit) to a communitarian standard (from each according to their ability, to each according to their need). But, as I see it, the breakdown of the social division of labor that dis-

tinguishes between mental and manual work, as well as the elimination of the sexual division of wage labor, will not occur automatically but will require explicit antiexpert and feminist empowerment strategies. I discuss these problems further in chapter 10 of *Sexual Democracy*.

4. The question whether there can be an international feminism that transcends national historical political cultures is an extremely difficult one. I would argue that we are saved from the specter of an unsolvable relativism about what would constitute the common goals of such a feminism by the development of international capitalism, which, through its spread of markets even to collectivist societies, has advanced the notion of individual rights. At the same time, the conflict between the movement of international capital and national interests of self-determination has raised the question of social equality with respect to the exercise of these rights. Thus, indirectly, two of the underlying values of feminism, the right of individual choice and of gender material equality, are increasingly being mandated as values that all national cultures must struggle for on the international level.

5. "Productive forces" is a concept that refers to available resources, including level of technology, know-how, and ability to exchange products on the international market to obtain needed goods.

6. For example, unlike West Germany, for twenty years East Germany had to pay reparations to the Soviet Union for World War II. Thus much of the productive resources of East Germany were exported and were not available to build up its own economy.

7. Just as there are many different types of capitalist society—from a complete laissez-faire, or unrestricted, market economy to welfare state or corporate capitalist economies such as those of Japan and Sweden—so there are different forms of socialism. Cf. Lane Kenworthy, "What Kind of Economic System? A Leftist's Guide," *Socialist Review* 20, no. 2 (April–June 1990): 102–24. Three models of socialism are a centrally planned, command economy (e.g., the USSR), a market socialist economy (e.g., Yugoslavia), and a council socialist economy (e.g., the anarchist collectives in Spain before the Spanish Civil War). For more on these models, see Michael Albert and Robin Hahnel, *Socialism Today and Tomorrow* (Boston: South End Press, 1981).

8. In some instances, where women have been those initially drawn into wage labor, as in the silk industry in China in the early twentieth century and currently in the textile and electronics industry in much of capitalist Asia, women have benefited as Engels predicted. Their wage labor has made them less dependent on male relatives and more able to resist arranged marriages and other patriarchal decisions. Even where some advantage is achieved by women in wage labor, however, great costs often ensue. For example, occupational hazards ruin their eyesight or health, or simply working (being a "loose" factory girl) ruins their reputation, making them unable to marry and forcing them to turn to prostitution or, ultimately, as un- or underemployed spinsters, dependence again on the earning power of a male relative (Barbara Ehrenreich and Annette Fuentes, "Life on the Global Assembly Line," in *Feminist Frameworks*, ed. Alison Jaggar and Paula Rothenberg [New York: Harper, 1984], pp. 279–91). The limited advantages gained by Third World women brought into wage labor obscure the fact that women wageworkers are typically young single women. The fate of married peasant women is worse under capitalist development: The common pattern, especially in Africa and Latin America, is for men to be drawn into production of cash crops or wage labor while women are left doing subsistence agriculture to support their children (hence the cash/use crops dynamic).

9. For their views, see John Locke's *Second Treatise on Civil Government*

(Chicago: Gateway Editions, distributed by H. Regnery Co.,1955); Mary Wollstonecraft's *Vindication of the Rights of Women* (Harmondsworth, Eng.; New York: Penguin Books, 1982); Thomas Jefferson's comments on *The Declaration of Independence* and the Virginia *Act for Establishing Religious Freedom, 1786,* and Jefferson's *Letters;* J. S. Mill's *On Liberty* (New York: Norton, 1975); and J. S. Mill and Harriet Taylor's *Subjection of Women* (Greenwich, Conn.: Fawcett Publications, 1971).

10. In chapter 9 of *Sexual Democracy*, on androgyny, I discuss the natural complement theory of gender roles. This view of the natural relations between men and women is grounded in the organic worldview.

11. See Wollstonecraft's *Vindication of the Rights of Women* and Mill and Taylor's *Subjection of Women.*

12. I owe the concepts of the choice and the equality paradigms to Sam Bowles. See his discussion of the need to acknowledge positive aspects of both the classical liberal and Marxist worldviews (Samuel Bowles and Herbert Gintis, *Democracy and Capitalism: Property, Community and the Contradictions of Modern Social Thought* [New York: Basic Books, 1986]).

13. Barbara Taylor, *Eve and the New Jerusalem: Socialism and Feminism in the Nineteenth Century* (New York: Pantheon, 1983).

14. Rather, he argued, the economic contradictions of capitalism had to develop to the point where the system could no longer function, at which point the workers would create a revolution, take over all the capitalists' property, and collectivize all productive property, with the force of the state on their side. Friedrich Engels, "Socialism, Utopian and Scientific," in *The Marx-Engels Reader*, ed. Robert C. Tucker (New York: W. W. Norton, 1978), pp. 683–717.

15. Taylor, *Eve.*

16. Joan B. Landes, "Marxism and the 'Woman Question,'" in *Promissory Notes: Women in the Transition to Socialism*, ed. Sonya Kruks, Rayna Rapp, and Marilyn B. Young (New York: Monthly Review, 1989), pp. 15–28.

17. Friedrich Engels, *The Origin of the Family, Private Property, and the State*, ed. Eleanor Leacock (New York, International Publishers, 1972).

18. Indeed, Engels points out that the Roman word *familia* originally meant a man's possessions in persons, whether they were wives, children, or slaves. Gerda Lerner, in *The Creation of Patriarchy* (New York: Oxford University Press, 1986), puts in a somewhat different but related hypothesis. She argues that women were the first slaves, as they could be more easily subjugated by rape and impregnation to develop kinship connections with their owners, which made them less likely to try to escape. Like Claude Lévi-Strauss, in *The Elementary Structures of Kinship* (Boston: Beacon, 1969), and Claude Meillassoux, in *Maidens, Meal and Money: Capitalism and the Domestic Economy* (New York: Cambridge University Press, 1981), Lerner suggests that women were the first property, traded to solidify kin ties with other tribes.

19. August Bebel, *Women Under Socialism* (New York: Schocken, 1971); Joseph Stalin, *The Woman Question: Selections from the Writings of Karl Marx, Friedrich Engels, V. I. Lenin, Joseph Stalin* (New York: International Publishers, 1951). As Weinbaum points out, Engels variously calls service production "family duties," "household management," "private housekeeping," and "care and education of children" (Batya Weinbaum, "Women in Transition to Socialism: Perspectives on the Chinese Case," *Review of Radical Political Economics* 8, no. 1 (1976): 34–58; cf. Engels, *Origin*, pp. 120–21; 137–39).

20. Engels, *Origin*, p. 121.

21. Though patriarchy is indeed social and historical, it is too simplistic to suppose that economic motives can fully explain the origins of patriarchy, as Jane Flax has made clear ("Do Feminists Need Marxism?" *Quest* 3, no. 1 [1976]: 174–86). Flax notes that Engels never really explains the economic motive for the transition from matriarchal to patriarchal society. The development of a domestic herding economy and the existent sexual division of labor in which men were in control of the social surplus would not explain why men should have desired to alter kinship inheritance practice so as to have their own biological children inherit their property, thus setting up patriarchal families. Economically, accumulation through inheritance could continue just as efficiently by continuing the matrilineal practice of the sister's children inheriting her brother's wealth. Only if one posits a psychological-cum-metaphysical reason, for example, the desire to perpetuate oneself symbolically in one's own biological offspring, does such a shift make sense (cf. Mary O'Brien, *The Politics of Reproduction* [London: Routledge, 1981]).

There were patriarchal aspects of many human cultures (wife capture, rape in war, etc.) prior to economic-class-divided societies. This suggests that for the human species, the organization of sexuality and nurturance occurs in systems that are semiautonomous from those that organize the production of material goods. Control of, and access to, sexuality and nurturance is a source of potential conflict in all human societies, independently of the economic consequences of reproductive sexual practices. Further, it seems likely that Engels was wrong on his stage theory of the evolution of patriarchy from matriarchy. Rather than the former evolving from the latter, it may well be that both patriarchies and matriarchies existed simultaneously, albeit in different tribes, and that patriarchal tribes gradually conquered matriarchal cultures, made the women slaves and wives, and thus ended the gender egalitarianism of these societies (Ann Ferguson, *Blood at the Root: Motherhood, Sexuality and Male Dominance* [London: Pandora/Unwin and Hyman, 1989]; Lerner, *Creation*). In any case, feminist anthropologists have made a good case for the view that relative male and female power in human societies is dependent on a number of factors in the way they organize sexuality, parenting, and social bonding, not merely the type of economic system and kinship inheritance they have (Peggy Reeves Sanday, *Female Power and Male Dominance: On the Origins of Sexual Inequality* [New York: Cambridge University Press, 1981]; Rayna Reiter, *Toward a New Anthropology of Women* [New York: Monthly Review, 1975]).

22. Carol Brown, "Mothers, Fathers and Children: From Private to Public Patriarchy," in *Women and Revolution*, ed. Lydia Sargent (Boston: South End Press, 1981), pp. 239–68; Zillah Eisenstein, *Feminism and Sexual Equality* (New York: Monthly Review,1984); Ferguson, *Blood at the Root*; MarilynYoung, "Chicken Little in China: Women After the Cultural Revolution, in Kruks et al., *Promissory Notes*, pp. 233–50. Gloria Joseph has argued that because male bonding does not occur across race in racist societies like the United States, such socialist-feminist arguments are too simplistic ("The Incompatible Ménage à Trois: Marxism, Feminism and Racism," in Sargent, *Women and Revolution*, pp. 91–108). Although Joseph has a point—race does divide men—it does not divide them absolutely. Both racist tendencies for men to bond only by race and sexist tendencies for men to bond across race coexist. In different specific contexts, one or the other tendency wins out. Theorizing public patriarchy is not meant to assume that all men inevitably bond with each other, regardless of race and class difference. Indeed, male

intra-race and -class bonding can create a problem for leftist attacks on the structures of public patriarchy and on welfare-state racism, as is demonstrated by racism and sexism in SDS, and sexism in SNCC and the Rainbow Coalition (cf. Michelle Wallace, *Black Macho and the Myth of the Super Woman* [New York: Dial/Warner, 1979]; Sara Evans, *Personal Politics* [New York: Random House, 1980]).

23. Jane Flax maintains that the Cuban family code, though it is radical in its elimination of the concept of the head of household, still valorizes the family as the necessary "cell" of socialist society. In this way, it supports compulsory heterosexuality and disparages both heterosexual singles and homosexual liaisons ("A Look at the Cuban Family Code," in Jaggar and Rothenberg, *Feminist Frameworks*, pp. 340–41). On the other hand, it should be said that the Cuban family code is the only legal code in the world that advocates the equal sharing of domestic labor. And though this has not resolved wage-earning women's double-shift problem (cf. Muriel Nazzari, "The 'Woman Question' in Cuba: An Analysis of Material Constraints on Its Resolution," in Kruks et al., *Promissory Notes*, pp. 109–26), it has certainly validated the concept of the personal as political in Cuba, and has allowed women a valuable way to challenge male machismo.

24. Wilhelm Reich, *Mass Psychology of Fascism* (New York: Farrar, Straus and Giroux, 1970).

25. Sheila Rowbotham, *Women, Resistance and Revolution* (New York: Random House, 1972); Hilda Scott, *Does Socialism Liberate Women?* (Boston: Beacon, 1974); Judith Stacey, *Patriarchy and Socialist Revolution in China* (Berkeley: University of California Press, 1983); Elizabeth Croll, *Feminism and Socialism in China* (New York: Schocken, 1978); Albert and Hahnel, *Socialism Today and Tomorrow*; Kruks et al., *Promissory Notes*.

26. Wilhelm Reich, *Mass Psychology of Fascism; The Discovery of the Orgone: The Function of the Orgasm* (New York: Farrar, Straus and Giroux, 1973); *The Sexual Revolution* (New York: Farrar, Straus and Giroux, 1974); Batya Weinbaum, *The Curious Courtship of Women's Liberation and Socialism* (Boston: South End Press, 1978).

27. Wendy Zeva Goldman, "Women, the Family and the New Revolutionary Order in the Soviet Union," in Kruks et al., *Promissory Notes*; Nazzari, "The 'Woman Question' in Cuba"; Sonya Kruks and Ben Wisner, "Ambiguous Transformations: Women, Politics and Production in Mozambique," in Kruks et al., *Promissory Notes*.

28. Taylor, *Eve*; Waters, Delia Davin, "Of Dogma, Dicta and Washing Machines: Women in the People's Republic of China," Kruks and Wisner, "Ambiguous Transformations," Barbara Einhorn, "The Women's Movement in the German Democratic Republic," Martha Lampland, "Biographies of Liberation: Testimonials to Labor in Socialist Hungary," Basu, Zillah Eisenstein, "Reflections on a Politics of Difference," all in Kruks et al., *Promissory Notes*.

29. Christina Gilmartin, "Gender, Politics and Patriarchy in China: The Experiences of Early Women Communists, 1920–27," in Kruks et al., *Promissory Notes*.

30. Scott, *Does Socialism Liberate Women?*; Weinbaum, "Women in Transition."

31. Heidi Hartmann, "The Unhappy Marriage of Marxism and Feminism," in Sargent, *Women and Revolution*; Christine Delphy, *Close to Home: A Materialist Analysis of Women's Oppression* (Amherst: University of Massachusetts Press, 1984); Young, "Chicken Little in China."

32. Goldman, "Women, the Family and the New Revolutionary Order in the Soviet Union."

33. Alexandra Kollontai, *The Autobiography of a Sexually Emancipated Communist Woman* (New York: Schocken, 1975).

34. Rowbotham, *Women, Resistance and Revolution.*

35. In Kruks et al., *Promissory Notes.*

36. Gilmartin argues that the Chinese Communist Party (CCP) initially prioritized feminist demands, such as for women's right to voluntary marriages and divorces, education, and property rights. The party supported independent women's organizations and schools in order to encourage cross-class collaboration between women. In the period 1925–1927, CCP training institutes for women organizers, particularly among the factory silk workers, involved 300,000 members. But the prioritizing of feminist demands was one of the main reasons the coalition with the nationalist Guomintang Party broke down. In the bloodbath by the Guomintang against the Communists on April 12, 1927, women, particularly feminists with bobbed hair, were singled out for particularly horrible sexual violence and murder.

Partly in reaction to these events and to the patriarchal backlash among their own male cadre, on the Long March in 1928 the CCP revised its women's liberation program. It denounced many of the united front feminist programs as bourgeois and counterrevolutionary. In the next twenty years peasant women were encouraged to support the civil war against the Guomintang by traditional women's activities such as sewing uniforms and nursing, but not by challenging the authority of their husbands, as had been the organizing tactic of the 1920s.

Other socialist struggles have had to contend with patriarchal political forces. Israel, which started off with a loose federation of socialist communes or collective farms (kibbutzim), is now a mixed economy with a strong central state. During its long rule, the Labor government, to maintain power, has ceded to the religious Right control over marriage and family law. Now that there is a more right-wing government composed of a coalition of Labor and the Likud, the situation is even more difficult for women. Recently, two different groups of women have conducted prayer services at the Western Wall in Jerusalem. Religious feminists have prayed to assert the right of women to pray in public. Others have prayed to express publicly their opposition to the occupations of the West Bank and Gaza. Both groups have met violent confrontations by right-wing rabbis, and the police have not protected the women from these assaults (personal communication from Batya Weinbaum).

37. Mary Buckley, in "The 'Woman Question' in the Contemporary Soviet Union," in Kruks et al., *Promissory Notes*, details the shifts in the Soviet Communist Party's ideology of the woman question as different male leaders redefine what women's interests are depending on how women's role in production and reproduction is seen to dovetail with other state priorities.

38. Capitalism in Western Europe, the United States, and China sought to develop a market sector of economies that were organized primarily for use by reorganizing women's household production and drawing them into wage labor there (e.g., textile production). It was primarily daughters who went into wage labor, for others in household production for use would lose either individually (fathers losing control of land, sons losing inheritance) or collectively (if the mother went, her organization of children in the putting-out system of labor was lost, and hence that source of income for the household). The conflict between production for use and capitalist production exacerbated conflicts

between women and men, as the female proletariat squeezed out skilled independent male artisans, for example, male weavers (cf. Weinbaum, "Women in Transition").

39. This shift in women's and men's sectors in the economy was not brought about because of a concerted patriarchal motive by men in Communist Party leadership positions to undercut women. Ironically, Weinbaum sees the move of men out of agriculture and into industrial work as in part due to the Communist reforms in marriage and family law to give women rights, such as outlawing arranged marriages and allowing women to own property and to retain it after divorce. The resulting instability in peasant households' abilities to aggregate large, stable holdings from arranged marriage caused men to leave agriculture in order to seek a more secure income from industrial wage labor.

40. Thus, to encourage women to make clothes at home, the production of sewing machines went up by 570 percent between 1952 and 1957, whereas the output of finished goods increased only a fraction (Weinbaum, "Women in Transition," p. 42).

41. Weinbaum argues that the perpetuation of an unequal sexual division of labor in China also occurs in the organization of communes, for women tend to spend more time in household than commune production and to be given fewer work points for the commune work they do. In addition to developing a less-secure relation to wage labor than men, and thus fewer skills (such as learning how to work machinery), women are often organized to do volunteer work for free (e.g., paraprofessional healthcare work). This keeps the wages of women working in this sphere lower than they would otherwise be.

42. Muriel Nazzari, in "The 'Woman Question' in Cuba," makes a complementary point. She argues that the Cuban state's turn from moral to material incentives to increase productivity, coupled with the existing differentials between men's and women's wages, gives women incentives to maximize the family income by no or only part-time wage work. Furthermore, generous maternity leave provisions that make women workers more costly than male workers deter state firms from hiring them. These are two economic reasons why both firms and women workers will support an imbalance in the housework load for men and women, thus undermining the goals of the Cuban family code requiring men and women to share housework equally.

43. Kruks and Wisner, "Ambiguous Transformations." Another example of a mechanistic application of a Marxist base/superstructure model is FRELIMO's critique of the patriarchal polygamous family. FRELIMO argues that the patrilocal polygamous family persists because of "feudal attitudes" that must be combated. But this blinds them to an economic analysis of how polygamy is not just a superstructural feature of the family but an actual relation of production. Thus FRELIMO cannot understand why most women want to continue polygamy, which is for an economic not merely ideological reason: In the current sexual division of labor, polygamy allows wives more help in the subsistence work they are expected to do. Consequently, FRELIMO and OMM are hampered in both their educational and economic strategies for challenging the existing patriarchal structures and finding a way to empower women.

44. V. I. Lenin, *State and Revolution* (New York: International Publishers, 1974).

45. Until the Sandinista (FSLN) electoral defeat in February 1990, Nicaragua had been involved in a socialist process with a democratic pluralism not seen in previous revolutions. Though the Sandinista Party initially conceived of its relation to mass organizations of women and peasants, local block organizations, and trade unions on the classic vanguard model, recent challenges by feminists and other grassroots activists have been

successful in giving the mass organizations more autonomy. For example, while *in* power the Sandinistas maintained a fragile alliance with the patriarchal Catholic Church by refusing to advocate abortion rights for women. But even before the FSLN's electoral defeat, the Associacion de Mujeres Nicaraguenses Luisa Amanda Espinosa (Luisa Amanda Espinosa Association of Nicaraguan Women, or AMNLAE) stepped up efforts to legalize abortion. Furthermore, there are now independent feminist projects such as the Ixchen family planning and abortion centers, the Masaya and Matagalpa all-purpose women's centers, and a Managua AIDS education group of lesbians and gays. These groups, though supportive of the FSLN, are also critical of its practices of machismo and homophobia. Ironically, because the FSLN has lost governmental power and must rebuild and strengthen its mass base, these popular feminist projects now have more influence on the FSLN to correct these practices in order to make a strong coalition with them. Thus there is a wide open window of opportunity for expanding feminism in Nicaragua at this moment, which nonetheless still depends for its ultimate success on the resurgence of the FSLN as a changed and strengthened coalition that can retake governmental power in the next presidential election.

46. Socialist revolutions have had notable success in attacking racism and ethnicism inherited from previous systems of slavery and colonialism. Cuba is a particularly good example of this (cf. Terry Cannon and Johnetta Cole, *Free and Equal: The End of Racial Discrimination in Cuba* [New York: Venceremos Brigade, 1978]). The Cuban Communist Party has revalidated the African roots of Cuban culture. The slogan "We are an Afro-Cuban people" has been backed up by incorporating African music and dance into mainstream education and culture. Because the darkest members of the multiracial Cuban people were also typically the poorest, much racism has been combated by attacking classism through free education, health care, affordable housing, and other welfare-state measures.

Socialist revolutions have been less successful in dealing with national and ethnic questions in situations which involve national minorities who have been forcibly included in the state or ethnic groups practicing fundamentalist religions. For example, the USSR includes the Baltic states of Latvia, Estonia, and Lithuania, incorporated in 1939 by the Hitler-Stalin pact and forcible occupation. Since the recent upheavals, these republics have begun fighting for their independence from the USSR. The Bolshevik Party was primarily based among ethnic Russians. They opposed both national liberation movements within the USSR and independence for ethnic religious sects. In part this was a consequence of the antireligious views of Marxism, but in hindsight it appears also to have been an ethnicist move to give Russians hegemony and to keep the Soviet Union from unraveling at the seams because of racial and ethnic rivalries. Thus the Soviet Communist party has consistently suppressed ethnic minorities such as Jews, Greek Orthodox Christians, and Moslems who have tried to preserve their religious cultures. Though the patriarchal nature of these religions raises serious questions of how to reconcile democracy for ethnic minorities with feminist goals, vanguard party repression of these elements is not the solution. Albert and Hahnel, in *Socialism Today and Tomorrow*, argue that Marxist Leninist theory of socialist revolution must be expanded from its focus merely on economic exploitation to deal with social domination based in racial and ethnic community power, as well as kinship and state power structures.

47. Gilles Deleuze and Felix Guattari, *Anti-Oedipus* (New York: Viking, 1977); Reich, *Mass Psychology of Fascism, The Discovery of the Orgone*, and *The Sexual Revolution*.

48. Ferguson, *Blood at the Root.*
49. Weinbaum, *The Curious Courtship.*
50. Einhorn, "The Women's Movement in the German-Democratic Republic."
51. Scott, *Does Socialism Liberate Women?*
52. Einhorn, "The Women's Movement in the German-Democratic Republic."
53. Christa Wolf, "Berührung: Maxi Wanders 'Guten Morgen, Du Schöne,'" *Neue Deutsche Literatur* 2 (1978): 53–63.
54. This information comes from a student paper by Steven Berrett, who received it from a talk given by Daniela Dahn, April 1990, at Mt. Holyoke College.

PART V.

DEMOCRACY AND COMMUNITY

13

IN WHAT SENSE MUST SOCIALISM BE COMMUNITARIAN?

DAVID MILLER

INTRODUCTION

This paper stands at the confluence of two streams in contemporary political thought. One stream is composed of those critics of liberal political philosophy who are often described collectively as "communitarians."[1] What unites these critics (we shall later want to investigate how deep their collegiality goes) is a belief that contemporary liberalism rests on an impoverished and inadequate view of the human subject. Liberal political thought—as manifested, for instance, in the writings of John Rawis, Robert Nozick, and Ronald Dworkin— claims centrally to do justice to individuality: to specify the conditions under which distinct individuals, each with his own view about how life should be lived, can pursue these visions to the best of their ability. But, the critics claim, liberalism is blind to the social origins of individuality itself. A person comes by his identity through participating in social practices and through his affiliation to collectivities like family and nation. An adequate political philosophy must attend to the conditions under which people can develop the capacity for autonomy that liberals value. This, however, means abandoning familiar preoc- cupations of liberal thought—especially the centrality it gives to individual rights—and looking instead at how social relationships of the desired kind can be created and preserved. It means, in short, looking at communities—their nature and preconditions.[2]

The other stream comprises various attempts to recast the principles of socialism with the aim, broadly speaking, of bringing it more closely into line

---

From *Socialism*, ed. Ellen Frankel Paul, Fred D. Miller Jr., Jeffrey Paul, and Dan Greenberg (Oxford: Basil Blackwell, 1989), pp. 51–73. Reprinted by permission of Cambridge University Press.

with the aspirations of the majority of people (including the majority of workers) in the advanced societies. This means not only discarding outdated policy proposals, such as extensive schemes of nationalization, but at a more fundamental level looking critically at traditional socialist ideals (for instance, the belief that it is intrinsically better for people to enjoy goods and services in common than to enjoy them privately as individuals). We can identify the central ideal of the new socialism as equality of effective choice: people should have the rights, opportunities, and resources that enable them to choose effectively how they are to live their lives. Socialism is not the enemy of freedom, but its best friend; whereas libertarians and liberals claim that their proposals provide people with the greatest equal liberty, only socialist policies can make that liberty effective.[3]

How are these two streams of thought related? In one, we find people attacking liberalism in the name of community: in the other, we find socialists trying to divest themselves of traditional commitments, including communitarian commitments, and to outflank liberals in their devotion to individual freedom. Should the communitarian critique give the new socialists any pause for thought? Are the ideas it advances in any way integral to socialism itself? Or should it be regarded as an essentially conservative response to liberal institutions with which a modernizing socialist should have nothing to do? To answer these questions, we need to look more closely and critically at the often obscure views of the "communitarians." First, though, I shall offer a schematic interpretation of the socialist tradition which is intended to bring the questions above into sharper focus.

I. TWO STRANDS IN THE SOCIALIST CRITIQUE OF CAPITALISM

It hardly needs saying that "socialism," like other terms designating ideologies, resists straightforward definition. It is impossible to provide a set of necessary and sufficient conditions for a political outlook to be socialist. Wittgenstein's strictures about family-resemblance terms like "game" apply with their full force here. We can, however, say uncontroversially that socialism arose as a radical reaction to nineteenth-century capitalism, and it is certainly a necessary condition for an outlook to be socialist that it advocate a major transformation of that order. For the purposes of the present discussion I want to isolate and contrast two strands in the socialist critique of capitalism, which I think on any reckoning would count as fairly central—though this is not to say that every socialist has embraced them both.[4]

The first element in the socialist critique focuses on the distributive inadequacies of capitalism. Capitalism, it is alleged, distributes resources, freedom, and power in a way that is grossly unfair and/or prevents a large section of the population from receiving decent quantities of these benefits. Socialist institutions would allocate such benefits in a far more egalitarian fashion, in order to conform with socialist criteria of justice (which, in the extreme view, would prescribe perfect equality—in less extreme views, those criteria would find a place for limited inequalities based on desert or merit). The most obvious target of this critique is the distribution of wealth and income in capitalist society. As I interpret it here, however, the critique also extends to issues such as the distribution of labor-time (workers sweat while capitalists stand idle), the distribution of power in economic enterprises (capitalists command while workers obey), and the distribution of power in society more generally (capitalists control the state, benefit from the legal system, etc.). If we construe "resources" *very* broadly to include benefits such as these, we can summarize the socialist charge as one of maldistribution of resources: the indictment of capitalism is not that it generates the wrong resources, but that it allocates them in a way that is unfair and inhumane.[5]

The second element in the socialist critique, in contrast, focuses on the quality of life in capitalist society, including the quality of the resources it generates. Included here, we find a number of different charges: for instance, capitalism involves production for profit rather than production for use, and therefore fails to provide people with the goods and services that they really need; it stifles creativity and robs work of its aesthetic content; it promotes the consumption of privately purchased commodities, rather than enjoyment of goods and services in common; it fosters competitive relationships between people rather than relations of cooperation and fraternity; it renders people's interactions instrumental and formal, rather than encouraging the spontaneous meeting of human hearts (and so forth). These claims, made singly or in combination, add up to the thesis that capitalism does not and cannot provide the good life for man, and that what must be brought about is not a mere reshuffling of resources, however radical, but a qualitative change in human relationships and motivations.

These two components of the socialist critique are not, of course, mutually exclusive, and can indeed be employed in tandem to good effect. In Marx, for instance, the first element is represented by the idea of exploitation—the claim that, under capitalism, the surplus value created by the labor of workers is systematically expropriated by capitalists—and the second is represented by the idea of alienation—the claim that work under the conditions of capitalism fails to realize man's "species-being" (i.e., his nature as a creative and communally oriented being). Nevertheless, it is in most cases possible to disentangle the two elements, and doing so may throw some light on the revisionary socialist project mentioned at the beginning of the paper. For that project can be interpreted as one of pursuing the distributive critique to the exclusion of what I have identified as the "quality of life" critique. Socialism, on this view, is entirely a matter of the fair distribution of resources, taking "resources" in the broad sense as above. It is not concerned with what people may do with the resources they are allocated, with what motivates them, or how they are related to one another—except insofar as these matters have repercussions for the allocation of resources itself.

It is not difficult to understand the pressures that push contemporary socialists in this direction. First of all, the distributive critique can be reconciled with major features of modern industrial societies far more readily than the "quality of life" critique. Consider two of these features: the market economy and the legal system. There is prima facie no incompatibility between the distributive critique and economic markets as such; that is, it seems a feasible project to reallocate resources in such a way that markets produce outcomes that are acceptable on grounds of distributive justice. How this could be done would depend on the criterion of distributive justice employed, but I am thinking generally of schemes such as equalization of capital holdings, the conversion of enterprises into worker cooperatives leasing capital, progressive income taxes, and so forth. To oppose this, one would have to hold that there was an inexorable connection between markets and capitalism such that, if markets are allowed to flourish, standard capitalist patterns of ownership must inevitably reemerge; or, on the other hand, if these arrangements are outlawed, markets will be unable to work effectively. (Although this view is sometimes expressed—both by Marxists and by libertarians—the argument for it remains obscure to me.)

By contrast, most versions of the "quality of life" critique—including the Marxian theory of alienation[6]—entail the condemnation of market relationships as a distortion of genuine human relationships. No matter how radically resources are redistributed, activity in the market must be governed by norms of instrumental rationality, people must behave nontuistically (that is, each must aim to maximize his holdings, regardless of the welfare of his partners in exchange), and so forth. The "quality of life" critique seems therefore inevitably to point beyond markets towards some other method of coordinating economic behavior. By the same token, however, it lays itself immediately open to a charge of utopianism. If we want a feasible form of socialism, it seems that we have to accept a major role for markets, and to that extent we must abandon the "quality of life" critique.[7]

A similar point can be made with respect to the legal system. A modern legal system can be regarded as a system of uniform general rules enforced by formal procedures, which confer rights on individuals. The distributive critique includes nothing at odds with this idea of legality itself. Socialists characteristically allege that, in capitalist societies, a particular set of rights favorable to capitalist interests is embodied in the law, and moreover that enforcement procedures favor those already well-endowed with resources. A socialist system would rectify these defects by, for instance, recognizing enforceable rights to welfare and allocating resources in such a way that access to the legal system was effectively equalized. In contrast, the "quality of life" critique contains elements hostile to the very idea of legality: rights are dismissed as "the prized possessions of alienated persons,"[8] and the formality of the law is contrasted with arrangements whereby people could deal with one another as complete human beings, each responding to the full particularity of the other. The problem, once again, is to see how an alternative to the legal system can be made to seem feasible in a modern industrial society.[9]

Considerations of realism, then, are one major pressure inducing contemporary socialists to abandon the "quality of life" critique in favor of the distributive critique of capitalism. A second pressure is loss of faith in the assumptions needed to back up the former critique. The "quality of life" critique requires us to judge some modes of human life as better than others, regardless of the preferences that people actually display. If we are going to condemn competition, say, or the kinds of goods produced for consumption in market economies, we must be able to deploy some theory of human good which allows us to make the necessary discrimination. But the contemporary intellectual climate is very hostile to any such theory. The high-minded assumptions about the nature of the good life that socialists made a century ago—as indeed did many liberals, most notoriously John Stuart Mill—now strike us as elitist and somewhat pious. We are far more self-critical in the matter of elevating our own preferred mode of life to the status of universal truth. And while most socialist intellectuals privately persist in their taste for improving literature, healthy hikes in the country, and political discussion as forms of recreation, they are far less keen to have those predilections held up as the image of socialism itself. The current preference is, if anything, for "designer socialism," that is a view of socialism that warmly allies itself to current fashions in clothes, music, and lifestyle generally. It is clearly impossible to celebrate modes of consumption thrown up by present-day capitalism while at the same time holding on to a view of socialism that embodies a strong "quality of life" critique of that very system.

These are two of the pressures, therefore, that incline contemporary socialists to put forward a slimmed-down version of socialism, defined more or less entirely in distributive terms. Socialism, then, is exclusively a matter of allocating resources (broadly conceived) in the appropriate manner. As examples of this tendency in political philosophy, I would cite the following: Hillel Steiner's proposals for a laissez-faire economy grounded in equal entitlements to natural resources;[10] Ronald Dworkin's conception of equality of resources, including an insurance scheme to compensate for inequalities in personal endowments;[11] John Roemer's argument for equality of productive assets as the best way of capturing the point of the Marxian theory of exploitation;[12] Robert van der Veen and Philippe Van Parijs's advocacy of a "Capitalist road to Communism" whereby returns to labor and capital are taxed at progressively higher rates to provide each person with an unconditional grant to satisfy their needs.[13] Although these proposals differ in important respects, they share the aim of radically altering the distributive outcome of conventional capitalism, but without requiring any corresponding change in the quality of human relationships that prevail under that system.

I should make it clear that I am broadly in sympathy with this tendency towards a justice-based socialism; in particular, I have been arguing for some time that markets are both an economically essential and an ethically acceptable component in a viable form of socialism.[14] Nevertheless, I do not believe that socialists can discard everything in the "quality of life" critique of capitalism; they especially need to hold on to *some* form of community as an essential part of their vision. *Which* form of community is the major issue addressed in this paper. But first let me present the minimalist case for communitarianism of some kind as an ineliminable part of the socialist project.[15]

In presenting this case, I make two assumptions which I hope are not controversial. The first is that we want our version of socialism to be democratically supported: whatever view is taken about the transition to socialism, socialist institutions should command the willing assent of at least the majority of the population once those institutions are installed. The second is that the rules of the system (the rules governing economic transactions, etc.) should, for the most part, be complied with voluntarily: the level of coercive enforcement should be no higher than, say, that prevailing under present-day capitalism, and preferably it should be a good deal lower. Clearly, if such assumptions are to hold good, the socialist arrangements we have in mind must be legitimated, in the sense that most people must hold a conception of justice that corresponds to the one that these arrangements embody. For instance, insofar as the arrangements we envisage rest on a conception of equality, the people subject to them must be, or become, egalitarians.

Now, on one view of the matter, this question of legitimation poses no real problem. If we think that good, rational arguments can be given for the view of justice that we favor, then we may believe that most people—given sufficient time, perhaps—will come to share this view, and so the appropriate conception of justice can be developed apart from, and prior to, the arrangements of socialism itself. In particular, the view of justice people hold doesn't depend on the kind of relationships they have with those around them, so the order of decision goes as follows: first, a consensus emerges on justice itself; second, this consensus is embodied in institutions which allocate resources to people; third, people use the resources they have been allocated to pursue their personal goals, perhaps including the goal of developing relationships of particular kinds. This, very crudely, is how John Rawls sees the matter,[16] and his idea has been influential among many, including some socialists who interpret the *substance* of justice in a more egalitarian way than he does himself.

I hold this view to be badly in error. Against it, I want to argue that our ideas of distributive justice are powerfully affected by our perception of the relationships generally prevailing in the set of people within which the distribution is going to occur. Perhaps this is best illustrated by starting with an extreme case. Suppose we conceived of a "society" made up of individuals who had no social relations with one another, each living an entirely independent and self-contained life—a set of Robinson Crusoes, each on his own island. What would justice mean to the inhabitants of such a "society"? They would endorse something like Nozick's view that justice means noninterference with the rights that each has acquired by his own legitimate efforts (where "legitimate" is in turn spelled out in terms of noninterference). Charles Taylor has put this point well:

> . . . there is a mode of justice which holds between quite independent human
> beings, not bound together by any society or collaborative arrangement. If two
> nomadic tribes meet in the desert, very old and long-standing intuitions about

justice tell us that it is wrong (unjust) for one to steal the flocks of the other. The principle here is very simple: we have a right to what we have.[17]

Conversely, any view that is more redistributive than Nozick's—any view holding that people can make claims on one another that go beyond simple non-interference—must presuppose a background set of social relationships against which claims of this sort would appear legitimate.[18] This, indeed, is the nub of Michael Sandel's criticism of Rawls.[19] Rawls advances a distributive principle— the difference principle—which gives people a claim on what others have produced by exercising their talents and skills, but says nothing about the communitarian relationships which, in practice, would be needed to underpin this principle. What applies to Rawls applies a fortiori to principles of distributive justice that are more strictly egalitarian. These principles may deprive some asset-holders of large quantities of the holdings they would have enjoyed under the "Nozick Constitution" which we are using as a benchmark. We can only expect them to consent to institutions that enforce the preferred distribution if they regard themselves as bound to the beneficiaries by strong ties of community: the stronger the ties, the more egalitarian the distribution can be.[20]

It is not an adequate answer to this line of thought to say that a distributive practice can, of itself, create the necessary ties. No doubt there is a process of reinforcement such that implementing a practice of distributive justice appropriate to a particular community will tend to buttress the sense of community that already exists. But if, starting from the Crusoe "society," an external agency were to impose an egalitarian redistribution of assets but do nothing else to change relationships between the Crusoes, I can see no reason to expect that they will begin to think of themselves as forming a community or to regard the redistribution as legitimate. The kind of ties we are looking for are not external and mechanical, but involve each person seeing his life as part and parcel of the life of the wider group, so that the question of how well his own life is going depends in some measure on how the community as a whole is faring. This brings in issues of common good, historical identity, and so forth which reach far beyond the scope of distributive justice. Rawls's notion that adherence to a shared conception of distributive justice could itself form a sufficient basis for community is quite implausible.[21]

I have not yet said anything about the idea of community that socialist proposals require, or about whether such an idea is feasible given the circumstances of an advanced industrial society. My argument so far is simply that a form of socialism which defines itself primarily in terms of distributive justice must still consider questions about the *quality* of social relationships if it wants to be something more than a nice intellectual construct. If socialism is to be politically feasible—if socialist arrangements once installed are to command the willing consent of the population—social relations generally must support the preferred conception of distributive justice. Even those who regard community as having no independent political value must rely on it in practice to underpin their distributive concerns. So at this point I turn to see whether there is anything in the recent communitarian literature that might be helpful to the socialist case.

II. THE AMBIVALENCE OF CONTEMPORARY COMMUNITARIANISM

I shall focus on the work of Alasdair MacIntyre, Charles Taylor, and Michael Sandel. Each of these writers would endorse the general argument I have just advanced: namely, that ideas of justice cannot be separated from a broader understanding of the community within which distributive practices exist.[22] It does not follow, of course, that the conceptions of justice and community they advance are socialist conceptions: indeed, in at least two out of the three cases, the evidence is rather to the contrary.[23] So our approach to their work must be a critical one. We can try to get clearer about socialist ideas of community, in part by seeing where they need to diverge from the ideas of MacIntyre, Taylor, and Sandel.

MacIntyre's understanding of community initially derives from his narrative view of the self. A person can only make sense of his actions, he argues, by placing them within a narrative structure—a self-told story which runs through the person's life from birth to death. The narrative I construct for myself, however, intersects with other people's narratives—I am a character in their stories and they figure in mine. This set of narratives, in turn, makes references to the wider communities within which the individuals in question bear social identities—say, as the occupants of kinship individuals in question bear social identities—say, as the occupants of kinship roles or as members of institutions. In particular, MacIntyre argues, moral activity itself depends upon an understanding of moral value which can only be provided within a particular community.

MacIntyre's claim, to sum up, is that people can only make sense of their lives by seeing themselves as members of large communities, which above all provide the preconditions of narrative unity. As to the *scope* of community, MacIntyre remains agnostic: he talks of "the family, the neighborhood, the city, and the tribe," and so forth.[24] What he does make clear, in contrast, is that the modern state is not an appropriate location for community. It cannot embody community, since in MacIntyre's view that would require a moral consensus at the political level which simply does not and cannot exist. Moreover, the mode of operation of the modern state tends to destroy such communal ties as still exist: bureaucratic procedures create individuals who are abstracted from any social identity, and whose residual sense of self is that of a pure chooser of ends. In his remarks on the Jacobins, MacIntyre does not exclude the possibility of an understanding of moral virtue that would give political participation a central place, but he argues that such an understanding is impossible to sustain in modern conditions. "The true lesson of the Jacobin Clubs and their downfall is that you cannot hope to reinvent morality on the scale of a whole nation when the very idiom of the morality that you seek to reinvent is alien in one way to the vast mass of ordinary people and in another to the intellectual elite."[25] So although patriotism—a special regard to the interests of my national community—remains a virtue for MacIntyre, it is no longer an idea which should inform my relations to the government of the day.[26] I should assess the state purely in instrumental terms: in terms of how effectively it keeps the peace between different communities, protects rights, and so forth.

It would be wrong to describe this outlook as politically conservative since, as MacIntyre notes, it involves a complete rejection of "modern systematic politics, whether liberal, conservative, radical, or socialist";[27] it can fairly be described, however, as morally conservative, in the sense that it defines moral virtue in terms of the traditions of such de facto communities as are salient for each particular person. Although MacIntyre, in his remarks on tradition, argues that living traditions always involve critical argument about the best way of carrying the tradition on, there is no wider forum within which the merits of different traditions might be debated—and, of course, MacIntyre rejects the idea that there are transcendent standards of justice which might be used to adjudicate between them.[28] From a socialist perspective, therefore, MacIntyre's view of community must appear dangerously tradition-bound, not so much in the sense that it starts with de facto communities as in the sense that it has no resources for getting beyond the notions of virtue embodied in each community except insofar as the community itself engages in critical reflection. I shall later connect this deficiency to MacIntyre's other view that political arrangements are irrelevant (in modern conditions) to communal life.

If we turn now to Taylor, we find once again that claims about the nature of personhood are advanced to underpin a (fairly unspecific) commitment to community. There is, however, this contrast with MacIntyre: whereas MacIntyre bases his account of the self on a premodern understanding of morality, Taylor assumes from the outset "the modern identity"—that is, a view of human nature which breaks decisively with the idea that human fulfillment can be understood as alignment with some given, cosmic order (as in older Christian views). Taylor accepts the modern idea that human self-realization involves choice as well as discovery; what he rejects are individualist accounts of that process of self-realization.

As far as I can discern, there are two major strands to Taylor's argument; I am not clear as to how these strands are supposed to be related. The first strand starts from a familiar liberal ideal, the ideal of personal autonomy. Taylor's claim is that individualist liberals fail to understand the preconditions for autonomy. They see it as unproblematically given and needing only protection against external constraints, whereas in fact it requires a certain kind of cultural background. People can only make authentic choices about their own lives against the background of a civilization in which, for example, moral questions are debated in public, certain aesthetic experiences are available, and so forth. Community makes its appearance here in the guise of a common culture, participation in which is a necessary condition of liberal aspirations to autonomy.[29]

The other strand in Taylor's argument moves further away from liberal premises. Taylor points to the importance, in the modern consciousness, of an attitude which he calls "expressivism."[30] This is the ambition to see the world around us as an expression of our authentic nature, an idea that was particularly prominent in the thought of the German Romantics and their followers. Now this attitude can take either private or public form, depending on whether the "nature" to be realized is the essence of a particular individual or a nature common to the members of some collectivity. Taylor, however, regards private versions of expressivism as somehow deficient: he points to the nuclear family as the current embodiment of the Romantic ideal of a life according to nature, but claims that the family lacks the moral resources to contain narrow self-absorption.

> . . . If the business of life is finding my authentic fulfilment as an individual, and my associations should be relativized to this end, there seems no reason why this relativization should in principle stay at the boundary of the family. If my development, or even my discovery of myself, should be incompatible with a long-standing association, then this will come to be felt as a prison rather than as a locus of identity.[31]

Hence, expressivist aspirations can only be fulfilled if we can discover some common identity that might be expressed in a public world. Where might such an identity be found? Taylor finds the answer in *language*, an institution that is necessarily public, and at the same time embodies a distinctive way of experiencing the world. The community here becomes the speech community. In talking to one another, we convey a shared view of the world: and this view is constantly open to modification as we change our language in order to express ourselves more adequately. Taylor summarizes:

> . . . The expressive conception gives a view of language as a range of activities in which we express/realize a certain way of being in the world. And this way of being has many facets. It is not just the reflective awareness by which we recognize things as—, and describe our surroundings: but also that by which we come to have the properly human emotions, and constitute our human relations, including those of the language community within which language grows.[32]

So we find two "communitarian" trains of thought in Taylor, one beginning with the liberal ideal of autonomy and ending with a view of community as common culture, the other beginning with expressivism and ending with a view of community as language-sharing. Rather than investigate the relationship between these conceptions, I want to point to three traits which they have in common.

First, on either view, the *scope* of the relevant community is exceedingly difficult to determine. How does one attempt to fix the boundaries either of a cultural or a linguistic community? On Taylor's first argument, there seems no reason to restrict the scope of community at all, since, presumably, the greater the cultural variety to which I am exposed, the more chance I have to develop my capacity for autonomous choice. The second argument does seem to imply a more particularistic view of community, but then we run into the familiar difficulties of individuating languages (is American-English the same language as English-English?). Taylor's communitarianism is unavoidably amorphous, and this immediately limits its power as a weapon in political philosophy.

Second, Taylor's view has the consequence of restricting the extent to which our communal relations are open to rational reflection. The ties that hold us together must, to some degree, remain opaque to critical investigation. Taylor makes this explicit when he describes languages as

> A pattern of activity . . . which can only be deployed against a background which we can never fully dominate; and yet a background that we are never fully dominated by, because we are constantly reshaping it. Reshaping it without dominating it, or being able to oversee it, means that we never fully know what we are doing to it; we develop language without knowing fully what we are making it into.[33]

Now it may turn out that communal relationships are indeed unavoidably opaque in the way that this view of language suggests; this is a matter requiring further investigation. But, prima facie, it undermines the belief held by some socialists, most notably Marx, that what we should be aiming for is a society in which human beings consciously and collectively control their destiny, and their relationships become entirely transparent. Community, on Taylor's view, is something that we are immersed in, but whose nature cannot be grasped fully and consciously, let alone shaped completely according to our will.

Anxieties about the potentially conservative character of Taylor's conception may be heightened when we notice that community has, for him, no necessary political dimension. It is true that he attempts to build a political argument onto his claim about the role of common culture in providing the conditions for autonomy. The logic of this argument must be that cultural forms and institutions are public goods, and it is unlikely that self-interested individuals will provide them voluntarily. That this is an empirical claim is made clear by Taylor's reply to the anarchist who thinks that these goods will be created spontaneously. "There is nothing in principle which excludes anarchism in the reflection that we owe our identity as free men to our civilization."[34] Political institutions, then, appear simply as instruments for protecting the elements of community by, for instance, subsidizing the arts. They are not part of the framework of community itself.

MacIntyre sees politics as irrelevant to community; Taylor sees it playing only an instrumental role. Sandel is, in contrast, more firmly set in the republican tradition. When he speaks of community, he appears to envisage a set of people engaged in, among other things, political deliberation. Corresponding to this is a stronger claim about the importance of community to personal identity. MacIntyre and Taylor both argue, in their different ways, that people's identities can't be satisfactorily defined without communal relationships in the background. Sandel's claim is that identity must, in part, be *constituted* by communal attachments. When people discover who they are (discover, not choose), part of what they discover is that they are members of this or that collectivity—a membership which they cannot relinquish without becoming different people in one important sense.

What is the status of Sandel's claim here? He presents it not as a description of present-day reality but as a presupposition of liberal theories of justice, especially the Rawlsian theory. His core argument is that the difference principle, which treats people's talents and abilities as common assets, can only be acceptable if we adopt the constitutive conception of community outlined above. He is far less sanguine about the practical feasibility of such a conception. In his brief remarks on the evolution of American politics, he traces a process whereby, starting with local political communities (which, by implication, were genuine communities), politics was progressively "nationalized" in response to economic pressures; but the attempt to foster a new sense of community at *this* level was unsuccessful. "Except for extraordinary moments, such as war, the nation proved too vast a scale across which to cultivate the shared self-understandings necessary to community in the formative, or constitutive sense."[35] Hence what we are left with is a liberal politics of rights that lacks a coherent communal underpinning.

What lies behind this conclusion? Sandel must be assuming that a sense of community strong enough to foster constitutive attachments can only exist where people have face-to-face relationships (as in the traditional town meeting) or perhaps have strong cultural affiliations. Clearly, a large modern nation cannot expect to meet either of these conditions. So the upshot of Sandel's argument must be uncongenial to the socialist. Although the link between community and politics is forged, community is seen as a phenomenon of localities, and this cannot satisfy the socialist, who needs it to underpin distributive justice across whole societies.[36] By strengthening the conditions for community, Sandel at the same time precludes it from playing the kind of political role that socialists want it to play.

None of the three "communitarians" we have considered advances a conception of community that seems well suited to socialist purposes. What lessons might we draw from this fact? For all three authors, the very idea of community is problematic in the modern world. MacIntyre sees us as clinging to fragments of community inherited from the pre-Renaissance period. Taylor sees communitarians as fighting a rear-guard battle against what he calls "Enlightenment naturalism"—a view of man as an agent who regards the surrounding world merely as an instrument to the optimal fulfillment of his freely chosen desires. Sandel, as we have just noted, is pessimistic about constitutive community in the face of the scale of modern politics. Now one lesson we might draw is to take these authors' findings as confirmation of a certain negative view of socialism, a view which sees the socialist project as anachronistic from the very moment of its conception. On this view, socialism became a popular ideology precisely in response to the breakup of traditional communities under the impact of the industrial revolution. It became popular because it promised to restore the coherent moral life found in the disappearing communities, while at the same time providing all the material (and other) benefits of industrialization. But these two promises could never be fulfilled together. In industrial societies the appeal to community is always nostalgic and backward-looking, whatever its proponents may think.

This is not the lesson I want to draw, though I feel the force of the argument in the last paragraph which, as noted, reflection on the ideas of MacIntyre, Taylor, and Sandel tends to support. We see, once again, the attractions of a purely distributive view of socialism, which aims to discard community as an essential element in the socialist framework. On this view, particular communities may flourish under a socialist distributive regime, but this is, so to speak, an optional extra, not something that the regime itself requires. I have explained already why this attractive view cannot, in the end, be maintained. Socialists must take up the quest for community, but they should do so in a chastened spirit, in full realization of the obstacles that lie in their path. In the final part of the paper, I sketch in a socialist view of community which I hope meets these strictures.

III. A SOCIALIST CONCEPTION OF COMMUNITY

A socialist who wants to avoid the charge that he is merely nostalgic for preindustrial forms of life cannot appeal to thick-textured, face-to-face community as the building block of his system. Where such communities still exist—as, for instance, in certain mining villages or other places where a fixed pattern of working life has persisted over decades—there is no reason to disparage them; equally, it would be wrong to make them integral to the socialist project, or in particular to suppose that the whole of a society could come to take on the character of these local communities. The tendency of an industrial economy is always to erode community in this strong sense, and, whether or not one thinks that economic policies should be designed to protect particular communities against such erosion, there is nothing here firm enough to support a socialist project.

It would be equally wrong to conclude that socialist community must comprise nothing less than humankind in general. Some socialists do seem to take it as their aim to extend fraternal sentiments to embrace all other human beings, and in the course of so doing to sweep away all local and particular attachments as relics of an unsavory past. This aim is often thought to embody a certain idea of rationality. There is no good reason to treat our neighbors or our compatriots any differently from equally needy people elsewhere in the world, so any sense that we owe them special loyalties must vanish under critical scrutiny.

This view neglects the fact, evident enough in the writings of the communitarians we have considered, that communities just are particularistic. In seeing myself as a member of a community, I see myself participating in a particular way of life marked off from other communities by its distinctive characteristics. Notions such as "loyalty" and "allegiance" make no sense unless there is an identifiable something towards which the attitudes are directed. Moreover, to say that such attitudes are necessary irrational is to adopt a contestable view of rationality, one that presents it as a property of the deliberations of a detached subject reasoning entirely from universal principles. Socialists need not and should not take up the view of ethical rationality implied here. They are better served by a form of ethical particularism that allows existing commitments and loyalties a fundamental place in ethical reasoning—which does not entail that every commitment must be accepted uncritically.[37] They should, in short, prefer the Hegelian idea of ethical life to the Kantian idea of morality as an account of practical reasoning vis-à-vis other members of the community.

There is a further implication to be drawn here. A realistic form of socialism must start out from actually existing communities. It cannot hope to invent the communities that it might be thought desirable to have on abstract grounds. Communal relationships, for reasons already given, are inevitably fragile in the circumstances of a modern industrial society; they must be husbanded with care. Now if we take this point together with the earlier point that community is needed to legitimize practices of distributive justice, our conclusion must be that the relevant communities are nations. On the one hand, people do, in general, identify themselves with national communities in a way that they rarely do with wider constituencies. On the other hand, community at this level is normally broad-based enough to provide the conditions for an effective practice of distributive justice. The nation as a form of community must have a privileged position in socialist thought, at least in any future we can envisage.[38] And this, of course, runs directly counter to a well-entrenched tendency in socialist thought, which regards nationality less as a resource than as a problem to be overcome. For many socialists, the future has seemed to lie either with local community or with global community, or with some combination of these, but in any case not with existing nationalities.

Why is there such a resistance in socialist thought to the idea of national community? There is the belief in moral universalism which I have already discussed (national boundaries are morally irrelevant). There is also, of course, the horrific experience of "national socialism" in its German incarnation. But there is a further point. If one starts out by thinking of a community as involving a set of face-to-face relationships in which each person has full and direct knowledge of the qualities of the other members, then the idea of a nation as a community must indeed seem peculiar. Nations are, in Benedict Anderson's phrase, "imagined communities."[39] They exist only because of beliefs each of us have about our compatriots, beliefs not acquired by direct experience but culturally transmitted. As Anderson points out, nations can't exist without mass media (originally the printed word) to disseminate an understanding of national identity. But with this comes the possibility of distortion. The picture of national life that becomes embedded in the culture may not accurately reflect what is actually the case, both now and historically. The extreme version of this is, of course, Orwell's *1984*, where the telescreens project a version of events that bears no relation at all to reality. But even in societies that are much more open than Orwell's Oceania, we find that national identities contain a greater or lesser admixture of myth. And this apparently contravenes an idea of rationality that the socialist must find attractive—not the abstract idea of reason that I have already rejected, but simply the idea that, to be rational, I must regard all of my beliefs as potentially subject to critical scrutiny. It seems that if I adopt this policy with respect to nationality, I am bound to end up by rejecting a good part of my existing national identity.

I have elsewhere tried to assess how far national identities can survive the critical rejection of certain of their components.[40] Here I want to develop a different point. There may be built-in limits to the process of critical scrutiny itself. We may simply not be able to formulate everything that goes to make up our nationality in a way that makes rational scrutiny possible. Here we see the significance of Taylor's conception of language as "a pattern of activity . . . which can only be deployed against a background which we can never fully dominate"; it is a conception which can, I think, be extended more widely to apply to many of the cultural phenomena which constitute nationality. Consider, for instance, the importance of symbols of various kinds—flags, emblems, festivities—in national life. When we respond to these symbols, as most of us do, we cannot spell out in propositional form precisely what it is we are responding to, although we may, of course, be able to say *something* about their significance. What passes through our minds as we stand before the Cenotaph to commemorate our war dead? Is it pride in the heroism of our soldiers, or horror at the carnage of war? Or perhaps both of these at once? If we can't be clear about what the ceremony means, how can we say whether it is rationally acceptable or not? Yet occasions such as these are an important component of national identity.

When assessing Taylor's view that communal relationships are unavoidably opaque, I pointed to its potentially conservative implications. Unquestionably, nationality is open to the same charge. If we define our community in terms of a spontaneously evolving national identity, we shall remain, to a large extent, the prisoners of our past. To avoid this implication, we must appeal to politics. The political forum must be the sphere in which we reshape our common identity through reasoned argument. A socialist view of community must therefore give a central place to citizenship. Not only should we be related as bearers of a common national identity, we should also be related as citizens, as codeterminers of our collective future.

Let me expand a little on this. It is important to see how nationality and citizenship are related in the view that I am outlining. Nationality is the identity we have in common, an identity in large measure inherited from the past, and not fully open to rational scrutiny. Citizenship is a political status which allows each of us to participate in reshaping that identity. For instance, we scrutinize our institutions and practices to see whether the meanings they convey (so far as these are determinate) are meanings we still want to endorse (to take a relatively trivial case, we may decide to abolish one public holiday and institute another); we decide which cultural activities are worthy of public support; more generally, our legislation may involve an attempt to influence future understanding of the meaning of membership in this society (consider the case of race-relations legislation). But this exercise never occurs in a vacuum. We take part in political debate already endowed with the shared understandings that come with a common nationality. Since critical reshaping starts with these understandings, we cannot get beyond them entirely, or certainly not beyond them all at once. Taylor's metaphor, borrowed from Neurath, of sailors rebuilding their ship at sea, seems to describe the case pretty well.

What must politics be like if it is to fulfill the function we are assigning to it? Socialists will certainly want to insist that citizenship must be a role available to everyone (or else the reshaping of communal identity won't be democratic), so we must envisage arrangements that permit everyone to be politically active. More significant for the present argument, people must engage in politics *as* citizens, that is, as members of a collectivity committed to advancing its common good. They cannot enter it in their capacity as private persons, each with a particular interest—say, an economic interest—to advance. This is a formidable requirement, as Rousseau understood in his pessimistic chapter on the silencing of the general will.[41] Socialism must draw on an ample stock of republican virtue. It must also become adept at what Michael Walzer has called the art of separation.[42] It must find ways of demarcating a person's role as citizen from other roles that he might perform, for instance, as enthusiast for a particular cause, or as spokesman for a sectional interest. A modern society will inevitably embrace a whole gamut of forms of private life (unless they are artificially suppressed), and these are bound to generate demands on public policy. There is always a danger that the force of these demands may obliterate citizenship. The sailors who are rebuilding their ship on the open sea may need to refurbish their tools at the same time.

This may indicate the distance between the form of communitarianism developed here, and the simpler view which sees community as a general, undifferentiated characteristic of relationships in socialist society. Community, on the present view, has a restricted character. It describes one respect in which members of a society may be related, but it does not exclude the possibility that they may also be related in other ways—say, as competitors in the marketplace. It also has an artificial character, at least to some extent.[43] I have argued that national identities will remain partially opaque to rational scrutiny; I have also argued that we may need devices—symbolic devices and so forth—to protect citizenship from invasion by private interests. This takes us very far from a view of community as the expression of natural sentiments, and of social relations as transparent to the participants. It is not clear to me, however, that socialists must disdain artifice, if that turns out to be the best way of achieving their essential goals. I draw comfort here from Jon Elster's recent discussion of the problem of constitutional choice, which takes up the idea that a constitution is a device for collective self-binding—a way of protecting ourselves from making certain kinds of decisions in the future—and applies it to the transition to socialism.[44] Socialists should discard the naive view that everything they want can be achieved by following majority opinion at each moment in time.

CONCLUSION

This paper began with the claim, made recently by several socialists, that socialism centers on the value of freedom of ensuring that each person enjoys equal effective freedom. In pursuing the implications of that claim, we may seem to have turned a somersault, for there is a well-established view that sees the politically organized community as essentially totalitarian in its upshot. If we are to concern ourselves with our collective identity, and use politics as a means of remodeling that identity, what place is left for the freedoms that liberals characteristically cherish: artistic freedom, religious freedom, privacy, and so forth? How can socialism with a communitarian face possibly claim to be freedom-maximizing?

The argument for that claim, to recall, runs as follows. Freedom depends on the distribution of resources. To equalize freedom, we need a system of distributive justice. But such a system can't be legitimized unless people see themselves as tied together communally. Politics enters the picture to prevent communal ties becoming merely traditional, to honor socialist demands for rationality.

Such a view does not entail a rejection of liberal forms of freedom, or of practices such as the creation and enforcement of rights which protect those freedoms. Communitarianism, in general, may differ from liberalism more radically in its basic premises than in the practical policies it recommends;[45] this applies a fortiori to the streamlined version defended here. That is not to say that a socialist set of rights would have precisely the same content as the standard liberal set. Socialism requires the introduction of new rights, especially in the field of economics. Equally, it may require the abrogation of some liberal rights particularly in areas in which forms of private culture threaten to have a destructive impact on the public culture which sustains a common identity.[46] So, for instance, a socialist society may wish to impose some limits on educational freedom, seeing the school as an important source of the political understandings that future citizens will bring to their public life. This may have implications both for the structure of the education system (should private schools be permitted?) and for the content of what is taught in certain fields (should teachers be permitted to transmit *any* version of the history and politics of their own country?). Where two sets of rights intersect but neither includes the other, there is the familiar problem of deciding which is the more extensive—in the present context, the problem of aggregating liberties. Although I have not tried to show here that the solution to this problem must favor the socialist case, I can see no reason why it should not. In that sense, there is nothing incoherent in beginning one's intellectual trajectory as a socialist from a commitment to freedom and ending up at the circumscribed form of communitarianism I have been delineating in this paper.

NOTES

I should like to thank the participants in the conference on "Capitalism and Socialism" organized by the Social Philosophy and Policy Center for helpful discussion of an earlier draft of this paper, and Jerry Cohen, Andrew Williams, and Lesley Jacobs for sending valuable written comments.

1. See, for instance, Amy Gutmann, "Communitarian Critics of Liberalism," *Philosophy and Public Affairs* 14 (1985): 308–22.

2. This sketch of communitarianism is deliberately ambiguous in one aspect. We may read the communitarian critics as basing their argument on a core liberal ideal—personal autonomy—but as proposing a more adequate account than mainstream liberalism of the conditions under which autonomy can be realized. Alternatively, we can read them as departing in a more fundamental way from liberal assumptions, substituting a different conception of the self, a different conception of freedom, and so forth. This ambiguity runs deep in communitarian writing (I return to the point later, particularly in relation to Charles Taylor): does communitarianism come to fulfill liberalism or to destroy it?

3. For statements of this view by two prominent members of the British Labour Party see Bryan Gould, *Socialism and Freedom* (London: Macmillan, 1985); Roy Hattersley, *Choose Freedom: The Future for Democratic Socialism* (London: Michael Joseph, 1987).

4. Nor do I want to say that the socialist critique is exhausted by the two elements I identify. It has other strands too: for instance one charge often made by socialists is that capitalism is a highly *inefficient* system, making poor use of the welfare-generating resources available to it. There is a good discussion of efficiency arguments in Allen Buchanan, *Ethics, Efficiency and the Market* (Oxford: Clarendon Press, 1985), chap. 2.

5. Marxists often claim that their critique of capitalism does not involve a charge of maldistribution. Their meaning, I think, is that they are not centrally concerned with the allocation of income; in particular, they want to dismiss the suggestion that capitalism can be made acceptably fair by income redistribution schemes. What this suggests is *either* that they see a fairly rigid connection between distribution in the narrow sense (income distribution) and the structural inequalities of capitalism (e.g., the power structure of enterprises) *or* that they see distribution in the former sense as a comparatively trivial matter. In my wider sense, however, the Marxist critique, in this aspect, would properly count as a distributive critique.

Marx himself recognized that his critique of capitalism could be expressed in distributive terms. For the evidence, see G. A. Cohen, "Freedom, Justice and Capitalism," *New Left Review* 126 (March–April 1981): 13–14 n. 7.

6. I have examined this theory critically in "Marx, Communism and Markets," *Political Theory* 15 (1987): 182–204.

7. Evidence for believing that a feasible form of socialism must allow a major role to markets is usefully presented in Alec Nove, *The Economics of Feasible Socialism* (London: Allen and Unwin, 1983).

8. Ruth Anna Putman, "Rights of Persons and the Liberal Tradition," in *Social Ends and Political Means,* ed. Ted Honderich (London: Routledge and Kegan Paul, 1976), p. 102.

9. I have argued this point briefly in *Anarchism* (London: Dent, 1984), chap. 12. For a fuller defense of the idea of legality against left-wing criticism, see Tom D. Campbell, *The Left and Rights* (London: Routledge and Kegan Paul, 1983), esp. chap. 3.

10. See Hillel Steiner, "The Natural Right to the Means of Production," *Philosophical Quarterly* 27 (1977): 41–49; "Slavery, Socialism and Private Property," in *Nomos XXII: Property,* ed. J. Roland Pennock and John W. Chapman (New York: New York University Press, 1970); "Liberty and Equality," *Political Studies* 29 (1981): 555–69.

11. Ronald Dworkin, "Equality of Resources," *Philosophy and Public Affairs* 10 (1981): 283–345.

12. John Roemer, "Equality of Talent," *Economics and Philosophy* 1 (1985): 151–87; "Should Marxists Be Interested in Exploitation?" *Philosophy and Public Affairs* 14 (1985): 30–65.

13. Robert J. van der Veen and Philippe Van Parijs, "A Capitalist Road to Communism," *Theory and Society* 15 (1986): 635–55.

14. See David Miller, "Socialism and the Market," *Political Theory* 5 (1977): 473–90; "Jerusalem Not Yet Built: A Reply to Lessnoff on Capitalism, Socialism and Democracy," *Political Studies* 28 (1980): 584–89; Miller, "Marx, Communism and Markets"; David Miller and Saul Estrin, "Market Socialism: A Policy for Socialists," in *Market Socialism: Whose Choice?* Fabian pamphlet No. 516, ed. I. Forbes [reprinted as "A Case for Market Socialism," *Dissent* (summer 1987): 359–67]. These ideas are developed more systematically in a forthcoming book, *Market, State and Community* (Oxford: Clarendon Press, 1989).

15. I call this the minimalist case because it hinges the argument for community entirely on elements drawn from the distributive critique; it makes no appeal to the inherent value of community. Now an argument of this kind might appear inherently paradoxical, at least insofar as it is addressed to the public at large. For either the addressees already see themselves as belonging to a community, or they do not. If they do, then it is redundant to offer them a justifying argument that appeals to extrinsic distributive considerations; if they do not, then a sense of community cannot be conjured out of thin air because it would be helpful from a distributive point of view were it to exist. Thus the argument that follows might seem to have an unavoidably esoteric character.

We may, however, take the addressees of the argument to be people who both see themselves as members of a community and espouse principles of distributive justice, but who as yet see no necessary relationship between these commitments. Community membership is felt to be inherently valuable, but irrelevant from a distributive point of view. The purpose of my argument is to enhance the value of community by connecting the two commitments. This has a practical point insofar as we are now in a position to make political decisions that will influence the nature of our community in the future—strengthening or weakening people's allegiance in the long run.

16. This is not the place to discuss the finer details of Rawls's theory. He expresses some concern about what he calls the "strains of commitment"—the possibility that

people might no longer be able to accept the principles of justice they have endorsed in the abstract when faced with their concrete results—but he sees this as a problem about justice and material interests: can people who do badly out of the application of a theory of justice be expected to continue embracing it? (See John Rawls, *A Theory of Justice* [Cambridge: Harvard University Press, 1971], esp. sec. 29.) He does not raise the question whether the practical acceptability of a theory of justice might not depend on the quality of social relationships *in general*.

17. Charles Taylor, "The Nature and Scope of Distributive Justice," *Philosophy and the Human Sciences: Philosophical Papers II* (Cambridge: Cambridge University Press, 1985), p. 289.

18. Let me stress that I am concerned here about the conditions under which a socialist system of distribution could be legitimate, in the sense of being congruent with widely held and spontaneously formed notions of justice. I am not directly concerned with the transition to socialism, i.e., with the circumstances under which those who are the chief beneficiaries of capitalism would be willing to renounce the privileges they already enjoy. Although democratic socialists will want both the transition and the ensuing arrangements to have broad popular support, it would be unrealistic to set the standard of consent as high for the former as for the latter.

19. See Michael Sandel, *Liberalism and the Limits of Justice* (Cambridge: Cambridge University Press, 1982), chap. 2.

20. Obviously, this is not a claim about logic but a claim about social psychology. Although social psychologists cannot create genuine communities in the laboratory, their simulations provide some support for the claim. In particular, people give less weight to merit and more weight to equality in distribution when they expect to interact with their partners over a period of time. See E. Gary Shapiro, "Effect of Expectations of Future Interaction on Reward Allocation in Dyads: Equity and Equality," *Journal of Personality and Social Psychology* 31 (1975): 873–80; Melvin J. Lerner, "The Justice Motive: 'Equity' and 'Parity' among Children," *Journal of Personality and Social Psychology* 29 (1974): 539–50.

21. Rawls, *A Theory of Justice*, sec. 79.

22. See Alasdair MacIntyre, *After Virtue* (London: Duckworth, 1981), chap. 17; Taylor, "The Nature and Scope of Distributive Justice"; Sandel, *Liberalism*, chap. 4.

23. Only Taylor seems in any way sympathetic to socialist views, and even he is mainly concerned to present socialism as trapped in the same modernist predicament as other outlooks: see Charles Taylor, "Socialism and Weltanschauung," in *The Socialist Ideal*, ed. Leszek Kolakowski and Stuart Hampshire (London: Quartet, 1977).

24. MacIntyre, *After Virtue*, p. 205.

25. Ibid., p. 221.

26. See ibid., pp. 236–37 and Alasdair MacIntyre, "Is Patriotism a Virtue?" Lindley Lecture, University of Kansas, 1984.

27. MacIntyre, *After Virtue*, p. 237.

28. For further reflection on the difficulties this entails, see my "Virtues and Practices," *Analyse und Kritik* 6 (1984): 49–60.

29. See Charles Taylor, "Atomism," in *Philosophy and the Human Sciences: Philosophical Papers II* (Cambridge: Cambridge University Press, 1985).

30. See Charles Taylor, *Hegel* (Cambridge: Cambridge University Press, 1975), esp. chaps. 1 and 20; "Legitimation Crisis?" in *Philosophy and the Human Sciences: Philosophical Papers II* (Cambridge: Cambridge University Press, 1985).

31. Taylor, "Legitimation Crisis?" p. 283.

32. Charles Taylor, "Language and Human Nature," in *Human Agency and Language: Philosophical Papers I* (Cambridge: Cambridge University Press, 1985), p. 234.

33. Ibid., p. 208.

34. Taylor, "Atomism," p. 207. Taylor later adds to his argument the claim that political deliberation forms an essential part of freedom, but this has the appearance of an afterthought. See ibid., p. 208.

35. Michael Sandel, "The Procedural Republic and the Unencumbered Self," *Political Theory* 12 (1984): 81–96.

36. If communal relationships foster a sense of justice that is relatively egalitarian, why shouldn't a society made up of small local communities develop a society-wide scheme of redistribution? Unfortunately, there is no reason to expect the *scope* of a practice of distributive justice to extend beyond the community that supports it. There is ample historical evidence of small communities (tribes, guilds, cooperatives) practicing quite radical forms of egalitarian redistribution internally, but dealing with outsiders on very different terms. Socialists must look for community at the level at which effective policies can be made for whole societies, which, in practice, means at the level of the nation-state.

37. I discuss ethical particularism more fully in "The Ethical Significance of Nationality," *Ethics* 98 (1987–88): 647–62. See also Andrew Oldenquist, "Loyalties," *Journal of Philosophy* 74 (1982): 173–93; John Cottingham, "Partiality, Favoritism and Morality," *Philosophical Quarterly* 36 (1986): 357–73; Philip Pettit, "Social Holism and Moral Theory," *Proceedings of the Aristotelian Society* 86 (1985–86): 173–97.

38. There is no need, I think, to commit ourselves on the question of whether it is ultimately preferable to have a world order made up of distinct national communities or a global community. On one side stands the value of diversity; on the other, the problems of international distributive justice. The point is that the most extensive communal identities that people currently have are national identities, and there is no sign that this is about to change. Insofar as there is any movement, it appears to be in the direction of smaller, more intense forms of nationality rather than towards internationalism.

39. Benedict Anderson, *Imagined Communities: Reflections on the Origin and Spread of Nationalism* (London: Verso, 1983).

40. See "The Ethical Significance of Nationality."

41. "In the end, when the state, on the brink of ruin, can maintain itself only in an empty and illusory form, when the social bond is broken in every heart, when the meanest interest impudently flaunts the sacred name of the public good, then the general will is silenced: everyone, animated by secret motives, ceases to speak as a citizen any more than as if the state had never existed; and the people enacts in the guise of laws iniquitous decrees which have private interests as their only end." Jean-Jacques Rousseau, *The Social Contract* (Harmondsworth: Penguin, 1968), p. 150.

42. Michael Walzer, "Liberalism and the Art of Separation," *Political Theory* 12 (1984): 315–30.

43. I use "artifice" here in its neutral, Humean sense.

44. Jon Elster, *Three Lectures on Constitutional Choice* (Oslo, 1981, mimeo).

45. For an attempt at conciliation, see Gutmann, "Communitarian Critics of Liberalism." See also the brief discussion in Michael Sandel, "Morality and the Liberal Ideal," *New Republic,* 7 May 1984, pp. 15–17.

46. I have grasped this nettle in "Socialism and Toleration," in *Justifying Toleration,* ed. Susan Mendus (Cambridge: Cambridge University Press, 1988).

14.

WHOSE SOCIALISM? WHICH DEMOCRACY?

FRANK CUNNINGHAM

Alexis de Tocqueville explained that his famous study, *Democracy in America*, was written "under the impulse of a kind of religious dread inspired by contemplation of this irresistible revolution."[1] Tocqueville was referring to democratic revolutions as in France and the United States. He saw these as the inexorable outcomes of a history of growing social and economic equality beginning as early as the twelfth century when, initially through the church, "equality began to insinuate itself into the heart of government."[2] By the beginning of the twentieth century the association of democracy and equality expressed by Tocqueville had taken the form of an association between democracy and socialism. But by the end of the century socialism had come to be paired in the public mind with authoritarianism (not without reason), while capitalism was regarded essential for democracy. As in nearly all such general conceptions, both in theories and in popular political culture, closer examination reveals complexities.

Madison, Jefferson, and Hamilton held very different views about how American democracy was best conceived and conducted. Not long after Tocqueville was writing, European socialists were locked into debate about whether socialism ought to be thought of in egalitarian terms, as the Lassallean wing of the German socialist movement maintained, or as a matter of the political dictatorship of the proletariat, as was argued by followers of Karl Liebknecht, most notably Marx and Engels.[3] In the next century, the "realist" school of democratic theory was launched with the publication in 1942 of Joseph Schumpeter's *Capitalism, Socialism and Democracy*, central to which is the idea, quite anemic compared to the engaged democracy Tocqueville had reported, that democracy is nothing but competition among would-be political leaders for the popular vote.[4] On this conception all that remains of equality among citizens is that each possesses the ability to vote.

Reprinted by permission of the author.

Notwithstanding periodic announcements of the "end of ideology," debates over the nature and value of democracy, socialism, and their relation continue. Regarding democracy this is evident in challenges to the realists by deliberative democrats, radical pluralists, civic republicans, and, at a more popular level, by renewed advocacy of participatory democracy on the part of radical environmentalists and social-movement veterans of "the battle of Seattle." Nor have debates among prosocialists been put to rest, as they see in the demise of Soviet and Eastern European Communism an opening for fresh socialist theory and activity now free of the albatross.[5]

In one sense of "ideology," namely having to do with motivating ideas of political culture, these debates are ideological. In another, pejorative sense they are also ideological when claims which in fact rationalize favored positions are announced as objective discoveries of eternal truths. Below I shall advance a "quasi-ideological" conception of democratic socialism that aims to explicate an ideal by reference to certain political values. Contrary to such an effort ideologically undertaken in the pejorative sense, links of this conception with specific and contestable value commitments will be acknowledged. A brief survey of standard political arguments will set the stage for the explication.

FORMS OF A CLASSIC STANDOFF

Stepping back from debates over the relation of socialism and democracy, the following controversies are thrown into relief. A standard argument of procapitalists has been that capitalism and democracy are clearly compatible (even if capitalism does not guarantee democracy), while none of the socialist regimes as in China or the former Soviet Union tolerated such things as genuinely free elections, constitutional protection of political and civil rights, or political party competition. Strong enough before the demise of Communism in the Soviet Union and Eastern Europe around 1989, this argument subsequently acquired more force. Before the demise, socialists in the tradition of Lenin countered that "real existing socialism" (as the regimes began desperately calling themselves toward the end) *were* democratic in a higher and truer form than capitalist, parliamentary democracy. From 1989 only strained attribution of mass false consciousness could sustain such a perspective as population after population rejected even Gorbachev's tame version of Communist socialism.

A contrasting argument to defend the compatibility of socialism and democracy notes that within liberal-democratic systems of government socialist political parties or coalitions sometimes mount electoral campaigns explicitly based on socialist platforms. From time to time these campaigns have enjoyed a certain measure of success, and one can imagine major electoral victories with large enough majority support to produce an enduring socialist government. (At least the procapitalist media can imagine it, as is seen in the extraordinary lengths to which they go to persuade people that programs with even the slightest hint of socialism are irrelevant, while shutting socialistic voices out of media exposure.) If this scenario is imaginable, it shows that there is no opposition *in principle* between socialism and democracy, and the question to ask is why socialism fails to enjoy electoral success.

One explanation is, of course, that voting populations are too wise to support socialistic political initiatives. An alternative explanation is that socialist electoral successes are reversed or prevented by undemocratic means when they are seen to challenge capitalist interests. A dramatic example is the 1973 military coup in Chile where a socialist government *was* elected and then overthrown with the well-documented support and planning of large U.S.-based capitalist enterprises and government agencies. Less violent is the realistic threat of economic penalties against a population that tries to implement socialistic policies through capital flight, refusal to extend credit to a socialist government, and other such measures. Socialist governments or parties are then in the bind of making concessions to the point that they are largely indistinguishable from alternatives or standing firm and then getting the blame for effects of threats carried out.

These observations shade into the most common argument against capitalism and for socialism with respect to democracy, namely that concentration of great wealth and power in the hands of a small minority of people in a capitalist system gives them the ability to manipulate electoral and party politics, to take disproportionate advantage of constitutionally protected rights, or to circumvent democratic procedures or legal constraints with relative impunity.[6] The mobility of capitalist enterprises and their ability to escape responsibility to any state afforded by globalization give new force to this argument.

Libertarian counters to the wealth-buys-democracy argument are less in vogue than during the heady days of Thatcher- and Reaganism, and in any case libertarians are at best ambiguously prodemocratic. Since the main argument of libertarianism is that unfettered markets offer those who deserve wealth the best chance of attaining it, they ought to be wary of the possibility of a majority voting for market constraints.[7] A procapitalist counter that does not depend upon embrace of libertarianism is that socialist policies involve long-range planning, which, in addition to placing excessive power in the hands of senior bureaucrats, requires that individual wishes be either sacrificed to the exigencies of plans or manipulated to conform to them. Thus does socialism constitute, in Friedrich Hayek's term, a road to serfdom.[8]

IDEALS, INSTITUTIONS, MOVEMENTS

Many, indeed in the current era of triumphant capitalism perhaps most, would not see a standoff in these arguments, since the authoritarianism and then the collapse of socialist governments in the Soviet Union and Eastern Europe are supposed to offer conclusive empirical proof against the socialist case. However, as in all political issues of large magnitude, the question of the compatibility of socialism and democracy is not settled by some analogue of a crucial experiment in science. Defenders of the erstwhile socialist societies can argue that their collapse fails to disprove the vision of communism of Marx and Engels. They thought that working-class revolutions in developed countries would quickly lead to participatory democracy as the dictatorship of the proletariat ("the first phase of communism") autodestructed in favor of the classless and cooperative societies of advanced communism.

That socialist revolutions took place instead in economically deprived countries changed everything, as they simply lacked the resources to effect a transition to the higher phase of communism, especially since they had to contend with opposition on the part of the more powerful, developed countries where revolutions were supposed to take place but instead became their capitalist foes. Reactions of the now overwhelming proportion of socialists who do not defend former incarnations of "real existing socialism" are even easier, since they can claim that these were depraved forms of socialism or even not true examples of socialism at all, and hence their experiences are irrelevant to the question at hand.

I do not intend directly to evaluate these charges and alternative counterclaims, though to the extent that they depend upon how democracy and socialism are to be interpreted the effort to disentangle various senses of these terms will bear on such evaluation. The reason that this effort will relate to the empirical arguments only indirectly is that the latter mainly address institutional matters, while the essay addresses normative and conceptual questions. In general one may distinguish three aspects of theories and debates regarding socialism: those that concern themselves with the "ideal" of socialism, that is, conceptions of its nature and value; projections of institutionalized governmental and economic frameworks within which a socialist ideal can (or must) be realized in ongoing practice; and proposals about the political activities required to secure the requisite institutions.

Most socialists today see some version of a parliamentary or presidential/congressional system with constitutional protection of rights and competition among political parties as appropriate to a socialist society, though there are differences about whether or how these should relate to nongovernmental organizations, and there are some more radical proposals, as, for instance, associative-democratic alternatives harkening back to guild socialism and suggestions for pyramiding systems of people's assemblies.[9] Regarding institutionalized economic practices, the most vital current debates among socialists are over the feasibility and best forms for achieving socialist goals within a market economy, usually conjoined with proposals for workers' self-management.[10] The main controversies about how socialist governments and economies are to be achieved are between those who favor the centrality of political activity by and within socialist or social-democratic political parties and champions of social-movement activism.

A similar three-way classification pertains to democracy, over which there are also debates about what it is and why it is to be valued, how it is best conducted, and how democracy can be attained or protected and enhanced. To be sure, both in the case of democracy and of socialism an approach to one of these aspects will have implications for treatments of the others. But failure to keep the treatments analytically separate not only makes for confusion but can have political implications. The Schumpeterian, "realist" conception of democracy fuses its ideal with one institution, namely of voting for leaders in a parliamentary system, and this fusion in turn facilitates unfortunate political practices and attitudes such as cynical manipulation of elections by politicians and public apathy (redescribed by later followers of Schumpeter as an unobjectionable part of normal democratic politics[11]). The authoritarianism of the late socialist societies was sustained, if not entirely caused, by generalizing militant and hierarchically organized socialist movement politics into the ideal of socialist democracy as proletarian dictatorship.

"Socialism" and "democracy," like "right," "justice," "freedom," "equality," and other key political terms are often said to designate contested concepts, but it is not always clear just what the nature of the contests is. On one interpretation they are over what such a term means when it captures the one, true essence of its putative referent. On another interpretation, any politically loaded term will be ambiguous or vague in popular discourse, and contests among political actors or theorists are attempts to focus thinking in accord with their favored uses. Like most theorists, Schumpeter mixes up these two contestatory strategies. He confronts those who think of democracy as popular self-government with challenging counterarguments, chief among which are that it requires unanimity of values not to be found in large modern societies and that it presupposes more rationality and political commitment among a citizenry than is warranted. Intermingled with these arguments are undefended assertions such as that the classical alternative to his conception of democracy is a "utilitarian rationalism" which "nobody accepts as a correct theory of the body politic."[12]

The second sort of argument is what I earlier called ideological in a pejorative sense: it advocates one conception under the guise of authoritatively reporting on the only coherent way of describing democracy. Clearly, however, there are alternatives (which need not suppose "utilitarian rationalism"). Town-hall type meetings, or on a larger scale electronic analogues, where people talk through issues and select leaders deliberately *avoiding* a vote in order to reach positive consensus are regarded by many as prototypes of democracy. Others think that an Athenian practice of selecting leaders by lot is sometimes superior to voting as a democratic procedure.[13] Schumpeter's definition confines democracy to formal, governmental elections, but this will be resisted by participatory democrats who think democracy appropriate to such institutions as neighborhoods, schools, families, or workplaces. On the realist definition such things as protest demonstrations and union or social-movement organization do not count as democratic activities, contrary to those who think of democracy more broadly as any form of joint action people take to gain some control over situations they share in common.

The other arguments Schumpeter deploys are also intended to shape public thinking, but the effort proceeds by linking his conception of democracy with views he thinks others will share and which will accordingly make them sympathetic to his conception. This approach was called quasi-ideological above because, while it aims to affect political opinions and does so by appeal to popular conceptions and values, it makes this explicit and invites debate and inter-rogation. For instance, someone with a richer notion of democracy in mind than Schumpeter's is obliged to show that it is realistic (either because sufficient con-sensus at least over political values can be counted on or because democracy does not require as much in the way of consensus as Schumpter seems to think) and that people are not as prone to political apathy as his view implies.

IDEALS OF DEMOCRACY

As employed in this essay an "ideal" of democracy (as of socialism) is a compo-nent or a potential component of popular culture in terms of which people orga-nize and prioritize their political thinking and practice, and it will be composed of two dimensions, a conception of what democracy is and of what it is for. I suppose that many people agree with theorists in the rational choice tradition in thinking that voting exhausts the nature of democracy. Some may agree with one or the other of two different views within this tradition of what voting is for, which are either to advance a voter's self-interest or to achieve a social aggregation of pref-erences.[14] That some people regard town-hall type efforts to reach consensus or mass actions as democratic is evidenced by the fact that these are often thus described by participants. Moreover, even among people who think of democracy only as voting, I suspect that those who value it simply for advancing their self-interest are rare. This is not because people do not look in part (or even exclusively for some all the time or for everyone sometimes) to their own interests when they vote, but because, as neo-Schumpeterians like Anthony Downs point out,[15] the chance of one's vote being decisive is almost always too small to offset the costs of voting; hence, people must be partly motivated to vote by the view that in doing so they participate in a worthwhile process. At the other end of a spectrum, there may be some for whom the value of democracy is as abstract as to aggregate pref-erences (or to participate in free and equal "discursive will-formation," to take another abstract theory of democracy's value), but, again, I suspect that most value democracy more for reasons of everyday morality than of high ethical theory.

Although in popular thinking, the two dimensions of democracy are not often clearly distinguished, this does not mean that political ideals are utterly value-laden. Full-fledged ideological contests would be hard to avoid if these were nothing but conflicting normative judgments, since people's conceptions of a sub-ject matter would then be no more than expressions of their political values. How-ever, in all the enduring disputes, the descriptive and normative dimensions can be distinguished. Those with differing value judgments can understand one another and agree that each of their characterizations succeeds, or in principle could suc-ceed, as descriptions of actual states of affair. Where they differ is in their views about what merits institutional and cultural promotion in current political societies. Contests are thus to be found at both normative and nonnormative levels.

David Beetham's discussion of what he calls democracy's two "principles" serves as a useful point of entry to the various dimensions of this topic regarding democracy. According to him, "a system of collective decision making" is democratic "to the extent that it is subject to control by all members of the relevant association . . . considered as equals."[16] Democracy on this conception includes two elements, control and equality, which, though they may on occasion be in conflict, are jointly required for full democracy. Beetham thus differs from those who think democracy is simply equal possession of democratic political rights and from those who see it exclusively as a means for individuals to gain control over environments they share with others by taking collective action. Of interest in this essay is not whether Beetham is justified in his claim that his concept is "uncontestable" but his focusing on these two features, whether regarded components of a single conception or as competing ones.

Political equality can be interpreted narrowly to refer to the possession of rights of political participation or broadly to include equal access to resources requisite for effective use of the rights. While there is room for debate over just which rights are to be included and how they are to be prioritized as there is over what resources in what amounts are necessary for meaningful democratic participation, any combination of stances on such issues will yield a descriptive conception amenable to assessment by those with different evaluations of democratic equality. Specific examples of collective control over a shared environment are also easy enough to identify, for example, when people vote for legislators or when workers engage in a strike, and of course each of these admits of finer differentiation depending on what voting rules are employed or how a social action is organized and conducted. It is more difficult, though in my view not impossible, to produce a generic characterization to describe what all such exercises share,[17] but at least a list of specific instances could be generated both by those who highly value collective activity and by those who do not.

Conceptions of democracy that are not easily molded into normatively neutral descriptions are offered among others by participationists, deliberative democrats, and civic republicans for whom it is essential for democracy that participants pursue the public good. If this qualification is accepted, then somebody who disagrees about what is identified as the good toward which a truly democratic society aims must also disagree that the society in question is democratic or else accept the normative description and reject democracy as something worthwhile. A moral relativist could avoid this alternative by interpreting the qualification to mean that democratic participants pursue goods as they perceive them, without passing judgment on the goods, or "public good" could be interpreted nonnormatively as interests members of a political society happen to have in common. But those who insist on this component of democracy properly conceived usually have in mind some objective and morally praiseworthy goals in mind, such as promotion of cooperation and cultivation of civically virtuous characters.

Less obviously normative are the interpretations that control and equality acquire when justifications for thinking of democracy in terms of one or both of them are entertained. Democracy for Schumpeter had to do with equality in a very restricted sense, namely at the ballot box. His main justification for this restriction was that anything more intrusive in the way of citizen involvement in politics impeded the free hand elected officials and the civil service required for efficient government. He thus supposed an image of democracy that values such things as efficiency and trust in bureaucratic expertise above citizen engagement. Most post-Schumpeterians have seen the principal merit of his thin conception as a way for citizens to have the negative control over politicians of being able to punish them if they too severely dissatisfied a majority.[18] This attitude toward democracy is labeled by some "protective" and criticized, again on normative grounds, for encouraging a merely reactive political culture which detracts from the potential of democratic engagement to enrich the lives of citizens. An alternative is "developmental" democracy, where, as in the views of C. B. Macpherson and Carol Gould, engaging with others in democratic participation is crucial in developing the full range of people's most important human potentials.[19]

Thomas Christiano identifies developmental-democratic theories as the most defensible version of democracy interpreted in terms of freedom or self-government, and he gives reasons to reject them for a conception of democratic equality, though one more robust than Schumpeter's since he allows for equality in access to means for effective participation. The justification Christiano gives for equality as the core conception of democracy is that by affording each an equal voice, the value of equal human worth is affirmed and government and its laws are thereby legitimized.[20] In tension, if not in contradiction, with this interpretation of democratic equality is one advanced by antioppressive theorists such as Iris Young.[21] While not disagreeing with the view that individuals are equally worthy of respect, she focuses on the potential for democracy to promote political inclusion, which is regarded especially vital for members of discriminated against or otherwise oppressed groups systemically excluded from full participation in public affairs. On this view inclusion is defended by reference to a mandate to end exclusion of those subject to systemic oppression or domination. This also makes the resulting conception a normative one, since terms like "oppression" and "subordination" are not value-free terms. (One does not describe thieves as oppressed though they are systematically impeded by the law and public opinion.)

To recap, in addition to the normatively neutral descriptions of democracy as political equality and/or joint control, five value-laden conceptions may be identified: the qualification that democracy must serve common goods; interpretations of democratic control as protective or as developmental; one justification of democratic equality for treating people with equal respect and another for providing political inclusion. Defense of a democratic-socialist orientation which generated a similar list of socialist ideals, and showed that socialism is necessary for democracy (or as I would prefer to put it for making significant democratic progress) while attending only to the normatively-neutral characterizations would have a certain finality about it. I have maintained that success in such a task is elusive and that putative demonstrations of this sort will employ unacknowledged value judgments and hence be objectionably ideological. The alternative is to defend one or more normative conceptions of each of democracy and socialism and to show them compatible or complementary in a way that would make the complex ideal of democratic socialism more attractive than any alternative.

IDEALS OF SOCIALISM

Two main generic uses of "socialism" have already been noted, namely that of the Lassalleans in terms of equality and of the Marxists as the dictatorship of the proletariat. Marxists and many in the egalitarian camp also advocate abolition of private property. Whether this should count as a third generic sense of a socialist ideal depends upon whether such abolition is regarded a conceptually essential part of socialism or, like economic planning or dependence on market mechanisms, part of institutionalized economic organization at least compatible with socialist goals. Also alluded to were some efforts to make out direct cases for socialism on democratic grounds: the Leninist claim that proletarian dictatorship is a higher form of democracy and the egalitarian socialist argument that economic equality is a necessary condition for effective use of democratic rights. However, not only is each claim contested in the ways reviewed, but as in the case of descriptive conceptions of democracy, each of these uses of "socialism" takes on normative connotations when interpreted and justified.

With the exception of a minority of utopian communalists, no socialist denies that people ought to have a legally protected right of personal *access* to some things, for instance, a car or house, where this means that the "owner" of such a thing enjoys a presumptive right to decide how it is to be used. Only on the most extreme of libertarian orientations, however, is this right absolute, since nearly everyone recognizes circumstances when the presumption can legitimately be overridden, most obviously when such use will or might harm others. A crucial question arises when it is asked whether "harming" in this context should be taken in part to mean "not helping."

In the case of a car or house, this would mean not that it would be an admirable instance of supererogation were I, for example, to turn over part of my house to a homeless person, but that I have a positive duty to help the homeless, if necessary by this means. For some who consider private property sacrosanct, recognition of such obligations already constitutes denial of it. Others may grant that holders of private property have positive duties, and consider the pivotal question to be whether these duties should be subject to public regulation. This might be by legal enforcement of positive duties or by planning, whereby something would cease to be my private property when I cease to be the locus of first decision making about its use, which role is instead assumed by public bodies.

My inclination is to include as part of a socialist ideal that, with respect to personal possessions like cars, people ought to be considered as having positive duties, but that these should neither be legally enforced nor planned, while in the case of profit-making institutions such as factories or banks, a duty to help should also be enforced. Whether the locus of first decision making with regard to such holdings should reside in public bodies rather than in the hands of individuals or (as would likely be more consistent with democratic principles) of collectives such as of farmers cooperatives or worker self-managed enterprises, I see as institutional questions. I shall return to this topic later in discussing the question of whether or how people should be considered as having property rights in themselves.

Marxists in the tradition of Lenin recognized that the proletariat as an entire class cannot literally govern and accordingly interpreted proletarian dictatorship to mean government by a political party representing the objective interests of the proletariat. But unless a strictly amoral, power-political stance is adopted, it must be averred that the objective interests of proletarians are consistent with those interests that *ought* to motivate people generally. This makes the claim of Marx and Engels that the proletarian movement is "of the immense majority in the interests of the immense majority"[22] plausible (on the assumption that success of this movement is in most people's true interests). I shall not pursue the controversies that exercised Marxist scholars for many decades about just how to interpret the dictatorship of the proletariat, because I think that from the point of view of articulating a democracy-friendly ideal of socialism any version of it suffers the fatal flaw of inconsistency with pluralism.

I take it as given that democratic institutions, policies, and habits must accommodate as far as possible people's abilities to pursue their own ends in their own ways. The many debates among liberal-democratic theorists over how far a democratic state may be neutral regarding conceptions of the good life or should tolerate antiliberal attitudes certainly address a hard problem, but they all presuppose the pluralist principle and are largely about how to interpret its "as far as possible" rider. The experience of politics informed by the dictatorship of the proletariat conception stands as a damning example of the attempt autocratically to control a society, paternalistically justifying this by reference to a theory of objective interests and disguising the paternalism as a higher form of democracy.[23]

Turning now to an egalitarian conception of socialism, it, too, confronts a theorist with several decisions, the first of which is to determine what sorts of things socialism is to equalize. Materially regarded, socialist equality is limited to things to which monetary value can be appropriately and directly assigned. Alternatives are "spiritual" or "cultural" things, such as friendship (to which it is inappropriate to assign monetary value) and political equality, the costs of which (for instance, to run an election) can be ascertained, though the equality itself is an entitlement which does not have a price directly attached to it. Some socialists object to limiting the concept of socialism to economic concerns, thinking that this makes it a crudely materialistic affair. Wary of efforts to build into the very conception of socialism everything one values (advocates of socialism's late incarnation were experts at this), I shall urge that the core descriptive notion of socialism should be regarded in terms of material or economic equality, the worth of which resides in promoting certain valued states of affairs.

A general and value-neutral description of socialism in this sense can be given by contrasting it with capitalism, that is, a society with a market-driven competitive economy in which private owners of major means of production, distribution, financial capital, and other such profit-generating assets are presumptively (though not entirely) free of state interference to dispose of their holdings and profits as they please. Socialism economically conceived is, then, an alternative to capitalism where the presumption that guides policy is to achieve material equality. Some wish to reserve the term "social democracy" for such an arrangement and often distinguish between "right-wing social democracy," which employs egalitarian rhetoric to cover policies compatible with ongoing capitalism, and "left social democracy," where the egalitarian presumption is sincere and policies actually challenge capitalism. To the extent that even left-wing social democracy has historically restricted itself to electoral politics and exhibited suspicion, if not outright hostility to extraparliamentary, movement politics (other than those of certain trade unions), it is also criticized by some egalitarian socialists, but with respect to economic egalitarianism this is a dispute over the means for realizing a socialist ideal, rather than over the ideal itself.

Just as notions of democracy as control and/or equality are challenged on normative grounds for leaving out of account commitment to the public good, so some challenge the egalitarian conception of socialism sketched above for detracting from what is seen as the more important potential of socialism to promote social solidarity.[24] This challenge expresses another ideal of socialism, which might be taken in a normative or a nonnormative sense depending upon whether one views solidarity as something to be valued in itself. Thought of as action motivated by a spirit of cooperation and mutual aid, solidarity might be seen as either or both a means to achieving equality (since support for egalitarian policies requires sacrifices on the part of some people) or a result of egalitarian redistribution, which lessens conflict over scarce resources by reducing the artificial scarcities created by extreme wealth in the midst of poverty. In its full-blown sense, solidarity involves a thoroughgoing coordination of individuals' interests so "the free development of each is the condition for the free development of all."[25] Solidarity in this full sense almost certainly runs afoul of the injunction imposed above to preserve pluralism. The notion of cooperative spirit as a means is, however, another matter shortly to be taken up.

Regarding economic equality, it, too, stands in need of interpretation. Equality enters the Marxist conception both of the lower and the advanced stages of communism, where in the latter material benefits and burdens are to be distributed according to need, while in the former they are to be distributed according to one's contribution to a socialist society as measured by productive work.[26] As stated, each of these criteria for distribution is incomplete. Regarding equality in the first phase of communism, there is the problem of ascertaining what counts as how much of a contribution; also an egalitarian must surely allow for subsidizing those who cannot work (a large proportion if one includes children, the very aged, and the ill). Distribution in accord with need raises the problem of determining what needs are and calls to mind current debates among egalitarian political theorists such as Ronald Dworkin or G. A. Cohen: Should equality be of resources or of results? Ought egalitarian policy to set welfare floors, income ceilings, or both? Is equality to be understood subjectively, or should objective standards be employed? Should people be held responsible for disadvantages they bring on themselves?[27] Different answers to these sorts of questions will generate alternative interpretations of equality and hence of ideals of socialism economically regarded.

Recapping this survey of candidates for a socialist ideal, a general distinction is among proletarian dictatorship, equality, solidarity, and rejection of some kind or degree of private property. Solidarity might be thought of as unity of interests or less contentiously as possession of a cooperative spirit and as a means to or an end of socialism interpreted in egalitarian fashion. Meanwhile, equality might be interpreted as any or all of a material, a cultural, or a political affair. A characterization of socialism in economic terms has been sketched, and in the next section some specific interpretations of cultural and political equality will be advocated as central to a satisfactory socialist ideal, as will a stance toward one kind of property.

A DEMOCRATIC-SOCIALIST IDEAL

The standard socialist argument summarized at the beginning of the essay regards democracy as a matter of substantive political equality and, defining socialism by reference to political equality, merges the two ideals. One problem with this approach is that capitalism can also coexist with some measure of democracy, even including limited access to means for political participation (for instance, tax exemptions for political parties, including socialist or social-democratic parties). Also, substantive political equality requires planned economic redistribution, which then confronts problems of bureaucratization, on the one hand, and the difficulty that this will be strenuously resisted by powerful capitalist opposition, on the other.

I see no solutions to the last-mentioned problems that do not involve active determination on the part of a large majority of a society's population to confront them. Dangers of capitalist retaliation for trying to implement socialist policies can only be met by a population prepared to call the bluff of what, in effect, are threats of blackmail. Since the threats are often real, this requires a population prepared actually to tighten its belt in a kind of prosocialist "battle of Britain." As even critics of Soviet-style plannification and defenders of market socialism allow, some measure of planning is unavoidable, both to solve economic problems that market transactions cannot and also to approximate equality. So the antidemocratic dangers that accompany planning must be addressed, and, again, a population with the right kinds of attitudes is required. Planning in which there is widespread public input and where individual members of the public take a broad and public-spirited view rather than each pushing recommendations out of narrow self-interest will be more durable than otherwise. Continuing public monitoring of plans and the means taken to implement them in the same spirit (and, where feasible, with direct citizen involvement) is required to prevent them from getting objectionably entrenched or taken advantage of by self-serving government officials.

These considerations make it tempting to promote ideals of democracy and/or of socialism that associate them with advancing the public good or achieving social solidarity. This tack, however, dangerously threatens pluralism, as when critics of a socialist plan are stigmatized or a socialist battle of Britain prompts a siege mentality where departures from democracy are accepted and critics are labeled traitors. In general, a conception is needed full enough to encourage active commitment in the right spirit but modest enough to avoid building valued goals into one's conception in such a way as to put pluralism at risk by encouraging paternalism or worse. Readers in sympathy with the project of integrating democratic and socialist campaigns (or even readers who are just intrigued by this puzzle of democratic and socialist theory) and who agree that the lists of candidates for democratic and socialist ideals are more or less accurate, will no doubt favor various combinations suitable for resolving this problem. This essay concludes by indicating my own choices.

Recalling that ideals are generated by interpreting and justifying descriptive core notions, I take as the descriptive core of socialism the economic definition given above in contrasting it with capitalism. As to democracy, I favor a core description in terms of collective actions to achieve joint control (though I think this notion best explicated by thinking of democracy as a matter of degree as sketched in note 17). Barring strained and implausible interpretations, these decisions rule out a proletarian dictatorship conception of socialism and a Schumpeterian notion of democracy. As noted, the first of these is objectionably antipluralist, while the Schumpeterian conception encourages political passivity, which not only dampens democratic initiative but is inimical to the active public involvement I have claimed to be essential to socialist politics. When normative ideas enter a conception of democracy, it seems to me there is much to be said for urging that democratic control encompass equality in both senses discussed. Joint control over shared environments is enhanced to the extent that none of those affected by the environment is excluded from participation in appropriate means of control over them, and equal possession of democratic rights is desirable as a presumptive base because this promotes a culture of mutual respect, which in addition to whatever moral virtues this embodies, is conducive to cooperative dispositions.

Macpherson's "developmental" conception of democracy as essentially involving the "equal effective right to live as fully as [one] may wish"[28] is similar to notions that insist democracy serve an objective public good. Their virtue is in offering a proactive ideal that can engage citizens in ways that seeing democracy as no more than a method for selecting leaders cannot. A problem in Macpherson's account is that he insists on prescribing the goals toward which democratic activity should be directed, namely that the development essential to democracy must be of people's "essentially human capacities,"[29] and this, again, has antipluralist implications. In keeping with Macpherson's view that political societies ought primarily to recognize people as "doers and creators" rather than just as "consumers of utilities," democracy may be valued for enabling people to take control of their lives, which at least means to be able to act on life projects important to them. If this ability is not to be confined to a few whose economic or political positions free them from the constraint of having democratically to coordinate their activities with those of others, it must be exercised in coopera-tive collective action, which, as participationists from Mill on have insisted, is not only an exigency but has rewards of its own. However, it is one thing to link democracy with the ideal of controlling one's life and another to link it with some specific end toward which this life should be directed, whether of the neo-Aris-totelian sort championed by Macpherson or some other goal.

Accordingly, I suggest a modification of Macpherson's conception comple-mented with one of Young's to yield, respectively, "proactive" and "reactive" conceptions that I think should be regarded integral to an ideal of democratic socialism. They begin with a generic conception offered by Cohen. For him egal-itarianism values people being provided with the "opportunities" and the "capac-ities" to enjoy life's advantages (provided that deficiencies in these things do not result from one's own uncoerced choices).[30] He deliberately leaves it vague what "advantages" are, and it would no doubt be very difficult to give a general defi-nition. But in the case of socialist equality, two candidates are suggested both by elements of a democratic ideal endorsed above. One "advantage" is overcoming systemic disadvantages. Being systemic such disadvantages apply to entire groups of people and have deep roots in the social, economic, cultural, and polit-ical structures of a society. As such they call for just the sorts of remedial mea-sures that socialist provision of resources and planning can offer. (So right-wing criticisms of affirmative action for being socialistic are in this respect on target.) Thus, a reactive conception of socialist equality is as provision of those material resources required for people to acquire the capacities and opportunities to over-come systemic disadvantage. With respect to democracy, this means that socialism serves the ideal of democratic equality in the sense of inclusion.

On a complementary, proactive sense, socialism may be regarded as the pro-vision of material resources requisite for the opportunities and capacities people need to live meaningful lives as they see them. Prominent among these are diverse and quality educational opportunities and resources necessary for free time. The intent here is to capture something of Macpherson's developmental view of democracy and of its potential to enable people to pursue life projects valued by them. The rider "as they see them" is included to protect pluralism. This, of course, confronts the problem faced by the liberal-democratic theorists about identifying limits to pluralism, but I think this problem less acute when confined in the way suggested. Claims about what makes a life meaningful are not like announcements of short-term preferences; more is needed to justify a polity's allocation of resources to its promotion. Such a polity would not be acting in an objectionable paternalistic way, it seems to me, if it denied allocation to someone whose life plan was clearly frivolous, hopelessly unrealistic, or blatantly harmful to others.

As urged earlier, a democratic-socialist society ought, in addition, to be one that places a high value on cooperation, provided this is not interpreted in a pluralist-threatening fashion. I think of two ways cooperation-endorsing ideals might be articulated, one pertaining to democracy and one to socialism. Drawing a cooperative ideal out of democracy is best achieved, in my view, by reviving the perspective of John Dewey that democracy is a matter of how groups of people collectively confront problems they face in common.[31] This notion does not suppose unanimity of values or purposes, but it does encourage a proactive approach to democratic politics and a disposition to try seeking out mutually acceptable solutions. In this way not only would socialism serve democratic ideals, but democracy could play a vital role in confronting the severe problems efforts to achieve and sustain a viable socialism can be counted on to face.

Socialist theorists are not in accord about whether people privately own themselves,[32] but I think rejection of an ethic of self-ownership in some, but not all, of the senses discussed above is an important component of a socialist ideal. Specifically, I think that this ideal should include the notion that people have positive duties to exercise their capacities in ways helpful to others. Confronted by those who consider this an outlandish intrusion into what is exclusively theirs, the social-scientific observation (obvious to all but megalomaniacs) that people's abilities, including the nurturing of whatever natural talents they inherit, are social products is appropriate. But even if some talents are somehow entirely self-created, people should be recognized as having obligations of mutual aid that supersede and hence vitiate supposed unfettered property rights in their abilities. Denying self-ownership in this sense does not entail that I refrain from using the capacities and talents I enjoy to promote my own well-being and satisfaction or insist in an antipluralist way on just what I should take satisfaction in, and it should be recognized that I am the locus of first decision making regarding deployment of my talents. Rather, this thesis suggests that I regard myself as the *custodian* of my capacities and that I undertake to discharge the duties of custodianship by exercising them in socially responsible ways.[33]

In a political-economic climate when selfish greed and consumerism are either fatalistically decried as hegemonic attitudes of current popular culture or promoted as true expressions of human nature, it is fashionable to regard any political ventures that depend upon widespread values favoring such things as equality, engaged collective action, or mutual aid as unrealistic. This, in turn, prompts some who classify themselves democrats and socialists to endorse minimalist, even Schumpeterian conceptions of democracy and/or versions of social democracy that could no more than soften the edges of capitalism. My own opinion is that people embrace possessive-individualist lifestyles or aspirations by default of the availability of resources to lead meaningful lives. On this view, it is not unrealistic to seek components among popular values of a democratic-socialist ideal as described in this essay or at least to look for kindred values amenable to cultivation. If, however, there is no purchase on such values in popular culture, democratic socialism of the form described here is not in the cards.

This is not the forum in which to defend an optimistic viewpoint on this question, about which readers will certainly have differing opinions. Nor is it the place to address the enormously challenging questions about socialist institutions or ways that successful socialist politics might be undertaken, though a defensible conception of a democratic-socialist ideal would bear on these tasks by setting goals and parameters. Instead I have advanced some hypotheses and sketched one strategy for addressing the question of the relation between democracy and socialism: Which democracy? One where joint and proactive control over shared environments is sought by people who enjoy political and inclusive equality and who approach democratic politics in a spirit of collective problem solving. Whose socialism? Of someone who values provision of material resources to facilitate counteroppressive equality and the ability of people to undertake life projects meaningful to them and for whom individuals should be regarded as custodians for the socially responsible use of their talents.

NOTES

1. Alexis de Tocqueville, *Democracy in America* (New York: Harper and Row, 1969), written in 1835–40, at p. 12.

2. Ibid., p. 10.

3. Karl Marx, *Critique of the Gotha Programme*, in Karl Marx and Frederick Engels, *Selected Works in One Volume* (New York: International Publishers, 1968), written in 1875, pp. 319–25. I discuss this document and debates it sparked in my *The Real World of Democracy Revisited and Other Essays on Democracy and Socialism* (Atlantic Highlands, N.J.: Humanities Press, 1994), essay 4, "The *Critique of the Gotha Programme* Again."

4. Joseph Schumpeter, *Capitalism, Socialism and Democracy* (New York: Harper and Row, 1962); his famous definition is at p. 269.

5. Some examples, of many, are Stephen Bronner, *Socialism Unbound*, 2d ed. (Boulder : Westview Press, 2001); Francois Hincker, *L'idée du socialisme: A-t-elle un avenir?*, a publication of Actuel Marx (Paris: Presses Universitaires de France, 1992); and contributions to *After the Fall: The Failure of Communism and the Future of Socialism*, ed. Robin Blackburn (London: Verso, 1992) and *Rethinking Marxism* 5, no. 2 (summer 1992).

6. Samples of extended arguments along these lines are in Andrew Levine, *Arguing for Socialism* (Boston: Routledge and Kegan Paul, 1984); Kai Nielsen, *Equality and Liberty: A Defense of Radical Egalitarianism* (Totowa, N.J.: Rowman and Allanheld, 1985); and Philip Green, *Retrieving Democracy* (Totowa, N.J.: Rowman and Allanheld, 1985).

7. Robert Nozick acknowledges this, *Anarchy, State, and Utopia* (New York: Basic Books, 1974), pp. 268–71.

8. Friedrich A. Hayek, *The Road to Serfdom* (Chicago: University of Chicago Press, 1944).

9. Paul Hirst advocates a renewed guild socialism in his defense of associative democracy, *Associative Democracy: New Forms of Economic and Social Government* (Cambridge: Polity Press, 1994); pyramidal models of people's assemblies are suggested by C. B. Macpherson, *The Life and Times of Liberal Democracy* (Oxford: Oxford University Press, 1977), chap. 5, and Alex Callinicos, "Socialism and Democracy," in *Prospects for Democracy*, ed. David Held (Stanford: Stanford University Press, 1993), pp. 200–12.

10. Discussions of workers' self-management and market socialism pertinent to the general topic of democracy and socialism are by Michael W. Howard, *Self-Management and the Crisis of Socialism: The Rose in the Fist of the Present* (Lanham, Md.: Rowman and Littlefield, 2000), and David Schweickart, *Against Capitalism* (Boulder: Westview Press, 1996), and see the debates in *Market Socialism: The Debate Among Socialists*, ed. Bertell Ollman, (New York: Routledge, 1998).

11. Macpherson refers to and criticizes several such neo-Schumpeterian theorists in *Life and Times*, pp. 88–89.

12. Schumpeter, p. 265.

13. John Burnheim argues the merits of election by lot in *Is Democracy Possible?* (Cambridge: Polity Press, 1985).

14. Emily Hauptmann uses the terms "public choice" and "social choice" to mark this distinction, where public choice theorists, employing economic models, interpret individuals' voting behavior as motivated by rational self-interest, while social choice theorists aim to promote social welfare and see voting as a way of aggregating preferences, *Putting Choice Before Democracy: A Critique of Rational Choice Theory* (Albany: State University of New York Press, 1996), p. 2.

15. Anthony Downs, *An Economic Theory of Democracy* (New York: Harper and Row, 1957), chap. 14.

16. David Beetham, *Democracy and Human Rights* (Cambridge: Polity Press, 1999), pp. 4–5.

17. In my view this is best accomplished by thinking of democracy as a matter of degrees of control people have over persisting sites of interaction (a country or region of the world, a city or neighborhood, a workplace, a school, a family, and so on). These things become more democratic when more of the people who make them up come to have effective control over what happens to and in them through any of a variety of joint actions they may take to this end. An ideally democratic situation (the articulation of which is required for methodological reasons on this approach, even if its attainment is not always possible or even desirable) is one where through their common actions people bring all aspects of such an environment into accord with all their uncoerced wishes (including ones generated in the process of democratic interaction) *or* they negotiate a mutually acceptable compromise, provided neither solution jeopardizes pursuit of strong consensus building or negotiation in the future. I first advanced this conception in my *Democratic Theory and Socialism* (Cambridge: Cambridge University Press, 1987), chap. 3; subsequent runs at the definition have encouraged me to think that I (or somebody) can adequately refine it.

18. An example is William Riker, *Liberalism Against Populism: A Confrontation*

Between the Theory of Democracy and the Theory of Social Choice (San Francisco: W. H. Freeman & Company, 1982).

19. C. B. Macpherson, *Democratic Theory: Essays in Retrieval* (Oxford: Clarendon Press, 1973); Carol Gould, *Rethinking Democracy: Freedom and Social Cooperation in Politics, Economy, and Society* (Cambridge: Cambridge University Press, 1988).

20. Thomas Christiano, *The Rule of the Many: Fundamental Issues in Democratic Theory* (Boulder: Westview Press, 1996), chap. 1.

21. Young's most recent exposition of this approach is her *Inclusion and Democracy* (Oxford: Oxford University Press, 2000).

22. Karl Marx and Frederick Engels, *Manifesto of the Communist Party,* in *Selected Works,* pp. 31–63, originally published in 1848, at p. 45.

23. It was a main burden of my *Democratic Theory and Socialism* to argue that structuring political leadership around a principle of paternalism was the core of socialist authoritarianism (as opposed to sympathetic explanations in terms of capitalist encirclement or hostile ones appealing to such as the iron law of oligarchy), see chap. 10.

24. For example, Ronald Beiner, *What's the Matter with Liberalism?* (Berkeley: University of California Press, 1992), chap. 6.

25. Marx and Engels, *Manifesto*, p. 53.

26. Marx, *Critique of the Gotha Programme*, pp. 324–25.

27. Ronald Dworkin, "What Is Equality?" *Philosophy and Public Affairs*, "Part I: Equality of Welfare," 10, no. 3 (summer 1981): 185–246, "Part II: Equality of Resources," 10, no. 4 (fall 1981): 283–345; G. A. Cohen, "On the Currency of Egalitarian Justice," *Ethics* 99, no. 4 (July 1989): 906–44.

28. Macpherson, *Democratic Theory*, p. 51.

29. Ibid., p. 53. Macpherson softens the pluralist-threatening aspect of this conception by giving an arguably innocuous list of "truly human capacities" as for such things as rational understanding, moral judgment, aesthetic creation, and friendship presented as open-ended (p. 4) and specifying that what is crucial for democracy about the capacities in question is that they are potentially able to be compatibly satisfied (p. 55).

30. Cohen, "Currency."

31. John Dewey, *The Public and Its Problems* (Denver: Allan Swallow, 1927).

32. For example, John Roemer, *Free to Lose: An Introduction to Marxist Economic Philosophy* (Cambridge, Mass.: Harvard University Press, 1988), p. 168. By contrast G. A. Cohen, also from a prosocialist perspective, argues for rejection of the self-ownership thesis, *Self-Ownership, Freedom, and Equality* (Cambridge: Cambridge University Press), chaps. 9 and 10.

33. A socialist would be ill-advised to recommend a general, legally enforced injunction that people discharge duties of mutual aid, since one point of advocating and trying to win people over to this aspect of a socialist ideal is to support cooperation in securing and defending socialism, and this must be voluntarily undertaken. However, if, as Cohen persuasively argues, in *Self-Ownership, Freedom, and Equality*, taxation for the purpose of providing social services and strictures on advantages that success in a market can confer on one are incompatible with self-ownership, then government policies in favor of these things constitute a sort of legal enforcement.

PART VI.

ART, CULTURE, AND RELIGION

15.

REIFICATION AND UTOPIA IN MASS CULTURE

FREDRIC JAMESON

The theory of mass culture—or mass audience culture, commercial culture, "popular" culture, the culture industry, as it is variously known—has always tended to define its object against so-called high culture without reflecting on the objective status of this opposition. As so often, positions in this field reduce themselves to two mirror images, which are essentially staged in terms of value. Thus the familiar motif of *elitism* argues for the priority of mass culture on the grounds of the sheer numbers of people exposed to it; the pursuit of high or hermetic culture is then stigmatized as a status hobby of small groups of intellectuals. As its anti-intellectual thrust suggests, this essentially negative position has little theoretical content but clearly responds to a deeply rooted conviction in American populism and articulates a widely based sense that high culture is an establishment phenomenon, irredeemably tainted by its association with institutions, in particular with the university. The value invoked is therefore a social one: it would be preferable to deal with TV programs, *The Godfather*, or *Jaws*, rather than with Wallace Stevens or Henry James, because the former clearly speak a cultural language meaningful to far wider strata of the population than what is socially represented by intellectuals. Populist radicals are however also intellectuals, so that this position has suspicious overtones of the guilt trip; meanwhile it overlooks the antisocial and critical, negative (although generally not revolutionary) stance of much of the most important forms of modern art; finally, it offers no method for reading even those cultural objects it valorizes and has had little of interest to say about their content.

This position is then reversed in the theory of culture worked out by the

Frankfurt School; as is appropriate for this exact antithesis of the populist position, the work of Adorno, Horkheimer, Marcuse, and others is an intensely theoretical one and provides a working methodology for the close analysis of precisely those products of the culture industry which it stigmatizes and which the radical view exalted. Briefly, this view can be characterized as the extension and application of Marxist theories of commodity reification to the works of mass culture. The theory of reification (here strongly overlaid with Max Weber's analysis of rationalization) describes the way in which, under capitalism, the older traditional forms of human activity are instrumentally reorganized and "taylorized," analytically fragmented and reconstructed according to various rational models of efficiency, and essentially restructured along the lines of a differentiation between means and ends. This is a paradoxical idea: it cannot be properly appreciated until it is understood to what degree the means/ends split effectively brackets or suspends ends themselves, hence the strategic value of the Frankfurt School term "instrumentalization" which usefully foregrounds the organization of the means themselves over against any particular end or value which is assigned to their practice.[1] In traditional activity, in other words, the value of the activity is immanent to it, and qualitatively distinct from other ends or values articulated in other forms of human work or play. Socially, this meant that various kinds of work in such communities were properly incomparable; in ancient Greece, for instance, the familiar Aristotelian schema of the fourfold causes at work in handicraft or *poeisis* (material, formal, efficient, and final) were applicable only to artisanal labor, and not to agriculture or war which had a quite different "natural"—which is to say supernatural or divine—basis.[2] It is only with the universal commodification of labor power, which Marx's *Capital* designates as the fundamental precondition of capitalism, that all forms of human labor can be separated out from their unique qualitative differentiation as distinct types of activity (mining as opposed to farming, opera composition as distinct from textile manufacture), and all universally ranged under the common denominator of the quantitative, that is, under the universal exchange value of money.[3] At this point, then, the quality of the various forms of human activity, their unique and distinct "ends" or values, has effectively been bracketed or suspended by the market system, leaving all these activities free to be ruthlessly reorganized in efficiency terms, as sheer means or instrumentality.

The force of the application of this notion to works of art can be measured against the definition of art by traditional aesthetic philosophy (in particular by Kant) as a "finality without an end," that is, as a goal-oriented activity which nonetheless has no practical purpose or end in the "real world" of business or politics or concrete human praxis generally. This traditional definition surely holds for all art that works as such: not for stories that fall flat or home movies or inept poetic scribblings, but rather for the successful works of mass and high culture alike. We suspend our real lives and our immediate practical preoccupations just as completely when we watch *The Godfather* as when we read *The Wings of the Dove* or hear a Beethoven sonata.

At this point, however, the concept of the commodity introduces the possibility of structural and historical differentiation into what was conceived as the universal description of the aesthetic experience as such and in whatever form. The concept of the commodity cuts across the phenomenon of reification—described above in terms of activity or production—from a different angle, that of consumption. In a world in which everything, including labor power, has become a commodity, ends remain no less undifferentiated than in the production schema—they are all rigorously quantified, and have become abstractly comparable through the medium of money, their respective price or wage—yet we can now formulate their instrumentalization, their reorganization along the means/ends split, in a new way by saying that, by its transformation into a commodity, a thing of whatever type has been reduced to a means for its own consumption. It no longer has any qualitative value in itself, but only insofar as it can be "used": the various forms of activity lose their immanent intrinsic satisfactions as activity and become means to an end.

The objects of the commodity world of capitalism also shed their independent "being" and intrinsic qualities and come to be so many instruments of commodity satisfaction: the familiar example is that of tourism—the American tourist no longer lets the landscape "be in its being" as Heidegger would have said, but takes a snapshot of it, thereby graphically transforming space into its own material image. The concrete activity of looking at a landscape—including, no doubt, the disquieting bewilderment with the activity itself, the anxiety that must arise when human beings, confronting the nonhuman, wonder what they are doing there and what the point or purpose of such a confrontation might be in the first place[4]—is thus comfortably replaced by the act of taking possession of it and converting it into a form of personal property. This is the meaning of the great scene in Godard's *Les Carabiniers* (1962–63) when the new world conquerors exhibit their spoils: unlike Alexander, "Michel-Ange" and "Ulysse" merely own images of everything, and triumphantly display their postcards of the Coliseum, the pyramids, Wall Street, Angkor Wat, like so many dirty pictures. This is also the sense of Guy Debord's assertion, in an important book, *The Society of the Spectacle,* that the ultimate form of commodity reification in contemporary consumer society is precisely the image itself.[5] With this universal commodification of our object world, the familiar accounts of the other-directedness of contemporary conspicuous consumption and of the sexualization of our objects and activities are also given: the new model car is essentially an image for other people to have of us, and we consume, less the thing itself, than its abstract idea, open to all the libidinal investments ingeniously arrayed for us by advertising.

It is clear that such an account of commodification has immediate relevance to aesthetics, if only because it implies that everything in consumer society has taken on an aesthetic dimension. The force of the Adorno-Horkheimer analysis of the culture industry, however, lies in its demonstration of the unexpected and imperceptible introduction of commodity structure into the very form and content of the

286   ART, CULTURE, AND RELIGION

work of art itself. Yet this is something like the ultimate squaring of the circle, the triumph of instrumentalization over that "finality without an end" which is art itself, the steady conquest and colonization of the ultimate realm of nonpracticality, of sheer play and antiuse, by the logic of the world of means and ends. But how can the sheer materiality of a poetic sentence be "used" in that sense? And while it is clear how we can buy the idea of an automobile or smoke for the sheer libidinal image of actors, writers, and models with cigarettes in their hands, it is much less clear how a narrative could be "consumed" for the benefit of its own idea.

In its simplest form, this view of instrumentalized culture—and it is implicit in the aesthetics of the *Tel Quel* group as well as in that of the Frankfurt School—suggests that the reading process is itself restructured along a means/ends differentiation. It is instructive here to juxtapose Auerbach's discussion of the *Odyssey* in *Mimesis,* and his description of the way in which at every point the poem is as it were vertical to itself, self-contained, each verse paragraph and tableau somehow timeless and immanent, bereft of any necessary or indispensible links with what precedes it and what follows; in this light it becomes possible to appreciate the strangeness, the historical unnaturality (in a Brechtian sense) of contemporary books which, like detective stories, you read "for the end"—the bulk of the pages becoming sheer devalued means to an end—in this case, the "solution" which is itself utterly insignificant insofar as we are not thereby in the real world and by the latter's practical standards the identity of an imaginary murderer is supremely trivial.

The detective story is to be sure an extremely specialized form: still, the essential commodification of which it may serve as an emblem can be detected everywhere in the subgenres of contemporary commercial art, in the way in which the materialization of this or that sector or zone of such forms comes to constitute an end and a consumption-satisfaction around which the rest of the work is then "degraded" to the status of sheer means. Thus, in the older adventure tale, not only does the *dénouement* (victory of hero or villains, discovery of the treasure, rescue of the heroine or the imprisoned comrades, foiling of a monstrous plot, or arrival in time to reveal an urgent message or a secret) stand as the reified end in view of which the rest of the narrative is consumed—this reifying structure also reaches down into the very page-by-page detail of the book's composition. Each chapter recapitulates a smaller consumption process in its own right, ending with the frozen image of a new and catastrophic reversal of the situation, constructing the smaller gratifications of a flat character who actualizes his single potentiality (the "choleric" Ned Land finally exploding in anger), organizing its sentences into paragraphs each of which is a subplot in its own right, or around the objectlike stasis of the "fateful" sentence or the "dramatic" tableau, the whole tempo of such reading meanwhile overprogrammed by its intermittent illustrations which, either before or after the fact, reconfirm our readerly business, which is to transform the transparent flow of language as much as possible into material images and objects we can consume.[6]

Yet this is still a relatively primitive stage in the commodification of narrative. More subtle and more interesting is the way in which, since naturalism, the best-seller has tended to produce a quasi-material "feeling tone" which floats about the narrative but is only intermittently realized by it: the sense of destiny in family novels, for instance, or the "epic" rhythms of the earth or of great movements of "history" in the various sagas can be seen as so many commodities towards whose consumption the narratives are little more than means, their essential materiality then being confirmed and embodied in the movie music that accompanies their screen versions.[7] This structural differentiation of narrative and consumable feeling tone is a broader and historically and formally more significant manifestation of the kind of "fetishism of hearing" which Adorno denounced when he spoke about the way the contemporary listener restructures a classical symphony so that the sonata form itself becomes an instrumental means toward the consumption of the isolatable tune or melody.

It will be clear, then, that I consider the Frankfurt's School analysis of the commodity structure of mass culture of the greatest interest; if, below, I propose a somewhat different way of looking at the same phenomena, it is not because I feel that their approach has been exhausted. On the contrary, we have scarcely begun to work out all the consequences of such descriptions, let alone to make an exhaustive inventory of variant models and of other features besides commodity reification in terms of which such artifacts might be analyzed.

What is unsatisfactory about the Frankfurt School's position is not its negative and critical apparatus, but rather the positive value on which the latter depends, namely the valorization of traditional modernist high art as the locus of some genuinely critical and subversive, "autonomous" aesthetic production. Here Adorno's later work (as well as Marcuse's *The Aesthetic Dimension*) marks a retreat over the former's dialectically ambivalent assessment, in *The Philosophy of Modern Music,* of Arnold Schoenberg's achievement: what has been omitted from the later judgments is precisely Adorno's fundamental discovery of the historicity, and in particular, the irreversible aging process, of the greatest modernist forms. But if this is so, then the great work of modern high culture—whether it be Schoenberg, Beckett, or even Brecht himself—cannot serve as a fixed point or eternal standard against which to measure the "degraded" status of mass culture: indeed, fragmentary and as yet undeveloped tendencies[8] in recent art production—hyper- or photo-realism in visual art; "new music" of the type of Lamonte Young, Terry Riley, or Philip Glass; postmodernist literary texts like those of Pynchon—suggest an increasing interpenetration of high and mass cultures.

For all these reasons, it seems to me that we must rethink the opposition high culture/mass culture in such a way that the emphasis on evaluation to which it has traditionally given rise—and which however the binary system of value operates (mass culture is popular and thus more authentic than high culture, high culture is autonomous and, therefore, utterly incomparable to a degraded mass culture) tends to function in some timeless realm of absolute aesthetic judgment—is replaced by a genuinely historical and dialectical approach to these phenomena. Such an approach demands that we read high and mass culture as objectively related and dialectically interdependent phenomena, as twin and inseparable forms of the fission of aesthetic production under capitalism. In this, capitalism's third or multinational stage, however, the dilemma of the double standard of high and mass culture remains, but it has become—not the subjective problem of our own standards of judgment—but rather an objective contradiction which has its own social grounding.

Indeed, this view of the emergence of mass culture obliges us historically to respecify the nature of the "high culture" to which it has conventionally been opposed: the older culture critics indeed tended loosely to raise comparative issues about the "popular culture" of the past. Thus, if you see Greek tragedy, Shakespeare, *Don Quijote,* still widely read romantic lyrics of the type of Hugo, and best-selling realistic novels like those of Balzac or Dickens, as uniting a wide "popular" audience with high aesthetic quality, then you are fatally locked into such false problems as the relative value—weighed against Shakespeare or even Dickens—of such popular contemporary auteurs of high quality as Chaplin, John Ford, Hitchcock, or even Robert Frost, Andrew Wyeth, Simenon, or John O'Hara. The utter senselessness of this interesting subject of conversation becomes clear when it is understood that from a historical point of view the only form of "high culture" which can be said to constitute the dialectical opposite of mass culture is that high culture production contemporaneous with the latter, which is to say that artistic production generally designated as *modernism.* The other term would then be Wallace Stevens, or Joyce, or Schoenberg, or Jackson Pollock, but surely not cultural artifacts such as the novels of Balzac or the plays of Molière which essentially antedate the historical separation between high and mass culture.

But such specification clearly obliges us to rethink our definitions of mass culture as well: the commercial products of the latter can surely not without intellectual dishonesty be assimilated to so-called popular, let alone folk, art of the past, which reflected and were dependent for their production on quite different social realities, and were in fact the "organic" expression of so many distinct social communities or castes, such as the peasant village, the court, the medieval town, the polis, and even the classical bourgeoisie when it was still a unified social group with its own cultural specificity. The historically unique tendential effect of late capitalism on all such groups has been to dissolve and to fragment or atomize them into agglomerations (*Gesellschaften*) of isolated and equivalent private individuals, by way of the corrosive action of universal commodification and the market system. Thus, the "popular" as such no longer exists, except under very specific and marginalized conditions (internal and external pockets of so-called underdevelopment within the capitalist world system); the commodity production of contemporary or industrial mass culture has nothing whatsoever to do, and nothing in common, with older forms of popular or folk art.

Thus understood, the dialectical opposition and profound structural interrelatedness of modernism and contemporary mass culture opens up a whole new field for cultural study, which promises to be more intelligible historically and socially than research or disciplines which have strategically conceived their missions as a specialization in this or that branch (e.g., in the university, English departments versus Popular Culture programs). Now the emphasis must lie squarely on the social and aesthetic situation—the dilemma of form and of a public—shared and faced by both modernism and mass culture, but "solved" in antithetical ways. Modernism also can only be adequately understood in terms of that commodity production whose all-informing structural influence on mass culture I have described above: only for modernism, the omnipresence of the commodity form, *not* to be a commodity, to devise an aesthetic language incapable of offering commodity satisfaction, and resistant to instrumentalization. The difference between this position and the valorization of modernism by the Frankfurt School (or, later, by *Tel Quel*) lies in my designation of modernism as reactive, that is, as a symptom and as a result of cultural crises, rather than a new "solution" in its own right: not only is the commodity the prior form in terms of which alone modernism can be structurally grasped, but the very terms of its solution—the conception of the modernist text as the production and the protest of an isolated individual, and the logic of its sign systems as so many private languages ("styles") and private religions—are contradictory and made the social or collective realization of its aesthetic project (Mallarmé's ideal of *Le Livre* can be taken as the latter's fundamental formulation[9]) an impossible one (a judgment which, it ought not to be necessary to add, is not a judgment of value about the "greatness" of the modernist texts).

Yet there are other aspects of the situation of art under monopoly and late capitalism which have remained unexplored and offer equally rich perspectives in which to examine modernism and mass culture and their structural dependency. Another such issue, for example, is that of *materialization* in contemporary art—a phenomenon woefully misunderstood by much contemporary Marxist theory (for obvious reasons, it is not an issue that has attracted academic formalism). Here the misunderstanding is dramatized by the pejorative emphasis of the Hegelian tradition (Lukács as well as the Frankfurt School) on phenomena of aesthetic reification—which furnishes the term of a negative value judgment—in juxtaposition to the celebration of the "material signifier" and the "materiality of the text" or of "textual production" by the French tradition which appeals for its authority to Althusser and Lacan. If you are willing to entertain the possibility that "reification" and the emergence of increasingly materialized signifiers are one and the same phenomenon—both historically and culturally—then this ideological great debate turns out to be based on a fundamental misunderstanding. Once again, the confusion stems from the introduction of the false problem of value (which fatally programs every binary opposition into its good and bad, positive and negative, essential and inessential terms) into a more properly ambivalent dialectical and historical situation in which reification or materialization is a key structural feature of both modernism and mass culture.

The task of defining this new area of study would then initially involve making an inventory of other such problematic themes or phenomena in terms of which the interrelationship of mass culture and modernism can usefully be explored, something it is too early to do here. At this point, I will merely note one further such theme, which has seemed to me to be of the greatest significance in specifying the antithetical formal reactions of modernism and mass culture to their common social situation, and that is the notion of *repetition*. This concept, which in its modern form we owe to Kierkegaard, has known rich and interesting new elaborations in recent poststructuralism: for Jean Baudrillard, for example, the repetitive structure of what he calls the simulacrum (that is, the reproduction of "copies" which have no original) characterizes the commodity production of consumer capitalism and marks our object world with an unreality and a free-floating absence of "the referent" (e.g., the place hitherto taken by nature, by raw materials and primary production, or by the "originals" of artisanal production or handicraft) utterly unlike anything experienced in any earlier social formation.

If this is the case, then we would expect repetition to constitute yet another feature of the contradictory situation of contemporary aesthetic production to which both modernism and mass culture in one way or another cannot but react. This is in fact the case, and one need only invoke the traditional ideological stance of all modernizing theory and practice from the romantics to the *Tel Quel* group, and passing through the hegemonic formulations of classical Anglo-American modernism, to observe the strategic emphasis on innovation and novelty, the obligatory break with previous styles, the pressure—geometrically increasing with the ever swifter temporality of consumer society, with its yearly or quarterly style and fashion changes—to "make it new," to produce something which resists and breaks through the force of gravity of repetition as a universal feature of commodity equivalence. Such aesthetic ideologies have, to be sure, no critical or theoretical value—for one thing, they are purely formal, and by abstracting some empty concept of innovation from the concrete content of stylistic change in any given period end up flattening out even the history of forms, let alone social history, and projecting a kind of cyclical view of change—yet they are useful symptoms for detecting the ways in which the various modernisms have been forced, in spite of themselves, and in the very flesh and bone of their form, to respond to the objective reality of repetition itself. In our own time, the postmodernist conception of a "text" and the ideal of schizophrenic writing openly demonstrate this vocation of the modernist aesthetic to produce sentences which are radically discontinuous, and which defy repetition not merely on the level of the break with older forms or older formal models but now within the microcosm of the text itself. Meanwhile, the kinds of repetition which, from Gertrude Stein to Robbe-Grillet, the modernist project has appropriated and made its own, can be seen as a kind of homeopathic strategy whereby the scandalous and intolerable external irritant is drawn into the aesthetic process itself and thereby systematically worked over, "acted out," and symbolically neutralized.

But it is clear that the influence of repetition on mass culture has been no less decisive. Indeed, it has frequently been observed that the older generic discourses—stigmatized by the various modernist revolutions, which have successively repudiated the older fixed forms of lyric, tragedy, and comedy, and at length even "the novel" itself, now replaced by the unclassifiable "livre" or "text"—retain a powerful afterlife in the realm of mass culture. Paperback drugstore or airport displays reinforce all of the now subgeneric distinctions between gothic, best-seller, mysteries, science fiction, biography, or pornography, as do the conventional classification of weekly TV series, and the production and marketing of Hollywood films (to be sure, the generic system at work in contemporary commercial film is utterly distinct from the traditional pattern of the 1930s and 1940s production, and has had to respond to television competition by devising new metageneric or omnibus forms, which, however, at once become new "genres" in their own right, and fold back into the usual generic stereotyping and reproduction—as, recently, with disaster film or occult film).

But we must specify this development historically: the older precapitalist genres were signs of something like an aesthetic "contract" between a cultural producer and a certain homogeneous class or group public; they drew their vitality from the social and collective status (which to be sure, varied widely according to the mode of production in question) of the situation of aesthetic production and consumption—that is to say, from the fact that the relationship between artist and public was still in one way or another a social institution and a concrete social and interpersonal relationship with its own validation and specificity. With the coming of the market, this institutional status of artistic consumption and production vanishes: art becomes one more branch of commodity production, the artist loses all social status and faces the options of becoming a *poète maudit* or a journalist, the relationship to the public is problematized, and the latter becomes a virtual "public introuvable" (the appeals to posterity, Stendhal's dedication "To the Happy Few," or Gertrude Stein's remark, "I write for myself and for strangers," are revealing testimony to this intolerable new state of affairs).

The survival of genre in emergent mass culture can thus in no way be taken as a return to the stability of the publics of precapitalist societies: on the contrary, the generic forms and signals of mass culture are very specifically to be understood as the historical reappropriation and displacement of older structures in the service of the qualitatively very different situation of repetition. The atomized or serial "public" of mass culture wants to see the same thing over and over again, hence the urgency of the generic structure and the generic signal: if you doubt this, think of your own consternation at finding that the paperback you selected from the mystery shelf turns out to be a romance or a science fiction novel; think of the exasperation of people in the row next to you who bought their tickets imagining that they were about to see a thriller or a political mystery instead of the horror or occult film actually underway. Think also of the much misunderstood "aesthetic bankruptcy" of television: the structural reason for the inability of the various television series to produce episodes which are either socially "realistic" or have an aesthetic and formal autonomy that transcends mere variation has little enough to do with the talent of the people involved (although it is certainly exacerbated by the increasing "exhaustion" of material and the ever-increasing tempo of the production of new episodes), but lies precisely in our "set" towards repetition. Even if you are a reader of Kafka or Dostoyevsky, when you watch a cop show or a detective series, you do so in expectation of the stereotyped format and would be annoyed to find the video narrative making "high cultural" demands on you. Much the same situation obtains for film, where it has however been institutionalized as the distinction between American (now multinational) film—determining the expection of generic repetition—and foreign films, which determine a shifting of gears of the "horizon of expectations" to the reception of high cultural discourse or so-called art films.

This situation has important consequences for the analysis of mass culture which have not yet been fully appreciated. The philosophical paradox of repetition—formulated by Kierkegaard, Freud, and others—can be grasped in this, that it can as it were only take place "a second time." The first-time event is by definition not a repetition of anything; it is then reconverted into repetition the second time round, by the peculiar action of what Freud called "retroactivity" [*Nachträglichkeit*]. But this means that, as with the simulacrum, there is no "first time" of repetition, no "original" of which succeeding repetitions are mere copies; and here too, modernism furnishes a curious echo in its production of books which, like Hegel's *Phenomenology* or Proust or *Finnegans Wake,* you can only *reread.* Still, in modernism, the hermetic text remains, not only as an Everest to assault, but also as a book to whose stable reality you can return over and over again. In mass culture, repetition effectively volatilizes the original object—the "test," the "work of art"—so that the student of mass culture has no primary object of study.

The most striking demonstration of this process can be witnessed in our reception of contemporary pop music of whatever type—the various kinds of rock, blues, country western, or disco. I will argue that we never hear any of the singles produced in these genres "for the first time"; instead, we live a constant exposure to them in all kinds of different situations, from the steady beat of the car radio through the sounds at lunch, or in the workplace, or in shopping centers, all the way to those apparently full-dress performances of the "work" in a nightclub or stadium concert or on the records you buy and take home to hear. This is a very different situation from the first bewildered audition of a complicated classical piece, which you hear again in the concert hall or listen to at home. The passionate attachment one can form to this or that pop single, the rich personal investment of all kinds of private associations and existential symbolism which is the feature of such attachment, are fully as much a function of our own familiarity as of the work itself: the pop single, by means of repetition, insensibly becomes part of the existential fabric of our own lives, so that what we listen to is ourselves, our own previous auditions.[10]

Under these circumstances, it would make no sense to try to recover a feeling for the "original" musical text, as it really was, or as it might have been heard "for the first time." Whatever the results of such a scholarly or analytical project, its object of study would be quite distinct, quite differently constituted, from the same "musical text" grasped as mass culture, or in other works, as sheer repetition. The dilemma of the student of mass culture therefore lies in the structural absence, or repetitive volatilization, of the "primary texts"; nor is anything to be gained by reconstituting a "corpus" of texts after the fashion of, say, the medievalists who work with precapitalist generic and repetitive structures only superficially similar to those of contemporary mass or commercial culture. Nor, to my mind, is anything explained by recourse to the currently fashionable term of "intertextuality," which seems to me at best to designate a problem rather than a solution. Mass culture presents us with a methodological dilemma which the conventional habit of positing a stable object of commentary or exegesis in the form of a primary text or work is disturbingly unable to focus, let alone to resolve; in this sense, also, a dialectical conception of this field of study in which modernism and mass culture are grasped as a single historical and aesthetic phenomenon has the advantage of positing the survival of the primary text at one of its poles, and thus providing a guide-rail for the bewildering exploration of the aesthetic universe which lies at the other, a message or semiotic bombardment from which the textual referent has disappeared.

The above reflections by no means raise, let alone address, all the most urgent issues which confront an approach to mass culture today. In particular, we have neglected a somewhat different judgment on mass culture, which also loosely derives from the Frankfurt School position on the subject, but whose adherents number "radicals" as well as "elitists" on the Left today. This is the conception of mass culture as sheer manipulation, sheer commercial brainwashing, and empty distraction by the multinational corporations who obviously control every feature of the production and distribution of mass culture today. If this were the case, then it is clear that the study of mass culture would at best be assimilated to the anatomy of the techniques of ideological marketing and be subsumed under the analysis of advertising texts and materials. Roland Barthes's seminal investigation of the latter, however, in his *Mythologies,* opened them up to the whole realm of the operations and functions of culture in everyday life; but since the sociologists of manipulation (with the exception, of course, of the Frankfurt School itself) have, almost by definition, no interest in the hermetic or "high" art production whose dialectical interdependency with mass culture we have argued above, the general effect of their position is to suppress considerations of culture altogether, save as a kind of sandbox affair on the most epiphenomenal level of the superstructure.

The implication is thus to suggest that real social life—the only features of social life worth addressing or taking into consideration when political theory and strategy is at stake—are what the Marxian tradition designates as the political, the ideological, and the juridical levels of superstructural reality. Not only is this repression of the cultural moment determined by the university structure and by the ideologies of the various disciplines—thus, political science and sociology at best consign cultural issues to that ghettoizing rubric and marginalized field of specialization called the "sociology of culture"—it is also and in a more general way the unwitting perpetuation of the most fundamental ideological stance of American business society itself, for which "culture"—reduced to plays and poems and highbrow concerts—is par excellence the most trivial and nonserious activity in the "real life" of the rat race of daily existence.

Yet even the vocation of the esthete (last sighted in the United States during the prepolitical heyday of the 1950s) and of his successor, the university literature professor acknowledging uniquely high cultural "values," had a socially symbolic content and expressed (generally unconsciously) the anxiety aroused by market competition and the repudiation of the primacy of business pursuits and business values: these are then, to be sure, as thoroughly repressed from academic formalism as culture is from the work of the sociologists of manipulation, a repression which goes a long way towards accounting for the resistance and defensiveness of contemporary literary study towards anything which smacks of the painful reintroduction of just that "real life"—the socioeconomic, the historical context—which it was the function of aesthetic vocation to deny or to mask out in the first place.

What we must ask the sociologists of manipulation, however, is whether culture, far from being an occasional matter of the reading of a monthly good book or a trip to the drive-in, is not the very element of consumer society itself. No society, indeed, has ever been saturated with signs and messages like this one. If we follow Debord's argument about the omnipresence and the omnipotence of the image in consumer capitalism today, then if anything the priorities of the real become reversed, and everything is mediated by culture, to the point where even the political and the ideological "levels" have initially to be disentangled from their primary mode of representation which is cultural. Howard Jarvis, Jimmy Carter, even Castro, the Red Brigade, B. J. Vorster, the Communist "penetration" of Africa, the war in Vietnam, strikes, inflation itself—all are images, all come before us with the immediacy of cultural representations about which one can be fairly certain that they are by a long shot not historical reality itself. If we want to go on believing in categories like social class, then we are going to have to dig for them in the insubstantial bottomless realm of cultural and collective fantasy. Even ideology has in our society lost its clarity as prejudice, false consciousness, readily identifiable opinion: our racism gets all mixed up with clean-cut black actors on TV and in commercials, our sexism has to make a detour through new stereotypes of the "women's libber" on the network series. After that, if one wants to stress the primacy of the political, so be it: until the omnipresence of culture in this society is even dimly sensed, realistic conceptions of the nature and function of political praxis today can scarcely be framed.

It is true that manipulation theory sometimes finds a special place in its scheme for those rare cultural objects which can be said to have overt political and social content: sixties protest songs, *The Salt of the Earth* (Biberman, 1954), Clancy Sigal's novels or Sol Yurick's, Chicano murals, the San Francisco Mime Troop. This is not the place to raise the complicated problem of political art today, except to say that our business as culture critics requires us to raise it, and to rethink what are still essentially thirties categories in some new and more satis-factory contemporary way. But the problem of political art—and we have nothing worth saying about it if we do not realize that it is a problem, rather than a choice or a ready-made option—suggests an important qualification to the scheme out-lined in the first part of the present essay. The implied presupposition of those ear-lier remarks was that authentic cultural creation is dependent for its existence on authentic collective life, on the vitality of the "organic" social group in whatever form (and such groups can range from the classical polis to the peasant village, from the commonality of the ghetto to the shared values of an embattled prerev-olutionary bourgeoisie). Capitalism systematically dissolves the fabric of all cohesive social groups without exception, including its own ruling class, and thereby problematizes aesthetic production and linguistic invention which have their source in group life. The result, discussed above, is the dialectical fission of older aesthetic expression into two modes, modernism and mass culture, equally dissociated from group praxis. Both of these modes have attained an admirable level of technical virtuosity; but it is a daydream to expect that either of these semiotic structures could be retransformed, by fiat, miracle, or sheet talent, into what could be called, in its strong form, political art, or in a more general way, that living and authentic culture of which we have virtually lost the memory, so rare an experience it has become. This is to way that of the two most influential recent Left aesthetics—the Brecht-Benjamin position, which hoped for the trans-formation of the nascent mass-cultural techniques and channels of communica-tion of the 1930s into an openly political art, and the *Tel Quel* position which reaf-firms the "subversive" and revolutionary efficacy of language revolution and modernist and postmodernist formal innovation—we must reluctantly conclude that neither addresses the specific conditions of our own time.

The only authentic cultural production today has seemed to be that which can draw on the collective experience of marginal pockets of the social life of the world system: black literature and blues, British working-class rock, women's literature, gay literature, the *roman québécois,* the literature of the Third World; and this production is possible only to the degree to which these forms of col-lective life or collective solidarity have not yet been fully penetrated by the market and by the commodity system. This is not necessarily a negative prog-nosis, unless you believe in an increasingly windless and all-embracing total system; what shatters such a system—it has unquestionably been falling into place all around us since the development of industrial capitalism—is however very precisely collective praxis or, to pronounce its traditional unmentionable name, class struggle. Yet the relationship between class struggle and cultural production is not an immediate one; you do not reinvent an access onto political art and authentic cultural production by studding your individual artistic discourse with class and political signals. Rather, class struggle, and the slow and inter-mittent development of genuine class consciousness, are themselves the process whereby a new and organic group constitutes itself, whereby the collective breaks through the reified atomization (Sartre calls it the seriality) of capitalist social life. At that point, to say that the group exists and that it generates its own specific cultural life and expression, are one and the same. That is, if you like, the third term missing from my initial picture of the fate of the aesthetic and the cultural under capitalism; yet no useful purpose is served by speculation on the forms such a third and authentic type of cultural language might take in situa-tions which do not yet exist. As for the artists, for them too "the owl of Minerva takes its flight at dusk," for them too, as with Lenin in April, the test of historical inevitability is always after the fact, and they cannot be told any more than the rest of us what is historically possible until after it has been tried.

This said, we can now return to the question of mass culture and manipula-tion. Brecht taught us that under the right circumstances you could remake any-body over into anything you liked (*Mann ist Mann*), only he insisted on the sit-uation and the raw materials fully as much or more than on the techniques stressed by manipulation theory. Perhaps the key problem about the concept, or pseudoconcept, of manipulation can be dramatized by juxtaposing it to the Freudian notion of repression. The Freudian mechanism indeed, comes into play only after its object—trauma, charged memory, guilty or threatening desire, anx-iety—has in some way been aroused, and risks emerging into the subject's con-sciousness. Freudian repression is therefore determinate, it has specific content, and may even be said to be something like a "recognition" of that content which expresses itself in the form of denial, forgetfulness, slip, *mauvaise foi,* displace-ment, or substitution.

But of course the classical Freudian model of the work of art (as of the dream or the joke) was that of the symbolic fulfillment of the repressed wish, of a complex structure of indirection whereby desire could elude the repressive censor and achieve some measure of a, to be sure, purely symbolic satisfaction. A more recent "revision" of the Freudian model, however—Norman Holland's *The Dynamics of Literary Response*—proposes a scheme more useful for our present problem, which is to conceive how (commercial) works of art can pos-sibly be said to "manipulate" their publics. For Holland, the psychic function of the work of art must be described in such a way that these two inconsistent and even incompatible features of aesthetic gratification—on the one hand, its wish-fulfilling function, but on the other the necessity that its symbolic structure pro-tect the psyche against the frightening and potentially damaging eruption of pow-erful archaic desires and wish-material—be somehow harmonized and assigned their place as twin drives of a single structure. Hence Holland's suggestive con-ception of the vocation of the work of art to *manage* this raw material of the drives and the archaic wish or fantasy material. To rewrite the concept of a man-agement of desire in social terms now allows us to think repression and wish-ful-fillment together within the unity of a single mechanism, which gives and takes alike in a kind of psychic compromise or horse-trading; which strategically arouses fantasy content within careful symbolic containment structures which defuse it, gratifying intolerable, unrealizable, properly imperishable desires only to the degree to which they can be momentarily stilled.

This model seems to me to permit a far more adequate account of the mech-anisms of manipulation, diversion, and degradation, which are undeniably at work in mass culture and in the media. In particular it allows us to grasp mass culture not as empty distraction or "mere" false consciousness, but rather as a transformational work on social and political anxieties and fantasies which must then have some effective presence in the mass cultural text in order subsequently to be "managed" or repressed. Indeed, the initial reflections of the present essay suggest that such a thesis ought to be extended to modernism as well, even though I will not here be able to develop this part of the argument further.[11] I will therefore argue that both mass culture and modernism have as much content, in the loose sense of the word, as the older social realisms; but that this content is processed in all three in very different ways. Both modernism and mass culture entertain relations of repression with the fundamental social anxieties and con-cerns, hopes and blind spots, ideological antinomies and fantasies of disaster, which are their raw material; only where modernism tends to handle this mate-rial by producing compensatory structures of various kinds, mass culture represses them by the narrative construction of imaginary resolutions and by the projection of an optical illusion of social harmony.

I will now demonstrate this proposition by a reading of three extremely suc-cessful recent commercial films: Steven Spielberg's *Jaws* (1975) and the two parts of Francis Ford Coppola's *The Godfather* (1972, 1974). The readings I will pro-pose are at least consistent with my earlier remarks about the volatilization of the primary text in mass culture by repetition, to the degree of which they are differ-ential, "intertextually" comparative decodings of each of these filmic messages.

In the case of *Jaws,* however, the version or variant against which the film will be read is not the shoddy and disappointing sequels, but rather the best-selling novel by Peter Benchley from which the film—one of the most successful box-office attractions in movie history—was adapted. As we will see, the adap-tation involved significant changes from the original narrative; my attention to these strategic alterations may indeed arouse some initial suspicion of the offi-cial or "manifest" content preserved in both these texts, and on which most of the discussion of *Jaws* has tended to focus. Thus critics from Gore Vidal and *Pravda* all the way to Stephen Heath[12] have tended to emphasize the problem of the shark itself and what it "represents": such speculation ranges from the psycho-analytic to historic anxieties about the Other that menaces American society—whether it be the Communist conspiracy or the Third World—and even to internal fears about the unreality of daily life in America today, and in particular the haunting and unmentionable persistence of the organic—of birth, copulation, and death—which the cellophane society of consumer capitalism desperately recontains in hospitals and old-age homes, and sanitizes by means of a whole strategy of linguistic euphemisms which enlarge the older, purely sexual ones: on this view, the Nantucket beaches "represent" consumer society itself, with its glossy and commodified images of gratification, and its scandalous and fragile, ever suppressed, sense of its own possible mortality.

Now none of these readings can be said to be wrong or aberrant, but their very multiplicity suggests that the vocation of the symbol—the killer shark—lies less in any single message or meaning than in its very capacity to absorb and organize all of these quite distinct anxieties together. As a symbolic vehicle, then, the shark must be understood in terms of its essentially polysemous function rather than any particular content attributable to it by this or that spectator. Yet it is precisely this polysemousness which is profoundly ideological, insofar as it allows essentially social and historical anxieties to be folded back into apparently "natural" ones, both to express and to be recontained in what looks like a conflict with other forms of biological existence.

Interpretive emphasis on the shark, indeed, tends to drive all these quite varied readings in the direction of myth criticism, where the shark is naturally enough taken to be the most recent embodiment of Leviathan, so that the struggle with it effortlessly folds back into one of the fundamental paradigms or archetypes of Northrop Frye's storehouse of myth. To rewrite the film in terms of myth is thus to emphasize what I will shortly call its Utopian dimension, that is, its ritual celebration of the renewal of the social order and its salvation, not merely from divine wrath, but also from unworthy leadership.

But to put it this way is also to begin to shift our attention from the shark itself to the emergence of the hero—or heroes—whose mythic task it is to rid the civilized world of the archetypal monster. That is, however, precisely the issue—the nature and the specification of the "mythic" hero—about which the discrepancies between the film and the novel have something instructive to tell us. For the novel involves an undisguised expression of class conflict in the tension between the island cop, Brody (Roy Scheider), and the high-society oceanographer, Hooper (Richard Dreyfuss), who used to summer in Easthampton and ends up sleeping with Brody's wife: Hooper is indeed a much more important figure in the novel than in the film, while by the same token the novel assigns the shark-hunter, Quint (Robert Shaw), a very minor role in comparison to his crucial presence in the film. Yet the most dramatic surprise the novel holds in store for viewers of the film will evidently be the discovery that in the book Hooper dies, a virtual suicide and a sacrifice to his somber and romantic fascination with death in the person of the shark. Now while it is unclear to me how the American reading public can have responded to the rather alien and exotic resonance of this element of the fantasy—the aristocratic obsession with death would seem to be a more European motif—the social overtones of the novel's resolution—the triumph of the islander and the yankee over the decadent playboy challenger—are surely unmistakable, as is the systematic elimination and suppression of all such class overtones from the film itself.

The latter therefore provides us with a striking illustration of a whole work of displacement by which the written narrative of an essentially class fantasy has been transformed, in the Hollywood product, into something quite different, which it now remains to characterize. Gone is the whole decadent and aristocratic brooding over death, along with the erotic rivalry in which class antagonisms were dramatized; the Hooper of the film is nothing but a technocratic whiz kid, no tragic hero but instead a good-natured creature of grants and foundations and scientific know-how. But Brody has also undergone an important modification: he is no longer the small-town island boy married to a girl from a socially prominent summer family; rather, he has been transformed into a retired cop from New York City, relocating on Nantucket in an effort to flee the hassle of urban crime, race war, and ghettoization. The figure of Brody now therefore introduces overtones and connotations of law-and-order, rather than a yankee shrewdness, and functions as a TV police-show hero transposed into this apparently more sheltered but in reality equally contradictory milieu which is the great American summer vacation.

I will therefore suggest that in the film the socially resonant conflict between these two characters has, for some reason that remains to be formulated, been transformed into a vision of their ultimate partnership, and joint triumph over Leviathan. This is then clearly the moment to turn to Quint, whose enlarged role in the film thereby becomes strategic. The myth-critical option for reading this figure must at once be noted: it is indeed tempting to see Quint as the end term of the threefold figure of the ages of man into which the team of shark-hunters is so obviously articulated, Hooper and Brody then standing as youth and maturity over against Quint's authority as an elder. But such a reading leaves the basic interpretive problem intact: what can be the allegorical meaning of a ritual in which the older figure follows the intertextual paradigm of Melville's Ahab to destruction while the other two paddle back in triumph on the wreckage of his vessel? Or, to formulate it in a different way, why is the Ishmael survivor-figure split into the two survivors of the film (and credited with the triumphant destruction of the monster in the bargain)?

Quint's determinations in the film seem to be of two kinds: first, unlike the bureaucracies of law enforcement and science-and-technology (Brody and Hooper), but also in distinction to the corrupt island Major with his tourist investments and big business interests, Quint is defined as the locus of old-fashioned private enterprise, of the individual entrepreneurship not merely of small business, but also of local business—hence the insistence on his salty Down-East typicality. Meanwhile—but this feature is also a new addition to the very schematic treatment of the figure of Quint in the novel—he also strongly associates himself with a now distant American past by way of his otherwise gratuitous reminiscences about World War II and the campaign in the Pacific. We are thus authorized to read the death of Quint in the film as the twofold symbolic destruction of an older America—the America of small business and individual private enterprise of a now outmoded kind, but also the America of the New Deal and the crusade against Nazism, the older America of the Depression and the war and of the heyday of classical liberalism.

Now the content of the partnership between Hooper and Brody projected by the film may be specified socially and politically, as the allegory of an alliance between the forces of law-and-order and the new technocracy of the multinational corporations: an alliance which must be cemented, not merely by its fantasized triumph over the ill-defined menace of the shark itself, but above all by the indispensable precondition of the effacement of that more traditional image of an older America which must be eliminated from historical consciousness and social memory before the new power system takes its place. This operation may continue to be read in terms of mythic archetypes, if one likes, but then in that case it is a Utopian and ritual vision which is also a whole—very alarming—political and social program. It touches on present-day social contradictions and anxieties only to use them for its new task of ideological resolution, symbolically urging us to bury the older populisms and to respond to an image of political partnership which projects a whole new strategy of legitimation; and it effectively displaces the class antagonisms between rich and poor which persist in consumer society (and in the novel from which the film was adapted) by substituting for them a new and spurious kind of fraternity in which the viewer rejoices without understanding that he or she is excluded from it.

Jaws is therefore an excellent example, not merely of ideological manipulation, but also of the way in which genuine social and historical content must be first tapped and given some initial expression if it is subsequently to be the object of successful manipulation and containment. In my second reading, I want to give this new model of manipulation an even more decisive and paradoxical turn: I will now indeed argue that we cannot fully do justice to the ideological function of works like these unless we are willing to concede the presence within them of a more positive function as well: of what I will call, following the Frankfurt School, their Utopian or transcendent potential—that dimension of even the most degraded type of mass culture which remains implicitly, and no matter how faintly, negative and critical of the social order from which, as a product and a commodity, it springs. At this point in the argument, then, the hypothesis is that the works of mass culture cannot be ideological without at one and the same time being implicitly or explicitly Utopian as well: they cannot manipulate unless they offer some genuine shred of content as a fantasy bribe to the public about to be so manipulated. Even the "false consciousness" of so monstrous a phenomenon of Nazism was nourished by collective fantasies of a Utopian type, in "socialist" as well as in nationalist guises. Our proposition about the drawing power of the works of mass culture has implied that such works cannot manage anxieties about the social order unless they have first revived them and given them some rudimentary expression; we will now suggest that anxiety and hope are two faces of the same collective consciousness, so that the works of mass culture, even if their function lies in the legitimation of the existing order—or some worse one— cannot do their job without deflecting in the latter's service the deepest and most fundamental hopes and fantasies of the collectivity, to which they can therefore, no matter in how distorted a fashion, be found to have given voice.

We therefore need a method capable of doing justice to both the ideological and the Utopian or transcendent functions of mass culture simultaneously. Nothing less will do, as the suppression of either of these terms may testify: we have already commented on the sterility of the older kind of ideological analysis, which, ignoring the Utopian components of mass culture, ends up with the empty denunciation of the latter's manipulatory function and degraded status. But it is equally obvious that the complementary extreme—a method that would cele- brate Utopian impulses in the absence of any conception or mention of the ideo- logical vocation of mass culture—simply reproduces the litanies of myth criti- cism at its most academic and aestheticizing and impoverishes these texts of their semantic content at the same time that it abstracts them from their concrete social and historical situation.

The two parts of *The Godfather* have seemed to me to offer a virtual text- book illustration of these propositions; for one thing, recapitulating the whole generic tradition of the gangster film, it reinvents a certain "myth" of the Mafia in such a way as to allow us to see that ideology is not necessarily a matter of false consciousness, or of the incorrect or distorted representation of historical "fact," but can rather be quite consistent with a "realistic" faithfulness to the latter. To be sure, historical inaccuracy (as, e.g., when the fifties are telescoped into the sixties and seventies in the narrative of Jimmy Hoffa's career in the 1978 movie *F.I.S.T.*) can often provide a suggestive lead towards ideological function: not because there is any scientific virtue in the facts themselves, but rather as a symptom of a resistance of the "logic of the content," of the substance of his- toricity in question, to the narrative and ideological paradigm into which it has been thereby forcibly assimilated.[13]

The Godfather, however, obviously works in and is a permutation of a generic convention; one could write a history of the changing social and ideo- logical functions of this convention, showing how analogous motifs are called upon in distinct historical situations to emit strategically distinct yet symbolically intelligible messages. Thus the gangsters of the classical thirties films (Robinson, Cagney, etc.) were dramatized as psychopaths, sick loners striking out against a society essentially made up of wholesome people (the archetypal democratic "common man" of New Deal populism). The postwar gangsters of the Bogart era remain loners in this sense but have unexpectedly become invested with tragic pathos in such a way as to express the confusion of veterans returning from

World War II, struggling with the unsympathetic rigidity of institutions, and ultimately crushed by a petty and vindictive social order.

The Mafia material was drawn on and alluded to in these earlier versions of the gangster paradigm, but did not emerge as such until the late fifties and the early sixties. This very distinctive narrative content—a kind of saga or family material analogous to that of the medieval *chansons de geste*, with its recurrent episodes and legendary figures returning again and again in different perspectives and contexts—can at once be structurally differentiated from the older paradigms by its collective nature: in this, reflecting an evolution towards organizational themes and team narratives which studies like Will Wright's book on the western, *Six Guns and Society*, have shown to be significant developments in the other sub-genres of mass culture (the western, the caper film, etc.) during the 1960s.[14]

Such an evolution, however, suggests a global transformation of postwar American social life and a global transformation of the potential logic of its narrative content without yet specifying the ideological function of the mafia paradigm itself. Yet this is surely not very difficult to identify. When indeed we reflect on an organized conspiracy against the public, one which reaches into every corner of our daily lives and our political structures to exercise a wanton ecocidal and genocidal violence at the behest of distant decision-makers and in the name of an abstract conception of profit—surely it is not about the Mafia, but rather about American business itself that we are thinking, American capitalism in its most systematized and computerized, dehumanized, "multinational," and corporate form. What kind of crime, said Brecht, is the robbing of a bank, compared to the founding of a bank? Yet until recent years, American business has enjoyed a singular freedom from popular criticism and articulated collective resentment; since the depolitization of the New Deal, the McCarthy era and the beginning of the Cold War and of media or consumer society, it has known an inexplicable holiday from the kinds of populist antagonisms which have only recently (white-collar crime, hostility to utility companies or to the medical profession) shown signs of reemerging. Such freedom from blame is all the more remarkable when we observe the increasing squalor that daily life in the United States owes to big business and to its unenviable position as the purest form of commodity and market capitalism functioning anywhere in the world today.

This is the context in which the ideological function of the myth of the mafia can be understood, as the substitution of crime for big business, as the strategic displacement of all the rage generated by the American system onto this mirror image of big business provided by the movie screen and the various TV series, it being understood that the fascination with the Mafia remains ideological even if in reality organized crime has exactly the importance and influence in American life which such representations attribute to it. The function of the Mafia narrative is indeed to encourage the conviction that the deterioration of the daily life in the United States today is an ethical rather than economic matter, connected, not with profit, but rather "merely" with dishonesty, and with some omnipresent moral corruption whose ultimate mythic source lies in the pure Evil of the Mafiosi themselves. For genuinely political insights into the economic realities of late capitalism, the myth of the mafia strategically substitutes the vision of what is seen to be a criminal aberration from the norm, rather than the norm itself; indeed, the displacement of political and historical analysis by ethical judgments and considerations is generally the sign of an ideological maneuver and of the intent to mystify. Mafia movies thus project a "solution" to social contradictions—incorruptibility, honesty, crime fighting, and finally law-and-order itself—which is evidently a very different proposition from that diagnosis of the American misery whose prescription would be social revolution.

But if this is the ideological function of Mafia narratives like *The Godfather,* what can be said to be their transcendent or Utopian function? The latter is to be sought, it seems to me, in the fantasy message projected by the title of this film, that is, in the family itself, seen as a figure of collectivity and as the object of a Utopian longing, if not a Utopian envy. A narrative synthesis like *The Godfather* is possible only at the conjuncture in which ethnic content—the reference to an alien collectivity—comes to fill the older gangster schemas and to inflect them powerfully in the direction of the social; the superposition on conspiracy of fantasy material related to ethnic groups then triggers the Utopian function of this transformed narrative paradigm. In the United States, indeed, ethnic groups are not only the object of prejudice, they are also the object of envy; and these two impulses are deeply intermingled and reinforce each other mutually. The dominant white middle-class groups—already given over to anomie and social fragmentation and atomization—find in the ethnic and racial groups which are the object of their social repression and status contempt at one and the same time the image of some older collective ghetto or ethnic neighborhood solidarity; they feel the envy and ressentiment of the *Gesellschaft* for the older *Gemeinschaft* which it is simultaneously exploiting and liquidating.

Thus, at a time when the disintegration of the dominant communities is persistently "explained" in the (profoundly ideological) terms of a deterioration of the family, the growth of permissiveness, and the loss of authority of the father, the ethnic group can seem to project an image of social reintegration by way of the patriarchal and authoritarian family of the past. Thus the tightly knit bonds of the Mafia family (in both senses), the protective security of the (god-) father with his omnipresent authority, offers a contemporary pretext for a Utopian fantasy which can no longer express itself through such outmoded paradigms and stereotypes as the image of the now extinct American small town.

The drawing power of a mass cultural artifact like *The Godfather* may thus be measured by its twin capacity to perform an urgent ideological function at the same time that it provides the vehicle for the investment of a desperate Utopian fantasy. Yet the film is doubly interesting from our present point of view in the way in which its sequel—released from the restrictions of Mario Puzo's best-selling novel on which Part I was based—tangibly betrays the momentum and the operation of an ideological and Utopian logic in something like a free or unbound State. *Godfather II,* indeed, offers a striking illustration of Pierre Macherey's thesis, in *Towards a Theory of Literary Production,* that the work of art does not so much *express* ideology as, by endowing the latter with aesthetic representation and figuration, it ends up enacting the latter's own virtual unmasking and self-criticism.

It is as though the unconscious ideological and Utopian impulses at work in *Godfather I* could in the sequel be observed to work themselves towards the light and towards thematic or reflexive foregrounding in their own right. The first film held the two dimensions of ideology and Utopia together within a single generic structure, whose conventions remained intact. With the second film, however, this structure falls as it were into history itself, which submits it to a patient deconstruction that will in the end leave its ideological content undisguised and its displacements visible to the naked eye. Thus the Mafia material, which in the first film served as a substitute for business, now slowly transforms itself into the overt thematics of business itself, just as "in reality" the need for the cover of legitimate investments ends up turning the Mafiosi into real businessmen. The climactic end moment of the historical development is then reached (in the film, but also in real history) when American business, and with it American imperialism, meet that supreme ultimate obstacle to their internal dynamism and structurally necessary expansion which is the Cuban Revolution.

Meanwhile, the utopian strand of this filmic text, the material of the older patriarchal family, now slowly disengages itself from this first or ideological one, and, working its way back in time to its own historical origins, betrays its roots in the precapitalist social formation of a backward and feudal Sicily. Thus these two narrative impulses as it were reverse each other: the ideological myth of the Mafia ends up generating the authentically Utopian vision of revolutionary liberation; while the degraded Utopian content of the family paradigm ultimately unmasks itself as the survival of more archaic forms of repression and sexism and violence. Meanwhile, both of these narrative strands, freed to pursue their own inner logic to its limits, are thereby driven to the other reaches and historical boundaries of capitalism itself, the one as it touches the precapitalist societies of the past, the other at the beginnings of the future and the dawn of socialism.

These two parts of *The Godfather*—the second so much more demonstrably political than the first—may serve to dramatize our second basic proposition in the present essay, namely the thesis that all contemporary works of art—whether those of high culture and modernism or of mass culture and commercial culture—have as their underlying impulse—albeit in what is often distorted and repressed unconscious form—our deepest fantasies about the nature of social life, both as we live it now, and as we feel in our bones it ought rather to be lived. To reawaken, in the midst of a privatized and psychologizing society, obsessed with commodities and bombarded by the ideological slogans of big business, some sense of the ineradicable drive towards collectivity that can be detected, no matter how faintly and feebly, in the most degraded works of mass culture just as surely as in the classics of modernism—is surely an indispensable precondition for any meaningful Marxist intervention in contemporary culture. (1979)

NOTES

1. See for the theoretical sources of this opposition my essay on Max Weber, "The Vanishing Mediator," in *The Ideologies of Theory,* vol. 2 (Minnesota: University of Minnesota Press, 1988), pp. 3–34.

2. The classical study remains that of J.-P. Vernant; see his "Travail et nature dans la Grece ancienne" and "Aspects psychologiques du travail," in *Mythe et pensee chez les grecs* (Paris: Maspéro, 1965).

3. Besides Marx, see Georg Simmel, *Philosophy of Money* (London: Routledge, 1978) and also his classic "Metropolis and Mental Life," translated in Simmel, *On Individuality and Social Forms* (Chicago: University of Chicago Press, 1971), pp. 324–39.

4. "[Bourgeois city-dwellers] wander through the woods as through the moist tender soil of the child they once were: they stare at the poplars and plane trees planted along the road, they have nothing to say about them because they are doing nothing with them, and they marvel at the wondrous quality of this silence," etc., J.-P. Sartre, *Saint Genêt* (Paris: Gallimard, 1952), pp. 249–50.

5. Guy Debord, *The Society of the Spectacle* (Detroit: Black and Red Press, 1973).

6. Reification by way of the *tableau* was already an eighteenth-century theatrical device (reproduced in Buñuel's *Viridiana*), but the significance of the book illustration was anticipated by Sartre's description of "perfect moments" and "privileged situations" in *Nausea* (the illustrations in Annie's childhood edition of Michelet's *History of France*).

7. In my opinion, this "feeling tone" (or secondary libidinal investment) is essentially an invention of Zola and part of the new technology of the naturalist novel (one of the most successful French exports of its period).

8. Written in 1976. A passage like this one cannot be properly evaluated unless it is understood that they were written before the elaboration of a theory of what we now call the postmodern (whose emergence can also be observed in [the essays in *Signatures of the Visible*]).

9. Jacques Scherer, *Le "Livre" de Mallarmé* (Paris: Gallimard, 1957).

10. My own fieldwork has thus been seriously impeded by the demise some years ago of both car radios: so much the greater is my amazement when rental cars today (which are probably not time machines) fill up with exactly the same hit songs I used to listen to in the early seventies, repeated over and over again!

11. Written before a preliminary attempt to do so in *The Political Unconscious* (Ithaca: Cornell University Press, 1981); see in particular chapter 3, "Realism and Desire."

12. Up to but not including: see Stephen Heath, "*Jaws:* Ideology and Film Theory," in *Framework,* vol. 4 (1976), pp. 25–27. Still, Heath's plea to study the filmic effect rather than the content does leave the "shark-effect" itself open to interpretation. It is meanwhile also worth mentioning the interpretation attributed to Fidel, in which the beleaguered island stands for Cuba and the shark for North American imperialism: an interpretation that will be less astonishing for U.S. readers who know this Latin American political

iconography. This image of the United States probably predates the classic "Fable of the Shark and the Sardines," published by the former Guatemalan President Juan Jose Arevolo in 1956, after the American intervention, and is still current, as witness Ruben Bladés's recent ballad.

13. See Adorno's thoughts on the "resistance" of chronology in a letter to Thomas Mann, quoted in *Marxism and Form* (Princeton: Princeton University Press, 1971), pp. 234–350.

14. See my review of Wright, in *Theory and Society*, vol. 4 (1977), pp. 543–59.

16

HEAVEN ON EARTH

A Conversation between a Political Radical and a Spiritual Seeker

ROGER S. GOTTLIEB

Radical: You talk about yoga, and meditation, and prayer, and seeking for the Ultimate Truth. But what is your spirituality in practice? It's the pursuit of personal satisfaction while escaping from the world's suffering and injustice—retreating into a sweet, spiritual cocoon. Do you realize that some folks can't afford to take time out for self-improvement workshops? Do you ever think about the battered women who are dying at the hands of the men in their lives? or the people being killed because of U.S. aid to military dictators? Do you ever meditate on how our society is destroying the natural world?

If you are really seeking The Truth, and not just escaping reality, then why are all the meditation centers out in the country? If you want to spread peace and love, why not put them where they're really needed? in the inner cities! Sure Yoga and meditation and incense and soft music feel good. So does a week on a Caribbean island.

Spiritual Seeker: You're so angry and sarcastic. Probably, underneath it all, you are very frightened. What kind of social change will you create if you are dominated by these feelings? Will the world *you* build be so different from the one we have now? You say it is radical social change you want. But what you *really* seek is power over others, and revenge for the real and imagined slights you have suffered in life. You say I'm escaping, but isn't a good deal of *your* politics an escape from the fact that you can't control life the way you'd like to, that sickness and aging and disappointment are part of *every* life, and that we all have to die, no matter what political system we live under?

Radical: Look, my suffering is nothing compared to what's going on in the

From *A New Creation: America's Contemporary Spiritual Voices,* ed. Roger S. Gottlieb (New York: Crossroad, 1990). Reprinted by permission of the author.

world. I see the pictures of children starving in Africa—not only because of a drought, but because rich corporations and their own corrupt governments have destroyed their agriculture. I know women who have been raped—because men hate women and think they can violate them at will. I know children who have been crippled by toxic wastes because corporate executives are trying to up their profit margin. I have seen single mothers locked into poverty, their kids hungry, any dreams of a decent life shattered.

And I know what makes these things happen. Capitalism. Imperialism. Bureaucratic Communism. Totalitarianism. Racism. Sexism. Sure it sounds silly when you say it like this. A lot of "isms" strung together. But they are not just words. They are names for the terrible powers that destroy the world. The terrible powers that must be fought. And beaten. And when we win we'll build a world where people have some real power over their own lives: where communities can protect their environment from greedy corporations; where people are valued as people, not just as a source of power and profits for the elite. We have to fight to do this, because the powerful never give up their privileges without a struggle. But we can win: make a real democracy instead of a sham, protect people's rights, make the economy work for us instead of against us.

Maybe I do sound stiff and self-righteous and angry. But is my shouting so important? Does it have to bother you so much? Why aren't you angry? Isn't there a tremendous amount to be angry about? This world could be so beautiful—and we're making it so ugly. And WHAT ARE YOU DOING ABOUT IT? What injustice does all your chanting and meditation change? What does it do for one starving child? How will it prevent one war?

Seeker: Slow down. Take it easy. Do you really think having contempt for me will help anyone? You seem to be as out of control as the people you oppose.

You and I actually agree on a great deal. We are sickened by cruelty and oppression. We yearn for a world of peace, justice, and cooperation. We are both opposed to a society that treasures only money, pleasure, and power. It makes us both very sad to see how lives are wasted.

And we also have some high hopes. You think a world of justice and peace are possible. I think people can be holy, can reach enlightenment. I think within each of us is a capacity to know God (or Truth, or The Goddess, put it any way you like). Neither of us is willing to just give up and say "the hell with it, people aren't capable of anything much better than we've got now."

Maybe we're not so far apart after all. We can both admit that terrible things have been done in the name of revolution and religion. We've both seen radical politics mask violence and a lust for power, and pretentious spirituality come from people who are really self-indulgent and self-deceived.

So why stress the obvious? You are serious about making a revolution to liberate human beings. So you are probably aware of the terrible history of radical movements: the awful successes of the ones that took power, and the series of failures of those that did not. I am serious about moving on the spiritual path towards an awakening of my True Self, and I am aware that much of what passes for spirituality is often a catering to the ego, not an attempt to transcend it.

But there is a simple truth that you political revolutionaries have always failed to understand: hatred and violence can only create more of the same. You may *think* that you can direct this angry, aggressive energy only towards the exploiters and oppressors. In the end, however, you will attack others who oppose your policies just because they do not agree or will not obey. Until you have purified yourself of your need for power over others, your fear, greed, hatred, and ignorance will only mirror the evil of those you seek to overcome.

Radical: I agree that we need to focus on the best that each of us has to offer; not the worst. But what you have just said is so naive and ignorant that it proves what I always suspected. Even when you are well-intentioned, people like you know nothing about politics, and about what really makes a difference in people's lives. You just care about how pleasant and peaceful and mellow it all is.

For very complicated historical reasons communist revolutions in Eastern Europe and the Third World turned into totalitarian states. You use that fact as a pretext to condemn every radical political movement not led by saints!

But let's look at some other things that happened a little closer to home. In the early years of the Depression in this country one out of four workers was unemployed, and one out of three people had no steady income. People were crushed by poverty, despair, and a deep sense of shame. The most important radical political response to all this came from the Communist Party. Now I have little real sympathy for the communists. They were in love with authority, rabid critics of anyone who disagreed, and allowed themselves to be completely dominated by the Soviet Communist Party. *But,* they also organized communities to prevent unemployed neighbors from being evicted; defended people's civil rights; and helped form industrial unions with blacks and whites—for the first time in American history—working together to get decent wages and working conditions. Were they angry? You bet. Did they get a little rough at times? Of course. Were they saints? Not in the least.

But they made a difference. Suppose you were out of work through no fault of your own, just another victim of a predictable depression produced by capitalism. You've got a sick wife or a sick husband, three or four young kids who need a home. The sheriff is coming to evict you because you can't pay the rent. And there's no place to go. Who you gonna call? Somebody who's busy meditating to purify his soul or chanting to raise his energy? No, you'll call the communist who's been organizing the neighbors after work. And she'll get her people. And in an hour you'll have a hundred angry—yes, angry—people there who won't let the sheriff put your kids out on the sidewalk.

Take another example. A little more recent. The women who created feminism in the 1960s and 1970s were pretty angry a lot of the time. They got really mad at rape and the threat of rape, sexism in books and religions and politics and schools, women condemned to poverty and self-hatred and subservience. Out of all that anger—and a lot of caring, too—came some important changes. For instance: suppose you're a married woman whose husband beats her. Nothing special in that, happens to millions of women. But suppose you just can't take it anymore: the terrible threats to you and the kids. Who you gonna call? The cops often do nothing or act as if it's your fault. The courts take forever. If you're lucky, you'll have a battered women's shelter to call: where other women will take you in, help you find your own place, help protect you from your husband. Now as sure as apples come from apple trees and not grape vines, it was all those angry feminists who made battered women's shelters possible.

You see, your problem is that you look at us and all you see is our anger. God knows we've made mistakes and failed. But you don't see what we've done. You don't see the love that's part of it. And you don't see that there is a certain kind of anger which is also a certain kind—and sometimes the best kind—of love.

Seeker: Perhaps, perhaps. But you tend to ignore what spiritual teachers have to give and get so caught up in the fact that we talk differently from you, that we're not part of your little club of political people, and then you miss what you have to learn from us.

You say you want to create a world in which people can be happy. I'm not sure you have ever really thought what that means. I don't believe that thinking about people *just* in terms of politics—in terms of rights, and freedom, and equality of opportunity, and the kinds of work they do—is enough.

I also want everyone to have enough to eat and a decent place to live. But most people in the United States have that. Are they happy? Have you ever taken a commuter train back out from New York City at five o'clock and looked at the faces of these well-off suburbanites? You see fatigue, anxiety, hostility, sadness, depression. Their bodies are pampered. No one is oppressing them. Don't they have what revolutionaries say everyone should have? Yet they are miserable!

And the reason they are miserable is that they identify with desires that can never be satisfied. What they have, they have, but they always want more. More money to buy more things. More pleasures to take their minds off the pleasures they have lost. More status. More privileges. More sex to make up for all that emptiness which they deny but cannot overcome. And they think that this is all there is to life.

Who will teach them anything different? Will you? I don't think so. It seems to me that radicals want to create a world in which desires are satisfied equally and fairly. But the sad truth is that desires just cannot be satisfied. Like the heroin addict, whose few hours of bliss after a shot guarantee his future misery when the drug wears off, so the life of possessions and desires makes for temporary satisfaction and long-term pain.

It is spiritual teachings—not political radicalism—which suggest something else is possible. If you practice Buddhist meditation, for example, you find yourself seeing the pattern of endless desires, confusions, and passion which your mind creates. And you can experience an awareness and a center of universal compassion which is not bound by the cycle of wanting, having, and wanting more. Or perhaps you could take seriously the Jewish practice of thanking God for our blessings: being alive when we wake up in the morning, rainbows and holidays and new fruits of each season. If you do this with attention and care, you start to replace craving and envy and the greedy pursuit of more and more with gratitude, acceptance, and peace.

Will you learn these things from angry words about imperialism, sexism, or exploitation? Will people really live fully just because their wages go up 15 percent, their working conditions get a little better, welfare benefits and social security payments rise, or blacks and women get equal opportunity to join the bored, anxious, and hostile upper middle class? Only a spiritual perspective and practice can help people see how ultimately hollow all that pursuit of superficial pleasure is, and can offer something to take its place.

Radical: You could be right. It's true, I sometimes get so caught up in my bitterness about what people don't have that I can't really enjoy what we *do* have. We like to talk about who'll run the steel mills and what to teach in the schools. But this stuff about the endlessness of desire, that's another story. It's possible that we who work to create a world of happiness don't really know what happiness is.

Sure it's wonderful to feel grateful for what you have. But—what about this?—maybe you shouldn't have it. Maybe you have it at someone else's expense. Maybe you only have it because society has given you privileges that it denies other people. Take your last example. Along with its wonderful appreciations, traditional Judaism also has men thanking God that they were not born women! And it's not surprising, because in that tradition social power and status belong to men.

And what's true of Judaism is also true of Christianity and Hinduism and Islam and all the rest. Your wise and enlightened and holy traditions give women a lot less influence and respect than men. And virtually all the supposedly great teachers talked about how to live a properly spiritual life as if someone else (not the profound, holy spiritual masters) was taking care of the children. I once heard a Zen Buddhist teacher say enlightenment is "sleeping when you're tired and eating when you're hungry." That's so silly. It could only come from someone who never changed a diaper at three in the morning or tried to eat dinner and feed two young children at the same time.

Spiritual teachers always act as if they're timeless, beyond the ugliness and greed and limitations of society. But guess what? They're like everyone else! They're not beyond society, they're part of it. They have their demeaning attitudes towards women. They pay taxes that support our government without understanding how our foreign policy hurts other countries. They don't seem to care about the way the rich exploit the poor. I asked a Taoist master what he thought about the effects of Reagan's budget cuts on the poor. "Teach Reagan to medi[t]ate," he said. I guess he just had nothing else to say. A friend of mine whose parents survived the Holocaust asked a famous Buddhist teacher how we can integrate knowledge of the Holocaust into our image of spiritual life. His answer? She should meditate on how *she* was like Hitler! How can these people claim to be "Masters" when they know so little about the real world?

Without a grounded understanding of politics you'll just repeat all the oppression of the society you live in. You'll think your sexist views are natural and that vast inequality of wealth and resources is just fine. You won't know what American imperialism does with your tax money and in your name—because it's not part of the here and now you concentrate on so much.

The fact is that you are trapped by the immediate contents of your mind, the moment-to-moment feelings you try to understand and detach from. The forces which shape the world don't come only from what people think and feel right in this moment. Suffering doesn't just come because of someone's desires and fears, but because of impersonal institutions and established social structures that everyone just takes for granted. While you spend all that time watching your mind for every possible sign of attachment, reading mystical stories, and purifying your energy, you ignore the ways social institutions shape who you are, how you live, and how you relate to other people. It's great to be kind and compassionate to those around you, but to some peasant in El Salvador who is being bombed by planes paid for by your tax money, it really doesn't make any difference how nice a person you are.

While you are healing yourself before you try to heal the world, large corporations are destroying our groundwater with toxic wastes. And it's not just *other* people; we *all* live like that. You drive a car and contribute to global warming. Your refrigerator and your air conditioning damage the ozone layer. Now you can't alter these things by yourself. It's hard to even see what's going on without a political analysis. And it's impossible to change without political action, community action, action aimed at the systematic way we do things, not just individual, conscious acts.

Like I said before, instead of some mountain retreat to teach meditation, why not the black ghetto? Instead of finding some sweet spot and proclaiming the joys of life, try shouting it out in the middle of a concentration camp. Tell me how the universe is just what it ought to be while you're fighting some big corporation that poisoned the water in a little town and tripled the cancer rates for the children.

And above all, don't tell me that everything happens to us because we choose it. At least, not until you go down to the slums in Latin America and try to help the wretchedly poor kids and watch the rich in those countries living like kings on their huge estates. Have a few children starve to death in your arms and watch their parents be shot for trying to start a union or get land reform, and see if you still think we all get what we choose.

Finding your own personal experience of bliss is just less important than the work to change all this. If I get uptight sometimes because the work is difficult or because the facts are so horrible—well, that's not such a terrible thing.

And you know something else? Maybe you'd reach enlightenment faster if you thought about it less, and more about making the world a better place. You spiritual types need politics to help you be a little more concerned for others. But you also need it in your search for your own enlightenment. You're never going to change yourself if you don't try to change the world. How else can you overcome that obsessive self-concern that only undermines everything you claim to stand for? "How's my mind? How's my breathing? How's my headstand? How's my bowel movement?" Enough already! Why not put your mind on something a little bigger?

Seeker: Look, I know I do have a tendency to want to escape at times. Don't we all? Don't you? When is the last time you went down to work with the dying children in Latin America? Sometimes when I meditate I feel such a calm, pure, healing energy—that's what I want to feel all the time. And then I'm not really sure how to do that and still think about the terrible things I read about in the newspaper.

But these big sweeping changes you're so sure will save the world, isn't that kind of an escape too? You've got all these plans; will they really amount to much? The only person I really know is me—and before I make the world so different I better start with my own life. How can I end war if I'm not peaceful myself? How can I save the environment if I don't recycle my own garbage: How can I expect love and clarity in all the great big institutions if I'm not loving and clear myself? And perhaps if I make some progress in these matters on my own, then I'll be able to share the gifts with those around me. Person by person. Heart by heart. That's how change takes place.

And you know something? I'm also a little scared of you. You say you're going to give me an understanding of society and politics so that my spiritual disciplines and teachings don't mask selfishness or escapism and I don't repeat the mistakes of the rest of society. O.K. Great. But who will help you to understand and be aware of *your* own anger and hatred, your lust for power? To put it simply: what's going to keep you from using the authority that you have in a destructive way? All the communists had great dreams, or so they said. But the ones who succeeded created murderous totalitarian states. And the ones in this country supported the Hitler-Stalin pact because they were so cowed by international communist authority, trashed everyone who questioned them in any way, and did all they could to dominate every group they joined. Contemporary feminism has led to some great changes; but a lot of women suffered from the competitiveness and backbiting that was part of the women's movement.

What would all you radicals do if you controlled the police, and the banks, and the armies? Wouldn't there simply be more arguing, and fighting, and struggling? You say you know how to make things work. But every radical group seems to self-destruct from its own in-fighting. Every leftist seems to hate other leftists because they've got the wrong ideas and the wrong strategy. If your little groups are models of the society you want to build, then pardon me for my doubts.

You talk a good game about participatory democracy and power to the people and empowering the disempowered. But what do you really know about how people change for the better? Where's your technology of self-awareness? How are you going to get a politics where people work towards the best in themselves and others and not just promote their anger and their point of view? You may have sophisticated theories of economic development, political institutions, and so on. But transformation on a personal level is all that can really happen; and it's what we know best.

We offer the discipline of prayer, the insights of meditation, the spiritual models of teachers, sages, and saints who acted from some other place than their own grasping and compulsive desires. Maybe some of this stuff is limited by elitism or sexism, but not all of it is. There are models of people wrestling with their greed and their passion and their anger—and winning. Experiencing their negativity and moving beyond it—not taking it out on someone else. Building their lives around compassion for others, connections that are felt despite all the obvious differences that we can all make such a fuss about.

When spiritual teachers move into the world, they bring love, and compassion, and calls for justice. But they don't do it because it's "right" in some abstract sense. No, they feel that this is what they are truly meant to do. That's why they don't end up resentful and self-righteous, violent and driven and burnt out. Go back to the Depression that you mentioned before. There was Dorothy Day and the Catholic Workers' movement. She served the people, organized, fought the good fight. But she did it as a child of God, not a servant of the Third International. Look at Gandhi and Martin Luther King. They weren't Marxists or socialists. They were spiritual leaders who made a difference. They saw real problems and they did something about them. And they did it without hate or violence. When things were desperate they had some faith in the power of that love which they called God or Truth—a love they saw in everyone, even their opponents. They were tuned into a resource which most people don't have. That's why they could bring people together by some other bond than anger. That's why they could help people rise up without trampling someone else down.

Spirituality isn't just meditation and soft music. It can help relieve the suffering in the world. Look what our teachings do for illness. When people get cancer, say, they usually feel totally helpless and passive, fall into despair, and let the doctors take over. But spiritual teachers have been changing that. They've gone into the cancer wards and talked to the patients and said: "Look: this is your body. You can heal yourself through meditation, visualization, a change of diet, and your own healing energies. You can see the cancer as a teacher: ask yourself if there is some part of you that wanted the cancer for some reason; or what lesson the illness might have for your life." When people do these things the cure rates go up. Even when they have to face death they can do it with dignity and peace.

Radical: Okay. I'll admit there *are* times when I've stepped back—at a demonstration, a meeting, a discussion of principles or tactics—and wondered what we were really there for: to end oppression or to have a little political club to belong to. And I appreciate what you say about cancer. My mother died of it last year; we just sat around the hospital feeling helpless and miserable. We certainly could have used *someone* who knew something else to do.

But cancer is a good example of your spiritual tendencies to avoid reality. Cancer is *not* a disease which strikes people for deep psychological reasons. Most of the cancer epidemic—60–80 percent according to some people—comes from the ways we abuse our environment: from the toxic wastes; poisoned air, water, and food; and radiation that *we* are creating. All the visualizations in the world won't affect those causes. You talk about what lessons cancer can teach us. The lesson is that we have to act, together, to change society so that the way we live doesn't end up killing us. And to do that we have to challenge the people who have the power—the greedy, arrogant corporations and their servants in the government. Put the corporations under real democratic control, and you can heal more cancer than a thousand prayer groups.

As for Gandhi and King, well, to start with, they were a little simplistic in their understanding of politics. Nonviolence can be a great tactic, but it's pretty limited in the long run. Gandhi had little real comprehension of the power of capitalism. He got the British out; but then a new ruling elite replaced the old one. It's the rich capitalists who have controlled India since independence. In the last months of his life King was moving a lot closer to something like a Marxist analysis of U.S. foreign policy in Vietnam. The old simple Christian understanding just didn't work anymore.

But if all spiritual people were like Gandhi and King—or the priests into liberation theology in Latin America, or the supporters of the Sanctuary movement in this country, or the people in the peace and ecology movements who challenge the government and the large corporations—I'd have no quarrel with spirituality. But they aren't. You know, Gandhi used to point to a picture of a starving peasant and say to his followers: "Examine what you did today; how much of it helped that man?" That was his measure of spirituality. How many spiritual seekers today can say the same? And I don't just mean giving him a handout, but trying to alter the system of power which keeps making him and millions of others like him. It's great to be charitable; but the real charity is social change.

As for your idea that politics can't liberate us on a deep and personal level, that's just not true. Personal change is exactly what happened when women in consciousness-raising groups started finding out that problems they thought were their own *personal* failures were *social* problems shared by a lot of other women. Personal change happened in Chile, before the army smashed the Left, for housewives and factory workers and peasants who felt for the first time they had some say about how their country was being run. Look at the pictures of blacks marching in civil rights demonstrations! There's personal transformation in action: self-hatred and submission shifting to pride; self-awareness replacing passivity; creativity winning over resignation.

Now is all this *personal?* You bet. But it's not just *individual*. It comes out of connecting to others. And it gives people an irresistible energy of solidarity: a sense that you and your pain are not alone. You feel that there are hundreds, thousands, maybe millions of others who will stand together with you. There is no feeling like it. It breaks through that devil of isolation you call the ego. It gives you the most purified sense of power—not power *over* others, but power *with* others, to help and be helped, to create a new and beautiful world. Isn't this part of spiritual life as much as meditating on your breath or singing God's praises?

Seeker: That makes sense. Perhaps there can be a spiritual dimension to political change. Political movements can certainly generate a feeling of human connection. But there is a communion possible—beyond that of people to people—that has to do with connecting to the universe as a whole, to God. If what you want is for people to move past the devil of isolation, don't you think it might help if they have some vision of union with something beyond their own immediate social situation? For thousands of years people in our traditions have had experiences of themselves as something deeper than simply a social identity or a lot of passions, even passions for justice. Whether it's a burning bush or prana or chi or Jesus, the idea is the same: you can connect to something beyond your own isolated ego—and something beyond the isolation of your tribe, your race, your country—because you *are* something besides your own isolated ego.

I know you want to go beyond selfishness, but you always proceed from confrontation and hatred. When you try to transcend the individual ego, it's to join some angry group, some collection of oppressed whom you try to motivate through their anger. "Look at your pain," you tell them, "it comes from someone else, your enemy. See how you've suffered. Fight back. Struggle. Triumph!" That's your basic message, isn't it?

But it's all so outmoded. With the threat of nuclear war, the damage to the ozone layer, global warming—*everyone* is "oppressed"; everyone is in danger. There is no enemy "out there." The enemy is a madness that afflicts us all. We need a global awareness, a global politics, because we all share the same fate. Your whole way of thinking—organize the oppressed, overcome exploitation, good guys fight the bad guys—it is out of date.

Radical: Well, things may have changed. It's certainly true that people like Marx never saw that we could have "global" interests. Or that human folly would reach the edge of the self-destruction of the species.

But if we're all connected, if politics really turns on "global" questions, how much more do we all need some kind of activism! We need to act in ways that connect us to real, living, breathing people, not just some infinite energy. I say: out of the meditation halls and into the streets!

Remember, we're *all* threatened by nuclear weapons and pollution; but only *some* of us get money and power through them. Agricultural laborers in Mexico harvest the crops and get cancer from the pesticides which we export even though they're banned here. How much do they have in common with the corporate executives who are getting rich off the transaction? Or their own wealthy landlords who own the farms?

Do you really think we can change our economies to take the environmental threat seriously if they are controlled by a tiny percentage of ridiculously rich people? What those people want is profits and power. And they want it now, in the short run. That's the system that got us into this mess. If we don't change that system, we'll probably never get out of it.

Or look at it the other way: the establishment can make the system manageable—and still keep its power. The barons and lords of the Middle Ages learned to band together under a king so they didn't waste their energy fighting each other, but stayed on top of the peasants. In the Depression the government took some control over the economy and gave workers social security and unemployment insurance. But capitalists kept their ownership of the economy. They only gave up what they did to keep the system from crumbling and the people from making a revolution. They got things back on an even keel—and then it was business as usual. It's not impossible for them to do the same things for these global threats you speak of. A little cooperation among the big powers; some exporting of cancer rates to the Third World by doing things there they are not allowed to do here; some big loans to protect the rainforests; some regulation on consumption, just the way they learned to regulate the stock market. Things will be a little less crazy, a little less dangerous. But the exploiters will still be at the top. Racism and sexism will still be used to oppress people and set them against each other. The culture will still train people to be passive and hate themselves and depend on powers and authority and values imposed from outside.

Seeker: Perhaps. Perhaps. All that seems a little far away. You can say what you say; and somebody else could come up with another analysis.

And in the meantime people live, and have children, and grow old and sick and die. What do you have to say about this? Not much. You know struggle, but not acceptance. You know how to try to control things, but not how to let go. I have friends whose child was born with a heart defect and died at three months. Their pain didn't come from injustice or oppression. It just came from life. There was no one to blame or get angry at. At that time it wasn't so important that they were white or black, rich or poor. It was just important that they were suffering. They didn't need a political organizer; they needed to know that others could accept their suffering. They needed to learn lessons of grief and acceptance, making a meaning out of pain and moving beyond it. What they told me afterwards was that they learned more about what real happiness is from having that sorrow—that they learned to feel real gratitude for the first time in their lives.

Maybe some spiritual people could use your political analysis to keep them honest, to keep them from self-indulgence and selfishness. But you could use a spiritual perspective to remind you of your humanness, to move you beyond the differences and antagonisms and help you accept and marvel at the special things which we face just as human beings, not as workers or bosses, women or men. People grow and get old, seasons change, babies are born, friends and parents die. What does all your political activism know about commemorating the mystery of all this, marking these moments and processes with a ritual, a celebration, a song, a prayer? Spiritual traditions can help us face and feel and accept these sorrows and to celebrate the joys. Your attitudes of confrontation and struggle, your goal of a society where life is always under our conscious control—they seem more than a little out of place for such things.

Silence.

Radical: When my mother was dying of cancer last year, I really didn't know what to do or how to feel. Of course, I can show the relation between pollution and cancer rates and criticize the patriarchal male medical hierarchy. Even basic issues of death have a political dimension.

But the death itself . . . I didn't know what to make of it. I wanted to pray for her soul after she died, even though God makes no sense to me. I prayed anyway. It made me feel that at least I had some place to put my love and my sorrow. When I see myself getting older I get scared. I see how little I've changed the world, I wonder what I'm alive for. . . .

Seeker: The world has become a very frightening place. I'd often like to escape to the eternal and forget I'm here among all the pain and problems. I've never had much faith in collective action for change.

Radical: As difficult as politics is, it has its satisfactions. If you once feel that you are really changing something, really stopping some pain and injustice and putting something else in their place, there is no joy like it.

Seeker: It sounds like heaven on earth. But I don't know if there's really hope that people will change, that the light will come through.

Radical: "I believe in the sun even when it is not shining. I believe in God even when God is silent." They found that scrawled on the wall of a bunker where Jews hid from Nazis during the Holocaust. People have always wondered if the light will banish the darkness. But it's not over yet. Have faith.[1]

NOTE

1. Readers interested in a fuller development of the political perspective presented here can consult Roger S. Gottlieb, *History and Subjectivity: The Transformation of Marxist Theory* (Philadelphia: Temple University Press, 1987).

PART VII.

ECOLOGY, SCIENCE, AND TECHNOLOGY

17.

SOCIALISM, NATURE, AND ECOLOGY

JAMES O'CONNOR

All philosophy lies in two words, sustain and abstain.

—Epictetus

There isn't anything that money can't fix, but everything stays broke.

—John Straley

SOCIALISM AND NATURE

A reasonable question is, given the extent of nature destruction in the ex-socialist countries, Why would anyone speak of "socialism and nature" in any but the most negative terms? After all, the socialist countries used up their nonrenewable resources as fast as (or faster than) the capitalist world and polluted the air, water, and land as much, if not more, than their capitalist counterparts. Many environmentalists therefore conclude that it is not capitalism and socialism as economic systems that deserve the onus for causing environmental degradation. Rather, they attribute blame to "industrialization," "urbanization," "technology," "bureaucracy," and a "production at all costs" mentality—all of which appear to be common in both the capitalist and the socialist worlds.[1]

Another axiom found in mainstream academia and the media is that the old socialist system exemplified by the Soviet Union and capitalism as exemplified by the United States were models that existed (as if in a laboratory) independently of each other. In fact, really existing socialism and capitalism were formed in interaction—often violent interaction—within and between each other during the twentieth

From James O'Connor, "Socialism and Nature," and "Socialism and Ecology," in *Natural Causes: Essays in Ecological Marxism* (New York: Guilford Press, 1998), pp. 255–79. Reprinted with permission.

century. The primary cause of environmental destruction in this century is war, and the most destructive wars (World Wars I and II) have been initiated by capitalist nations, or between imperial powers and Third World liberation movements or fledgling states. In 1945, the United States detonated two nuclear weapons over Japan and for decades thereafter its (and the USSR's) testing of nuclear weapons continued to degrade land, sea, and air. These were ecological watersheds.

In the post–World War II era, U.S. war-fighting policies in Vietnam did mayhem to the environment. In much of Central America in the 1980s, the United States, in support of right-wing allies such as the Contras, drenched agricultural areas with toxic pesticides and chemical fertilizers that made the region into a zone of ecodisaster. In the African subcontinent, South Africa did not hesitate to destroy agricultural areas in the front-line states as part of its military strategy to deprive liberation forces of cover, and to weaken governments sympathetic to democratic goals in the region. The ecodestruction caused by aggressive expansionist socialist states, for example, the old Soviet Union in Afghanistan or the Chinese in Tibet, pales in comparison with that produced by intercapitalist wars and imperial wars of counterrevolution.

To put the point as bluntly as possible, socialist revolution has proven to be less ecologically harmful than capitalist imperialist rivalry and counterrevolution. And, while the ecological history of war in the twentieth century needs to be written in terms of this rivalry and of revolution and counterrevolution, we do not as yet have any such general history, nor any general complementary account of the integration of war into political economy and political ecology.

While "socialism" and "capitalism" should not be compared as if they developed independently of one another, they *can* be legitimately compared insofar as they developed on the basis of different property relations, legal relations, ideologies, and relations of political power. In fact, the standard Western view that "industrialization," "technology," and so on are the causes of environmental destruction in both the West and the East fails to distinguish between a society's productive forces and its production relations, that is, its technological base, labor, and production system, on the one hand, and its property, legal, and political relations, on the other. In any comparison between socialism and capitalism, such a comparison, and the theoretical implications of different property and political systems for the causes and consequences of environmental degradation, is useful to make.

To the degree that socialist countries imported technology and systems of production and labor control (indeed, root *conceptions* of technology and production) from the West, the causes of environmental destruction in socialist countries were similar to those in the capitalist countries. Also, to the extent that economic growth and development were overriding priorities in the socialist world, the causes and consequences of nature degradation were roughly the same. Finally, insofar as the socialist countries integrated themselves into the world capitalist market, the same kind of systemic forces were at work in the East as in the West.

To the degree that property and legal relations were different in the socialist countries than in the capitalist world, however, the causes and effects of environmental destruction were not the same. This can also be said about the two political systems and the corresponding differences in the relationship between civil society and the state.

In fact, in the ex-socialist countries, the productive *forces* were not that dissimilar to those in the West, excepting that they were typically less "advanced." The production *relations* in the socialist world *were* quite different from those in the capitalist countries, hence the specific forms of technology, and the particular ways in which agriculture, mining, industry, and so on, developed within the socialist world, were also different. Finally, the differences in political systems had important effects on the processes of both ecological degradation and environmental struggle and reconstruction. The causes for environmental destruction in capitalist and socialist societies were thus both the same and different.

Since the similarities between capitalism and socialism are fairly well known (just because they are similarities), it is important to focus on the differences between the two systems. What were the main ways in which socialist property/production relationships and political systems led to different or modified technological choices, industrial structures, allocations of social labor, patterns of scientific development and application, forms of consumption and urbanization, and so on? And, in what ways were socialist *solutions* to environmental problems different than those in the advanced capitalist countries?

There were many variations in the forms of the production relations and productive forces, and their relation to the conditions of production, within the socialist world. The extent and kinds of market relationships, cultural traditions, and political systems also varied widely. Yet there were certain broad similarities. First, in all socialist countries the major means of production were nationalized although not socialized—that is, there was no strong tradition of democratic control of the means of life, even though there existed substantial degrees of local control of resources in their presocialist past. Nationalization, or state ownership, without socialization, or democratic social control, of the means of production meant that the socialist countries were characterized by central planning and party/bureaucratic political rule. Second, all socialist countries had constitutional guarantees, not always practiced, especially in the last years of liberalization, that workers have the right to access, utilize, and exercise control over the means of production.

Third, most, if not all, socialist countries had a history of extensive rather than intensive economic development based on educated labor and high-tech production, because socialism appeared in relatively "backward" regions of world capitalism. Thus, the socialist countries attempted to "catch up with the West" (they called this effort "socialist construction"). This was determined by the Communist Party's perceived need for national security against the West and its proclaimed goal of surpassing the West's ability to improve the material and social conditions of the producing classes. An uncritical acceptance of certain aspects of Western-style development often led to their mechanical imitation in the socialist countries—a "mistake" that present-day red green movements and political parties do not make. In the course of the East-West conflict, the idea of a qualitatively different type of progress, one measured by the quality of life rather than by the quantity of technology or consumer goods, or by use value rather than by exchange value, was systematically suppressed; this was another "error" that red Greens today avoid like the plague (or should).

Further, nearly all of the socialist countries collapsed in the face of economic and political crisis associated with the phasing out of extensive economic development and the transition to more intensive types of development in the context of a supply-constrained economy. In this crisis, the demand for Western capital equipment, including pollution control and abatement technology and consumer goods, was high and rising rapidly. Meanwhile, in the West, the hypercapitalistic, obsessively cost-cutting major economies found themselves with a surplus of both capital and consumer goods. This was due mainly to increased rates of labor exploitation and growing income and wealth inequalities, together with intensified competition from Asia. These basic economic facts helped to set the stage for political moves in both the East and the West to end the Cold War, and to renew investment and trade between the old socialist and new capitalist worlds, which have had important effects on the ways that the ex-socialist countries exploit their environments and conditions of production generally.

In principle, state ownership and central planning permit the state to minimize resource depletion, "negative externalities" such as pollution, and the destruction of environmental amenities. The key role of science and scientists in socialist planning reinforces this principle. Thus, huge sums can be allocated to pollution abatement investments by political fiat (e.g., the Brezhnev-era decision in the USSR to reduce pollution by industry located on Lake Baikal). Also, industry can be removed by fiat (e.g., Gorbachev talked about dismantling the Baikal mills), and decentralized by fiat, partly transforming harmful pollution into harmless waste. Further, the leaders of the USSR for over two decades stated that ecological science is one key basis for rational, scientific, economic planning.

No matter how enlightened or unenlightened those at the top of the old socialist hierarchies may have been, workers, farmers, scientists, and technicians trained to recognize and deal with ecological problems had little or no political power. The combination of state ownership/planning and party/bureaucratic rule—or the absence of popular power with an "ecological consciousness"—meant that managers, technicians, and workers in particular enterprises were politically divided from those in other enterprises. There was thus a structural tendency to be indifferent to the environmental effects of one's own enterprises on other enterprises and communities "downstream." Insofar as ecologically conscious cadres had no common organization, the root of this problem was clearly political.

A further point is that the political division of the working class in party/

bureaucratic-ruled socialist states was associated with the weak development of internal democracy; absence of freedom to organize and agitate independently around specific environmental issues; lack of public information about pollution levels; bureaucratic secrecy and disinformation about the environmental effects of new investments; and, last but not least, political cynicism and indifference. "Negative externalities" or "social costs" were often not identified as such because of the lack of a free flow of information, of ministry and enterprise accountability, of independent access to technical data, and of institutional channels that could be used to change existing practices. Thus, environmental problems were comparatively speaking, invisible; hence the kinds and extent of pollution and resource depletion were relatively unknown. There were certain obvious exceptions to this rule, for example, Chernobyl, the drying up of the Aral Sea, and the salinization of soils in drained areas.

Yet ecological science traditionally played a role in economic planning. Historically, because the Soviet conservation movement was dominated by scientists, it had more legitimacy within the state than conservationism historically had in the capitalist world. Moreover, "ecological glasnost" opened up independent channels of protest and organization, within student movements in particular, which began to make the invisible more visible and the uncertain more knowable.

Central planning itself had both positive and negative implications for the environment. On the positive side, the absence of "economic crises" of the type inherent in capitalism—hence the absence of capitalist-type struggles between enterprises for market shares—meant that enterprises had less incentive to pollute than do capitalist companies, which are often forced to externalize costs as the price of survival in the market. On the negative side, central planning encouraged large, ecologically unsound mining, construction, and other projects, and centralized energy production and distribution. The worst example is nuclear power production which everywhere is associated with centralized political power, military ambition, secrecy, and rule by technocrats. In the last analysis, Chernobyl (where the reactor's design was copied from an American model) might have been as much the result of a powerful state and a weak society (i.e., the lack of democracy) as a lack of quality control and weak worker motivation, which, in turn, were related to undemocratic and inefficient forms of politics and economy, respectively.

In socialist countries, full employment and job security were the norm and not the exception (as they are in the capitalist world). Full employment and job security had profound effects on the ways that socialist economies worked. These effects included limited horizontal, upward, and downward mobility of labor; limited ability of enterprise managers to use laborpower in flexible ways (as "variable capital" in Marxist terms); and limited ability of enterprises to draw on surplus labor reserves. With little "slack" and much "rigidity" in the economy (which probably could not have been removed without subverting norms of full employment and job security), socialist economic growth (as Kornai theorized) was *resource constrained*. "Resource constraint" is here defined in the economic sense, not as an "ecological constraint." This is in sharp contrast with capitalist economies which historically have been *demand constrained*. The effects of resource-constrained economies on the environment in principle seem to depend on a number of factors. First, enterprises in resource-constrained economies were notorious for "hoarding" labor, raw materials, fuels, component parts, and other inputs. Markets were infamous for "shortages" and "queuing," which seemed to have both positive and negative effects on the environment. On the minus side, natural resources were appropriated even when there was no immediate use for them. On the plus side, resource-constrained economies were likely to grow slowly until the shift to intensive development was made (and also during the transition to intensive development), hence they were likely to deplete and pollute resources at a slower rate.

Second, full employment and job security constraints reduced management incentives to make labor-saving technological changes (hence the relative stagnation of the Soviet economy). A priori, there is no way to know whether older technologies depleted resources and/or polluted more than new technologies. On the one hand, in China, small iron foundries and other industrial facilities constructed in the countryside with the purpose of integrating agriculture and industry and evening out economic development were famous "polluters." Technical backwardness was also associated with the absence of up-to-date pollution control equipment. On the other hand, the relative backwardness of East Europe and the USSR in high-tech sectors minimized the kind of high-tech pollution that is common in the Western industrialized economies. In general, full employment and job security and the relative absence of capitalist-type market discipline meant that socialist enterprises were not driven by the need to continuously adopt new technology of any kind. This is, of course, a comparative judgment. The USSR, for example, exported manufacturing licenses for water purification plants, blast furnace evaporation plants, and other innovations to Western firms, and many "ecologically clean technologies" were adopted in dozens of Soviet industries. However, the USSR was technologically backward in most respects compared with the leading Western capitalist countries.

Third, full employment and job security meant that management, technicians, and workers had powerful incentives to keep their enterprises going at all costs independent of changes in technology and market conditions. As already indicated, workers and management were basically "enterprise conscious," not "society conscious," hence had incentives to externalize costs, for example, by polluting. On the other hand, full employment and job security constraints (with central planning) also limited processes of uneven and combined economic development that are characteristic in the capitalist world (hence limited the resulting ecological horror stories). Some socialist countries used central planning mechanisms to try to reduce regional inequalities of wealth and productive capacity, which appeared to have had both positive and negative effects on the environment. On the positive side was the dispersion of "waste," which helped to prevent waste from becoming "pollution." One negative effect was that economies of scale in waste disposal systems were difficult to realize when industry is decentralized—which led to severe local pollution problems. As a rule, though, socialist industry was centralized, and had environmental effects similar to those under capitalist industry.

There are other important differences between resource- and demand-constrained economies. One is that the latter waste resources through advertising, packaging, style changes, model changes, product differentiation, product obsolescence, and credit buying—all of which are needed to keep the system afloat. This "sales effort" not only wastes resources but also results in more pollution of the environment. Socialist economies were much less guilty in this respect. Another difference is that demand-constrained economies are based on the wage form of labor and on the commodity form of need satisfaction. By contrast, socialist economies stressed collective consumption, for example, mass transit, collective recreational and vacation facilities, and apartment living. On these grounds, socialist economies used and wasted fewer resources than capitalist economies, and socialist personal consumption created less pollution. Still another difference is that capitalist economies are subject to the rule, "accumulate or die." Growth is not a means to the end of economic and social well-being but an end in and of itself. Although economic growth was also a key goal in socialist countries, the same *systemic economic* imperative to grow was absent. Growth was rather a political decision pertaining to economic development and the desire to "catch up with the West." The relentless and unplanned nature of resource extraction/pollution in capitalism may not be inherent in socialist economies, where in principle production was for use, not profit, and growth was regarded as a means, not an end in and of itself—although in *practice* this clearly has not been true. Yet it is worthwhile to stress that enterprises seeking to fulfill their quotas under a central plan in theory operate under different performance principles than capitalist firms whose profit margins must continuously expand.

Finally, in these socialist societies, norms of economic and social equality governed political and economic decisions more than in capitalist societies. In the latter, the tragedy of poverty-stricken masses pushed into marginal lands by international capital and forced to degrade the environment out of sheer survival needs has little or no counterpart in the socialist world. A comparison of Cuba with, for example, the Dominican Republic or much of Central America would be instructive in this connection.

In most socialist countries, the Party came to power in relatively backward peripheral, or semiperipheral regions of world capitalism. The socialist countries underwent a period of extensive development—capital-widening investments, heavy industry, huge power projects, proletarianization of the peasantry, and so on—which the developed capitalist countries experienced in an earlier period. "Socialist construction" and "catching up with the West" in the context of the Cold War and Western hostility to the USSR reinforced the environmental effects of extensive economic development, especially in the resource-rich USSR. All major countries passing through extensive development have "specialized" in polluting industries, for example, paper and pulp, fossil fuel power production, oil refining, heavy chemicals, petrochemicals, and other basic capital goods industries. Thus the "miracle" of Eastern European industrial growth from the end of World War II through most of the 1960s was environmentally costly because of the rapidity of extensive development. This was more apparent in East Germany, for example, than it was in the USSR, because population density and per capita income was much lower in the latter. Also, smaller countries (e.g., Denmark) with much better environmental records have benefited by situating themselves in an environmentally more favorable position within the international division of labor. They have been able to import oil and gas, chemicals, and so on, without having to suffer the costs of pollution and pollution prevention and control characteristic of the big industrial countries.

The shift to intensive development—the start of which was symbolized by *glasnost* and *perestroika* in the USSR—would have produced different environmental problems and opportunities. First, many socialist countries would have been likely to make much greater use of price mechanisms, which would lead enterprises to economize on natural resources, that is, to stop undervaluing resources, hence utilizing them too rapidly or inefficiently, or utilizing the wrong kinds of resources. Second, the demand for Western goods included high-tech capital goods to modernize manufacturing facilities and also environmental protection equipment. Third, it is interesting to speculate on what the goals and strength of the environmental movement in the socialist world might have been. The base of the early environmental movement in the advanced capitalist countries is the urban/suburban salariat, professionals, and educated groups generally. These classes exist because of two generations of intensive industrial development and because of the subsequent rapid growth of financial services, communications, corporate administration, research and development, and so on—all a consequence of the new international division of labor since the early 1970s. The capitalist salariat has no intrinsic material interest in heavy industry. In the USSR, by contrast, engineers, managers, and others employed in heavy manufacturing industries were important in the environmental movement. They were not "cut off " so much from interests in continued industrialization as were their Western counterparts, which might have limited their capacity to support an economic shift from "socialist construction" to "socialist reconstruction."

It is impossible to say in principle whether resource-constrained economies deplete resources and pollute the environment more or less than demand-constrained economies *in similar stages of development*. It can be said that some of the main *reasons* for depletion and pollution are different in the two types of economies, and also that depletion and pollution in socialist countries were more political than economic questions; that is, that massive environmental degradation is probably not *inherent* in socialism (although no socialist country ever demonstrated this proposition), as it appears to be in capitalism. Certainly, environmental degradation was intrinsic to industrial progress in the USSR because its leaders believed that their country had to match the United States bomb for bomb, hence had much less to spend on environmental protection because the Soviet economy was so much smaller than that of the United States. Centrally planned economies, with or without extensive market mechanisms, can, in principle, coerce enterprises into internalizing possible negative externalities and social costs generally. This is true, however, only to the degree that the central planners and enterprises, and the politicians and people, want it to be true. In the USSR, what emerged in current debates on the economy in the Soviet press was that (in William Mandel's words) the planners' "lodestar has been growth rates, and everything else be damned." The emphasis on growth is obviously connected with the USSR's perceived need to catch up with the West, in the context of the Cold War, anticommunism, hostility to socialism by the capitalist powers, and, last but not least, the arms race. In other words, as stated earlier, any real understanding of the environmental issue in socialist countries must be framed within the context of the political-economic-military-ideological struggles against socialism by the leading Western powers since the early twentieth century, and also in the context of the Cold War since the end of World War II. It is too early to tell whether new "reforms" in the ex-socialist world that aim to produce "slack" in the economy in order to give management more incentives to economize on labor and resources, more flexibility in production, and so on will lead to increases or decreases in rates of and kinds of depletion/pollution. This will depend on the exact nature of the "reforms," methods of implementation, and development of democratic political forms. It is also too early to assess the effects of the global ecology movement, especially the (to date, weak and divided) international movement for ecological socialism, on traditional socialist attitudes against the "idealization of virgin nature," that is, in favor of what are regarded as scientifically based "rational" attitudes toward nature. It is, however, the right moment to try to debunk *some* of the standard views on the political economy of ecology of socialism and capitalism.

In sum, the party/state made it difficult and often impossible for environmental organizations to develop and grow, to organize protests and pressure the government, and even to find needed basic information. Second, the party/state system meant that workers, technicians, and managers had little or no power within the central planning mechanisms, a situation that prevented the development of an ecological and social consciousness that went beyond the enterprise. Third, the party/state legitimated itself by guaranteeing full employment and job security, which reduced or eliminated both pressures and opportunities to make technological improvements of a type that would not impact the environment unfavorably. In these senses, the gap between government rhetoric and the potential for ecological planning, on the one hand, and the reality of the structure of the state, on the other hand, sabotaged whatever good intentions were held by top planners and the party apparatus. Present-day ecological socialists, beware—and live and learn.

[The next section], "Socialism and Ecology," attempts to identify some points of contrast and comparison between the labor and environmental movements, and also between traditional socialist thought and modern ecological thinking. . . .

SOCIALISM AND ECOLOGY

It seems to me that today there are three general socioeconomic trends giving rise to the possibility of a red green politics. The first is a global economy that is undergoing a process of "accumulation through crisis" that is impoverishing tens of millions of people, destroying communities, degrading hundreds of thousands of bioregions, and exacerbating a global ecological crisis. Crisis-ridden and crisis-driven capitalist accumulation is wrecking the conditions of production, and creating more poverty, unemployment, inequality, and economic insecurity and marginalization, on the one hand, and (often fatally) harming human health, urban and rural communities, and ecological systems, on the other. The second trend is the rise of environmental, urban, labor, peasant, and other social movements to defend the conditions of production and the conditions of life for workers and peasants, women, communities, and the environment. These movements are divided in a thousand ways, running ideologically from religious fundamentalism and reactionary nationalism to old-style Marxist-Leninist-Maoist armed struggle to a broad range of "new social movements." The third premise is that solutions to the ecological crisis presuppose solutions to the economic crisis (and the problem of global capital generally) and vice versa. Red green politics is premised on the belief that both sets of solutions presuppose some kind of ecological socialism and socialist ecology.[2]

Ecological socialism, in turn, presupposes the development of a specifically global class politics, first, because of growing economic oppression and exploitation, and second, because ecological degradation is increasingly a class issue (but rarely *only* a class issue). This is indicated, for example, by the growth of movements for environmental (and economic and social) justice in the North and the "environmentalism of the poor" in the South, where dominant groups owe an "ecological debt" to oppressed minorities and the Third World as a whole, respectively (because the prosperity of dominant groups in the North is in some part based on the ecological damage done to minorities in the North and South). It is also indicated by the fact that present-day labor, community, and environmental struggles seek to make the workplace a healthier and safer place for both workers and communities, hence fight for more influence or control of technology, work relations, and the conditions of work generally. Labor, community, and environmental groups challenge in various ways (implicitly if not explicitly) criteria of production based on market values and profit. Also, human laborpower, community organization, and the environment are all "conditions of production," hence politicized and regulated in various ways by the state.

In the minds of most labor, community, and environmental leaders, however, socialism (of any type) and ecology remain contradictions in terms. Socialists are still seen as "productivist," Greens as "antiproductivist." Most socialists still believe that ecology is merely an ideology of austerity or is simply a system for ensuring amenities for the middle and upper middle classes. Most Greens think that socialism is an ideology promoting growth without limit or end. The effect: business and other groups use the false choices between "jobs versus environment" "the capitalization of land and economic growth versus community values" and "economic development versus sustainable society" as a handy scheme to divide and conquer.

Historically, Western socialists have sought two remedies for the condition of labor. The first is a more equitable distribution of wealth and income. The second is higher levels of productivity and production (which sometimes have been seen as a condition of more equality). Greater productivity is needed to create more free or leisure time; greater production is required to expand the economic pie to mute struggles over the share of the pie appropriated by different classes. These remedies roughly approximate the programs of the old socialist, social democratic, and labor parties as they functioned through the 1970s (and in some countries through the 1980s).

There are at least two major problems with this way of thinking. One is that in a capitalist society (no matter how "reformed") an equitable distribution of wealth and income is almost certain to harm economic incentives and also to promote political unrest from the right, thus impairing productivity and production. The second is that expanding productivity and production usually presupposes a higher (not a lower) level of exploitation of labor, which itself is premised on more (not less) economic inequality.

For their part, Greens, too, have two general remedies for the degraded condition of nature. The first is the same as that promoted by labor and old-style socialism: a more suitable distribution of wealth and income such that poverty no longer leads producers to degrade nature out of material necessity. Even in the North, environmentalists have shown increasing sensitivity to equity concerns because the impact of environmental reform typically has been regressive: workplace pollution and toxic waste contamination disproportionately affect minorities and lower income strata. The second remedy is the opposite of that of labor and socialists: slow growth, no growth, or sustainable growth (there are different versions). Slow or zero growth of production scales down the use of nature as tap and sink for human production, thus (it is thought) reducing both the depletion and the exhaustion of resources and pollution of all kinds.

Since a significantly more equal distribution of wealth and income would harm economic incentives, it would seem that increased equity would lower production and slow down the economic growth rate. Seen this way, the green position is fully coherent. The problem is that in a capitalist economy, a low- or no-growth policy would create an economic crisis, which, in turn, would lead to more ecological degradation as business scrambled to reduce costs in various ways. An alliance between labor (and socialists) and Greens around the redistribution of wealth and income might be possible. But in capitalist economy such a redistribution would harm productivity and production and generate economic crisis, which would adversely affect both labor (and socialists) and Greens.

Clearly, no way exists to make an alliance between labor (and socialists) and Greens, *given the way the whole problem is usually framed.* (The main exceptions are labor-community alliances against workplace and community pollution.) For Greens, socialists are part of the problem, not the solution; for labor and socialists, Greens are part of the problem, not the solution. The former associate Greens with cutbacks and austerity; the latter identify labor and socialists with higher rates of economic growth, hence ecological unsustainability. The only way out of this trap is to redefine productivism: a society can achieve higher levels of productivity via more efficient reuse, recycling, and so on, of materials; via reducing energy use and the commute to work within reformed green cities; via preventing the "pesticide treadmill" by using organic agriculture; and so on, including and especially decommodifying labor and land. *Ecological* socialist productivism and ecological rationality are thus not mutually incompatible.

"Real socialism" in theory and practice has been declared by nonsocialists and many ex-socialists to be "dead on arrival." In theory, post-Marxist theorists of radical democracy are completing what they think is the final autopsy of socialism. In practice, in the North, socialism has been banalized into a species of welfare capitalism. In Eastern Europe, the moment for democratic socialism seems to have been missed almost thirty years ago and socialism has been overthrown. In the South, most socialist countries are introducing market incentives, reforming their tax structures, and taking other measures that they hope will enable them to find their niches in the world market. Everywhere market economy and liberal democratic ideas on the right, and radical democratic ideas on the left, seem to be defeating socialism and socialist ideas.

Meanwhile, a powerful new force in world politics has appeared, an ecology or green movement, that puts the earth first and makes the preservation of the ecological integrity of the planet the primary issue. The simultaneous rise of the free market and the Greens, together with the decline of socialism, suggests that capitalism has an ally in its war against socialism. This turns out to be the case, in fact. Most, if not all, Greens dismiss socialism as irrelevant. Some Greens attack socialism as dangerous. They are especially quick to condemn those whom they accuse of trying to appropriate ecology for Marxism.[3] The famous green slogan, "Neither left nor right, but out front," speaks for itself.[4]

But most Greens are not friends of capitalism, either, as the green slogan makes clear. The question then arises, Who or what are the Greens allied with? The crude answer is "the small farmers and independent business," that is, those who used to be called the "peasantry" and "petty bourgeoisie"; "liveable cities" visionaries and planners; "small is beautiful" technocrats; and artisans, cooperatives, and others engaged in ecologically friendly production. In the South, Greens typically support decentralized production organized within village communal politics; in the North, Greens are identified with municipal and local politics of all types.

By way of contrast, mainstream environmentalists might be called "fictitious Greens."[5] These environmentalists support environmental regulations consistent with profitability and the expansion of global capitalism, for example, resource conservation for long-run profitability and profit-oriented regulation or abolition of pollution. They are typically allied with national and international interests. In the United States, they are environmental reformers, lobbyists, lawyers, and others associated with most of the organizations making up the famous "Group of Ten."

As for ecology, everywhere it is at least tinged with populism, a politics of resentment against not only big corporations and the national state and central planning but also against mainstream environmentalism.

Ecology (in the present usage) is thus associated with "localism," which typically has been opposed to the centralizing powers of capitalism. If we put two and two together, we can conclude that ecology and localism in all of their rich varieties have combined to oppose both capitalism and socialism. Localism uses the medium of ecology and ecology uses the vehicle of localism. They are both the content and context of one another. Decentralism is an expression of a certain type of social relationship of production historically associated with self-earned property and small-scale enterprise. Ecology is an expression of a certain type of relationship between human beings and nature—a relationship that stresses biodiversity, the integrity of local and regional ecosystems, and the like. Together, ecology and localism constitute the most visible political and economic critique of capitalism (and traditional state socialism) today.

Besides the fact that both ecology and localism oppose global capital and the national state, there are two main reasons why they appear to be natural allies. First, ecology stresses the site-specificity of the interchange between human material activity and nature, hence opposes both the abstract valuation of nature made by capital and the idea of central planning of production, as well as centralist approaches to global issues generally.[6] The concepts of site-specificity of ecology, local subsistence or semiautarkic economy, communal self-help principles, and direct forms of democracy all seem to be highly congruent.

Second, the socialist concept of the "masses" has been deconstructed and replaced by a new "politics of identity" and "politics of place" in which cultural and ecological factors, respectively, are given the place of honor. The idea of the specificity of cultural identities seems to meld easily with the site-specificity of ecology in the context of a concept of social labor defined in ecogeographic terms. The most dramatic examples today are the struggles of indigenous peoples to keep both their cultures and subsistence-type societies intact. In this case, the struggle to save local cultures and local ecosystems turns out to be two different sides of the same fight.

For their part (as noted above), most of the traditional Left, as well as the unions, remain focused on enhanced productivity, growth, and international competitiveness, that is, on jobs and wages, or more wage labor—not to abolish exploitation but (if anything) to be exploited less. This part of the Left does not want to be caught any more defending policies that can be identified with "economic austerity" or policies that labor leaders and others think would endanger past economic gains won by the working class. (Union and worker struggles for healthy and safe conditions inside and outside of the workplace obviously connect in positive ways with broader ecological struggles.) Most of those who oppose more growth and development are mainstream environmentalists from the urban middle classes who have the consumer goods that they want and also have the time and knowledge to oppose ecologically dangerous policies and practices. It would appear, therefore, that any effort to find a place for the working class in this equation, that is, any attempt to marry labor (and socialism) and ecology, is doomed from the start.

Yet, left green politics of different types has made an appearance in all of the major countries of the world. One bold initiative in the "developed" world is New Zealand's Alliance, organized in 1991, uniting the Greens, the movement for Maori self-determination, the New Labour Party, and other small parties. In the 1980s, Germany's Green Party was perhaps the most influential left green grouping in the world. In general, Western European countries have a wide variety of left green and green left tendencies. Holland's Green Left Party and Norway's Green Socialist Party, for example, are conscious attempts to fuse red green political tendencies via the parliamentary route. France's Red Green Alternative and Great Britain's Red-Green Network are minuscule groupings which, however, have generated influential theoretical and practical ideas. One might also mention Canada's New Democratic Party's green caucuses, and the movements in the United States to reduce and eliminate toxics and fight for environmental justice; these latter are deeply influenced by the work of Barry Commoner, who calls for source reduction, the "social governance of technology," and economic planning based on a "deep scientific understanding of nature." In the North, there are also many left green/green left solidarity groups, as well as a greening of Labor, Socialist, and (ex-)Communist Parties, even if reluctantly and hesitatingly. In the South, there are thousands of organizations, electoral and otherwise, that have a green left perspective; both rural and urban movements (e.g., Brazil's Landless Rural Workers Movement and Mexico's Zapatistas) raise ecological along with socioeconomic and political issues. In the big subimperialist countries of the South (e.g., Brazil, Mexico, India) where the contradictions of combined and uneven development are most acute, there are new ecological movements that engage many in the traditional working class and also new "peasant" movements concerned with ecological issues. And we should not forget the Nicaraguan and Cuban experiments, which combined policies aimed at deep environmental reforms with populism and traditional state socialism, respectively.[7]

There are good reasons to believe that these and other ecosocialist tendencies, however tentative and experimental, are no flash in the pan, and that they permit us to discuss ecology and socialism as if they are *not* a contradiction in terms (this is obviously especially true of radical *urban* ecology movements). Or, to put the point differently, there are good reasons to believe that the contradictions of world capitalism themselves have created the conditions for an ecological socialist tendency. These reasons can be collected under two general headings. The first pertains to the causes and effects of the world social and ecological crisis from the mid-1970s to the present. The second pertains to the nature of the key ecological issues, most of which are national and international, as well as local, in scope.

First, the vitality of Western capitalism since World War II has in large part been based on the massive externalization of social and ecological costs of production. Since the slowdown of world economic growth in the mid-1970s, the concerns of both socialism and ecology have become more pressing than ever before in history. "Accumulation of capital through crisis" during the past two decades of slow growth in the West has produced even more devastating effects, not only on wealth and income distribution, norms of social justice, treatment of minorities, and so on, but also on the integrity of community and the environment. An "accelerated imbalance of (humanized) nature" is a phrase that neatly sums this up. Socially, there has been more wrenching poverty and violence, and rising misery in all parts of the world, especially the South; and, environmentally, the toxication of whole regions, the production of drought, the thinning of the ozone layer, the greenhouse effect, the assault on biodiversity, rainforests, and wildlife. The issues of socioeconomic and ecological justice have surfaced as in no other period in history; in fact, it is increasingly clear that they are two sides of the same historical process.

Given the relatively slow rate of growth of worldwide market demand since the mid-1970s, capitalist enterprises have been less able to defend or restore profits by expanding their markets and selling more commodities in booming markets. Instead, big and small capitals alike have attempted to rescue themselves from a deepening crisis mainly by expanding exports and cutting costs, by raising the rate of exploitation of labor, by depleting and exhausting resources, and by subverting the integrity of local community.

This "socioeconomic restructuring" has a two-sided effect. Cost-cutting has led many, if not most, capitals to externalize more social and environmental costs, or to pay less attention to the global environment, pollution, depletion of resources, worker health and safety, and product safety (meanwhile, increasing efficiency in energy and raw material use in the factories). The modern ecological crisis is thus aggravated and deepened as a result of the way that capitalism has reorganized itself to get through its latest economic crisis.

In addition, new and deeper inequalities in the distribution of wealth and income are the result of a worldwide increase in the rate of exploitation of labor. In the United States during the 1980s and early 1990s, for example, property income increased three times as fast as average wage income, which has been stagnant for twenty years. Higher rates of exploitation have also depended upon the ability to abuse undocumented workers and set back labor unions, social democratic parties, and struggles for social justice generally, especially in the South. It is no accident that in those parts of the world where ecological degradation is greatest—Central America, for example—there is greater poverty and heightened class struggle. The feminization of poverty is also a crucial part of this trend of ecological destruction. The working class, oppressed minorities, women, and the rural and urban poor worldwide are the groups who suffer most from both economic and ecological exploitation. The burdens of "economic adjustments" and ecological destruction alike fall disproportionately on these groups.

Crisis-ridden and crisis-dependent capitalism has forced the traditional issues of socialism and the relatively new issues ("new" in terms of public awareness) of ecology to the top of the political agenda. Capitalism itself turns out to be a kind of marriage broker between socialism and ecology, or to be more cautious, if there is not yet a prospect for marriage, there are at least openings for an engagement.

The second point is that most ecological problems worldwide cannot be adequately addressed at the local (ecological/geographical) level. One reason pertains to the green concept of "site-specificity," which means that in any given area or region a wide diversity of conditions exists, hence that an ecologically rational unit of production is necessarily small in scale; that is, site-specificity is (wrongly) equated with the "local." But the former does not refer only or mainly to the scale of operations involved in productive activity, but also (or rather) to the necessary relationship between this activity and its necessary *conditions*, which in terms of scale may be regional, national, or even global in scope. The reproduction of fisheries, for example, presupposes that the fishing industry is able to deal with the consequences of its fishing activity for its own necessary conditions (e.g., a clean ocean, healthy fisheries elsewhere, etc.). These conditions cannot be ignored, nor can the costs be externalized, without harming the reproductive capacity of the activity in question. Even (or especially) when the degradation of local ecological systems has local solutions, some planning mechanism is needed to integrate the local into the "general" or "total." Concerning agriculture, Richard Levins writes that "it may seem that large-scale production is itself inimical to ecological sensitivity to local conditions and to the imperative of diversity. But this is a misconception. The unit of planning (e.g., of pest control) must be large enough to allow precisely for the integration of diversity of conditions, while the unit of production will be much smaller and reflect the needs for the mosaic, alley, and polyculture patterns."[8]

Most ecological problems, as well as the socioeconomic problems that are both cause and effect of the ecological problems, cannot be solved at the local level *alone*. Regional, national, and international planning is *also* necessary. The heart of ecology, after all, is the *interdependence* of specific sites and problems and the need to situate local responses in regional, national, and international contexts, that is, to sublate the local and the central into new democratic socioeconomic and political forms.

National and international priorities are needed to deal with the problem of energy supplies and supplies of nonrenewal resources in general, not just for the present generation but especially for future generations. The availability of other natural resources, for example, water, is mainly a regional issue, but in many parts of the globe it is a national or an international issue. The same is true of many forests. Or take the problem of soil depletion, which seems to be local or site-specific. Insofar as there are problems of soil quantity and quality, or water quantity or quality, in big food exporting countries, for example, the United States, food importing countries are also affected. Further, industrial and agricultural pollution of all kinds spills over local, regional, and national boundaries. Ocean pollution, acid rain, ozone depletion, and global warming are obvious examples.

Localism also raises the danger that people will ground their resistance to neoliberalism and globalism in a sense of place alone—not also in the subjectivity of labor, women, peasant cultures, oppressed minorities, and so on.[9]

There is, finally, the problem of equity or distribution. Resource endowments vary widely from place to place, necessitating some central authority to redistribute wealth and income from rich to poor districts. Also, "a valid argument for channeling resources to certain segments of the population and to have a tight control over the resource flow is the high degree of inequality that usually exists in Third World countries [and between these countries and the North—J. O'C.]."[10]

If we broaden the concept of ecology to include urban environments, problems of urban transport and congestion, high rents and housing, and drugs (seemingly local issues amenable to local solutions) turn out to be global issues pertaining to financial speculation, and the ways that mortgage markets work and that money capital is allocated worldwide; the loss of foreign markets for "legal" raw materials and foodstuffs in drug-producing countries; and the absence of regional, national, and international planning of infrastructures oriented to the direct needs of the people.

If we broaden the concept of ecology even more to include the relationship between human health and well-being and environmental factors, given the increased mobility of labor nationally and internationally, and greater emigration and immigration, and an explosion of foreign trade and investment, we are also talking about problems with only or mainly national and international solutions.

Finally, if we address the question of technology and its transfer, and the relationship between new technologies and local, regional, and global ecologies, given that the dominant technology and its transfer are more or less monopolized by international corporations and nation states, we have another national and international issue.

In sum, we have good reasons to believe that both the causes consequences of, and also the solutions to, most ecological problems are national and international (i.e., pertain to national economies and the global economy). Hence, that far from being incompatible, socialism and ecology might make a good fit. Socialism needs ecology because the latter stresses site-specificity and reciprocity, as well as the central importance of the material interchanges within nature and between society and nature. Ecology needs socialism because the latter stresses democratic planning and the key role of the social interchanges between human beings. By contrast, popular organizations or movements confined to the community, municipality, or village cannot by themselves deal effectively with most of both the economic and ecological aspects of the general destructiveness of global capitalism, and still less with the destructive dialectic between economic and ecological crisis.

If we assume that ecology and socialism presuppose one another, the logical question is, Why haven't they gotten together before now? Why is Marxism especially regarded as unfriendly to ecology and vice versa? To put the question another way, Where did socialism go wrong, ecologically speaking?

The standard and (in my opinion) correct view is that socialism defined itself as a movement that would complete the historical tasks of fulfilling the promises of capitalism. This meant two things: first, socialism would put real social and political content into the formal claims of capitalism concerning equality, liberty, and fraternity. Second, socialism would realize the promise of material abundance that crisis-ridden capitalism was incapable of doing. The first pertains to the ethical and political meanings of socialism, the second, to the economic meaning.

It has been clear for a long time to almost everyone that this construction of socialism failed on both counts. First, instead of an ethical political society, in which the state is subordinated to civil society, we have the party bureaucratic state—and thus one justification for the post-Marxist attempt to reconcile social justice demands with liberalism.

Second, and related to the first point, in place of material abundance, we have the economic crisis of socialism—thus the post-Marxist attempt to reconcile not only social justice demands and liberalism but also both of these with markets and market incentives.

However, putting the focus on these obvious failures obscures two other issues that have moved into the center of political debates in the past decade or two. The first is that the ethical and political construction of socialism borrowed from bourgeois society ruled out any ethical or political practice that is not more or less thoroughly human-centered, as well as downplayed or ignored reciprocity and "discursive truth." The second is that the economic concept of abundance borrowed (with some modifications, of course) from capitalism ruled out any material practice that did not advance the productive forces, even when these practices were blind to nature's economy. Stalin's plan to green Siberia, which fortunately was never implemented, is perhaps the most grotesque example.

These two issues, or failures, one pertaining to politics and ethics, the other to the relationship between human economy and nature's economy, are connected to the failure of historical materialism itself. Hence they need to be addressed in methodological as well as theoretical and practical terms.[11]

Historical materialism is flawed in two big ways. Marx tended to abstract his discussions of social labor, that is, the divisions of labor, from both culture and nature. A rich, developed concept of social labor that includes both society's culture and nature's economy cannot be found in Marx or traditional historical materialism.

The first flaw is that the traditional conception of the productive forces ignores or plays down the fact that these forces are *social* in nature, and include the mode of cooperation, which is deeply inscribed by particular cultural norms and values.

The second flaw is that the traditional conception of the productive forces also plays down or ignores the fact that these forces are *natural* as well as social in character.

It is worth recalling that Engels himself called Marxism the "materialist conception of history," where "history" is the noun and "materialist" is the modifier. Marxists know the expression "in material life social relations between people are produced and reproduced" by heart, but they know another important expression much less well: "in social life the material relations between people and nature are produced and reproduced." Marxists are very familiar with the "labor process" in which human beings are active agents, and much less familiar with the "waiting process" or "tending process" characteristic of agriculture, forestry, and other nature-based activities in which human beings are more passive partners and, more generally, where both parties are "active" in complex, interactive ways.

Marx constantly hammered away on the theme that the material activity of human beings is two-sided, that is, a social relationship as well as a material relationship; in other words, that capitalist production produced and reproduced a specific mode of exploitation and a particular class structure as well as the material basis of society. But in his determination to show that material life is also social life, Marx tended to play down the opposite and equally important fact that social life is also material life. To put the same point differently, in the formulation "material life determines consciousness." Marx stressed the idea that since material life is socially organized, the social relationships of production determine consciousness. He muted the equally true fact that since material life is also the interchange between human beings and nature, these material or natural relationships also determine consciousness. These points have been made in weak and strong ways by a number of people, although they have never been integrated and developed into a revised version of the materialist conception of history.

It has also been suggested *why* Marx played up history (albeit to the exclusion of culture) and played down nature. The reason is that the problem facing Marx in his time was to show that capitalist property relationships were historical, not natural. But so intent was Marx to criticize those who naturalized, hence reified, capitalist production relationships, competition, the world market, and the like that he failed to emphasize sufficiently the fact that the development of human-made forms of "second nature" does not make nature any less natural. This was the price he paid for inverting Feuerbach's passive materialism and Hegel's active idealism into his own brand of active materialism. As Kate Soper has written, "The fact is that in its zeal to escape the charge of biological reductionism, Marxism has tended to fall prey to an antiethical form of reductionism, which in arguing the dominance of social over natural factors literally spirits the biological out of existence altogether."[12] Soper then calls for a "social biology." We can equally call for a "social chemistry," "social hydrology," and so on, that is, a "social ecology," which for socialists means "socialist ecology."

Greens are forcing reds to pay close attention to the material interchanges between people and nature and to the general issue of biological exploitation, including the biological exploitation of labor, and also to adopt an ecological sensibility. Some reds have been trying to teach Greens to pay closer attention to capitalist production relationships, competition, the world market, and so on—to sensitize Greens to the exploitation of labor and the themes of economic crisis and social labor. And feminists have been teaching both Greens and reds to pay attention to the sphere of reproduction and women's labor generally.

What does a green socialism mean politically? Green consciousness would have us put "earth first," which can mean anything you want it to mean politically. As mentioned earlier, what most Greens mean in practice most of the time is the politics of localism. By contrast, pure red theory and practice historically have privileged the "central."

To sublate socialism and ecology does not mean in the first instance defining a new category that contains elements of both socialism and ecology but that is, in fact, neither. What needs to be sublated politically is localism (or decentralism) and centralism, that is, self-determination and the overall planning, coordination, and control of production. To circle back to the main theme, localism per se won't work politically and centralism has self-destructed. To abolish the state will not work; to rely on the liberal democratic state in which "democracy" has merely a procedural or formal meaning will not work, either. In my view, the only political form that might work, that might be eminently suited to both ecological problems of site-specificity and global issues, is a democratic state—a state in which the administration of the division of social labor is democratically organized.[13]

Finally, the only *ecological* form that might work is a sublation of two kinds of ecology, the "social biology" of the coastal plain, the plateau, the local hydrological cycle, and the like, and the energy economics, the regional and international "social climatology," and so on, of the globe—that is, in general, the sublation of nature's economy defined in local, regional, and international terms. To put the conclusion somewhat differently, we need "socialism" *at least* to make the social relations of production transparent, to end the rule of the market and commodity fetishism, and to end the exploitation of human beings by other human beings; we need "ecology" *at least* to make the social productive forces transparent, to end the degradation and destruction of the earth.

NOTES

1. "Socialism" and "capitalism" in this account are constructed from the experiences of the industrial capitalist and socialist countries. Although some references are made to other countries (e.g., in the South), many of these cannot be wholly subsumed under the respective imaginaries of "socialism" and "capitalism."

2. Ecological socialism means, generally, an ecologically rational and sensitive society based on democratic control of the means and objects of production, information, and so on, and characterized by a high degree of socioeconomic equality, and peace and social justice, where land and labor are decommodified and exchange value is subsumed under use value. "Socialist ecology" means (again roughly) a dialectical ecological science and sociopolitical practice that successfully sublates the local and the central, the spontaneous and the planned, and the like—in other words, the premises of traditional anarchism and traditional socialism.

3. This is a crude simplification of green thought and politics, which vary from country to country, and which are also undergoing internal changes. In the United States, for example, where Marxism historically has been hostile to ecology, "left green" is associated with anarchism or libertarian socialism.

4. This slogan was coined by a conservative cofounder of the German Greens and was popularized in the United States by the antisocialist "New Age" Greens, E. Capra and C. Spretnak. Needless to say, it was never accepted by left Greens of any variety.

5. "Mainstream environmentalists" is used to identify those who are trying to save capitalism from its ecologically self-destructive tendencies. Many individuals who call themselves "environmentalists" are alienated by, and hostile to, global capitalism, and also do not necessarily identify with the "local" (see below).

6. Martin O'Connor writes, "One of the striking ambivalencies of many writers on 'environmental' issues is their tendency to make recourse to authoritarian solutions, e.g., based on ethical elitism. An example is the uneasy posturings found in the collection by Herman Daly in 1973 on *Steady-State Economics.*"

7. "Social movements inscribed in the environmental perspective of development in Third World countries incorporate . . . a concept of environment that is much richer and more complex than that manifested by conservationist politics and ecological movements of the core countries. . . . The claims of environmental movements, even when incorporating the right to democratic access to resources and conditions for ecological equilibrium for a sustained development, are not guided by an ecological rationality. Environmentalism does not pretend to reestablish the 'natural' conditions of the human species' insertion in nature, but rather to incorporate ecological and natural conditions into the conjuncture of social conditions that determine human development, and that of each community, to satisfy culturally defined needs and demands" (Enrique Left, "The Environmental Movement in Mexico and Latin America," *Ecologia: Politica/Cultura* 2, no. 6 [November 1988], trans. by Margaret Villanueva).

8. Richard Levins, "The Struggle for Ecological Agriculture in Cuba," *Capitalism, Nature, Socialism* 5 (October 1990).

9. For example: "The only political vision that offers any hope of salvation is one based on an understanding of, a rootedness in, a deep commitment to, and a resacrilization of, *place.* Here is where any strategy of resistance to the industrial monolith and its

merchants of death must begin; here is where any program of restoration and revitalization must be grounded" (Kirkpatrick Sale, "What Columbus Discovered," *Nation,* [22 October 1990]: 446).

10. Jan Lundquist, "Right Food, Right Way, and Right People," a revised version of a paper presented at a study group, "Famine Research and Food Production Systems," Freiburg University, 10–14 November 1989.

11. See *Natural Causes*, chap. 1.

12. Quoted by Ken Post, "In Defense of Materialistic History," *Socialism in the World* 74–75 (1989): 67.

13. I realize that the idea of a "democratic state" seems to be a contradiction in terms, or at least immediately raises difficult questions about the desirability of the separation of powers, the problem of scale inherent in any coherent description of substantive democracy, and also the question of how to organize—much less plan—a nationally and internationally regulated division of social labor without a universal equivalent for measuring costs and productivity (however "costs" and "productivity" are defined) (courtesy of John Ely). On the other hand, we presently live under a bureaucratic democracy, so why cannot we have a democratic bureaucracy?

18.

MARCUSE OR HABERMAS
Two Critiques of Technology[1]

ANDREW FEENBERG

INTRODUCTION

In this essay I confront Marcuse and Habermas's views on technology and propose an alternative which combines elements of both. A synthesis is possible because the two different traditions of critique on which these thinkers draw are complementary. However, as we will see, neither thinker comes out of the confrontation unscathed.

The *critique of technology as such* characterizes the Frankfurt School and especially its leading members, Adorno and Horkheimer. In *Dialectic of Enlightenment* they argue that instrumentality is in itself a form of domination, that controlling objects violates their integrity, suppresses and destroys them. If this is so, then technology is not neutral, and simply using it involves taking a valuative stance.[2]

The critique of technology as such is familiar not only from the Frankfurt School but also from Heidegger, Jacques Ellul, and a host of social critics who might be described unkindly as technophobic. Generally this sort of critique is placed in a speculative framework.[3] Heidegger's theory of technology is based on an ontological understanding of being; a dialectical theory of rationality does the same work for the Frankfurt School. These sweeping theories are not entirely convincing, but they are a useful antidote to positivist faith in progress and bring into focus the need for limits on technology. However, they are too indiscriminate in their condemnation of technology to guide efforts to reform it. The critique of technology as such usually ends in retreat from the technical sphere into art, religion, or nature.

Reform of technology is the concern of a second approach which I call *design critique*. Design critique holds that social interests or cultural values influence the realization of technical principles. For some critics, it is Christian or masculinist values that have given us the impression that we can "conquer" nature, a belief that shows up in ecologically unsound technical designs; for others it is capitalist values that have turned technology into an instrument of domination of labor and exploitation of nature.[4]

These theories are sometimes generalized into versions of the critique of technology as such. Then their relevance to design is lost in favor of essentialist condemnation of any and all technical mediation. But where the essentialist temptation is avoided and the critique confined to *our* technology, this approach promises a radically different technical future based on different designs embodying a different spirit. On this account technology is social in much the same way as law or education or medicine insofar as it is similarly influenced by interests and public processes. Critics of the Fordist labor process and environmentalism have challenged technical designs on these terms for twenty-five years.[5] More recently, this view has found broad empirical support in constructivist sociology of science and technology.[6]

Although he is often seen as a romantic technophobe, Marcuse belongs in this camp. He argues that instrumental reason is historically contingent in ways that leave a mark on modern science and technology. He mentions the assembly line as an example; however, his aim is not to challenge any particular design but rather the epochal structure of technological rationality which, unlike Heidegger and Adorno, he regards as changeable. He claims that there could be forms of instrumental reason other than that produced by class society. A new type of instrumental reason would generate a new science and new technological designs freed of the negative features of our science and technology. Marcuse is an eloquent advocate of this ambitious position, but today the notion of a metaphysically inspired transformation of science has a vanishingly small audience and discredits his whole approach.

Habermas offers a modest demystified version of the critique of technology as such. Instrumental action, including technical action, has certain characteristics which are appropriate in some spheres of life, inappropriate in others. Habermas's approach implies that in its proper sphere technology is neutral, but outside that sphere it causes the various social pathologies that are the chief problems of modern societies. Although his position too is powerfully argued, the idea that technology is neutral, even with Habermas's qualifications, is reminiscent of the naive instrumentalism so effectively laid to rest by constructivism.

The question I address here is, what can we learn from these two thinkers assuming that we are neither metaphysicians nor instrumentalists, that we reject both a romantic critique of science and the neutrality of technology?

In the following discussion, I work through the argument in three phases. I start with Habermas's critique of Marcuse in "Technology and Science as 'Ideology,'" the locus classicus of this debate.[7] Then I consider the deeper presentation of similar themes in Habermas's *The Theory of Communicative Action* where he reformulates the problems in Weberian terms.[8] Of course Marcuse was not able to reply to these arguments so my procedure is anachronistic, but I will do my best to imagine how he might have responded on the basis of his own critique of Weber. Next, I discuss aspects of Habermas's theory that can be reconstructed to take the Marcusian critique into account. Finally, I offer my own formulation of an alternative approach.[9]

FROM "SECRET HOPES" TO NEW SOBRIETY

Marcuse follows Adorno and Horkheimer's *Dialectic of Enlightenment* in arguing that both inner and outer nature are suppressed in the struggle for survival in class society. To carry any critical weight, this position must imply, if not an original unity of man nature, at least the existence of some natural forces congruent with human needs and that have been sacrificed in the course of history. Like his Frankfurt School colleagues, Marcuse believes such forces are manifested in art. But today even consciousness of what has been lost in the development of civilization is largely forgotten. Technical thinking has taken over in every sphere of life, human relations, politics, and so on.

Although *One-Dimensional Man* is often compared to *Dialectic of Enlightenment*, it is far less pessimistic.[10] In putting forward a more hopeful view, Marcuse appears to be influenced by Heidegger, although he does not acknowledge this influence, perhaps because of their deep political disagreements. In Heideggerian terms, Marcuse proposes a new disclosure of being through a revolutionary transformation of basic practices.[11] This would lead to a change in the very nature of instrumentality, which would be fundamentally modified by the abolition of class society and its associated performance principle. It would then be possible to create a new science and technology which would be fundamentally different, which would place us in harmony with nature rather than in conflict with it. Nature would be treated as another subject instead of as mere raw materials. Human beings would learn to achieve their aims through realizing nature's inherent potentialities instead of laying it waste in the interest of narrow short-term goals such as power and profit.

Aesthetic practice offers Marcuse a model of a transformed instrumentality, different from the "conquest" of nature characteristic of class society. The early twentieth-century avant-garde, especially the surrealists, seems to be the source of this idea. Like them, Marcuse believed that the separation of art from daily life could be transcended through the fusion of reason and imagination. *An Essay on Liberation* proposes the *Aufhebung* of art in a new technical base. Although this program sounds wildly implausible, it makes a kind of intuitive sense. For example, the contrast between the architecture of Mies van der Rohe and Frank Lloyd Wright suggests the difference between technology as a manifestation of untrammeled power and another kind of technology that harmonizes with nature, that seeks to integrate human beings with their environment.[12]

Habermas is not convinced. In "Technology and Science as 'Ideology'" he denounces the "secret hopes" of a whole generation of social thinkers—Benjamin, Adorno, Bloch, Marcuse—whose implicit ideal was the restoration of the harmony of man and nature. He attacks the very idea of a new science and technology as a romantic myth; the ideal of a technology based on communion with nature applies the model of human communication to a domain where only instrumental relations are possible. Habermas follows the anthropologist Gehlen, for whom technical development supplements the human body and mind with one device after another. Thus technology is a generic project, "a 'project' of the human species *as a whole*," not of some particular historical epoch like class society or of a particular class like the bourgeoisie.[13]

In defense of Marcuse, it should be said that he nowhere proposes that a qualitatively different technical rationality would substitute an interpersonal relationship to nature for the objectivity characteristic of all technical action. It is Habermas who uses the phrase "fraternal relation to nature" to describe Marcuse's views. Marcuse does advocate relating to nature as to another subject, but the concept of subjectivity implied here owes more to Aristotelian substance than to the idea of personhood. Marcuse does not recommend chatting with nature but, rather, recognizing it as possessing potentialities of its own with a certain inherent legitimacy. That recognition should be incorporated into the very structure of technical rationality.

Of course Habermas would not deny that technological development is influenced by social demands, but that is quite different from the notion that there are a variety of technical rationalities, as Marcuse believes. Thus Habermas could agree that technology might be designed differently, for example, out of respect for ecological constraints, but he would still insist that it remains *essentially* unchanged by this or any other particular realization. Technology, in short, will always be a nonsocial, objectivating relation to nature, oriented toward success and control. Marcuse would argue, on the contrary, that the very essence of technology is at stake in the reform of the modern industrial system.

In any case, Habermas does not simply dismiss Marcuse, who no doubt had a considerable influence on him. In fact he finds in the concept of one-dimensionality the basis for a much better critique of technology than the one he rejects. This is Marcuse's version of the technocracy thesis according to which there is a tendency toward total administration in advanced societies. He developed this idea in terms of the overextension of technical modes of thinking and acting. For Habermas, this implies the need to bound the technical sphere so as to restore communication to its proper place in social life.

Paradoxically, although the germ of Habermas's famous "colonization thesis" appears to derive at least in part from Marcuse's critique of technology, technology itself drops out of the Habermasian equation at this point in time, and never reappears. As I will show, Habermas's theory could accommodate a critique of technology in principle, but the index of *The Theory of Communicative Action* does not even contain the word. This oversight is related to his treatment of technology as neutral in its own sphere. The neutrality thesis obscures the social dimensions of technology on the basis of which a critique could be developed.

What is the outcome of this first encounter? Despite the problems in his position, Habermas comes out best. Marcuse's views were forgotten in the late seventies and eighties. Of course there was something right about Habermas's critique, but it also had a favorable historical context. That context was the retreat from the utopian hopes of the sixties in the eighties, a kind of *neue Sachlichkeit*, or "new sobriety." Habermas's views suited a time when we tamed our aspirations.

RATIONALITY IN THE CRITIQUE OF MODERNITY

Habermas regards the sixties radicals as antimodern while defining his own position as critical of the "incompleteness" of modernity. Accordingly, *The Theory of Communicative Action* develops an implicit argument against Marcuse and the New Left in the name of a redeemed modernity.

I will review here one important version of Habermas's argument which I will explain in terms of Chart I (Habermas's figure 11), drawn from *The Theory of Communicative Action*.[14] Along the top, Habermas has listed the three "worlds" in which we participate as human beings, the objective world of things, the social world of people, the subjective world of feelings. We switch constantly between the three worlds in our daily life. Along the side are listed the "basic attitudes" we can take up with respect to the three worlds: an objectivating attitude which treats things, or people, or feelings as things; a norm-conformative attitude which views them in terms of moral obligation; and an expressive attitude which approaches them emotively. Crossing the basic attitudes and worlds yields nine world-relations. Habermas follows Weber in claiming that only those world-relations can be rationalized that can be clearly differentiated and that can build on their past achievements in a progressive developmental sequence. Modernity is based on precisely those rationalizable world-relations. They appear in the stepped double boxes: cognitive-instrumental rationality, moral-practical rationality, and aesthetic-practical rationality.

Of the three possible domains of rationalization, only the objectivating relation to the objective and social worlds, which yields science, technology, markets, and administration, has been allowed fully to develop in capitalist societies. Habermas concludes that the problems of capitalist modernity are due to the obstacles it places in the way of rationalization in the moral-practical sphere.

There are also three X's (at 2.1, 3.2, 1.3) on the chart which refer to nonrationalizable world-relations. Two of these are of interest to us: 2.1 is the norm-conformative relation to the objective world, i.e. the fraternal relation to nature. Although he is not explicitly mentioned here, Marcuse is clearly consigned to box 2.1. Another X is placed over 3.2, the expressive relation to the social world, bohemianism, the counterculture, exactly where Marcuse and his allies in the

New Left sought the alternative to modernity. In sum, the sixties are placed under X's in zones of irrationality which are incapable of contributing to the reform of a modern society. This figure explains more precisely than his early essay on "Technology and Science as 'Ideology'" why Habermas rejects Marcuse's most radical critique of technology.

How might Marcuse have replied? He could have drawn on the arguments against the neutrality of science and technology developed in his essay on "Industrialization and Capitalism in the Work of Max Weber" and in *One-Dimensional Man*.[15] In Habermas as in Weber, scientific-technical rationality is nonsocial, neutral, and formal. By definition it excludes the social (which would be 1.2). It is neutral because it represents a species-wide interest, a cognitive-instrumental interest which ignores the specific values of every subgroup of the human species. And it is formal as a result of the process of differentiation by which it abstracts itself from the various contents it mediates. In sum, science and technology are not

CHART I

Worlds / Basic Attitudes	1 Objective	2 Social	3 Subjective	1 Objective
3 Expressive	Art			
1 Objectivating	Cognitive-Instrumental rationality Science	Social Technologies	X	
2 Norm-conformative	X	Moral-practical rationality Law	Morality	
3 Expressive		X	Aesthetic-practical rationality Eroticism	Art

essentially responsive to social interests or ideology but only to the objective world which they represent in terms of the possibilities of understanding and control.

Marcuse addresses this conception of the neutrality of the cognitive-instrumental sphere in his essay on Weber, where he shows that it is a special kind of ideological illusion. He concedes that technical principles can be formulated in abstraction from any content, that is to say, in abstraction from any interest or ideology. However, as such, they are merely abstractions. As soon as they enter reality, they take on a socially and historically specific content. Efficiency, to take a particularly important example, is defined formally as the ratio of inputs to outputs. This definition would apply in a communist or a capitalist society, or even in an Amazonian tribe. It seems, therefore, that efficiency transcends the particularity of the social. However, concretely, when one actually gets down to the business of applying the notion of efficiency, one must decide what kinds of things are possible inputs and outputs, who can offer and who acquire them and on what terms, what counts as waste and hazards, and so on. These are all socially specific, and so, therefore, is the concept of efficiency in any actual application. As a general rule, formally rational systems must be practically contextualized in order to be used at all. This is not merely a matter of classifying particular social contents under universal forms, but involves the very definition of those forms which, as soon as they are contextualized in a capitalist society, incorporate capitalist values.

This approach is a generalization from Marx's original critique of the market. Unlike many contemporary socialists, Marx did not deny that markets exhibit a rational order based on equal exchange. The problem with markets is not located at this level, but in their historical concretization in a form which couples equal exchange to the relentless growth of capital at the expense of the rest of society. Economists might concede the bias of actual market societies, but they would attribute the difference between ideal models and vulgar realities to accidental "market imperfections." What they treat as a kind of external interference with the ideal-type of the capitalist market, Marx considers an essential feature of its operation. Markets in their perfect form are simply an abstraction from one or another concrete context in which they take on biases reflecting specific class interests.

Marcuse adopts a similar line in criticizing Weber's notion of administrative rationality, a fundamental aspect of rationalization. Administration in the economic domain presupposes the separation of workers from the means of production. That separation eventually shapes technological design as well. Although Weber calls capitalist management and technology rational without qualification, they are so only in a specific context where workers do not own their own tools. This social context biases Weber's concept of rationality however much he continues to talk about a universal process of rationalization. The resulting slippage between the abstract formulation of the category and its concrete social instantiation is ideological. Marcuse insists on the distinction between rationality in general and its historical realization in a concrete, socially specific rationalization process. "Pure" rationality is an abstraction from the life process of a historical subject. That process necessarily involves values that become integral to rationality as it is realized.

Habermas too finds Weber's rationalization theory equivocating between abstract categories and concrete instances, but his critique differs from Marcuse's. Habermas argues that behind the modern developmental process there lies a structure of rationality that is realized in specific forms privileged by the dominant society (see Chart I above). Weber overlooked systematic moments of potential normative rationalization suppressed by capitalism, and as a result confused the limits of capitalism with the limits of rationality as such.

Because Habermas does not challenge Weber's account of technical rationalization, he too appears to identify it with its specifically capitalist forms. Marcuse, on the contrary, attacks Weber's understanding of technical rationalization itself. Weber's error is not simply to identify one type of rationalization with rationalization in general, but more deeply to overlook the biasing of any and all rationality by social values. Weber's account of science and technology as nonsocial and neutral, which Habermas shares, masks the interests that preside over their original formulation and later applications. Hence Marcuse would consider even Habermas's ideal of across-the-board rationalization, including both technical and normative moments, to be value-laden.

I can imagine Habermas responding that these problems are mere sociological details inappropriate at the fundamental theoretical level. Raising them at that level might risk making a Trojan Horse of them for a romantic critique of rationality. The best way to keep the horse outside the city walls is to maintain a clear distinction between principle and application. Just as ethical principles must be applied if they are to enter reality, so must technical, economic, or political principles. That the applications never correspond exactly to principles is not a serious objection to formulating the latter in purified ideal-types. At that essential level, there is no risk of confusion between formal properties of rationality as such and particular social interests.

This formalistic account of the relation of principle to application is more persuasive in ethics than in technology studies. Ethical principles formulated in abstraction from particular applications provide criteria for judging the latter. Even where the principles themselves require revision to remove deficiencies in their current formulation, the revision proceeds in the name of the principles. Thus a flawed understanding of equality is criticized from the standpoint of a more adequate understanding of equality. But the "principles" underlying technologies are instrumental rather than normative, and therefore can only correct instrumental deficiencies. The point of Marcuse's theory is to show that these principles are insufficient by themselves to determine the contours of a specific technical form of life. For that, other factors must enter into the equation that have nothing to do with efficiency.

This theory is indeed a critique of rationality, but not a romantic regression to immediacy. Rather, it addresses the deceptive claims to neutrality that are made in the name of rationality. The point of criticizing this form of appearance is to bring technology under the judgment of normative principles, to raise its normative dimension to consciousness so that it can be discussed and challenged. There is no comparable problem in the application of moral principles because their biased implementation falls under the norm that is being applied. For example, if one invokes the principle of fairness selectively to perpetuate discrimination, as in the current attack on affirmative action, that is itself unfair. By contrast, technical changes introduced in the workplace to enhance managerial power may be justified by reference to efficiency, in the sense that they may increase the return on capital even as they render the job more difficult and painful. The moral dimension of this outcome is occluded rather than revealed by the application of technical norms.

Indeed, the use of technical alibis to justify what are in reality relations of force is a commonplace in our society. Typically, considerations of efficiency are invoked to remove issues from normative judgment and public discussion. The very formulation of moral norms is distorted where they are arbitrarily excluded from significant domains of life. Thus the failure of our society to judge work settings according to norms of democracy and respect for persons reacts back on our understanding of these norms themselves and renders them hollow and "formalistic" in the bad sense. The point then is that the neutrality thesis supports a different type of mystification than ethical formalism, one that may sometimes involve formalistic abuses but which in any case blocks public dialogue with technical alibis.

Marcuse's critique of science and technology was presented in a speculative context, but its major claim—the social character of rational systems—is a commonplace of recent constructivist research on science and technology. The notion of underdetermination is central to this approach.[16] If several purely technical solutions to a problem are available, with different effects on the distribution of power and wealth, then the choice between them is both technical and political. The political implications of the choice will be embodied in some sense in the technology.

Although he is not a constructivist, Langdon Winner offers a particularly clear illustration of the political implications of the underdetermination thesis.[17] Robert Moses's plans for an early New York expressway included a height specification for overpasses that was a little too low for city buses. Poor people from Manhattan, who depended on bus transportation, were thereby prevented from visiting the beaches on Long Island. In this case a simple number on an engineering drawing contained a racial and class bias. We could show something similar with many other technologies, the assembly line for example, which exemplifies capitalist notions of control of the workforce. Reversing these biases would not return us to pure, neutral technology, but simply alter its valuative content in a direction less visible to us because more in accord with our own preferences.

Habermas himself at one time focused on this very phenomenon. In an early essay, he argued that science cannot help us decide between functionally equivalent technologies, but that values must intervene. He showed that the application of decision theory does not supply scientific criteria of choice, but merely introduces different valuative biases. Even in "Technology and Science as 'Ideology'"

Habermas recognizes that "social interests still determine the direction, functions, and pace of technical progress." He does not explain how this affirmation squares with his belief, expressed in the same essay, that technology is a "'project' of the human species *as a whole*." Even this (no doubt resolvable) inconsistency seems to disappear in the later work where technology is defined as nonsocial.[18]

But surely the earlier position was correct. If this is true, then what Habermas calls the fraternal relation to nature, 2.1, should not have an X over it. If 1.1, that is, the objective relation to the objective world, is already social, the distinction between it and 2.1 is softened. Pure instrumentality is not opposed to social norms since all attitudes have a social dimension. Objectivity of the sort involved in natural scientific research would no doubt differ from the relation to nature which Marcuse recommends, but along a different axis from that identified by Habermas. The issue is not, as Habermas thinks, whether a teleological philosophy of nature makes sense today: it concerns our self-understanding as subjects of technical action.

This is the argument of Steven Vogel, who points out that Habermas's chart omits an obvious domain of normative relations to the objective world: the built environment. The question of what to build, and how to build it, engages us in normative judgments concerning factual states of affairs. While there is no science of such judgments, they are at least as capable of rationalization as the aesthetic judgments Habermas classifies under 3.1 on his chart.[19] Here we can give a rational content to Marcuse's demand for a new relation to nature.

Nature would be treated as another subject where humans took responsibility for the well-being of the materials they transform in creating the built environment. There is nothing about this proposition that offends against the spirit of modern science. On the contrary, to carry out this program science is needed. Methodologically, the case is similar to medicine, which involves a normative relation to the objectified human body.

What is the result of this second phase of the debate? I think Marcuse wins this one. We are no longer in the new sobriety eighties, but have entered the social constructivist nineties, and his views sound much more plausible than they did twenty or thirty years ago. However there are still problems with Marcuse's position. Even if Habermas's conception of technology falls under this constructivist counterattack, his rejection of romantic metaphysics stands. Rather than simply returning to Marcuse's original formulations, perhaps elements of his critical theory of technology can be reconstructed so that it no longer depends on a speculative basis. Does one really need a new science to get a Frank Lloyd Wright technology rather than a Mies van der Rohe technology? Couldn't one work toward such a transformation gradually, using existing technical principles but reforming them, modifying them, applying them somewhat differently? Environmentalism has shown us that this is a practical approach to a long-term process of technological change.

In the remainder of this essay I propose to reformulate the Marcusian design critique inside a version of Habermas's communication theory modified to include technology.

REFORMULATING THE MEDIA THEORY

Habermas's media theory provides the basis for a synthesis. This theory is designed to explain the emergence in modern societies of differentiated "subsystems" based on rational forms such as exchange, law, and administration. These "media" make it possible for individuals to coordinate their behavior while pursuing individual success in an instrumental attitude toward the world. Media-steered interaction is an alternative to coordinating social behavior through communicative understanding, through arriving at shared beliefs in the course of linguistically mediated exchanges. Roughly summarized, Habermas's aim is to right the balance between these two types of rational coordination, both of which are required by a complex modern society.

The media concept is generalized from monetary exchange along lines first proposed by Parsons. Habermas claims that only power resembles money closely enough to qualify as a full-fledged medium. Together, money and power "delinguistify" social life by organizing interaction through objectifying behaviors. Common understandings and shared values play a diminished role on a market, because the market mechanism yields a mutually satisfactory result without discussion. Something similar goes on with the exercise of administrative power.

It is important not to exaggerate Habermas's concessions to systems theory.[20] In his formulation media do not eliminate communication altogether, merely the need for "communicative action." This term does not refer to the general faculty of using symbols to transmit beliefs and desires, but to the special form of communication in which subjects pursue mutual understanding.[21] Media-related communication is quite different. It consists in highly simplified codes and stereotyped utterances or symbols which aim not at mutual understanding but at successful performance. Action coordination is an effect of the structure of the mediation rather than a conscious intention of the subjects.

This is the basis for the contrast that runs through *The Theory of Communicative Action* between *system*, media regulated rational institutions, and *lifeworld*, the sphere of everyday communicative interactions. The central pathology of modern societies is the colonization of lifeworld by system. The lifeworld contracts as the system expands into it and delinguistifies dimensions of social life which should be linguistically mediated. Habermas follows Luhmann in calling this the "technicization of the lifeworld."

The media theory allows Habermas to offer a much clearer explanation of the technocratic tendencies of modern societies than *Dialectic of Enlightenment* and *One-Dimensional Man*. His strategy here is the same as in his early critique of Marcuse: to limit the instrumental sphere, to bound it so that communicative action can play its proper role. But, surprisingly, even though he protests the "technicization" of the lifeworld, Habermas scarcely mentions technology. That seems to me an obvious oversight. Surely technology, too, organizes human action while minimizing the need for language.

There is a strong objection to this view, namely that technology involves causal relations to nature while the other media are essentially social. The codes that govern money and power are conventional, and possess communicative significance, however impoverished, whereas those that govern technology seem to lack communicative content. Or, put in another way, technology "relieves" physical, not communicative effort.

But in fact technology operates at both levels. It has several different types of communicative content. Some technologies, such as automobiles and desks, communicate the status of their owners; others, such as locks, communicate legal obligations; most technologies also communicate through the interfaces by which they are manipulated.[22] A computer program, for example, transmits the designer's conception of the problems to which the program is addressed while also helping to solve those problems.[23] In any transportation system, technology can be found organizing large numbers of people without discussion; they need only follow the rules and the map. Again, workers in a well-designed factory find their jobs almost automatically meshing because of the structure of the equipment and buildings—their action is coordinated—without much linguistic interaction.

Indeed, it is quite implausible to suggest as Habermas does, at least by implication, that one could completely describe action coordination in the rationalized spheres of social life simply by reference to money and power. Certainly no one in the field of management theory would subscribe to the view that a combination of monetary incentives and administrative rules suffices to coordinate economic activity. The problem of motivation is far more complex, and unless the technical rationality of the job brings workers together harmoniously in pursuit of the same goals, mere rules will be impotent to organize their activity.

To reduce technology to a mere causal function is to miss the results of a generation of research in the sociology of technology. By the same token, it would be a mistake to ignore the importance of a grasp of causal mechanisms in the control of human behavior in the administrative sphere: the phrase "social technologies" is well chosen. But if one cannot reduce technology to natural causality, why exclude it from the list of media which it resembles in so many respects? Of course it is quite different from money, the paradigm medium, but if the loose analogy works for power, I would argue that it can be extended to technology as well. In Chart II (Habermas's figure 37), where Habermas defines money and power as media, I have listed technology alongside them and found a parallel for each of the terms he uses to describe them.[24] I will not go over the whole chart, but will focus on three of the most important functions.

First, consider "generalized instrumental value." In the case of money it is utility, in the case of power it is effectiveness, and I call it productivity in the case of technology. Those in charge of technological choices (who are not necessarily technicians) interpose devices and associated behaviors between the members of the community which unburden them at both the communicative and the physical levels. This generates two types of value: first, the enhanced command of resources of the equipped and coordinated individuals, and second, the enhanced

CHART II

Components / Medium	Standard situation	Generalized value	Nominal claim	Rational criteria	Actors' attitude	Real value	Reserve backing	Form of institutionalization
Money	Exchange	Utility	Exchance value	Profitableness	Oriented to success	Use value	Gold	Property and contract
Power	Directives	Effectiveness	Binding decision	Success (sovereignty)	Oriented to success	Relatization of collective goals	Means of Enforcement	Organization of official positions
Technology	Applications	Productivity	Prescriptions	Efficiency	Oriented to success	Realization of goals	Natural consequences	Systems

command of persons gained by those who mediate the technical process. This technical authority resembles political power but cannot be reduced to it. Nor is it as vague as influence or prestige, media suggested by Parsons which Habermas does not retain. I believe it is *sui generis*.

Second, each of these media makes a "nominal claim": with money it is exchange value, that is, money demands an equivalent; power yields binding decisions which demand obedience; and technology generates what I call, following Bruno Latour, "prescriptions," rules of action which demand compliance.[25] Complying with instructions in operating a machine is different both from obeying political commands and from accepting an exchange of equivalents on the market. It is characterized by its own unique code. The defining communication, the one which corresponds most closely to the simplified codes of money (buy, not buy), and power (obey, disobey), is pragmatic rightness or wrongness or action.

Third, there is the sanction column, which Habermas calls the "reserve backing." In claiming that money is backed by gold Habermas skips twenty-five years of economic history, but of course monetary value must refer to something people have faith in. Power requires means of enforcement; in the case of technology, the natural consequences of error have a similar function, often mediated by organizational sanctions of some sort. If you refuse the technical norms, say, by driving on the wrong side of the street, you risk your life. You burden those who would have been relieved by your compliance and who must now waste time signaling to avoid a crash. Failing the success of this communicative intervention, nature takes its course and an accident enforces the rules encoded in law and in the technical configuration of highways and cars.

If technology is included in the media theory, the boundaries Habermas wants to draw around money and power can be extended to it as well. It certainly makes sense to argue that technical mediation is appropriate in some spheres and inappropriate in others, just as Habermas claims for money and power.

However, it has been objected that despite certain similarities to money and power, technology is so thoroughly intertwined with them, and with the lifeworld, that it defies a simple bounding strategy. It is better understood as a means or mediator by which the media penetrate the lifeworld, than as a medium in its own right. Technologizing a domain of life opens it to economic and political control; technology serves system expansion without itself being a medium.[26]

But is technology uniquely intertwined? This objection confuses two levels of the media theory. Habermas distinguishes the media as ideal-types, but in practice, of course, money and power are constantly intertwined. With money one can obtain power, with power one can obtain money; money is a means to power, power to money. Technology is no different. It can be distinguished from money and power as an ideal-type with no difficulty, although empirically it is intertwined with them just as they are intertwined with each other. All media are mediations in this sense, all media serve as means for each other.

Historical considerations also argue for this view. In each phase or type of modern development, one or another of the media plays the mediating role, facilitating general system advance. Polanyi's description of the predatory market offers a model of market-led system expansion.[27] Foucault's discussion of the origins of the disciplinary society relies on the "capillary spread" of techniques.[28] State power is the mediator for the extension of market and technical relations into traditional lifeworlds in most theories of Japanese and Russian modernization.

Juridification plays the mediating role in the contemporary welfare state according to *The Theory of Communicative Action*. Law, Habermas claims, is both a "complex medium" and an "institution." As a complex medium law appropriately regulates system functions. A society with contracts obviously needs laws and means of enforcement. But, as an institution, law also regulates lifeworld functions, for example through welfare and family legislation. To some extent that is necessary, but regulating the lifeworld can have pathological consequences: communication is blocked or bypassed, mistrust enters, and so on. Then law becomes an instrument of colonization of lifeworld by system.

In these respects technology offers an exact parallel to law. It, too, mediates both system and lifeworld functions. On this account, technical improvements in production would be unobjectionable. But the application of technology to lifeworld functions sometimes gives rise to pathologies. Consider, for example, the medical offensive against breast feeding in the 1930s and 1940s. In this instance, an aspect of family life was technologized in the mistaken belief that formula was healthier than breast milk. This technical mediation complicated infant care unnecessarily while opening huge markets. The widespread use of formula in countries without pure water supplies spread infant diarrhea which in turn required medical treatment, further intruding technology on infant care. This is a clearly pathological intervention of technology into the lifeworld.[29]

This section has suggested a way of developing a critical theory of technology on a communication-theoretic basis. Instead of ignoring the growing technologization of advanced societies, it can be subjected to analysis and critique. I hope that this approach will enable Critical Theory to resume the interrupted discussion of technology it pursued until the early debate between Marcuse and Habermas recounted above.

VALUE AND RATIONALITY

This treatment of technology as a medium improves Habermas's theory of communicative action without shattering its framework. Nevertheless, it suggests some deeper problems in the theory which do place its framework under tension. I would like to address those problems in the concluding sections of this essay.

The synthesis sketched so far concerns only the extent and the range of instrumental mediation and not technological design. This is because Habermas's system theory offers no basis for criticizing the internal structure of any of the media. He can challenge their overextension into communicative domains but not their design in their own domain of competence. Nothing in his theory corresponds to Marcuse's critique of the neutrality thesis. But it is difficult to see how a critical theory of technology can avoid addressing questions of design. Is it possible to recapture the essential point of Marcuse's critique without defending the controversial metaphysical assumptions with which he supports it? I will argue that this goal can be achieved but only by abandoning both the specifics of Marcuse's quasi-Heideggerian approach and the notion of formal rationality which Habermas takes over from Weber.

What I am aiming at is a two-level critique of instrumentality. At one level I will follow Habermas and the critique of technology as such in claiming that the media have certain general characteristics which qualify their application. This justifies the demand for boundaries on their range. But a second-level critique is also needed because the design of the media is shaped by the hegemonic interests of the society they serve. Markets, administrations, technical devices have what I will call an *implementation bias*: the form in which they are realized embodies specific valuative choices. These designed-in biases leave a mark on the media, even in those domains where they appropriately regulate affairs. Therefore, critique must not cease at the boundary of the system but must extend deep inside it.

Is this two-level approach to the critique of the media consistent? Can critique at the second level be reconciled with Habermas's distinction between system and lifeworld? Blurring the boundary between the two appears to undermine the colonization thesis, diminishing the critical potential of the Habermasian theory. We can no longer protest against the extension of pure technological rationality into communicatively regulated domains if there is no fundamental difference between system and lifeworld in the first place.

This objection is related to the question of whether the system/lifeworld distinction is analytic or real. Axel Honneth, among others, objects to Habermas's identification of the terms of this distinction with actual institutions, e.g. state, market, family, school.[30] In reality there is no clear institutional line between system and lifeworld. Production as much as the family is constituted by a promiscuous mixture of cognitive, normative, and expressive codes, success-oriented and communicative action. The distinction is therefore purely analytic.

It seems to me that several different considerations are confused in these objections. Surely Habermas is right to argue that there is a fundamental difference between institutional contexts that are preponderantly shaped by markets or bureaucracies (and, I would add, technologies), and others in which personal relations or communicative interaction are primary. The fact of mixed motives and codes notwithstanding, without some such distinction one can make no sense at all of the process of modernization.

The problem is not the distinction per se, but the identification of one of its terms with neutral formal rationality. Contemporary feminist theory, organizational sociology, and sociology of science and technology have abundantly demonstrated that no such rationality exists. For example, Nancy Fraser has shown that the high level of abstraction at which Habermas defines his categories only serves to mask their gendered realization in concrete societies.[31] System and lifeworld, material production and symbolic reproduction, public and private, all such abstractions hide distinctions of male and female roles which invest even the apparently pure administrative and political rationality of the modern economy and state. Failing to grasp that fact leads to an overestimation of the centrality of the pathologies of colonization (reification), and a corresponding underestimation of the oppression of social groups such as women.

We need a way of talking about designed-in norms of the sort that characterize all rationalized institutions without losing the distinction between system and lifeworld. I propose to develop the concept of "implementation bias" for this purpose. Implementation bias enters media in media-specific forms, not as communicative understandings of the sort that characterize the lifeworld. Latour calls this sort of bias delegation: norms are delegated to technology through the design and configuration of devices and systems.[32] This notion can be generalized to the other media, so that one can talk about the delegation of norms to markets, laws, etc. The two forms of action-coordination Habermas identifies and the corresponding domains of system and lifeworld can thus be kept meaningfully separate without the need for an unconvincing notion of pure rationality.

However, so far as I can tell, this is not Latour's agenda. Rather than reconstruct the notion of rationality in this way, Latour and his colleagues seem to be trying to blur the line between rationality and everyday practice. Like constructivist microsociology, they reduce the specificity of system functions to the lifeworld without regard for the macro-sociological consequences of system expansion in modern societies. Indeed, Latour has entitled one of his books *We Have Never Been Modern*. I believe this is an overreaction to the notion of pure rationality. Even in Latour's book, the "nonmodern" sociologist finds it necessary to introduce substitutes for the system/lifeworld, modern/premodern distinctions.[33] It is pointless to deny the differences, however "constructed" they may be, between rationalized operations such as modern technology makes possible, and nontechnological modes of action. There is a point, however, to showing that despite the differences, the rationalized operations are still value-laden to the core.

Precisely how do normativity and system rationality coexist in the media? The conundrum only appears so difficult because our conception of valuative bias is shaped by lifeworld contexts and experiences. We think of values as rooted in feelings or beliefs, as expressed or justified, as chosen or criticized. Values belong to the world of "ought," in contrast to the factual world of "is." Of course, this commonsense notion of values overlooks the institutional realization of norms in an objectified background consensus which makes social life possible. Organizational sociology insists on this point, and Habermas agrees that rationalized activities require a shared normative background of some sort, for example, consensus on the meaning and worth of the activities. Yet the question goes deeper. We need to know how institutions based on system rationality realize objectified norms in devices and practices, and not merely in individual beliefs or shared assumptions.

A somewhat similar conceptual difficulty arises in relation to equitable treatment of racial or ethnic groups. A culturally biased test may be fairly administered and yet favor one group unfairly at the expense of another. In such cases the bias need not be present in the everyday form of prejudice, nor is it merely a background assumption of the testers. Rather, it is actually there in the test itself, and yet no amount of study of the test and the testing conditions will reveal it since it is a relational property of the test in its social context.

I propose to call this sort of inequity a "formal bias," in contrast to the "substantive bias" that commonly appears in the lifeworld.[34] Formal bias is a consequence of the formal properties of the biased activity, not of substantive value choices. In the case of a culturally biased test, for example, the choice of testing language or supposedly familiar questions suffices to bias the outcome. There is no need for a substantive intervention such as underhanded downgrading of members of the minority group, or quotas excluding them from the positions to which the test gives access.

The concept of formal bias can be generalized to cover biases in the implementation of technically rational systems. Their internal workings may be exhaustively described without reference to values other than efficiency and cognitive correctness; however, their design reveals an implicit normative content when placed in its social context.

Critical theory has struggled to raise that content to consciousness ever since Marx's original critique of the neutrality of the market. Much that is obscure and challenging in Marx and in such radical Marxists as Marcuse stems from the complexity of that critique. I am not sure whether Habermas's theory of communicative action adequately reflects that complexity. The notion of a nonsocial instrumental rationality seems to put the critique out of action. Where technical designs embody normative biases that are taken for granted and placed beyond discussion, only a type of critique Habermas's theory excludes can open up a truly free dialogue.

In the case of technology, this critique is still largely undeveloped although some work has been done on the labor process, reproductive technologies, and the environment. The research seems to show that modern technological rationality exhibits fundamental deficiencies in its handling of labor, gender, and nature. These deficiencies are systematically related to the nature of our social order. They determine the way in which we think about technical action and design technical devices. Social critique of these general deficiencies is therefore necessary.

It is true that this pattern is often condemned in totalizing critiques of technology as such. Habermas is right to want to avoid the technophobia sometimes associated with that approach. However, Marcuse's historicized critique identifies a similar pattern without foreclosing the possibility of future change in the structure of technological rationality.[35] As we have seen, it is based on the quasi-

Heideggerian distinction between technology as reduction to raw materials in the interest of control, and a differently designed technology that would free the inherent potential of its objects in harmony with human needs. We have already discussed some of the unsolved problems with this theory.

These problems do not, however, justify returning to an essentialist approach which defines technology in abstraction from any sociohistorical context. Nor will it work to claim, as Habermas would, that there is a level of technical rationality that is invariant regardless of changes in that context. While there is some core of attributes and functions that enables us to distinguish technical rationality from other relations to reality, he wants to get too much—a whole social critique—out of the few abstract properties belonging to that core. No doubt it includes, as he affirms, the objectifying, success-oriented relation to nature—but it must be embodied in technical disciplines that include much else besides to provide a basis for application. It is the rationality of those disciplines that is in question, since that is the concrete institutional form in which reason becomes historically active.

Is it possible to develop a critique of technical rationality at that institutional level while avoiding the pitfalls of Marcuse's theory? I believe this can be done through analysis of the reflexive properties of technical practice. This approach can capture something of Marcuse's contribution while also clarifying problems in Habermas's notion of rationality.

Admittedly, the claim that technology has reflexive properties is surprising. Yet if we are serious about saying that technology is essentially social, then like all social institutions it too must be characterized by its reflexivity. That this is not generally recognized is due to the identification of technology as such with a particular *ideology* hostile to reflection. Heidegger practically admits as much when he affirms that the essence of technology is nothing technological. Ellul too warns us off early on in his major work: the "technical phenomenon" is not so much a matter of devices as of the spirit in which they are appropriated. But in the end, these thinkers and their followers fail to develop an independent theory of technology. They seem to conclude that because technology harbors the evils they have identified in positivism, instrumentalism, behaviorism, mechanism, and all the other doctrines they so effectively criticize, the critique of the one can take the place of a theory of the other. Habermas is no different from these predecessors in this regard: his model of the technical relation to the world is positivism and takes over from that doctrine assumptions about the possibility of a nonsocial, neutral rationality. He identifies that ideology with the eternal essence of technology.

It is true that, abstractly conceived, technology does bear an elective affinity for positivism, but that is precisely because every element of reflexivity has been left behind in extracting its essence from history. The essence of technique in the broadest sense is not simply those constant distinguishing features identified in extrahistorical conceptual constructions such as Habermas's. To be sure, such constructions can sometimes yield insight, but only into what I will call the "primary instrumentalization" that distinguishes technical action generally. Technique includes those features in historically evolving combinations with variable ones. Those few determinations shared by all types of technical practice are not an essence prior to history, but are merely abstractions from the various historically concrete essences of technique at its different stages of development, including its modern technological stage.

The reflexive properties of technique enable it to turn back on itself and its users as it is embedded in its social and natural context. I am thinking of such attributes as aesthetic forms, workgroup organization, vocational investments, and various relational properties of technical artifacts. I call these reflexive features of technique "secondary instrumentalizations"; their configuration characterizes distinct eras in the history of technical rationality.[36] The passage from craft to industrial production offers a clear example: productivity increased rapidly, a quantitative change of great significance at the level of the primary instrumentalization, but just as importantly, secondary instrumentalizations such as product design, management, and working life suffered a profound qualitative transformation. These transformations are not merely sociological accretions on a presocial relation to nature but are essential to industrialization considered precisely in its technical aspect.

This position appears more plausible by contrast with Habermas's as soon as one asks what he actually means by the essence of technology, i.e., the objectivating, success-oriented relation to nature. Is there enough substance to such a definition to imagine it implemented? Is it not rather an abstract classification so empty of content as to tolerate a wide range of realizations, including Marcuse's notion of relating to nature as to another subject? Unless, that is, one smuggles in a lot of historically specific content. That is the only way one can get from the excessively general concept of a success-oriented relation to nature to the specific assertion that technology necessarily excludes respect for nature along the lines Marcuse proposes. But this move repeats the very error of which Habermas accuses Weber, identifying rationality in general with a specific historical realization of it.

The essence of technology can only be the sum of all the major determinations it exhibits in its various stages of development. That sum is sufficiently rich and complex to embrace numerous possibilities through shifts of emphasis and exclusions. One might treat it as a structure or formal logic in very much the way Habermas treats the different types of rationalization (see Chart I). The various technical rationalities that have appeared in the course of history would each be characterized by a formal bias associated with its specific configuration. A critical account of modern technical rationality could be developed on this basis with a view to constructive change rather than romantic retreat.

Can such an approach be reconciled with discourse ethics? It suggests the need for the type of demystifying critique Habermas endorsed in his earlier *Knowledge and Human Interests*. There Habermas was more willing than he is now to recognize the political nature of the systematic distortions of communication in our society which render most dialogue empty and useless. To the extent that a certain distribution of social power is rooted in the given technological rationality, which in turn forms the unquestioned horizon of discussion, no amount of debate can make much difference. But how can that horizon be subverted? What type of critique, based on what kinds of practical challenges to everyday forms of oppression in a technological society, can make a difference? I doubt that Habermas's theory of communicative action has all the resources needed to answer these questions, so tied is it to an inadequate concept of technical rationality.[37]

CONCLUSION

In this essay I have presented the basis for a position which resolves major problems in both Marcuse and Habermas. Let me summarize it in a sentence. Technology is a medium in which instrumental action-coordination replaces communicative understanding through interest-biased designs. Simply put, sometimes technology is overextended, sometimes it is politically biased, sometimes it is both. Several different critical approaches are needed, depending on the case. This position involves neither a repudiation of science, nor a metaphysics, neither instrumentalism, nor claims to neutrality. It solves what I think are the chief problems in Marcuse and Habermas's theories of technology, and it offers the basis for radical critique.

Many of Habermas's significant advances are compatible with this enlargement of the media theory to include technology. Indeed, in recent writings, he has already taken a significant step toward what I would describe as a two-level critique of law. Habermas distinguishes between the "pure" moral norms that describe "possible interactions between speaking and acting subjects in general," and legal norms that "refer to the network of interactions in a specific society." Because they are the concrete expression of a people at a particular time and place, committed to a particular conception of the good life, these latter must incorporate substantive values. But they do so in a legally salient manner, not in a way that would erase the distinction between law and politics. Habermas concludes, "Every legal system is also the expression of a particular form of life and not merely a reflection of the universal content of basic rights."[38] Is this not rather similar to the approach to technology proposed here? I have argued that every particular instantiation of technical principles is socially specific, just as Habermas claims of law. Both are open to criticism not only where they are inappropriately applied, but also for the defects of the form of life they embody.

On this account *bounding* the system is not enough; it must also be layered with demands corresponding to a publicly debated conception of the good life.[39] It is unclear how to do this in the original Habermasian media theory because of the lack of a concept of implementation bias, but it follows directly from the revision of the theory proposed here. Where technical design is layered with democratic demands, deep socio-technical changes are foreshadowed. We need a method that can appreciate these occasions, even if they are few and far between, even if we cannot predict their ultimate success. This essay has attempted to create a theoretical framework for doing precisely that.

364 **ECOLOGY, SCIENCE, AND TECHNOLOGY**

One can only wonder why the problem of technology was not addressed earlier, on these or similar terms, in response to the desire of so many in the Frankfurt School tradition for a widening of the horizon of critique. Could it be that old disciplinary boundaries between the humanities and the sciences have determined the fundamental categories of social theory? If so, it is time to challenge the effects of those boundaries in our field, which is condemned to violate them by the very nature of its object.

NOTES

1. This paper is based on a talk given at the TMV Centre of the University of Oslo and the Center for the Study of the Sciences and the Humanities of the University of Bergen. The current version reflects discussion at those sessions, and with Torben Hviid Nielsen, Thomas Krogh, David Ingram, and Gerald Doppelt, to whom I am deeply grateful for many helpful criticisms.

2. Theodor Adorno and Max Horkheimer, *Dialectic of Enlightenment*, trans. J. Cummings (New York: Herder and Herder, 1972).

3. Martin Heidegger, *The Question Concerning Technology*, trans. W. Lovitt (New York: Harper and Row, 1977); Jacques Ellul, *The Technological Society*, trans. J. Wilkinson (New York: Vintage, 1964).

4. Lynn White, "The Historical Roots of Our Ecological Crisis," in *Philosophy and Technology: Readings in the Philosophical Problems of Technology*, ed. C. Mitcham and R. Mackey (New York: Free Press, 1972); Carolyn Merchant, *The Death of Nature: Women, Ecology, and the Scientific Revolution* (New York: Harper and Row, 1980); Harry Braverman, *Labor and Monopoly Capital* (New York: Monthly Review, 1974).

5. Larry Hirschhorn, *Beyond Mechanization: Work and Technology in a Post-Industrial Age* (Cambridge, Mass.: MIT, 1984); Barry Commoner, *The Closing Circle* (New York: Bantam, 1971).

6. *The Social Construction of Technological Systems*, ed. Wiebe Bijker, Thomas Hughes, and Trevor Pinch (Cambridge, Mass.: MIT Press, 1989).

7. Jürgen Habermas, "Technology and Science as 'Ideology,'" in *Toward a Rational Society*, trans. J. Shapiro (Boston: Beacon Press, 1970).

8. Jürgen Habermas, *Theory of Communicative Action*, 2 vols., trans. T. McCarthy (Boston: Beacon Press, 1984–1987).

9. I discuss a number of related issues in the interpretation of Habermas in "The Technocracy Thesis Revisited: On *The Critique of Power*," Inquiry 37, no. 1 (1994): 85–102.

10. Herbert Marcuse, *One-Dimensional Man* (Boston: Beacon Press, 1964).

11. Hubert Dreyfus, "Heidegger on Gaining a Free Relation to Technology," in *Technology and the Politics of Knowledge*, ed. A. Feenberg and A. Hannay (Bloomington and Indianapolis: Indiana University Press, 1995).

12. Herbert Marcuse, *An Essay on Liberation* (Boston: Beacon Press, 1969). For a fuller treatment of Marcuse's views, see Andrew Feenberg, "The Bias of Technology," in *Marcuse: Critical Theory and the Promise of Utopia*, ed. R. Pippin, A. Feenberg, and C. Webel (South Hadley, Mass.: Bergin & Garvey Press, 1987).

13. Habermas, "Technology and Science as 'Ideology,'" p. 13.

14. Habermas, *Theory of Communicative Action.* This chart is the object of an interesting debate between Habermas and Thomas McCarthy. See *Habermas and Modernity*, ed. Richard Bernstein (Cambridge: Polity Press, 1985), pp. 177ff, 203ff. Habermas rather confuses the issues here by apologizing for using the chart to present his own views when in fact it was meant primarily as an explanation of Weber; but then he goes on to use it once again to present his own views. The debate is inconclusive since, as I will explain in more detail below, it poses the question of a normative relation to the objective world in terms of the possibility of a natural philosophy rather than in terms of a reconceived technical reason. Cf. also John B. Thompson and David Held, eds., *Habermas: Critical Debates* (Cambridge, Mass.: MIT Press, 1982), p. 238ff. Marcuse was none too clear on what he intended, but at least he explicitly rejected regression to a "qualitative physics" (*One-Dimensional Man*, p. 166).

15. Herbert Marcuse, "Industrialization and Capitalism in the Work of Max Weber," in *Negations*, trans. J. Shapiro (Boston: Beacon Press, 1968).

16. Trevor Pinch and Wiebe Bijker, "The Social Construction of Facts and Artefacts: or How the Sociology of Science and the Sociology of Technology Might Benefit Each Other," *Social Studies of Science* 14 (1984): 339–441.

17. Langdon Winner, "Do Artifacts Have Politics?" in *The Whale and the Reactor* (Chicago: University of Chicago, 1986).

18. Jürgen Habermas, "Dogmatism, Reason, and Decision: On Theory and Praxis in Our Scientific Civilization," in *Theory and Practice*, trans. J. Viertel (Boston: Beacon Press, 1973), pp. 270–71; Habermas, "Technology and Science as 'Ideology,'" pp. 105, 87.

19. Steven Vogel, *Against Nature: The Concept of Nature in Critical Theory* (Albany: SUNY Press, 1996), p. 388.

20. For a discussion of this issue, see Thomas McCarthy, "Complexity and Democracy: or the Seducements of Systems Theory," in *Communicative Action*, ed. A. Honneth and H. Joas, trans. J. Gaines and D. Jones (Cambridge, Mass.: MIT Press, 1991). Cf. also Habermas's reply in Jürgen Habermas, "A Reply," in *Communicative Action*.

21. Habermas, *Theory of Communicative Action*, vol. 1, p. 286.

22. Adrian Forty, *Objects of Desire* (New York: Pantheon, 1986).

23. Lucy Suchman, *Plans and Situated Actions: The Problem of Human-Machine Communication* (Cambridge, England: Cambridge University Press, 1987).

24. Habermas, *Theory of Communicative Action*, vol. 2, p. 274.

25. Bruno Latour, "Where Are the Missing Masses? The Sociology of a Few Mundane Artifacts," in *Shaping Technology/Building Society: Studies in Sociotechnical Change*, ed. W. Bijker and J. Law (Cambridge, Mass.: MIT Press, 1992).

26. This objection has been suggested to me by Torben Hviid Nielsen and Thomas Krogh.

27. Karl Polanyi, *The Great Transformation* (Boston: Beacon Press, 1957).

28. Michel Foucault, *Discipline and Punish*, trans. A. Sheridan (New York: Pantheon, 1977).

29. Before leaving this point, it is perhaps necessary to forestall a possible misunderstanding. It would be misleading to identify technology (or any of the other media) with instrumentality as such. If all instrumentality is designated as technological, one has no basis on which to distinguish between the various media. Furthermore, one cannot distinguish the broad realm of technique in general from its specifically modern technological form. In particular, traditional craft, with its premodern technologies, and what might be called personal technique must be distinguished from modern technology, i.e., handwork and ordinary life-

world activities carried out by individuals or small groups with small-scale means under individual control, as opposed to unusually complex activities mediated by semiautomatic devices and systems under some sort of management control. No doubt the line is fuzzy, but this general distinction is useful and allows us to judge the degree of technicization of the lifeworld in Habermas's sense. This is clear from the example of breast feeding which is not without its own *techne*, different from formula but "success oriented" too. On these terms baby formula is modern technology and as such a mediation, unlike breast feeding which is a personal technique. The realm of technical action is thus broader than the realm of media.

30. Axel Honneth, *The Critique of Power: Reflective Stages in a Critical Social Theory*, trans. K. Baynes (Cambridge, Mass.: MIT Press, 1991).

31. Nancy Fraser, "What's Critical about Critical Theory," in *Feminism as Critique*, ed. S. Benhabib and D. Cornell (Cambridge, England: Polity Press, 1987).

32. Latour, "Where Are the Missing Masses? The Sociology of a Few Mundane Artifacts."

33. Bruno Latour, *Nous n'avons jamais été modernes* (Paris: La Découverte, 1991), p. 181.

34. For a fuller treatment of this concept see Andrew Feenberg, *Critical Theory of Technology* (New York: Oxford University Press, 1991), chap. 8.

35. Marcuse, *One-Dimensional Man*.

36. For a fuller treatment of this concept see Feenberg, *Critical Theory of Technology*. A very different alternative is represented by Lorenzo Simpson's *Technology, Time, and the Conversations of Modernity* (New York: Routledge, 1995), pp. 15–16, 18. Simpson denies that he is essentializing technology, and yet he works throughout his book with a minimum set of invariant characteristics of technology as though they constituted a "thing" he could talk about independent of the sociohistorical context. That context is then consigned to a merely contingent level of influences or conditions rather than being integrated to the conception of technology itself.

37. Jürgen Habermas, *Knowledge and Human Interests* (Boston: Beacon Press, 1971). For an interesting attempt to defend discourse ethics by enlarging its scope to include technical relations, see David Ingram, *Reason, History, and Politics: the Communitarian Grounds of Legitimation in the Modern Age* (Albany: State University of New York Press, 1995), chap. 5.

38. Jürgen Habermas, "Struggles for Recognition in the Democratic Constitutional State," in *Multiculturalism*, ed. A. Gutman (Princeton: Princeton University Press, 1994), p. 124.

39. For more on the concept of layering, see Andrew Feenberg, *Alternative Modernity: The Technical Turn in Philosophy and Social Theory* (Los Angeles: University of California Press, 1995), especially chap. 9.

PART VIII.

NEW DIRECTIONS

19.

THE NEW AGENDA

ANDRÉ GORZ

In the developed late-capitalist societies the reality of class as organized power is destroyed on the terrain of class society.
—Detlev Claussen[1]

Everyday solidarity is based on the search for open communication free of domination. It is, therefore, from the first, more comprehensive than workers' solidarity; it does not have the latter's constantly reemerging limitations, indeed it even has universalist tendencies.
—Rainer Zoll[2]

The socialist movements, and later the socialist parties, developed out of the struggle against the exploitation and oppression of the wage-earning masses, but also against the social goals and conceptions of the bourgeois leading strata. The socialist project of a new society at first contained two elements. On the one hand, there was the claim to leadership by a class of skilled workers, which tested its ability to direct the production process itself in daily practice; it was simultaneously determined to seize power from the class of owners, whom it regarded as parasites and exploiters, in order to place the development of the productive forces at the service of emancipation and human needs. And on the other hand, there was the resistance of a disenfranchised and oppressed proletariat of women, children, and men who toiled in workshops and factories at starvation wages, and had to fight for their political and economic rights. These unskilled laboring masses could only achieve the cultural and social perspectives with which to over-

Translated by Martin Chalmers and first published in *New Left Review* 184 (November–December 1990): 37–46; reprinted in *After the Fall: The Failure of Communism and the Future of Socialism*, ed. Robin Blackburn (London: Verso, 1991). Reprinted by permission of *New Left Review*.

come oppression through an alliance with the skilled workers. Equally, the potential leading class of skilled workers drew, in part, legitimation for its claim to leadership from the unbearable immiseration of the proletarian masses, for whom the elimination of capitalist domination was a question of life and death; however, legitimation was also provided by man's domination of the forces of nature, embodied in the worker—above all in the versatile craft worker. The real subject of this domination was the worker himself, not only as "global worker," but also as individualized bearer of irreplaceable human capacities and human skills.

Beyond the historicity of the central conflict between labor and capital, however, socialism signified more than its manifest political and social contents: more than emancipation of the disenfranchised, oppressed, and exploited; more than just the claim to power of the immediate masters of nature. Resistance and the claim to power of the working class contained a fundamental critique, not only of the capitalist relations of production, but also of capitalist rationality itself, as expressed in commodity, market, and competitive relationships.

Actions are economically rational insofar as they aim at the maximization of productivity. But this only becomes possible under two conditions: (1) productivity has to be separated from the individual singularity of the laborer, and it must be expressed as a calculable and measurable quantity; and (2) the economic goal of the maximization of productivity cannot be subordinated to any noneconomic social, cultural, or religious goals; it must be possible to pursue it ruthlessly. Only unlimited competition in a free market makes such ruthlessness possible, indeed compels it. Only the "free-market economy" permits economic rationality to make itself independent of the demands of sociality, in which it is embedded in all noncapitalist societies, and to withdraw from society's control—in fact, even to put society at its service.

The socialist workers' movement came into being as the positive negation of capitalist development. Against the principle of the maximization of output, it set the necessary self-limitation of the amount of labor performed by the workers; against the principle of competitive struggle between isolated individuals, it set the principle of solidarity and mutual support, without which self-limitation would be practically impossible. The socialist workers' movement aimed, therefore, to place limits on economic rationality, and ultimately to place them at the service of a humane society.

THE CENTRAL CONFLICT

The central conflict out of which the socialist movement has developed, revolves, then, around the expansion or limitation of the areas in which economic rationality is allowed to evolve unhindered in market and commodity relationships. It is characteristic of capitalist society that relationships conducive to the realization of capital predominate in conceptions of value, in everyday life and in politics. The socialist movement opposes this with the striving after a society in which the rationality of the maximization of productivity and profit is locked into a total social framework in such a way that it is subordinated to nonquantifiable values and goals, and that economically rational labor no longer plays the principal role in the life of society or of the individual. Socialism, understood as the abolition of economic rationality, assumes, consequently, that this has already fully evolved. Where, in the absence of market and commodity relations, it has not yet established itself, "socialism" cannot put economic rationality at the service of a social project intended to dissolve it. Where "socialism" understands itself as the planned development of not-yet-existing economic structures, it necessarily turns into its opposite: it reconstructs a society so that it is devoted to the economic development of capital accumulation. Such a society cannot assert its independence of economic rationality. It is "economized" through and through.

The central conflict over the extent and limits of economic rationality has lost nothing of its sharpness and historical significance. If one understands socialism as a form of society in which the demands deriving from this rationality are subordinated to social and cultural goals, then socialism remains more relevant than ever. Nevertheless, the concrete historical contents as well as the actors of the central conflict have changed. This used to be conducted, culturally and politically, at the level of workplace struggles; it has gradually spread to other areas of social life. Other kinds of antagonism have been superimposed on the contradiction between living labor and capital, and have relativized it. The striving after emancipation, after free self-development, and to shape one's own life cannot assert itself without trade-union struggles for a reshaping of work and conditions of work, but it also demands actions on other levels and on other fronts, which may be equally important and at times even more so. The question as to the "subject" that will decide the central conflict, and in practice carry out the socialist transformation, can consequently not be answered by means of traditional class analysis.

In Marxian analysis, the class of skilled workers was destined to rule over a totality of productive forces, so that a totality of human capacities would develop in each worker. The all-round developed individual would consequently be able to make himself the subject of that which he already was; that is, he would resist every external determination, take command of the production process, and set himself the goal of the "free development of individuality" within and outside productive cooperation. Now unfortunately actual developments have not confirmed these predictions. Although in parts of industry an "integral adaptation of tasks" (Kern/Schumann) becomes possible or even necessary, there can be no question—even in the case of the new, versatile, skilled production workers—of a totality of skills commanding a totality of productive forces. The integrally adapted task always affects only the manufacture of parts of an end product (for example, of crankshafts, cylinder heads, gearboxes) or of their assembly and control. As a consequence of its ever greater complexity the total social production process demands a functional specialization of tasks in all areas. Max Weber spoke in this context of *Fachmenschenrum* (specialized mankind). But specialization always stands in contradiction to the free all-round unfolding of individual capacities, even if it demands initiative, responsibility, and personal commitment to the job. A computer specialist, a maintenance worker, a chemicals worker, or a postman cannot experience and develop themselves in their work as creative human beings, materially shaping with hand and mind the world experienced through their senses. They can only succeed in doing so outside their professional employment. Specialization—that is, the total social division of labor beyond the level of the individual plant—renders the production process opaque. In the course of their work the operatives can hardly influence at all the decisions which relate to the character, determination, use-value, and social utility of the end products. A process worker is in no way different, according to Oskar Negt, from the civil servant in a public body, who is also responsible only for sections of work cycles and for the precise execution of tasks that are placed before him. He makes a contribution to the functioning of areas which as a rule he knows nothing about.[3]

The concept, which appears in Hegel and is then taken over by Marx, according to which labor is the material shaping of the world experienced by the senses, through which man becomes the producer of himself, was still valid seventy years ago for the overwhelming majority of the working class: it was employed in nonformalized activities in which individual know-how, physical strength, planning, and self-organization of the sequence of tasks played a decisive role. Today the majority of wage-earners work in administration, banks, shops, transport, postal, caring, and education services, where individual performance is usually not measurable, and labor has lost its materiality.

The "modern male and female workers," who now take the place of the former versatile skilled worker, are not in a position, on the basis of their own direct experience of work, to question the meaning and social purpose of production simply by identifying themselves with their work. With "modern male and female workers," the "transformation of labor-process power" into a political claim to power can no longer develop, if at all, through an identification with their position in the production process. Rather, starting from the total social relationships of society, it demands a distancing from the experienced work task. Such a capacity is founded on the socialization of male and female workers, because this socialization does not in the first instance pass by way of learning a social role. In addition, professional training develops capacities which are never utilized to the full within labor. This may require a sense of responsibility and independence, but always only to fulfil predetermined functions: it demands "autonomy within heteronomy."

However, the capacity to put capitalist relations of production fundamentally in question does not, at the same time, automatically incorporate practical possibilities that could lead in this direction. Such possibilities cannot be grasped by the male and female workers as such at the workplace (one thinks of the maintenance specialists in automated plants, of employees in nuclear power stations or in the chemical industry), but only in their capacity as citizen, as consumer, as tenant, or as the user of private and public facilities; here they participate in social relationships outside the workplace and experience themselves as belonging to a much larger community.

NEW CULTURES OF RESISTANCE

It can or should be the task of trade-union work to animate this feeling of an expanded belonging, responsibility, and solidarity, and the related distancing from a predetermined professional role. However, the trade-union movement's understanding of itself would have to change. Its task would then no longer consist solely of representing and defending the interests of modern workers as such, but also of giving them the possibility of seeing their professional activity in relationship to an economic and political development determined by the logic of capital realization. This can happen in many forms: through working groups; through public discussions and critical investigations, whose content is the social and political implications of technological innovations and their effect on the environment. What may be advantageous to the employees of one company, writes Hinrich Ötjen, may under certain circumstances involve disadvantages or reduced future opportunities for others; and he continues: "If the trade unions want to remain relevant, then at the very least a public debate on such conflicts of interest should be organized on the spot, because otherwise new movements, in which the workers can draw on their various interests, will be more relevant to them than the trade unions. Up to now, trade-union immobility has frequently given workers cause to set up citizens' initiatives; they capitulate in the face of the trade unions' difficulties in organizing such a dialogue internally."[4]

At this point it becomes clear: for modern workers, socialist consciousness and the critique of capitalism do not usually have any direct connection with, or derive from, the lived experience of work. The "subject" of a socialist project of society therefore no longer develops in the capitalist relation of production as class consciousness of the worker as such, but rather in a worker who as a citizen, for example, in his neighborhood, is deprived of his social and natural life-world by the consequences of capitalist development, just as are most of the rest of his fellow human beings. It's very much in this sense that Horst Kern writes that there is no such thing as "the natural recalcitrance of experience in the face of hegemonic limitations." It is rather the case that modern workers' critical reflections are set free by the fact that they "are confronted by the imperfection of the capitalist version of modern life not within, but largely outside, their actual professional roles."[5] Alain Touraine's thesis may also be valid here.

According to him, the central conflict is no longer the antagonism between living labor and capital, but that between the large scientific-technical-bureaucratic apparatuses,[6] which I—following Max Weber and Lewis Mumford—have called the "bureaucratic-industrial megamachine," and a population which feels itself robbed of the possibility of shaping its own life by a culture of experts, by external determination of its interests, by professional know-alls, and by technological appropriation of the environment. However, nothing should prevent one recognizing the bureaucratic-industrial megamachine and its leading stratum as also the expression of an economic rationality characteristic of capitalism, which takes the shape of industrial growth, the realization of ever larger quantities of capital, the monetarization and professionalization of social and interpersonal relationships.

The inadequacy of an analysis that relies principally on the cultural resistance to the "colonization of the lifeworld" contained in the "new social movements" is that these movements do not consciously and concretely attack the domination of the economic rationality embodied in capitalism. These movements are certainly antitechnocratic, that is, directed against the cultural hegemony of the leading stratum of the ruling class, but they only strike at the cultural assumptions and social consequences of the relation of domination, not, however, at their economic-material core. The new social movements will become the bearers of socialist transformation when they ally themselves not only with the "modern worker" but also with the contemporary equivalent of the disenfranchised, oppressed, and immiserated proletariat—that is, with the postindustrial proletariat of the unemployed, occasionally employed, working short-term or part-time, who neither can nor want to identify themselves with their employment or their place in the production process. Estimates, according to which this group is likely to make up 50 percent of the wage-earning population in the 1990s, are proving by now to be realistic: in West Germany, as well as in France, more than half of the workers newly started in recent years are employed in precarious or part-time jobs. Workers who are employed in this way already constitute in total more than a third of the wage-earning population. Together with the unemployed, that makes a "post-industrial proletariat" of 40–45 percent in Great Britain, and in the United States as much as 45–50 percent. The two-thirds society has already been left behind.[7]

Now it would be a mistake to see in the 40 percent excluded from normal full-time working relationships only people who long for a full-time job. In its most recent research into the subject of the thirty-five-hour week,[8] the Italian metalworkers' union, FIOM-CGIL, comes to the same conclusion as similar studies in France and West Germany. According to this, we are dealing with a social transformation that is leading to a situation in which work occupies only a modest place in people's lives. Work as wage-labor is losing its centrality, though it is more a question of a decline of the socialization function of work than of a refusal to work. Work is only desired if it possesses the character of autonomous and creative activity. Otherwise it is viewed solely with respect to the income deriving from it, and for women also as a way of achieving independence from the family.

Rainer Zoll also came to similar conclusions as a result of exhaustive research with reference above all to young people. He concludes that "the breaking up of the old identity structures" throws young people back on themselves "in their search for an identity of their own." They could never achieve the total, fixed identity that results from traditional family and corporate professional roles, but at best an open one, based on "self-realization," legitimated by communicative intercourse, but never definitive. The choice of professions potentially available to a young person was greater than ever, but the chances of actually finding what s/he was looking for—namely a job with creative and socially useful aspects in which s/he could realize him/herself—were extremely limited. The number of such workplaces is estimated at 5 percent. It was therefore understandable that many had already given up the race before it had even begun. The evident consequence of this situation was that individuals transferred the search for self-realization to other terrains.[9] It should therefore be no surprise that, according to an Italian survey already a few years old, young people frequently prefer to take part-time work, to enter precarious or short-term work situations, and to pursue if possible, by turns, a variety of activities; even among university students with limited means, the professional activity most frequently preferred was that which left most time for one's own cultural activities.[10] The impossibility of creating stable, socially useful, and economically rational full-time jobs for almost half of the wage-earning population corresponds, therefore, to the desire of a significant proportion of younger wage-earners not to be tied, either full-time or for life, to a career or professional employment which only very rarely makes use of all personal capacities and cannot be regarded as self-realization.

LIMITING THE SPHERE OF ECONOMIC RATIONALITY

Now what connects this postindustrial proletariat of wage-earners, who cannot identify themselves with their position in the productive process, with the "modern worker"? Both strata experience the fragility of a wage relation based on measurable work performance. It is the case, both for those not working full-time or all the year round, or precariously employed, as it is for the core workforces of "modern workers," that their effective labor is not constantly required. The first group is needed for limited, usually short-term, foreseeable units of time; the second is needed for situations that are frequently quite unpredictable, which can occur several times a day or only relatively seldom. "Process workers," maintenance specialists, also firemen or caring professionals, must be constantly available, and in an emergency also work twenty hours without a break. They are paid for their availability and not only for their qualifications. They are on duty even when they are not active. In the case of the precariously employed, by contrast, only that time is paid during which they are performing effective work, even though it is of the utmost importance to industry and services that flexible, willing, and capable labor is available at short notice. It is for exactly this reason that the demand of the precariously employed—usually less than six months a year—that they also be paid for their availability during interruptions of the wage relation, which are no fault of theirs but advantageous to business, is quite legitimate.

It is therefore a question of uncoupling income and work time, and not income and work itself. This demand is altogether rational, since as a consequence of increases in productivity through technical innovation the total economic production process requires less and less labor. Under these circumstances it is absurd to continue to make the wages paid out by the economy as a whole dependent on the volume of labor performed, and the individual income dependent on individually performed work time. Work time as the basis for the distribution of socially produced wealth is clung to solely for reasons of ideology and political domination. For the postindustrial proletariat that is not employed full-time or all the year round, the wage relation becomes the manifest expression of a relation of dominance whose previous legitimacy derived from the now untenable rationality of the production ethic. The common goal of the "modern workers" and the postindustrial proletariat is to free themselves from this relation of dominance. However, this goal is pursued by them in very different ways. For the postindustrial proletariat of marginal men and women workers, it is principally a matter of being able to transform the frequent interruptions to their wage-labor relationship into new areas of freedom; that is, to be entitled to periodic unemployment, instead of being condemned to it. For this purpose they need the right to a sufficient basic income which permits new lifestyles and forms of self-activity. For the core workforces of "modern male and female workers," as for others with full-time jobs, forms of control over working time, such as self-determined flexibility of working hours or even linear reductions in the length of the working week, may seem more attractive.

This may appear to be a new form of the earlier social stratification, with its distinction between skilled workers on the one side and proletariat on the other. As in earlier times, the contemporary proletariat is rebelling principally against the arbitrariness of relations of dominance that express themselves in the absurd compulsion to live from wage labor of which not enough is available; while autonomy within and outside professional life becomes the main desire of "modern male and female workers." The divisions between the two strata are consequently much more fluid than they may first appear to be, and could to a great extent be removed. Progressive general reductions in working hours must logically lead to a redistribution of work, whereby the skilled jobs would be made available to a much larger number of wage-earners; and at the same time the right and the possibility of interruptions of the wage-labor relation could apply to everyone. An alliance of both strata does indeed seem feasible, especially on the question of the demand for reduced working hours, provided that such a demand does not become a straitjacket but enhances autonomy within and outside labor.

Reduction in the average annual working time, or even in the quantity of labor performed in the course of four or six years, entitling the wage-earner to an uncut income, offers in this respect the greatest scope and possibilities of choice. The thirty-hour week, for example, whose achievement the trade unions and left-wing parties of most European countries have set themselves as a goal, corresponds to an annual working time of approximately 1,380 hours, and combined with the right to a sabbatical year, an average of approximately 1,150 hours annually. A society that no longer needs all its labor-power full time and all the year round can also easily provide for reductions in working hours, without loss of income, in the form of the right to longer breaks from work. Until the beginning of the twentieth century, journeymen and skilled workers always took this right. Variety, tramping, collecting experiences, were for them part of human dignity. Consequently a reduction in working time must be regarded "not only as a technocratic means to a more just distribution of work," which allows everyone to acquire an indisputable right to their share of social wealth, "but as the society-transforming goal of procuring more 'disposable time' for human beings."[11] This time may be used however one likes, depending on one's situation in life, to experiment with other lifestyles or a second life outside work. In any case it limits the sphere of economic rationality. It has a socialist significance insofar as it is combined with a social project that puts economic goals at the service of individual and social autonomy.

Jacques Delors has pointed out that forty years ago a twenty-year-old worker had to be prepared to spend a third of his waking life at work. Today his working time only amounts to a fifth of his waking time, and it will shrink further. From the age of fifteen, one spends more time in front of the television today than at work.[12] If a socialist movement does not focus on cultural, interpersonal, community life as intensively as it does on working life, it will not be able to succeed against the capital-realizing leisure and culture industry. It only has a chance if it consciously insists on the creation of expanding free spaces for the development of a many-sided, communicative, everyday culture and everyday solidarity liberated from commodified relations of buying and selling.

The expansion of areas freed from economic calculation and immanent economic necessities cannot mean that a socialist economy or alternative economy is taking the place of the capitalist one. There exists, up till now, no other science of management except the capitalist one. The question is solely to what extent the criteria of economic rationality should be subordinated to other types of rationality within and between companies. Capitalist economic rationality aims at the greatest possible efficiency, which is measured by the "surplus" obtained per unit of circulating and fixed capital. Socialism must be conceived as the binding of capitalist rationality within a democratically planned framework, which should serve the achievement of democratically determined goals, and also, of course, be reflected in the limitation of economic rationality within companies.

Consequently, there can be no question of dictating to public or private companies conditions which make the calculation of real costs and performance impossible, or which are incompatible with initiatives aiming at economic efficiency, and consequently prevent economically rational company management. Reduction in working time cannot, if it is to have general validity—which on the grounds of justice it must have—take place purely at the individual company level and be dependent on a particular company's increases in productivity. The equalization of incomes, together with a general reduction in working hours guaranteed to all, can also not be financed by a general taxation on increases in company productivity (machine tax), but must be guaranteed by indirect taxes, applicable to every European Community country, which are cost-neutral for the businesses. But that is already another chapter.

NOTES

1. Detlev Claussen, "Postmoderne Zeiten," in H. L. Krämer and C. Leggewie, eds., *Wege ins Reich der Freiheit* (Berlin: Rotbuch, 1989), p. 51.

2. Rainer Zoll, "Neuer Individualismus und Alltagssolidarität," in ibid., p. 185.

3. Oskar Negt, *Lebendige Arbeit, enteignete Zeit* (Frankfurt and New York: Campus Verlag, 1984), p. 188.

4. Hinrich Ötjen, *Krise der Gewekschaften* (Manuscript, Hattingen, 1989).

5. Horst Kern, "Zur Aktualität des Kampfs um die Arbeit," in Krämer and Leggewie, *Wege ins Reich der Freiheit*, p. 217.

6. Alain Touraine, *Le Retour de l'acteur* (Paris: Fayard, 1984).

7. W. Lecher, "Zum zukünftigen Verhältnis von Erwerbsarbeit und Eigenarbeit aus gewerkschaftlicher Sicht," *WSI Mitteilungen* 3 (1986): 256.

8. According to the report by Bruno Vecchi in *Il Manifesto*, 1 July 1989.

9. Rainer Zoll, *Nicht so wie unsere Eltern?: Ein neues kulturelles Modell?* (Opladen and Wiesbaden: Westdeutscher Verlag, 1989).

10. S. Benvenuto and R. Scartenazzi, *Verso la fine del Giovanilism Inchiesta* (Bari: 1981), p. 72.

11. Peter Glotz, "Die Malaise der Linken," in *Der Spiegel*, no. 51 (14 December 1987): 128–46.

12. Jacques Delors, *La France par l'Europe* (Paris: B. Grasset, 1988), p. 107.

BIBLIOGRAPHY

Adorno, Theodor, and Max Horkheimer. *Dialectic of Enlightenment*. Translated by J. Cummings. New York: Herder and Herder, 1972.

Albert, Michael, and Robin Hahnel. *Looking Forward: Participatory Economics for the Twenty-First Century*. Boston: South End Press, 1991.

———. *The Political Economy of Participatory Economics*. Princeton, N.J.: Princeton University Press, 1991.

———. *Quiet Revolution in Welfare Economics*. Princeton, N.J.: Princeton University Press, 1990.

———. *Socialism Today and Tomorrow*. Boston: South End Press, 1981.

Allen, Robert. *Black Awakening in Capitalist America: An Analytic History*. Garden City, N.Y.: Anchor, 1969.

Althusser, Louis. *For Marx*. New York: Pantheon, 1969.

Anderson, Benedict. *Imagined Communities: Reflections on the Origin and Spread of Nationalism*. London: Verso, 1983.

Arato, Andrew. "The Democratic Theory of the Polish Opposition: Normative Intentions and Strategic Ambiguities." Unpublished paper, 1983.

Arévalo, Juan José. *The Shark and the Sardines*. New York: L. Stuart, 1961.

Arnold, Matthew. "Democracy" [1861]. In *The Portable Matthew Arnold*, edited by Lionel Trilling. New York: Viking Press, 1949.

Arrow, K., L. Hurwicz, and H. Uzawa. *Studies in Linear and Non-Linear Programming*. Stanford, Calif.: Stanford University Press, 1958.

Asbaugh, Carolyn. *Lucy Parsons: American Revolutionary*. Chicago: Charles H. Kerr, 1976.

Atkinson, A. B. *Unequal Shares: Wealth in Britain*. London: Allen Lane, Penguin Press, 1972.

Auerbach, Erich. *Mimesis: The Representation of Reality in Western Literature*. Princeton, N.J.: Princeton University Press, 1971.

Avineri, Shlomo, ed. *Karl Marx on Colonialism and Modernization*. Garden City, N.Y.: Anchor Books, 1969.

Babeuf, Gracchus. *Manifeste des égaux* [1796]. In *Les Précurseurs français du socialisme de Condorcet à Proudhon*. Edited by M. Leroy. Paris: *Editions du temps présent*, 1948.

Bannock, Graham, R. E. Baxter, and Evan Davis. *The Penguin Dictionary of Economics*. 5th ed. London: Penguin Books, 1992.

Barthes, Roland. *Mythologies*. Paris: Éditions du Seuil, 1957.

Bazarov, Vladimir. *Kapitalisticheskiye tsikly i vosstanovitel'nyi protsess Khozyaistua SSSR*. Moscow: GIZ, 1927.

Beard, Charles A. *An Economic Interpretation of the Constitution of the United States*. New York: Macmillan, 1913.

Bebel, August. *Women Under Socialism*. New York: Schocken, 1971.

Beetham, David. *Democracy and Human Rights*. Cambridge, England: Polity Press, 1999.

Beiner, Ronald. *What's the Matter with Liberalism?* Berkeley: University of California Press, 1992.

Benchley, Peter. *Jaws*. New York: Bantam Books, 1991.

Benjamin, Walter. "The Work of Art in the Age of Mechanical Reproduction." In *Illuminations: Essays and Reflections*, edited with an introduction by Hannah Arendt, translated by Harry Zohn. New York: Schocken Books, 1968.

Benvenuto, S., and R. Scartenazzi. *Verso la fine del Giovanilism Inchiesta*. Bari: 1981.

Bernstein, Eduard. *Evolutionary Socialism*. New York: Schocken Books, 1961.

Bernstein, Richard, ed. *Habermas and Modernity*. Cambridge, England: Polity Press, 1985.

Bijker, Wiebe, Thomas Hughes, and Trevor Pinch, eds. *The Social Construction of Technological Systems*. Cambridge, Mass.: MIT Press, 1989.

Blackburn, Robin, ed. *After the Fall: The Failure of Communism and the Future of Socialism*. London: Verso, 1992.

Blau, P. M., and O. D. Duncan. *The American Occupational Structure*. New York: John Wiley, 1967.

Bloom, Harold. *How to Read and Why*. New York: Scribner, 2000.

Bober, M. M. *Karl Marx's Interpretation of History*. New York: W. W. Norton, 1965.

Bond, Julian. *A Time to Speak, a Time to Act*. New York: Simon and Schuster, 1972.

Bowles, Samuel, and Herbert Gintis. *Democracy and Capitalism: Property, Community, and the Contradictions of Modern Social Thought*. New York: Basic Books, 1986.

Brandt, Willy, Bruno Kreisky, and Olof Palme. *La Social-Démocratie et l'avenir*. Paris: Gallimard, 1976.

Braverman, Harry. *Labor and Monopoly Capital: The Degradation of Work in the Twentieth Century*. New York: Monthly Review Press, 1975.

Brentlinger, John. "Revolutionizing Spirituality: Reflections on Marxism and Religion." *Science and Society* 64, no. 2 (summer 2000): 171–93.

Bronner, Stephen. *Socialism Unbound*. 2d ed. Boulder, Colo.: Westview Press, 2001.

Brown, Carol. "Mothers, Fathers and Children: From Private to Public Patriarchy." In *Women and Revolution*, edited by Lydia Sargent. Boston: South End Press, 1981.

Brown, Norman O. *Life against Death: The Psychoanalytical Meaning of History*. New York: Vintage Books, 1959.

Buchanan, Allen E. *Ethics, Efficiency, and the Market*. Totowa, N.J.: Rowman and Littlefield; and Oxford: Clarendon Press, 1985.

———. *Marx and Justice: The Radical Critique of Liberalism*. Totowa, N.J.: Rowman and Littlefield, 1982.

Burnheim, John. *Is Democracy Possible?* Cambridge, England: Polity Press, 1985.

Callinicos, Alex. "Socialism and Democracy." In *Prospects for Democracy*, edited by David Held. Stanford: Stanford University Press, 1993.

Campbell, Tom D. *The Left and Rights.* London: Routledge and Kegan Paul, 1983.

Cannon, Terry, and Johnetta Cole. *Free and Equal: The End of Racial Discrimination in Cuba.* New York: Venceremos Brigade, 1978.

Cantor, Milton. *The Divided Left: America Radicalism, 1900–1975.* New York: Hill and Wang, 1978.

Carr, Edward H. *The New Society.* London: Oxford University Press, 1961.

Christiano, Thomas. *The Rule of the Many: Fundamental Issues in Democratic Theory.* Boulder, Colo.: Westview Press, 1996.

Clark, T. J. *Farewell to an Idea: Episodes from the History of Modernism.* New Haven: Yale University Press, 1999.

Claussen, Detlev. "Postmoderne Zeiten." In *Wege ins Reich der Freiheit*, edited by H. L. Krämer and C. Leggewie. Berlin: Rotbuch, 1989.

Cockshott, W. Paul, and Allin Cottrell. *Towards a New Socialism.* Nottingham, England: Spokesman, 1993.

Cohen, G. A. "Freedom, Justice and Capitalism." *New Left Review* 126 (1981): 3–16.

———. "On the Currency of Egalitarian Justice." *Ethics* 99, no. 4 (July 1989): 906–44.

———. *Self-Ownership, Freedom, and Equality.* Cambridge: Cambridge University Press, 1995.

Coleman, James S. "Equality of Opportunity and Equality of Results." *Harvard Educational Review* 43 (February 1973): 129–37.

Commoner, Barry. *The Closing Circle.* New York: Bantam, 1971.

Condorcet, Jean-Antoine-Nicolas de Caritat Marquis de. *Sketch for the Progress of the Human Mind* [1793], translated by June Barraclough. London: Weidenfeld and Nicolson, 1955.

Conyers, John. "The Economy Is the Issue, Planning for Full Employment." *Freedomways* 17 (spring 1977): 71–78.

Cottingham, John. "Partiality, Favoritism and Morality." *Philosophical Quarterly* 36 (1986): 357–73.

Croll, Elizabeth. *Feminism and Socialism in China.* New York: Schocken, 1978.

Crosland, C. A. R. *The Future of Socialism.* London: Cape, 1956.

Cruse, Harold. *Rebellion or Revolution.* New York: William Morrow, 1968.

Cunningham, Frank. *Democratic Theory and Socialism.* Cambridge: Cambridge University Press, 1987.

———. *The Real World of Democracy Revisited and Other Essays on Democracy and Socialism.* Atlantic Highlands, N.J.: Humanities Press, 1994.

Dahrendorf, Ralf. "On the Origin of Social Inequality." In *Philosophy, Politics and Society: Second Series*, edited by P. Laslett and W. G. Runciman. Oxford: Blackwell, 1962.

Dalton, H. *Some Aspects of Inequality of Incomes in Modern Communities.* London: Routledge, 1925.

Daniels, Norman. "Equal Liberty and Unequal Worth of Liberty." In *Reading Rawls: Critical Studies on Rawls' "A Theory of Justice,"* edited by Norman Daniels. New York: Basic Books, 1975.

Davis, Angela. *Angela Davis: An Autobiography.* New York: Random House, 1974.

Davis, Angela. *Women, Race, and Class*. New York: Random House, 1981.

Davis, K., and W. E. Moore. "Some Principles of Stratification." In *Class Status and Power: Social Stratification under State Socialism*, edited by R. Bendix and S. M. Lipset. London: Routledge, 1967.

Debord, Guy. *The Society of the Spectacle*. Detroit: Black and Red Press, 1973.

Deere, Carmen Diana, and Mieke Meurs. "Markets, Markets Everywhere? Understanding the Cuban Anomaly." *World Development* 20, no. 6 (1992): 825–39.

Deleuze, Gilles, and Felix Guattari. *Anti-Oedipus*. New York: Viking, 1977.

Dellums, Ronald. "Black Leadership: For Change or for Status Quo?" *Black Scholar* 8 (January–February 1977): 2–5.

Delors, Jacques. *La France par l'Europe*. Paris: B. Grasset, 1988.

Delphy, Christine. *Close to Home: A Materialist Analysis of Women's Oppression*. Amherst: University of Massachusetts Press, 1984.

Deutscher, Isaac. *Stalin: A Political Biography*. New York: Oxford University Press, 1949.

Devine, P. J. *Democracy and Economic Planning: The Political Economy of a Self-governing Society*. Boulder, Colo.: Westview Press, 1988.

Dewey, John. *The Public and Its Problems*. Denver: Allan Swallow, 1927.

Downs, Anthony. *An Economic Theory of Democracy*. New York: Harper and Row, 1957.

Dreyfus, Hubert. "Heidegger on Gaining a Free Relation to Technology." In *Technology and the Politics of Knowledge*, edited by A. Feenberg and A. Hannay. Bloomington and Indianapolis: Indiana University Press, 1995.

Du Bois, W. E. B. "Along the Color Line." *Crisis* 2 (October 1911): 227–33.

——. *The Autobiography of W. E. B. Du Bois*. New York: International Publishers, 1968.

——. "The Battle of Europe." *Crisis* 12 (September 1916): 216–18.

——. "Christmas Gift." *Crisis* 3 (December 1911): 68

——. "Colonialism and the Russian Revolution." *New World Review* (November 1956): 18–22.

——. "The Dream of Socialism." *New World Review* (November 1959): 14–17.

——. "A Field for Socialists." *New Review* (11 January 1913): 54–57

——. "Forward." *Crisis* 18 (September 1919): 234–35.

——. "The Negro and Radical Thought." *Crisis* 22 (July 1921): 202–204.

——. "The Negro Mind Reaches Out." In *The New Negro*, edited by Alain Locke. New York: Atheneum, 1977.

——. "Postscript." *Crisis* 34 (August 1927): 203–204.

——. "Postscript." *Crisis* 36 (July 1929): 242–45.

——. "Postscript." *Crisis* 39 (June 1932): 190–91.

——. "Problem Literature." *Crisis* 8 (August 1914): 195–96.

——. "Russia, 1926." *Crisis* 33 (November 1926): 8.

——. "Socialism and the Negro Problem." *New Review* 1 (1 February 1913): 138–41.

——. "The Socialists." *Crisis* 1 (March 1911): 15.

——. "The Stalin Era." *Masses and Mainstream* 10 (January 1957): 1–5.

——. "To Black Voters." *Horizon* 3 (February 1908): 17–18.

——. "The World Last Month." *Crisis* 13 (March 1917): 215.

During, Simon, ed. *The Cultural Studies Reader*. New York: Routledge, 1993.

Dworkin, Ronald. "What Is Equality? Part I: Equality of Welfare." *Philosophy and Public Affairs* 10, no. 3 (summer 1981): 185–246.

———. "What Is Equality? Part II: Equality of Resources." *Philosophy and Public Affairs* 10, no. 4 (fall 1981): 283–345.

Ehrenberg, John. *The Dictatorship of the Proletariat: Marxism's Theory of Socialist Democracy*. New York: Routledge, 1992.

Ehrenreich, Barbara, and Annette Fuentes. "Life on the Global Assembly Line." In *Feminist Frameworks*, edited by Alison Jaggar and Paula Rothenberg. New York: Harper, 1984.

Eisenstein, Zillah. *Feminism and Sexual Equality*. New York: Monthly Review, 1984.

Ellacuría, Ignacio, and Jon Sobrino. *Mysterium Liberationis: Fundamental Concepts of Liberation Theology*. Maryknoll, N.Y.: Orbis, 1993.

Ellul, Jacques. *The Technological Society*, translated by J. Wilkinson. New York: Vintage, 1964.

Elster, Jon. *Three Lectures on Constitutional Choice*. Mimeo. Oslo, 1981.

Engels, Friedrich. *The Origin of the Family, Private Property, and the State*, edited by Eleanor Leacock. New York: International Publishers, 1972.

———. "Socialism, Utopian and Scientific." In *The Marx-Engels Reader*, edited by Robert C. Tucker. New York: W. W. Norton, 1978.

Esping-Anderson, Gösta. "Comparative Social Policy and Political Conflict in Advanced Welfare States: Denmark and Sweden." *International Journal of Health Services* 9 (1979): 269–93.

Evans, Sara. *Personal Politics*. New York: Random House, 1980.

Eysenck, H. J. *The Inequality of Man*. London: Temple Smith, 1973.

Feenberg, Andrew. *Alternative Modernity: The Technical Turn in Philosophy and Social Theory*. Los Angeles: University of California Press, 1995.

———. "The Bias of Technology." In *Marcuse: Critical Theory and the Promise of Utopia*, edited by R. Pippin, A. Feenberg, and C. Webel. South Hadley, Mass.: Bergin & Garvey Press, 1987.

———. *Critical Theory of Technology*. New York: Oxford University Press, 1991.

———. "The Technocracy Thesis Revisited: On *The Critique of Power*." *Inquiry* 37, no. 1 (1994): 85–102.

Ferguson, Ann. *Blood at the Root: Motherhood, Sexuality and Male Dominance*. London: Pandora/Unwin and Hyman, 1989.

Fisk, Milton. *The State and Justice*. Cambridge: Cambridge University Press, 1989.

Flax, Jane. "Do Feminists Need Marxism?" *Quest* 3, no. 1 (1976): 174–86.

———. "A Look at the Cuban Family Code." In *Feminist Frameworks*, edited by Alison Jaggar and Paula Rothenberg. New York: Harper, 1984.

Foner, Philip S. *Organized Labor and the Black Worker, 1619–1973*. New York: International Publishers, 1974.

Foreman, James. *The Making of Black Revolutionaries*. New York: Macmillan, 1972.

Forty, Adrian. *Objects of Desire*. New York: Pantheon, 1986.

Foucault, Michel. *Discipline and Punish*, translated by A. Sheridan. New York: Pantheon, 1977.

Franklin, John Hope. *From Slavery to Freedom*. New York: Random House, 1969.

Fraser, Nancy. "What's Critical about Critical Theory?" In *Feminism as Critique*, edited by S. Benhabib and D. Cornell. Cambridge, England: Polity Press, 1987.

Fried, Albert, ed. *Socialism in America*. Garden City, N.Y.: Anchor, 1970.

Friedman, Milton. *Capitalism and Freedom.* Chicago: University of Chicago Press, 1962.

Friedman, Milton, and Rose Friedman. *Free to Choose.* New York: Harcourt, 1980.

Froude, James Anthony. *History of England from the Fall of Wolsey to the Death of Elizabeth.* New York: Scribner, Armstrong, and Co., 1875.

Gellner, Ernest. "The Pluralist Anti-levelers of Prague." *European Journal of Sociology* tome XII (1971): 312–25.

Glotz, Peter. "Die Malaise der Linken." *Der Spiegel* 51 (1987): 128–46.

Godwin, William. *Enquiry Concerning Political Justice and Its Influence on Morals and Happiness* [1793]. 3d edition. Vol. 1. London: G. G. and J. Robinson, 1798.

Goldthorpe, J. H. "Social Stratification in Industrial Society." Reprinted in *Class, Status, and Power: Social Stratification in Comparative Perspective*, edited by R. Bendix and S. M. Lipset. London: Routledge, 1967.

Gordon, M. J. "China's Path to Market Socialism." *Challenge* 35 (January–February 1992): 53–56.

Gottlieb, Roger S. *History and Subjectivity: The Transformation of Marxist Theory.* Philadelphia: Temple University Press, 1987.

Gould, Bryan. *Socialism and Freedom.* London: Macmillan, 1985.

Gould, Carol. *Rethinking Democracy: Freedom and Social Cooperation in Politics, Economy, and Society.* Cambridge: Cambridge University Press, 1988.

Gramsci, Antonio. *Selections from the Prison Notebooks*, edited by Q. Hoare and G. Nowell Smith. New York: International, 1971.

Green, Philip. *Retrieving Democracy.* Totowa, N.J.: Rowman and Allanheld, 1985.

Gutmann, Amy. "Communitarian Critics of Liberalism." *Philosophy and Public Affairs* 14 (1985): 308–22.

Habermas, Jürgen. "Dogmatism, Reason, and Decision: On Theory and Praxis in Our Scientific Civilization." In *Theory and Practice*, translated by J. Viertel. Boston: Beacon Press, 1973.

———. "A Reply." In *Communicative Action*, edited by A. Honneth and H. Joas, translated by J. Gaines and D. Jones. Cambridge, Mass.: MIT Press, 1991.

———. "Struggles for Recognition in the Democratic Constitutional State." In *Multiculturalism*, edited by A. Gutmann. Princeton, N.J.: Princeton University Press, 1994.

———. "Technology and Science as 'Ideology.'" In *Toward a Rational Society*, translated by J. Shapiro. Boston: Beacon Press, 1970.

———. *Theory of Communicative Action*, translated by T. McCarthy. 2 vols. Boston: Beacon Press, 1984–1987.

Hahn, Frank. "On Involuntary Unemployment." *Conference Papers:* Supplement to *Economic Journal* 97 (1987): 1–16.

———. "Of Marx and Keynes and Many Things." *Oxford Economic Papers* 38 (July 1986): 354–61.

Hattersley, Roy. *Choose Freedom: The Future for Democratic Socialism.* London: Michael Joseph, 1987.

Hauptmann, Emily. *Putting Choice Before Democracy: A Critique of Rational Choice Theory.* Albany: State University of New York Press, 1996.

Hayek, Friedrich A. *The Constitution of Liberty.* Chicago: University of Chicago Press, 1960.

———. *Individualism, True and False.* Dublin: Hodges, Figgis, & Co., and Oxford: Blackwell, 1946.

——. *The Road to Serfdom*. Chicago: University of Chicago Press, 1944.

Heal, G. M. *The Theory of Economic Planning*. Amsterdam: North Holland, 1973.

Heath, Stephen. "*Jaws*: Ideology and Film Theory." *Framework* 4 (1976): 25–27.

Heidegger, Martin. *The Question Concerning Technology*, translated by W. Lovitt. New York: Harper and Row, 1977.

Hegel, G. W. F. *The Philosophy of Right*, translated by T. M. Knox. Oxford: Clarendon, 1942.

Heller, Agnes. *The Theory of Need in Marx*. London: Allison & Busby, 1974.

Herndon, Angelo. *Let Me Live*. New York: Arno Press, 1969.

Herrnstein, R. *IQ in the Meritocracy*. London: Allen Lane, Penguin Press, 1973.

Higgins, Winton, and Nixon Apple. "How Limited Is Reformism? A Critique of Przeworski and Panitch." *Theory and Society* 12 (1983): 603–30.

Hincker, Francois. *L'idee du socialisme: A-t-elle un avenir?* Paris: Presses Universitaires de France, 1992.

Hirschhorn, Larry. *Beyond Mechanization: Work and Technology in a Post-Industrial Age*. Cambridge, Mass.: MIT, 1984.

Hirst, Paul. *Associative Democracy: New Forms of Economic and Social Government*. Cambridge, England: Polity Press, 1994.

Hobgood, Mary E. *Dismantling Privilege: An Ethics of Accountability*. Cleveland, Ohio: Pilgrim Press, 2000.

Hodgson, Geoff. "On the Political Economy of Socialist Transition." *New Left Review* 133 (1982): 52–67.

Holland, Norman Norwood. *The Dynamics of Literary Response*. New York: Oxford University Press, 1968.

Honneth, Axel. *The Critique of Power: Reflective Stages in a Critical Social Theory*, translated by K. Baynes. Cambridge, Mass.: MIT Press, 1991.

Horkheimer, Max, and Theodor Adorno. *Dialectic of Enlightenment*. London: Allen Lane, 1973.

Howard, Michael W. *Self-Management and the Crisis of Socialism: The Rose in the Fist of the Present*. Lanham, Md.: Rowman & Littlefield, 2000.

Huaco, G. A. "The Functionalist Theory of Stratification: Two Decades of Controversy." *Inquiry* 9 (autumn 1966): 215–40.

Hudson, Hosea. *Black Worker in the Deep South*. New York: International Publishers, 1972.

Ingram, David. *Reason, History, and Politics: The Communitarian Grounds of Legitimation in the Modern Age*. Albany: State Univeristy of New York Press, 1995.

James, C. L. R. *The Black Jacobins: Toussaint L'Ouverture and the San Domingo Revolution*. New York: Vintage, 1963.

James, Henry. *The Wings of the Dove*. Oxford: Oxford University Press, 1984.

Jameson, Fredric. *Marxism and Form*. Princeton, N.J.: Princeton University Press, 1971.

——. *The Political Unconscious*. Ithaca, N.Y.: Cornell University Press, 1981.

——. Review of *Six Guns and Society*, by Will Wright. *Theory and Society* 4 (1977): 543–59.

Jaures, Jean. *L'Esprit de socialisme*. Paris: Denoel, 1971.

Jencks, Christopher, et al. *Inequality: A Reassessment of the Effects of Family and Schooling in America*. London: Allen Lane, Penguin Press, 1974.

Jensen, Arthur R. *Educability and Group Differences*. London: Methuen, 1973.

Kenworthy, Lane. "What Kind of Economic System? A Leftist's Guide." *Socialist Review* 20, no. 2 (April–June 1990): 102–24.

Kern, Horst. "Zur Aktualität des Kampfs um die Arbeit." In *Wege ins Reich der Freiheit*, edited by H. L. Krämer and C. Leggewie. Berlin: Rotbuch, 1989.

Kerr, C., et al. *Industrialism and Industrial Man*. Cambridge, Mass.: Harvard University Press, 1960.

Khor, Martin. "Growing Consensus on Ills of Globalization." <http://www.twnside.org.sg/souths/twn/title/ills-cn.htm> (12 March 1999).

Kirzner, Israel M. "Some Ethical Implications for Capitalism of the Socialist Calculation Debate." *Social Philosophy & Policy* 6, no. 1 (autumn 1988): 165–82.

Kolakowski, Leszek. "The Myth of Human Self-Identity: Unity of Civil and Political Society in Socialist Thought." In *The Socialist Idea: A Reappraisal*, edited by Leszek Kolakowski and Stuart Hampshire. New York: Basic Books, 1974.

Kollontai, Alexandra. *The Autobiography of a Sexually Emancipated Communist Woman*. New York: Schocken, 1975.

Kornai, Janos. *The Economics of Shortage*. Amsterdam: North Holland, 1980.

———. *The Socialist System: The Political Economy of Communism*. Princeton, N.J.: Princeton University Press, 1992.

Korpi, Walter. *The Working Class in Welfare Capitalism: Work, Unions, and Politics in Sweden*. London: Routledge & Kegan Paul, 1978.

———. *The Democratic Class Struggle*. London: Routledge & Kegan Paul, 1983.

Kruks, Sonya, Rayna Rapp, and Marilyn B. Young, eds. *Promissory Notes: Women in the Transition to Socialism*. New York: Monthly Review, 1989.

Lane, David. *The End of Inequality? Stratification under State Socialism*. Harmondsworth: Penguin Education, 1971.

Lang, Berel. *Marxism and Art: Writings in Aesthetics and Criticism*. New York: McKay, 1972.

Lange, Oskar, and Frederick M. Taylor. *On the Economic Theory of Socialism*, edited with an introduction by Benjamin Evans Lippincott. New York: Monthly Review Press, 1964; A. M. Kelley, 1970.

Lappé, Frances Moore, Joseph Collins, and Peter Rosset, with Luis Esparza. "Twelve Myths About Hunger." *Food First Backgrounder* 5, no. 3 (summer 1998): 1–4. Based on Lappé, Frances Moore, Joseph Collins, and Peter Rosset, with Luis Esparza. *World Hunger: Twelve Myths*. 2d ed. New York: Grove/Atlantic and Food First Books, 1998.

Latour, Bruno. *Nous n'avons jamais été modernes*. Paris: La Découverte, 1991.

———. "Where Are the Missing Masses? The Sociology of a Few Mundane Artifacts." In *Shaping Technology/Building Society: Studies in Sociotechnical Change*, edited by W. Bijker and J. Law. Cambridge, Mass.: MIT Press, 1992.

Lecher, W. "Zum zukünftigen Verhältnis von Erwerbsarbeit und Eigenarbeit aus gewerkschaftlicher Sicht." *WSI Mitteilungen* 3 (1986): 256.

Left, Enrique. "The Environmental Movement in Mexico and Latin America." Translated by Margaret Villanueva. *Ecologia: Politica/Cultura* 2, no. 6 (November 1988).

Lenin, V. I. *State and Revolution*. New York: International Publishers, 1974.

Lerner, Gerda. *The Creation of Patriarchy*. New York: Oxford University Press, 1986.

Lerner, Melvin J. "The Justice Motive: 'Equity' and 'Parity' among Children." *Journal of Personality and Social Psychology* 29 (1974): 539–50.

Lerner, Michael. "Jewish Liberation Theology and Emancipatory Politics." In *Religion and Economic Justice*, edited by Michael Zweig. Philadelphia: Temple, 1991.

Levine, Andrew. *Arguing for Socialism*. Boston: Routledge and Kegan Paul, 1984.

Levins, Richard. "The Struggle for Ecological Agriculture in Cuba." *Capitalism, Nature, Socialism* 5 (October 1990).

Lévi-Strauss, Claude. *The Elementary Structures of Kinship*. Boston: Beacon, 1969.

Locke, John. *Second Treatise on Civil Government*. Chicago: Gateway Editions, 1955.

Lukács, Georg. *History and Class Consciousness: Studies in Marxist Dialectics*. Cambridge: MIT Press, 1968.

Lukes, Steven. *Individualism*. Oxford: Blackwell, 1973.

———. "Political Ritual and Social Integration." *Sociology* 9, no. 2 (May 1975): 289–308.

———. *Power: A Radical View*. London: Macmillan, 1974.

Lundquist, Jan. "Right Food, Right Way, and Right People." A revised version of a paper presented at the study group "Famine Research and Food Production Systems." Freiburg University, 10–14 November 1989.

Luxemburg, Rosa. *The Russian Revolution and Leninism or Marxism?* Ann Arbor: University of Michigan Press, 1967.

———. *The Mass Strike, the Political Party, and the Trade Unions*. In *Rosa Luxemburg Speaks*, edited by M. A. Waters. New York: Pathfinder Press, 1970.

Lydall, H. F. *The Structure of Earnings*. Oxford: Oxford University Press, 1968.

Macherey, Pierre. *A Theory of Literary Production*. London: Routledge & Kegan Paul, 1978.

Machonin, P. "Social Stratification in Contemporary Czechoslovakia." *American Journal of Sociology* 75 (1970): 725–41.

MacIntryre, Alasdair. *After Virtue*. London: Duckworth, 1981.

———. "Is Patriotism a Virtue?" Lindley Lecture, University of Kansas, 1984.

———. *Marxism and Christianity*. New York: Schocken, 1968.

Macpherson, C. B. *Democratic Theory: Essays in Retrieval*. Oxford: Clarendon Press, 1973.

———. *The Life and Times of Liberal Democracy*. Oxford: Oxford University Press, 1977.

Marable, Manning. *Blackwater: Historical Studies in Race, Class Consciousness, and Revolution*. Dayton, Ohio: Black Praxis Press, 1981.

———. *From the Grassroots: Social and Political Essays Towards Afro-American Liberation*. Boston: South End Press, 1980.

Marcuse, Herbert. *Eros and Civilization*. New York: Vintage Books, 1962.

———. *An Essay on Liberation*. Boston: Beacon Press, 1969.

———. "Industrialization and Capitalism in the Work of Max Weber." In *Negations*, translated by J. Shapiro. Boston: Beacon Press, 1968.

———. *One-Dimensional Man*. Boston: Beacon Press, 1964.

Marković, Mihailo. *From Affluence to Praxis; Philosophy and Social Criticism*. Ann Arbor: University of Michigan Press, 1974.

Martin, Andrew. "Is Democratic Control of Capitalist Economies Possible?" In *Stress and Contradiction in Modern Capitalism*, edited by Leon Lindberg. Lexington, Mass.: Lexington Books, 1975.

Marx, Karl. "Critique of the Gotha Programme" [1875]. In *Selected Works in One Volume*. New York: International Publishers, 1968.

———. *Grundrisse*. Edited by Martin Nicolaus. New York: International Publishers, 1973.

———. *Karl Marx: Selected Writings*, edited by David McLellan. Oxford: Oxford University Press, 1977.

Marx, Karl, and Frederick Engels. *The Communist Manifesto* [1888]. Chicago: Charles H. Kerr Publishing Co., 1984.

―――. *Manifesto of the Communist Party* [1848]. In *Selected Works in One Volume*. New York: International Publishers, 1968.

Matthews, R. C. O. "The Economics of Institutions and the Sources of Growth." *Economic Journal* 96 (December 1986): 903–18.

Maurois, André. "The Sage of Verney: An Appreciation." In Voltaire. *Candide*, translated by Lowell Blair. New York: Bantam Books, 1959.

McCarthy, Thomas. "Complexity and Democracy: Or the Seducements of Systems Theory." In *Communicative Action*, edited by A. Honneth and H. Joas, translated by J. Gaines and D. Jones. Cambridge, Mass.: MIT Press, 1991.

McLellan, David. *Karl Marx: His Life and Thought.* New York: Harper and Row, 1973.

―――. *The Thought of Karl Marx.* New York: Harper & Row, 1977.

Medvedev, Pavel. "Ekonomiko-matematicheskie metody v plamrovanii." *Voprosy ekonomiki* 12 (1986).

Meier, August. "Booker T. Washington and the Negro Press." *Journal of Negro History* 38 (January 1953): 68–82.

―――. *Negro Thought in America, 1880–1915*. Ann Arbor: University of Michigan Press, 1963.

Meillassoux, Claude. *Maidens, Meal, and Money: Capitalism and the Domestic Economy.* New York: Cambridge University Press, 1981.

Merchant, Carolyn. *The Death of Nature: Women, Ecology, and the Scientific Revolution.* New York: Harper and Row, 1980.

Michelet, Jules. *History of France*. New York: D. Appleton, 1867.

Mill, John Stuart. *On Liberty*. New York: Norton, 1975.

―――. "Socialism and Liberty." In *Essential Works of Socialism*, edited by Irving Howe. 3d ed. New Haven: Yale, 1986.

Mill, John Stuart, and Harriet Taylor. *Subjection of Women*. Greenwich, Conn.: Fawcett Publications, 1971.

Miller, David. *Anarchism*. London: Dent, 1984.

―――. "The Ethical Significance of Nationality." *Ethics* 98 (1987–88): 647–62.

―――. "Jerusalem Not Yet Built: A Reply to Lessnoff on Capitalism, Socialism and Democracy." *Political Studies* 28 (1980): 584–89.

―――. *Market, State and Community*. Oxford: Clarendon Press, 1989.

―――. "Marx, Communism and Markets." *Political Theory* 15 (1987): 182–204.

―――. "Socialism and the Market." *Political Theory* 5 (1977): 473–90.

―――. "Socialism and Toleration." In *Justifying Toleration*, edited by Susan Mendus. Cambridge: Cambridge University Press, 1988.

―――. "Virtues and Practices." *Analyse und Kritik* 6 (1984): 49–60.

Miller, David, and Saul Estrin. "Market Socialism: A Policy for Socialists." In *Market Socialism: Whose Choice?* edited by I. Forbes. Fabian Pamphlet No. 516. Reprinted as "A Case for Market Socialism." *Dissent* (summer 1987): 359–67.

Mischel, Lawrence, Jared Bernstein, and John Schmitt. *The State of Working America 1998–99*. Ithaca, N.Y.: Cornell University Press, 1999.

Mitchell, Juliet. "Women: The Longest Revolution." *New Left Review* 40 (1966): 11–37.

Moore, Stanley. *Marx versus Markets*. University Park: Pennsylvania State University Press, 1993.

Morris, William. "Art and Socialism," "The Lesser Arts," and "Useful Work versus Useless Toil." Http://www.marxists.org/archive/morris/works/ index.htm. 15 January 2000.
———. *Letters on Socialism* [1888]. London: privately printed, 1894.
Morrison, Roy. *We Build the Road as We Travel.* Philadelphia: New Society Publishers, 1991.
Moss, Jr., Alfred A. *The American Negro Academy: Voice of the Talented Tenth.* Baton Rouge: Louisiana State University Press, 1981.
Negt, Oskar. *Lebendige Arbeit, enteignete Zeit.* Frankfurt and New York: Campus Verlag, 1984.
Ngo, Vinh Long. "China: Ten Years after the Tiananmen Crackdown." *New Political Science* 21, no. 4 (1999): 463–73.
Nielsen, Kai. *Equality and Liberty: A Defense of Radical Egalitarianism.* Totowa, N.J.: Rowman and Allanheld, 1985.
Nolan, Peter. "The Chinese Puzzle." *Challenge* 37 (January–February 1994): 25–31.
Nove, Alec. *The Economics of Feasible Socialism.* London: Allen and Unwin, 1983.
———. *The Soviet Economy.* London: Allen & Unwin, 1961.
Nozick, Robert. *Anarchy, State, and Utopia.* New York: Basic Books, 1974.
Nuti, D. M. "Socialism on Earth." *Cambridge Journal of Economics* 5 (1981): 391–403.
O'Brien, Mary. *The Politics of Reproduction.* London: Routledge, 1981.
Oldenquist, Andrew. "Loyalties." *Journal of Philosophy* 74 (1982): 173–93.
Ollman, Bertell, ed. *Market Socialism: The Debate Among Socialists.* New York: Routledge, 1998.
O'Neill, John. *The Market: Ethics, Knowledge, and Politics.* New York: Routledge, 1998.
Orwell, George. *Homage to Catalonia.* London: Secker and Warburg, 1938; Penguin edition, 1962.
Ötjen, Hinrich. *Krise der Gewekschaften.* Manuscript, Hattingen, 1989.
Ovington, Mary White. "The National Association for the Advancement of Colored People." *Journal of Negro History* 9 (April 1924): 107–16.
———. "The Negro in the Trade Unions in New York." *Annals of the American Academy of Political and Social Science* 27 (June 1906): 551–58.
———. "Vacation Days on San Juan Hill—A New York Negro Colony." *Southern Workman* 38 (November 1909): 627–34.
Painter, Nell Irvin. *The Narrative of Hosea Hudson: His Life as a Negro Communist in the South.* Cambridge: Harvard University Press, 1979.
Parkin, Frank. *Class, Inequality, and Political Order.* London: MacGibbon and Kee, 1971.
———. "Class Stratification in Socialist Societies." *British Journal of Sociology* (December 1969): 355–74.
Petrović, Gajo. "Philosophy and Politics in Socialism." In *Marxist Humanism and Praxis,* edited and translated by Gerson S. Sher. Amherst, N.Y.: Prometheus Books, 1978.
Pettit, Philip. "Social Holism and Moral Theory." *Proceedings of the Aristotelian Society* 86 (1985–86): 173–97.
Pinch, Trevor, and Wiebe Bijker. "The Social Construction of Facts and Artefacts: or How the Sociology of Science and the Sociology of Technology Might Benefit Each Other." *Social Studies of Science* 14 (1984): 339–441.
Polanyi, Karl. *The Great Transformation.* Boston: Beacon Press, 1957.
Post, Ken. "In Defense of Materialistic History." *Socialism in the World* 74–75 (1989).
Putman, Ruth Anna. "Rights of Persons and the Liberal Tradition." In *Social Ends and Political Means,* edited by Ted Honderich. London: Routledge and Kegan Paul, 1976.

Radner, Roy. "The Internal Economy of Large Firms." *Conference Papers:* Supplement to *Economic Journal* 96 (1986): 1–22.

Rawls, John. *A Theory of Justice.* Cambridge: Harvard University Press, 1971.

Reich, Wilhelm. *Mass Psychology of Fascism.* New York: Farrar, Straus and Giroux, 1970.

———. *The Discovery of the Orgone: The Function of the Orgasm.* New York: Farrar, Straus and Giroux, 1973.

———. *The Sexual Revolution.* New York: Farrar, Straus and Giroux, 1974.

Reiter, Rayna. *Toward a New Anthropology of Women.* New York: Monthly Review, 1975.

Rethinking Marxism 5, no. 2 (summer 1992).

Riker, William. *Liberalism Against Populism: A Confrontation Between the Theory of Democracy and the Theory of Social Choice.* San Francisco: W. H. Freeman & Company, 1982.

Roemer, John. "Equality of Talent." *Economics and Philosophy* 1 (1985): 151–87.

———. *Free to Lose: An Introduction to Marxist Economic Philosophy.* Cambridge: Harvard University Press, 1988.

———. *A Future for Socialism.* Cambridge: Harvard University Press, 1994.

———. "Should Marxists Be Interested in Exploitation?" *Philosophy and Public Affairs* 14 (1985): 30–65.

Roemer, John, and Pranab Bardhan, eds. *Market Socialism: The Current Debate.* Oxford: Oxford University Press, 1993.

Rousseau, Jean-Jacques. *The Social Contract.* Harmondsworth: Penguin, 1968.

Rowbotham, Sheila. *Women, Resistance and Revolution.* New York: Random House, 1972.

Russell, Bertrand. "Science and Art Under Socialism." In *Essential Works of Socialism,* edited by Irving Howe. 3d ed. New Haven: Yale University Press, 1986.

Said, Edward W., and Christopher Hitchens. *Blaming the Victims: Spurious Scholarship and the Palestinian Question.* London: Verso, 1988.

Sale, Kirkpatrick. "What Columbus Discovered." *Nation,* 22 October 1990.

Sales, William. "New York City: Prototype of the Urban Crisis." *Black Scholar* 7 (November 1975): 20–39.

Samuels, Wilfred D. "Hubert H. Harrison and 'The New Negro Manhood Movement.'" *Afro-Americans in New York Life and History* 5 (January 1981): 29–41.

Sanday, Peggy Reeves. *Female Power and Male Dominance: On the Origins of Sexual Inequality.* New York: Cambridge University Press, 1981.

Sandel, Michael. *Liberalism and the Limits of Justice.* Cambridge: Cambridge University Press, 1982.

———. "The Procedural Republic and the Unencumbered Self." *Political Theory* 12 (1984): 81–96.

———. "Morality and the Liberal Ideal." *New Republic* 190 (7 May 1984): 15–17.

Sargent, Lydia, ed. *Women and Revolution.* Boston: South End Press, 1981.

Sartre, Jean-Paul. *Critique de la raison dialectique.* Paris: Gallimard, 1960.

———. *Critique of Dialectical Reason.* 2 vols. Vol. 1 translated by A. Sheridan-Smith. Vol. 2 translated by Q. Hoare. London: New Left Books, 1976; Verso, 1991.

———. *Nausea.* London: H. Hamilton, 1971.

———. *Saint Genêt.* Paris: Gallimard, 1952.

Scheiner, Seth M. "Early Career of T. Thomas Fortune, 1879–1890." *Negro History Bulletin* 28 (April 1964): 170–72.

Scherer, Jacques. *Le "Livre" de Mallarmé.* Paris: Gallimard, 1957.

Schlesinger, Arthur M. "Orestes Brownson, American Marxist Before Marx." *Sewanee Review* 47 (July–September 1939): 317–23.

Schumpeter, Joseph. *Capitalism, Socialism, and Democracy*. New York: Harper and Row, 1962.

Schweickart, David. *Against Capitalism*. Boulder, Colo.: Westview Press, 1996.

Scott, Hilda. *Does Socialism Liberate Women?* Boston: Beacon, 1974.

Shapiro, E. Gary. "Effect of Expectations of Future Interaction on Reward Allocation in Dyads: Equity and Equality." *Journal of Personality and Social Psychology* 31 (1975): 873–80.

Shaw, George Bernard, ed. *Fabian Essays in Socialism*. London: Fabian Society, 1931.

———. "Socialism and Liberty." In *Essential Works of Socialism*, edited by Irving Howe. 3d ed. New Haven: Yale University Press, 1986.

Simmel, Georg. *On Individuality and Social Forms*. Chicago: University of Chicago Press, 1971.

———. *Philosophy of Money*. London: Routledge, 1978.

Simpson, Lorenzo. *Technology, Time, and the Conversations of Modernity*. New York: Routledge, 1995.

Sirianni, Carmen. "Councils and Parliaments: The Problem of Dual Power and Democracy in Comparative Prospective." *Politics and Society* 12, no. 1 (1983): 83–123.

Skilling, H. Gordon, and Franklyn Griffiths, eds. *Interest Groups in Soviet Politics*. Princeton, N.J.: Princeton University Press, 1971.

Smith, Damu I. "The Upsurge of Police Repression: An Analysis." *Black Scholar* 12 (January–February 1981): 35–37.

Solomon, I. "Red and Black: Negroes and Communism, 1929–1932." Ph.D. diss., Harvard University, 1972.

Stacey, Judith. *Patriarchy and Socialist Revolution in China*. Berkeley: University of California Press, 1983.

Stalin, Joseph. *The Woman Question: Selections from the Writings of Karl Marx, Friedrich Engels, V. I. Lenin, Joseph Stalin*. New York: International Publishers, 1951.

Stauber, Leland. *A New Program for Democratic Socialism*. Carbondale, Ill.: Four Willows Press, 1987.

Steiner, Hillel. "Liberty and Equality." *Political Studies* 29 (1981): 555–69.

———. "The Natural Right to the Means of Production." *Philosophical Quarterly* 27 (1977): 41–49.

———. "Slavery, Socialism and Private Property." In *Nomos XXII: Property*, edited by Roland Pennock and John W. Chapman. New York: New York University Press, 1970.

Stephens, John D. *The Transition from Capitalism to Socialism*. London: Macmillan, 1979.

Strickland, William. "Whatever Happened to the Politics of Black Liberation?" *Black Scholar* 7 (October 1975): 20–26

Suchman, Lucy. *Plans and Situated Actions: The Problem of Human-Machine Communication*. Cambridge: Cambridge University Press, 1987.

Taylor, Barbara. *Eve and the New Jerusalem: Socialism and Feminism in the Nineteenth Century*. New York: Pantheon, 1983.

Taylor, Charles. *Hegel*. Cambridge: Cambridge University Press, 1975.

———. *Human Agency and Language: Philosophical Papers I*. Cambridge: Cambridge University Press, 1985.

Taylor, Charles. *Philosophy and the Human Sciences: Philosophical Papers II.* Cambridge: Cambridge University Press, 1985.

———. "Socialism and *Weltanschauung.*" In *The Socialist Idea*, edited by Leszek Kolakowski and Stuart Hampshire. London: Quartet, 1977.

Tawney, R. H. *Equality.* 4th ed. London: Allen and Unwin, 1952.

———. "Liberty and Equality." In *Essential Works of Socialism*, edited by Irving Howe. 3d ed. New Haven: Yale University Press, 1986.

Theobald, Robert, ed. *The Guaranteed Income: Next Step in Economic Evolution?* Garden City, N.Y.: Anchor, 1967.

Thompson, Frank. "Would Roemer's Socialism Equalize Income from Surplus?" Conference paper, University of Wisconsin, 13–15 May 1994.

Thompson, John B., and David Held, eds. *Habermas: Critical Debates.* Cambridge, Mass.: MIT Press, 1982.

Thornbrough, Emma Lou. "More Light on Booker T. Washington and the *New York Age.*" *Journal of Negro History* 43 (January 1958): 34–49

Ticktin, Hillel. "The Problem of Market Socialism." Unpublished manuscript, 1993.

Tillich, Paul. "Marxism and Christian Socialism." In Tillich, Paul. *The Protestant Era*, translated with a concluding essay by James Luther Adams. Chicago: University of Chicago Press, 1948.

Tocqueville, Alexis de. *Democracy in America.* New York: Harper and Row, 1969.

Touraine, Alain. *Le Retour de l'acteur.* Paris: Fayard, 1984.

Tucker, Robert C., ed. *Stalinism: Essays in Historical Interpretation.* New York: W. W. Norton, 1977.

van der Veen, Robert J., and Philippe Van Parijs. "A Capitalist Road to Communism" *Theory and Society* 15 (1986): 635–55.

Vaksberg, Arkadi. "Pravda v glaza." *Literaturnaya gazeta* 51 (December 1986).

Vaughan, Michalina. "Poland." In *Contemporary Europe: Class, Status and Power*, edited by Margaret Scotford Archer and Salvador Giner. London: Weidenfeld and Nicolson, 1971.

Vernant, J.-P. *Mythe et pensee chez les grecs.* Paris: Maspéro, 1965.

Vogel, Steven. *Against Nature: The Concept of Nature in Critical Theory.* Albany: State University of New York Press, 1996.

Wallace, Michelle. *Black Macho and the Myth of the Super Woman.* New York: Dial/Warner, 1979.

Walzer, Michael. *Exodus and Revolution.* New York: Basic Books, 1984.

———. "Liberalism and the Art of Separation." *Political Theory* 12 (1984): 315–30.

Weber, Max. "The Vanishing Mediator." In vol. 2 of *The Ideologies of Theory*, edited by Fredric Jameson. Minnesota: University of Minnesota Press, 1988.

Wedderburn, D., and C. Craig. "Relative Deprivation in Work." Paper presented at the British Association for the Advancement of Science, Exeter, 1969.

Weil, Robert. "China at the Brink: Class Contradictions of 'Market Socialism'—Part 1." *Monthly Review* 4 (December 1994): 10–35.

Weinbaum, Batya. *The Curious Courtship of Women's Liberation and Socialism.* Boston: South End Press, 1978.

———. "Women in Transition to Socialism: Perspectives on the Chinese Case." *Review of Radical Political Economics* 8, no. 1 (1976): 34–58.

Westergaard, John, and Henrietta Resler. *Class in Contemporary Britain.* London: Heinemann, 1975.

Wilde, Oscar. "The Soul of Man under Socialism." In *Essential Works of Socialism*, edited by Irving Howe. 3d ed. New Haven: Yale University Press, 1986.

Wiles, P. J. D., and S. Markowski. "Income Distribution under Communism and Capitalism: Some Facts about Poland, the UK, the USA, and the USSR." *Soviet Studies* 22 (1971): 334–69.

Williams, Bernard. "The Idea of Equality." In *Philosophy, Politics and Society: Second Series*, edited by P. Laslett and W. G. Runciman. Oxford: Blackwell, 1962.

Winner, Langdon. *The Whale and the Reactor*. Chicago: University of Chicago, 1986.

White, Lynn. "The Historical Roots of Our Ecological Crisis." In *Philosophy and Technology: Readings in the Philosophical Problems of Technology*, edited by C. Mitcham and R. Mackey. New York: Free Press, 1972.

Whyte, William Foote, and Kathleen King White. *Making Mondragon: The Growth and Dynamics of the Worker Cooperative Complex*. Ithaca, N.Y.: Cornell University Press, 1988.

Wolf, Christa. "Berührung: Maxi Wanders 'Guten Morgen, Du Schöne.'" *Neue Deutsche Literatur* 2 (1978): 53–63.

Wollstonecraft, Mary. *Vindication of the Rights of Women*. New York: Penguin Books, 1982.

Woodward, C. Vann. *Tom Watson: Agrarian Rebel*. New York: Oxford University Press, 1970.

Wright, Will. *Six Guns and Society: A Structural Study of the Western*. Berkeley: University of California Press, 1975.

Young, Iris. *Inclusion and Democracy*. Oxford: Oxford University Press, 2000.

Yunker, James. *Socialism Revised and Modernized: The Case for Pragmatized Market Socialism*. New York: Praeger, 1992.

Zoll, Rainer. "Neuer Individualismus und Alltagssolidarität." In *Wege ins Reich der Freiheit*, edited by H. L. Krämer and C. Leggewie. Berlin: Rotbuch, 1989.

———. *Nicht so wie unsere Eltern?: Ein neues kulturelles Modell?* Opladen and Wiesbaden: Westdeutscher Verlag, 1989.

CONTRIBUTORS

MICHAEL ALBERT and ROBIN HAHNEL are coauthors of *Looking Forward: Participatory Economics for the Twenty-First Century* (South End Press), *The Political Economy of Participatory Economics* (Princeton University Press), and *Socialism Today and Tomorrow* (South End Press). Hahnel is professor, Department of Economics, American University. Albert is coeditor and cofounder of *Z Magazine*.

FRANK CUNNINGHAM is professor, Department of Philosophy, University of Toronto. He is the author of *Democratic Theories: A Critical Introduction* (Routledge), *Democratic Theory and Socialism* (Cambridge University Press), *The Real World of Democracy Revisited* (Humanity Books), and other work.

ANDREW FEENBERG is professor of philosophy at San Diego State University. He is the author of *Critical Theory of Technology* (Oxford University Press), *Alternative Modernity* (University of California Press), *Questioning Technology* (Routledge), and other work.

ANN FERGUSON is professor, Department of Philosophy, University of Massachusetts, Amherst. She is the author of *Blood at the Root: Motherhood, Sexuality and Male Dominance* (Pandora), *Sexual Democracy: Women, Oppression, and Revolution* (Westview), and other work.

ANDRÉ GORZ is the author of many works on economics and philosophy, including *Critique of Economic Reason* (Verso), *Capitalism, Socialism, Ecology* (Verso), and *Farewell to the Proletariat* (South End Press). He lives in Paris.

ROGER S. GOTTLIEB is professor, Department of Humanities and Arts, Worcester Polytechnic Institute. He is the author of *Marxism, 1844–1990: Origins, Betrayal, Rebirth* (Routledge), *History and Subjectivity: The Transformation of Marxist Theory* (Temple), *This Sacred Earth: Religion, Nature, Environment* (Routledge), and other books.

FREDRIC R. JAMESON is William A. Lane Jr. Professor of Comparative Literature, professor of Romance Studies (French), and chair of the Literature Program at Duke University. His most recent books include *Postmodernism, or, The Cultural Logic of Late Capitalism* (Duke University Press), *Brecht and Method* (Verso), and *The Cultural Turn* (Verso).

STEVEN LUKES is professor, Department of Sociology, New York University. He is the author of *The Category of the Person: Anthropology, Philosophy, History*, coedited with M. Carrithers and S. Collins (Cambridge University Press), *Power: A Radical View* (Macmillan), *Marxism and Morality* (Clarendon Press), and other works.

ROSA LUXEMBURG was a founder of the Social Democratic Party of Poland and Lithuania, and a prominent critic of revisionism and militarism in the German Social Democratic Party from the turn of the century until her assassination in 1919. She was also a Marxist theoretician and a critic of excessive centralization and dictatorship by the Bolsheviks.

C. B. MACPHERSON was professor of political science at the University of Toronto and the author of *The Political Theory of Possessive Individualism* (Oxford University Press), *Democratic Theory: Essays in Retrieval* (Oxford University Press), *The Life and Times of Liberal Democracy* (Oxford University Press), and other books.

MANNING MARABLE is professor, Department of History, and director of African American Studies, Columbia University. He is the author of *Beyond Black and White: Transforming African-American Politics* (Verso), *How Capitalism Underdeveloped Black America: Problems in Race, Political Economy, and Society* (South End Press), *Speaking Truth to Power: Essays on Race, Resistance, and Radicalism* (Westview), and other books.

KARL MARX, author of *Capital*, *The Communist Manifesto* (with Friedrich Engels), and scores of other works, was one of the founders of modern communism and its chief theoretician. Marx invented the theory of surplus value and historical materialism.

DAVID MILLER is Official Fellow in Social and Political Theory at Nuffield College, Oxford. He is the author of *Market, State and Community* (Clarendon), *On Nationality* (Clarendon), *Principles of Social Justice* (Harvard University Press), and other books.

ALEC NOVE was professor of economics and director of the Institute of Soviet and East European Studies at the University of Glasgow, and the author of *The Soviet Economic System* (G. Allen & Unwin), *Economic History of the USSR* (Penguin Books), *The Economics of Feasible Socialism* (G. Allen & Unwin), and other books.

JAMES O'CONNOR is cofounder and editor-in-chief of *Capitalism, Nature, Socialism: A Journal of Socialist Ecology*, and director of the Center for Political Ecology in Santa Cruz, California. He is retired from teaching sociology, economics, and environmental studies at the University of California, Santa Cruz. He is the author of *Natural Causes: Essays in Ecological Marxism* (Guilford), and other books.

ADAM PRZEWORSKI is professor, Department of Politics, New York University. He is the author of *Capitalism and Social Democracy* (Cambridge University Press), *Democracy and the Market* (Cambridge University Press), and other books.

DAVID SCHWEICKART is professor, Department of Philosophy, Loyola University of Chicago. He is the author of *Against Capitalism* (Cambridge University Press and Westview), *Capitalism or Worker Control? An Ethical and Economic Appraisal* (Praeger), and other work.

RAYMOND WILLIAMS was a Fellow of Jesus College, Cambridge University, and the author of *The Long Revolution* (Columbia University Press), *The English Novel from Dickens to Lawrence* (Oxford University Press), *Culture and Society 1780–1950* (Columbia University Press), and other work.

INDEX

accumulation, 23, 93–94, 160, 197, 199, 203–205, 233n.21, 330, 335, 371; socialist, 223–24

aesthetics, 37n.33, 166, 243, 249, 280n.29, 284–97, 345, 352, 362

Afghanistan, 322

Africa, 18, 185, 192, 194, 202, 231, 294, 322

African Americans: and capitalism (*see* capitalism, racism and); and feminism, 186; historical impediments to socialist consciousness of, 195–98; and labor, 188–89, 193, 196, 198–99, 204–205; and nationalism, 189, 191, 197–99, 205n.12, 208n.43, 208n.48; and religion, 196; and socialism, 189–95

agriculture, 336, 108–109. *See also* class, peasant

Albert, Michael, 131–45

alienation, 24–26, 29–30, 32–33, 101, 108, 244; of labor, 25, 93, 96, 101, 243; religion and, 24. *See also* fetishism, reification

altruism 277

America, 20–22, 32, 181, 185–87, 194, 198, 200, 202–203, 263, 278, 298,

300, 312–13, 315, 322, 327, 336, 341

anarchism, 41–42, 74, 75, 191, 251, 341n.2, 341n.3

antihumanism, 35n.4

art, 37n.33; as commodity, 286, 291; community and, 299; as end, 284; folk, 288; nature and, 345; political, 295. *See also* culture; aesthetic

Asia, 18, 185, 194, 231, 324

atheism, 20, 32, 40, 196

authoritarianism, 78, 123–125, 131, 168, 220, 226, 263, 265, 267, 280n.23, 303, 341n.6

automation, 94

autonomy, 72, 96, 130, 166–68, 227, 241, 249–51, 258n.2, 372–77; of art, 287, 292; of enterprises, 20, 114n.8; of movements, 90, 201, 212, 215, 225, 227, 233, 237

base and superstructure, 19, 35n.4, 47, 50–51, 57, 187, 238n.43, 339

Benjamin, Walter, 18, 31, 201, 295

Bernstein, Eduard, 21, 28, 64, 66–74, 86, 90, 365

Bolsheviks, 28, 81, 84–85, 193